SETTLEMENT AND SOCIETY IN WALES

ANGLESEY
(SIR FÔN)

GWYNEDD

FLINTSHIRE
(SIR Y FFLINT)

DENBIGHSHIRE
(SIR DDINBYCH)

CLWYD

CAERNARVONSHIRE
(SIR GAERNARFON)

FLINTS.
(deu)

MERIONETH
(MEIRIONNYDD)

MONTGOMERYSHIRE
(SIR DREFALDWYN)

---- Old Counties
-·- New Counties

CARDIGANSHIRE
(SIR ABERTEIFI)

RADNORSHIRE
(SIR FAESYFED)

POWYS

DYFED

PEMBROKESHIRE
(SIR BENFRO)

CARMARTHENSHIRE
(SIR GAERFYRDDIN)

BRECKNOCKSHIRE
(SIR FRYCHEINIOG)

MONMOUTHSHIRE
(SIR FYNWY)

GLAMORGAN
(MORGANNWG)

GWENT

0   10   20   30
MILES

WEST GLAMORGAN
(GORLLEWIN MORGANNWG)

MID GLAMORGAN
(MORGANNWG GANOL)

CARDIFF
(CAERDYDD)

SOUTH GLAMORGAN
(DE MORGANNWG)

The main administrative units of Wales, showing 'old' and 'new' county boundaries.
E. G. Bowen

Settlement and Society
in
Wales

edited by
D. HUW OWEN

UNIVERSITY OF WALES PRESS
CARDIFF
1989

© University of Wales, 1989

British Library Cataloguing in Publication Data

Settlement and society in Wales.
  1. Wales. Human settlements, to 1987
  I. Owen, D. Huw, *1941–*
  307′.09429

ISBN 0–7083–0985–2

Jacket design by Design Principle, Cardiff
Printed in Great Britain by The Alden Press, Oxford

Er Cof am
In memory of
E.G. BOWEN

Contents

Figures

Plates

Preface

THIS volume seeks to satisfy a demand which has arisen as a result of the remarkable growth of interest displayed, in recent years, in the study of local history. There has been a proliferation of local history societies, adult education classes and publications concentrating on various aspects of the historical development of specific localities. Local history studies also feature increasingly in courses taught at universities, colleges and schools and there has been a marked increase in the use made of local collections in libraries, museums and record offices.

The volume comprises a collection of essays which examine various aspects of the emergence and development of the landscape, settlement patterns and social framework of Wales. A synthesis is provided of current views on specified subjects or periods, available sources and techniques are evaluated, and detailed studies, with illustrations, are presented of selected localities in various parts of Wales.

The conventions of modern Welsh orthography have been adopted for personal and place-names. It is appreciated that in some cases this may cause difficulties but Anglicized forms, with suitable cross-references, appear in the Index (e.g. Wrecsam/Wrexham, Rhuthun/Ruthin, Cydweli/Kidwelly).

A number of individuals have assisted the editor and the contributors in various ways. They include Dr Stephen Green and Mr R. Gwynn Ellis, National Museum of Wales, and Dr J. Gwynfor Jones, University College, Cardiff. We also wish to record our appreciation of the assistance and guidance provided by the staff of numerous libraries and record offices, and especially those of the institutions with which we are associated. The index was prepared by Annette Musker. The compilation of the Select Bibliography benefited from the constructive comments of Dr Matthew Griffiths and Mrs Mary Owen: however the editor accepts full responsibility for this section, as he does for the whole volume.

The editor wishes to express his appreciation of the ready co-operation of the contributors to this volume and the unfailing support of Mr John Rhys and Susan Jenkins of the University of Wales Press.

We were all saddened to learn of the sad and untimely death of Frank Emery. His colleague, Dr K. Addison, agreed to read the galley-proofs. This exceptionally kind and thoughtful action was greatly appreciated, as also was his observation that Chapter 3 'in many ways a synthesis of Frank Emery's range of work on "landscape" and Wales, was a fitting posthumous work'.

We were conscious of another sad loss when these chapters were being prepared. It is therefore considered appropriate that this book should be dedicated to the memory of the late Professor E.G. Bowen who made such a diverse and immense contribution to our understanding of a number of the subjects examined in this volume.

Aberystwyth
August 1988

D. HUW OWEN

Acknowledgements

The individuals and institutions named below are thanked for their permission to include the following material:

The Cambrian Archaeological Society and the editor of *Archaeologia Cambrensis* for the frontispiece. E.G. Bowen's map of the administrative units of Wales was published in *Index to Archaeologia Cambrensis, 1901–1960* (Cardiff, 1976), compiled by T. Rowland Powell, with lists and notes by Donald Moore;

The editors of *Welsh History Review* for Chapter 1, much of which was first published in *WHR*, V (1970), and for Figure 47;

The Royal Commission on Ancient and Historical Monuments in Wales and Her Majesty's Stationery Office: for the figures and plates previously published in P. Smith, *Houses of the Welsh Countryside* (1975); *An Inventory of the Ancient Monuments in Caernarvonshire*, II (1960) for Figure 41, and III (1964) for Figures 38a and 38b; *An Inventory of the Ancient Monuments in Glamorgan*, I, Pt. ii (1976), for Figures 39, 40a and 40b; Plates II–IX are from the National Monuments Record Collection and are mainly the work of the Commission's staff photographers;

Cambridge University Collection (copyright reserved) for Plate X;

The National Library of Wales for Plate XI;

Cadw—Welsh Historic Monuments for Plate XII;

The editor of the *Transactions of the Honourable Society of Cymmrodorion* for Figures 48a and 48b;

Professor Harold Carter, Dr C.R. Lewis and The Open University Press for Figure 54 first published in *Aspects of Historical Geography* (1983);

Dr P.E. Jones and the editor of the *Transactions of the Caernarvonshire Historical Society* for Figure 56a;

Mr J.B. Lowe, Mr David Anderson and the Welsh School of Architecture, UWIST, Cardiff for Figure 59;

Dr P.N. Jones and the University of Hull for Figure 60 first published in *Colliery Settlement in the South Wales Coalfield* (1969).

Abbreviations

Ag. Hist.	*The Agrarian History of England and Wales*, I (ii) ed. H.P.R. Finberg (Cambridge, 1972); IV ed. Joan Thirsk (Cambridge, 1967); VIII ed. Edith H. Whetham (Cambridge, 1978); V (Cambridge 1984).
Ag. Hist. Rev.	*Agricultural History Review*
A.C.	*Archaeologia Cambrensis*
Arch. Jnl.	*The Archaeological Journal*
Arch. in Wales	*Archaeology in Wales*
B.A.R.	British Archaeological Reports
B.L.	The British Library
B.B.C.S.	*Bulletin of the Board of Celtic Studies*
Caern. Inv.	The Royal Commission on Ancient and Historical Monuments in Wales, *An Inventory of the Ancient Monuments in Caernarvonshire*, 3 vols. (1956–64).
Carms. Antiq.	*The Carmarthenshire Antiquary*
C.B.A.	Council of British Archaeology
Ec.H.R.	Economic History Review
E.H.R.	English Historical Review
E.A.N.C.	R.J. Thomas, *Enwau Afonydd a Nentydd Cymru* (Cardiff, 1938)
E.P.N.E.	A.H. Smith, *English Place-Name Elements*, 2 vols. (1956)
G.C.H.	*Glamorgan County History*, gen. ed. Glanmor Williams, I (1936, repr. 1971), II (1984), III (1971), IV (1974), V (1980).
Glam. Inv.	The Royal Commission on Ancient and Historical Monuments in Wales. *An Inventory of the Ancient Monuments in Glamorgan*, I, Parts 1, 2, 3 (1976); IV, Part 1 (1981); III, Part 2 (1982).
G.P.C.	*Geiriadur Prifysgol Cymru* (University of Wales, Dictionary of the Welsh Language)
Jnl. Brit. Arch. Ass.	*Journal of the British Archaeological Association*
Jnl. Flints. H.S.	*Journal of the Flintshire Historical Society*
Jnl. Mer. H.R.S.	*Journal of the Merioneth Historical and Record Society*
M.W.S.	T. Jones Pierce, *Medieval Welsh Society*, ed. J. Beverley Smith (Cardiff, 1972).
Mon. Antiq.	*The Monmouthshire Antiquary*
Mont. Coll.	*Montgomeryshire Collections*
N.C.P.N.	B.G. Charles, *Non-Celtic Place-Names in Wales* (1938).
N.L.W.	National Library of Wales
N.L.W.Jnl.	*Journal of the National Library of Wales*
N.M.W.	National Museum of Wales

N.T.C.B.	Margaret Gelling, W.F.H. Nicolaisen and Melville Richards, *The Names of Towns and Cities in Britain* (1970).
Pembs. Hist.	*The Pembrokeshire Historian*
P.N.D.P.	G.O. Pierce *The Place-Names of Dinas Powys Hundred* (Cardiff, 1968).
Proc. Pre. Soc.	*Proceedings of the Prehistoric Society*
P.R.O.	Public Record Office
R.C.A.H.M.	Royal Commission on Ancient and Historical Monuments in Wales
S.W.M.R.S.	South Wales and Monmouth Record Society
T.A.A.S.	*Transactions of the Anglesey Antiquarian Society and Field Club*
T.C.S.	*Transactions of the Honourable Society of Cymmrodorion*
T.C.H.S.	*Transactions of the Caernarvonshire Historical Society*
T. Cardiff Nat. Soc.	*Transactions of the Cardiff Naturalists' Society*
T.D.H.S.	*Transactions of the Denbighshire Historical Society*
T. Inst. Brit. Geog.	*Transactions of the Institute of British Geographers*
T.R.H.S.	*Transactions of the Royal Historical Society*
U.C.N.W.	University College of North Wales, Bangor
W.H.R.	*Welsh History Review*

Introduction

L OCAL pride and regional allegiance contribute today, as in the past, to the cultural diversity (and also political divisions) of Wales. Over the centuries the Welsh, and also visitors to Wales, have recorded their impressions and reminiscences in word, on canvas, and (in recent years) on film. Collectively, these dispersed literary and visual productions illuminate various aspects of the development of local communities. Attachment to one's own locality (*bro*) has been a powerful sentiment passionately expressed over the centuries, and it thus forms a recurring and abiding theme in Welsh literature. An early example of this is found in 'Edmyg Dinbych' a ninth-century poem in praise of Tenby found in the Book of Taliesin, while Hywel ab Owain Gwynedd, a poet of the twelfth century, was acutely aware of the beauty of the Welsh landscape. Twentieth-century poets have again reflected this deep-rooted consciousness of the complex relationship between man and his natural environment, even though the approach varies from the romanticism of Eifion Wyn to the realism of Gwenallt and Sir Thomas Parry-Williams. Novels, containing a wealth of material forged out of personal experience, together with memoirs and autobiographical works, again constitute valuable sources for an understanding of the character of diverse communities; writings which stand out in this respect include those of Jack Jones, Kate Roberts and D. J. Williams.[1]

Interest in the history of a locality may be seen as either the product of a well-developed sense of local allegiance or a commitment to identify with a particular community: the latter phenomenon explains the involvement of recently-settled families in the activities of local history societies. The existence of a long and honourable tradition of local history studies in Wales is emphasized in Glanmor Williams's comprehensive résumé of relevant activities and publications (Chapter 1). In this chapter attention is also focused on the complex relationship between the study of local and that of national history, and reference is made to a once strongly-felt uncertainty concerning the validity of the study of Welsh history. Fortunately, hostile attitudes and prejudices of this kind are now largely rejected, and a similar development may be seen in local history studies. Disparaging comments, such as that which referred to local histories forming 'so much dead weight on library shelves' reflected a belief in the inferior status of local history and accounted for the description of the subject as the 'Cinderella among historical studies'.[2] The quality of publications, extent of activities, and range of academic courses ensure that the value of the study of local history is now widely-accepted and appreciated.

Definitions of local history and the local community have also attracted attention. The Committee, established under the chairmanship of Lord Blake to review the state of local history in England and Wales, reported in 1979 that 'There is no one accepted definition of local history' but ventured to present a tentative definition 'that local history is a study of man's past in relation to his locality, locality being determined by an individual's interests and experience'.[3]

Differing standpoints adopted by local historians were discussed by V. Skipp whose new definition of local history involves the construction of a three-dimensional model formed of locality (village, town, county, region), theme (e.g. topography, demography) and methodology (fact-collecting, narrative writing, rigorous analysis).[4] An earlier and well-known definition of local history, enunciated by the 'Leicester School', was proclaimed in 1952 by W. G. Hoskins and H. P. R. Finberg who emphasized the local community as an appropriate area of study for the local historian. Hoskins referred to the need to study the 'origin and growth of the local community or society' while Finberg considered the local historian's role 'to re-enact in his own mind, and to portray for his readers, the Origin, Growth, Decline, and Fall of a Local Community'. The local community, whether it was a village or town, was seen as a distinct entity 'an organism with a continuous, ordered, coherent life of its own'.[5] The definition of a 'community' has again aroused debate and uncertainty. An enquiry conducted from a sociological standpoint considered ninety-four definitions of the concept of 'community' and concluded that 'all of the definitions deal with people'.[6] Finberg defined the 'community' as 'a set of people occupying an area with defined territorial limits and so far united in thought and action as to feel a sense of belonging together, in contradiction from the many outsiders who do not belong'.[7] Such a definition is appropriate for a local and national community, but in his justification for local history studies Finberg attacked those who argued that the value of local history should be seen in relation to that of national history and that 'local history . . . is not or ought not to be an end in itself'.[8]

The approach of the Leicester School has been criticized by advocates of a regional approach and one of these critics has stressed the importance of comparative methods and the desirability of examining 'common historical problems and developments'.[9] However, Hoskins had referred in 1952 to the need for the local historian to be concerned with problems.[10] In this respect he echoed the views of the distinguished French historians, Lucien Fevre and Fernand Braudel. Braudel's *The Mediterranean and the Mediterranean World in the Age of Philip II*, described as 'the most remarkable historical work to have been written this century', had a profound impact on French historical studies.[11] His outstanding pupil, Emmanuel Le Roy Ladurie, has published remarkable studies of the peasants of Languedoc from the fifteenth century to the eighteenth and also of the medieval community of Montaillou. These local studies, with the latter an international best-seller, contributed immensely to an enhanced understanding of the social history of France.[12]

Braudel had argued in 1949 that the problem, not the region, should be the unit for research, and in 1963 he criticized the regional approach adopted by the disciples of the influential French geographer, Vidal de la Blache.[13] The latter's influence on French regional studies, and in particular his use of the word *pays*, was considered by E. G. Bowen in 1959. Reference was made to the dual use of the word in signifying either a country, as in *le Pays de Galles*, or a region with its distinctive characteristics but not always corresponding to a political or administrative unit. Bowen identified several *pays* (in the second sense of the word) within Wales, with south Pembrokeshire a medieval creation, the Rhondda a product of the modern period, and the predominantly Welsh-speaking areas in north-west and south-west Wales forming the 'true *Pays de Galles* in the sense in which the term *pays* is used by French geographers'.[14]

For centuries attention has been drawn to the dualism which prevailed in Glamorgan. *Bro Morgannwg* and *Blaenau Morgannwg* (the lowland Vale and upland Glamorgan) may again be considered as further examples of *pays* in Wales. In the sixteenth century Rice Merrick distinguished between the Vale which was renowned 'as well for the fertility of the soil, and abundance of all things serving to the necessity or pleasure of man, as also for the temperature and wholesomeness of the air. And was a champion and open country, without great store of inclosures', and the uplands which were suitable for 'great breeding of cattle, horses and sheep: but in the elder time therein grew but small store of corn'.[15] Merrick's contemporary, William Camden commented in 1578 on the characteristic features of the area, known as the Border Vale, which separated lowland and upland Glamorgan: 'On the north it is very rugged with mountains, which inclining towards the south become by degrees more tillable, at the roots whereof we have a spacious Vale or plain open to the South Sun . . . For this part of the County is exceeding pleasant, both in regard to the fertility of the soil and the number of towns and villages'.[16]

In Glamorgan, therefore, three *pays* may be identified in addition to the administrative units which comprised the Dark Age kingdom of Morgannwg — the medieval lordship of Glamorgan, the shire of Glamorgan created in 1536, and the three counties of West Glamorgan, Mid Glamorgan and South Glamorgan which came into existence in 1974. Despite the recent reorganization of local government, familiarity with older institutions explains the inclusion of maps which illustrate, for purposes of clarity, the two major systems under which Wales has been administered in the modern period.[17]

The boundaries of both historical *pays* and administrative units have been largely determined by topographical conditions: the rivers Conwy, Dyfi, Teifi and Llwchwr today constitute, as they have formed in the past, important lines of demarcation. In south-west Wales the *Landsker* is a frontier separating distinctive cultural and social entities.[18] A feature of the reorganization of local government in 1974 was the apparent correlation, in some instances, of historical *pays* and administrative units; this may be observed in south Pembrokeshire, the Vale of Glamorgan, the Rhondda and Blaenau Gwent. The names of seven of the eight Welsh counties (Clwyd being the exception) remind us of the complex political framework of Dark Age Wales. Gwynedd, Powys, Dyfed and Gwent were kingdoms in sixth-century Wales, and whilst there is uncertainty concerning the derivation of the name 'Morgannwg' it is possible that Morgan ab Owain, a ruler in south-east Wales in the tenth century, may have given his name to 'Gwlad Forgan' or Morgannwg (Glamorgan).[19] The names of some of the districts today are again associated with the Dark Ages. Ceredigion and Meirionnydd are traditionally reputed to have been established by the sons of Cunedda who came to Wales from northern Britain in the fourth century to combat the threat presented from Ireland. The boundaries of present-day Ceredigion correspond, to a large extent, to those of Dark Age Ceredigion, but this is not true of some of the other administrative units with marked differences between the boundaries of Dark Age Dyfed and Powys, and their modern counterparts.

The nomenclature, boundaries and territorial extent of a number of administrative units reflect a remarkable degree of continuity. The significance of this element has been emphasized in the valuable studies which have been published on various Welsh communities.[20] Continuity, in terms of settlement history, forms a major theme of this volume. The title reflects the continuing but fluctuating interaction in Wales of physical environment and human activities, with settlement forms and patterns critically influenced by the exploitation of territorial resources and by the intervention of political and administrative organizations. These subjects are examined over an extended period of time. A wide perspective is also adopted in the consideration of demographic changes and of patterns of population-mobility. These modify and counter those features which contribute to the underlying stability and continuity of Welsh life, whilst the features themselves are subject to pressures, innovation and change.

The complex nature of both physical and human development is illustrated in the two studies which comprise Chapter 2. Geological processes which account for the Welsh landform were substantially affected by global climatic changes. The survey of vegetation history includes the identification of both native and introduced species. Local climatic and soil conditions are again of critical importance, but human action and intervention are also potent and formative influences. These themes are again developed in Chapter 3 which considers the dramatic effects of human activity on the natural landscape, as in woodland–clearance and tree-planting enterprises. The opening chapters thus indicate the value of the adoption of an interdisciplinary approach and this is further emphasized in Chapter 4 which examines place-name evidence. The principles of place-name study, basically a philological discipline, are clearly formulated and its importance in respect of social and settlement history amply demonstrated. Finberg had urged the local historian to exploit the varied contributions of diverse disciplines and Braudel had stressed the importance of 'total history'.[21] It is also of interest here to recall Marc Bloch's emphasis on the significance of human settlement in relation to historical studies as well as his reference to place-name study as an appropriate subject for co-operative interdisciplinary research-work.[22] Another fruitful area in this respect is the study of houses and building-styles. An awareness of a building's social position, together with the geographical and historical context, again contributes immensely to an understanding of the history of a local community. Regional variations within Wales are examined in Chapter 5, together with a consideration of related developments in other parts of the British Isles and of Europe.

Each of the first five chapters covers an extended period of time and this is also true of the remaining chapters. These however form part of a chronological sequence, and it is envisaged that this arrangement will assist and benefit the reader. The sixth chapter, which forms a bridge between the two major sections of the volume, presents a summary of exciting recent discoveries which have been responsible for a reappraisal of developments in the prehistoric period. However, the accompanying discussion on the specialized scientific and photographic techniques employed by contemporary archaeologists explains why this chapter bears the title of 'Archaeology'. The concluding comments on Dark Age and medieval Wales prepare the reader for the next two chapters which are concerned with these periods.

In Chapter 7 attention is focused on the nature and stability of territorial arrangements and on the distribution of settlements. Tenurial and agrarian practices are considered in Chapter 8, which is largely concerned with the expansion and decline of rural, urban and industrial communities in the Middle Ages. Changing patterns of agricultural organization and rural and urban settlements are discussed in Chapter 9, and reference is made to the relationship between nucleation and dispersal in the early-modern landscape. An assessment of demographic trends is presented in this chapter and also in the succeeding two chapters which examine relevant trends in the modern period.

Chapter 10 contains a study of tenurial trends and the role of religion and education in shaping the identity of rural communities whose distribution, growth and decay are charted. There is an inevitable connection between the two final chapters and this may be seen in the reference in Chapter 10 to the relationship between rural settlements and both market centres and industrial areas. In Chapter 11 there is an identification of the analytical procedures involved in understanding the transformation of Welsh towns in the period 1750–1914 and also an examination of the distribution, structure and expansion of towns and industrial centres in Wales.

The arrangement and format of the volume, together with the nature of the subject-matter, account for the discussion of several relevant aspects in more than one chapter. Reference has already been made to some of the major themes which include continuity of settlement, population-mobility, land use and the interaction of physical environment and human behaviour. Buildings used for domestic, occupational and religious purposes are discussed in several chapters in addition to the one devoted to this subject. Demographic trends inevitably engage the attention of several contributors and the kindred system, and its collapse, are discussed in three chapters. Moreover, the Leicester formula of 'origin, growth and decline' forms a recurring theme in studies of diverse local communities in different periods of time.

Relevant problems are identified and a synthesis presented of current views on specific subjects or periods. Scientific, technical, photographic and philological techniques are described and assessed and a range of documentary, literary and visual sources are evaluated. Detailed references and the select bibliography are designed to guide the reader to specialist literature on related subjects. An essentially general approach is often accompanied by detailed studies of one or more localities. The volume is specifically aimed at those interested in settlement studies or in local history studies, and it is hoped that local historians will derive benefit from the discussion of sources and techniques, and the local case-studies. On several occasions contributors have drawn attention to the means whereby local historians may, through their detailed topographical knowledge, contribute effectively to a more complete appreciation of certain subjects. It is envisaged that the volume will cater for a wide range of students and local historians: both 'amateur' and 'professional' and also for the custodians of local collections in libraries, museums and record offices. It is also intended that the volume will appeal to the proverbial 'intelligent layman' interested in the fascinating and intriguing themes and problems which are of central importance for an understanding of the character and history of the country and people of Wales.

NOTES

[1] Thomas Parry, *A History of Welsh Literature*, trans. H.I. Bell (Oxford, 1955); Gwyn Williams, *An Introduction to Welsh Literature* (Cardiff, 1978).

[2] M. de W. Hemmeon, *Burgage Tenure in Mediaeval England* (Cambridge, Mass, 1914), 9; H.P.R. Finberg, 'The Local Historian and his Theme' in H.P.R. Finberg and V. Skipp, *Local History. Objective and Pursuit* (Newton Abbot, 1967), 1–2.

[3] *Report of the Committee to Review Local History* (1979), 3.

[4] V. Skipp, 'Local History: a new definition', *The Local Historian*, 14 (1981), 6 and 7, 325–31, 392–9.

[5] W.G. Hoskins, 'The Writing of Local History', *History Today*, 11 (1952), 490; Finberg and Skipp, op. cit., 10.

[6] George A. Hillery 'Definitions of Community', *Rural Sociology*, XX (1955), 111–23. A valuable discussion on general approaches to the analysis of communities appears in A. McFarlane, *Reconstructing Historical Communities* (Cambridge, 1977).

[7] H.P.R. Finberg, 'Local History' in Finberg and Skipp, op. cit., 33.

[8] Ibid., 28–41; R.B. Pugh, *How to write a Parish History* (1954).

[9] J.D. Marshall, 'Local or Regional History—or both? A Dialogue', *The Local Historian*, 13, 1 (1978), 7, 10.

[10] Hoskins, art. cit., 490.

[11] F. Braudel, *The Mediterranean and the Mediterranean World in the Age of Philip II* (1972–3); P. Burke, 'Fernand Braudel' in J. Cannon (ed.), *The Historian at Work* (1980), 188.

[12] E. Le Roy Ladurie, *The Peasants of Languedoc* (Urbania, Illinois 1974); Idem, *Montaillou, Cathars and Catholics in a French village, 1294–1324* (1978).

[13] J.H. Hexter, *On Historians* (1979), 105–6; *Annales: Economies, sociéties, civilisations*, 8 (1949), 496; ibid. 18 (1963), 778.

[14] E.G. Bowen, 'Le Pays de Galles', *T. Inst. Brit. Geog.*, 26 (1959), 1–23, and in H. Carter and W.K.D. Davies (eds.), *Geography, Culture and Habitat, Selected Essays (1925–1975) of E. G. Bowen* (Llandysul, 1976), 244–71.

[15] Rice Merrick, *Morganiae Archaiographia, A Book of the Antiquities of Glamorganshire*, B.Ll. James (ed.), South Wales Record Society, 1 (Barry, 1983), 14–15.

[16] W Camden, *Britannia*, published by Edmund Gibson, (1695), 610.

[17] Frontispiece.

[18] B. John, *Pembrokeshire* (Newton Abbott, 1976), 159–63.

[19] Wendy Davies, *Wales in the Early Middle Ages* (Leicester, 1982), 92–7.

[20] Elwyn Davies and Alwyn D. Rees (eds.), *Welsh Rural Communities* (Cardiff, 1960); Isabel Emmett, *A North Wales village* (1964); Ronald Frankenberg, *Village on the Border* (1957); David Jenkins, *The Agricultural Community in south-west Wales at the turn of the twentieth century* (Cardiff, 1971); Trefor M. Owen, 'Community Studies in Wales: an Overview' in Ian Hume and W.T.R. Pryce (eds.), *The Welsh and their Country* (Llandysul, 1986).

[21] Hexter, op. cit., 106–7; Finberg, 'Local Historian' in Finberg and Skipp, *Local History*, 10–11.

[22] M. Bloch, *The Historian's Craft* (Manchester, 1976), 48–78; H. Loyn, 'Marc Bloch' in J. Cannon (ed.), *Historian at Work*, 131.

Local and National History in Wales*

GLANMOR WILLIAMS

THE founding fathers of modern British history, it might generally be agreed, were that race of diligent and scholarly antiquaries who made their appearance in the first Elizabeth's reign. They had their lively and enthusiastic representatives in Wales. Indeed, in the person of a Welsh squire, Sir Edward Stradling of St Donat's in Glamorgan, William Lambarde, whose *Perambulation of Kent* (1576) takes pride of place among our county histories, had a potentially close rival for the honour. A letter written to Stradling in 1574 by his friend and fellow-member of a circle of keen Glamorgan antiquaries, Rice Merrick, suggests that he was engaged on an ambitious work 'wherein the state of Glamorgan for a long time in many things is preserved from oblivion'.[1] There are some indications that Stradling's history had been encouraged by and was intended for that prince of antiquaries, William Camden; but, unfortunately, it has not survived, if indeed it was ever completed. On the other hand, the work of Merrick himself, who wrote an accomplished topographical and historical survey of Glamorgan, completed soon after Lambarde's book on Kent, has come down to us and is of great interest and value.[2] Even more distinguished are the treatises produced by a younger Welsh contemporary, George Owen of Henllys, who was the mainspring of a west Wales group of antiquaries and whose writings will bear favourable comparison with those of comparable scholars elsewhere in the queen's realm.[3] It was in this same generation, too, that the first of the modern histories of Wales as a whole, David Powel's *History of Cambria*, made its appearance in print in 1584. Influential as this work was in its own time and afterwards, it now has only a limited scholarly value but merits notice, nevertheless, as an earnest of widespread interest, however misinformed and unsceptical, in the Welsh past.[4]

This interest in Welsh history continued to flourish with greater or less vigour throughout the seventeenth and eighteenth centuries. Some of it was of the highest scholarly calibre. The explorations of that prodigious polymath, Edward Lhuyd (1660–1709) — linguist, littérateur, lawyer, topographer, archaeologist, geologist, naturalist, and historian — could, if they had been succeeded by investigations of the same excellence, have produced an early history of Wales on impeccably scholarly lines. The only other eighteenth-century antiquary to rival Lhuyd at all was Thomas Pennant, a gifted scholar though his Welsh was poor. He began to publish his *Tours in Wales* in 1778, and this work has been aptly described as 'not strict history, but an informal history lesson, ranging widely back and forth in

* Much of the substance of this chapter was first published in *The Welsh History Review*, V (1970). I am grateful to the editors, Dr K. O. Morgan and Professor R. A. Griffiths, for their permission to reprint large parts of the original.

Welsh history as points of topography prompted'.[5] On a more modest scale, if each of the Welsh counties had inspired an historian like Breconshire's Theophilus Jones (1759–1812), whose two-volume account of his native county is a minor classic,[6] we should have had an altogether securer foundation on which to build.

Unhappily, however, the eighteenth and the early nineteenth century produced more than their fair share of history shaped more by imagination than discipline. Henry Rowlands of Anglesey, out of the fervour of his passion for his native island, gave it an altogether too vivid and romantic past, blithely confusing its Druidic associations with all kinds of megalithic monuments in his *Mona Antiqua Restaurata* (1723).[7] But much the most astonishing 'creative artist' of this kind was the one and only Edward Williams (1747–1826). Known to his admiring contemporaries as 'The Bard' and immortalized in Wales by his self-bestowed bardic title, 'Iolo Morganwg', he was a stonemason by calling, a scholar by inclination and a poet by instinct.[8] He is Wales's arch-romantic and a literary forger of genius, compared with whom the more celebrated Chatterton and MacPherson were mere tyros. For all Iolo's faults, he had an unrivalled knowledge of the literature and history of Wales. He and his friend, William Owen (Pughe), and others like them injected into their own and later generations a potent stimulus to historical curiosity and delight. They also infected Wales with the much less desirable virus of an uncritical and over-romanticized excitement about the past.[9]

Nineteenth-century Wales itself was changing fast. Up until the end of the previous century the country had been a poor, thinly-peopled, pastoral land, the slenderness of whose resources had understandably restricted the publication of much in the way of historical writing.[10] Great changes were wrought by the rapid industrialization of the last century. This gave Wales a comfortably wider margin of prosperity and a higher concentration of middle-class and professional men. A massive spread of literacy in Welsh and English created an unprecedented market for books and journals in both languages; and printing-presses and publishing houses proliferated to supply the demand.[11] In Wales, as in a number of other European countries, a sharp increase in the literate element in the population was paralleled by a heightened awareness of national identity based on language, literature and antiquities. This in turn kindled a widening curiosity concerning local and national history.[12]

Nevertheless, no small share of the impetus came from major developments in England. New ventures like the Rolls series, the volumes published by the Record Commission and the Record Office, and the publications of the Camden Society, the Royal Historical Society and the Historical Manuscripts Commission, had a considerable impact. Some of the books published had a particular significance for Wales. In 1838 Henry Ellis published his *Record of Caernarvon*, in 1843 the Record Commissioners issued the two-volume *Ancient Laws and Institutes of Wales* edited by Aneurin Owen, and in 1860 the Rolls series sponsored an edition of *Brut y Tywysogyon* and *Annales Cambriae* edited by John Williams (*ab Ithel*). Though the standards of editing leave much to be desired when judged by modern criteria, the appearance of such volumes constituted a considerable gain. Even more valuable was J. Gwenogvryn Evans's still indispensable *Catalogue* of Welsh manuscripts, published by the Historical Manuscripts Commission between 1898 and 1910.[13]

Regrettably, one of the greatest nineteenth-century ventures, the Victoria County History, did not extend its activities to Wales, despite suggestions that it might have done so. The role of these great achievements of nineteenth-century scholarship has, in general, increased in scope within Wales. By today no historian with the slightest pretension to serious interest in his subject can be unaware of the significance of the Public Record Office, the British Library, or other comparable institutions associated with the study of history.

Among nineteenth-century Welshmen themselves, ever a gregarious group by nature, there emerged the characteristic Victorian passion for founding scholarly publishing societies. The earliest, and still one of the most vigorous, was the Cambrian Archaeological Association, founded in 1846,[14] whose journal, *Archaeologia Cambrensis*, after more than 130 years of publication contains an enormous wealth of material — miscellaneous in quality as well as content, admittedly — on the history and archaeology of all parts of Wales. The other outstanding name is that of the Honourable Society of Cymmrodorion. Founded first by patriotic London Welshmen of the eighteenth century, this society has, since 1877, had a distinguished record of publication in which historical writing has always had a primary place. In addition to its *Transactions* and its annual journal, *Y Cymmrodor*, it also undertook for forty years, between 1893 and 1936, an ambitious programme of publishing historical records and calendars of primary importance for the history of Wales.[15] Its most notable achievement was the 1,100-page single-volume *Dictionary of Welsh Biography*, published in its Welsh version in 1953 and in English in 1959, a venture to which more than 300 scholars contributed.

Of recent years the most interesting development in the founding of societies has been the establishment in every historic Welsh county of a county history society — though Montgomeryshire's Powisland Club could boast a series of transactions going back as far as 1868. Nearly all these former county societies aimed at publishing an annual journal.[16] Their activity was greatly strengthened by a general move towards the setting up of county record offices. Out of thirteen former Welsh counties (Monmouthshire is unhesitatingly included!) eight had their own record offices. The others were mostly too poor and sparsely-populated to justify expenditure for the purpose; but where that was the case the National Library of Wales did a great deal to look after their interests. In this context of county activity a word of praise should go to the old Welsh local authorities for their encouragement of local history. Most of them contributed handsomely towards the cost of publishing county history transactions. Without such subventions the transactions, if they could have been published at all, would have appeared only in severely attenuated and undernourished condition. Some of these counties also had ambitious schemes for official county histories. The last of the old-style, big-scale histories by an individual author was Sir Joseph Bradney's admirable four-volume history of Monmouthshire (1904–1933), though A. H. Dodd also brought out an interesting one-volume history of Caernarfonshire which covers the period between 1284 and 1900.[17] Most of the more recent county histories, however, are co-operative ventures. Carmarthenshire published a two-volume history edited by Sir John Edward Lloyd in the 1930s.[18] Merioneth, one of the least wealthy and populous historic counties of Wales, published the first handsome volume of its projected history in 1967.[19] Glamorgan, the wealthiest of the former counties, embarked on a six-volume scheme in the 1930s but only got one volume through the press before the outbreak of war. In recent years that first volume has been reprinted and four more have been published.[20] Pembrokeshire and Cardiganshire have also made advanced plans for the publication of county histories. Even so, the absence of an organization like the Victoria County History is sorely felt in Wales. Getting a county history launched is hard going; keeping it on course is an even more formidable responsibility for a voluntary part-time editor and contributors, all of whom have many other commitments to fulfil.

The share taken by local authorities in helping to finance these publications reflects the growing scarcity of individuals rich or interested enough to publish on their own initiative and the soaring cost of printing. This marks off our own age from the last century, which was nothing if not an age of rugged individual enterprise. Some of it was really breathtaking. Two quite outstanding examples were the studies of Thomas Stephens and G. T. Clark. Stephens was a largely self-educated chemist at Merthyr Tudful, who won a European reputation for himself as the result of his writings on Welsh literature and Welsh history.[21] G. T. Clark, a Londoner by birth and an engineer by training, settled in Wales almost by chance as manager of the Dowlais Iron Company's Works; but few immigrants can ever have done as well by the history of their adopted county and country. His *Cartae et Alia Munimenta quae ad Dominium de Glamorgan Pertinent* is an astonishingly full and surprisingly accurate compilation of documents relating to Glamorgan history from AD 447 to 1721.[22] Its contents were drawn from a wide range of sources in the Public Record Office and the British Library (then British Museum) as well as a diverse miscellany of private collections.

The last century was also an era of intense civic, municipal and parochial pride. It produced in Wales, as elsewhere, an almost overpoweringly prolific crop of town and parish histories, in Welsh and English, of wildly disparate value, from John Hobson Matthews's six-volume *Records of the County Borough of Cardiff* (1898–1911) downwards. However, histories like A. N. Palmer's *History of the Town of Wrexham* (1893) or William Spurrell's *Carmarthen and its Neighbourhood* (1879), to name but two, are still distinctly valuable. Another characteristic of Victorian Wales was its passionate religiosity which, in turn, led to an almost insatiable thirst for religious and denominational history. Some authors found it worthwhile publishing vast multi-volume histories of individual denominations. Among the more impressive are those of the Independents by Thomas Rees and John Thomas, the Baptists by Spinther James, and the Methodists by John Hughes and by Hugh Jones.[23] To modern readers these may be tedious chronicles of the minutiae of the deeds of the faithful, yet they, too, like some of the town and parish histories, frequently contain invaluable material which lends itself to analysis and interpretation of a kind never envisaged by the original authors. So, too, do the hundreds of biographies (hagiographies might be a better description) of eminent divines. This kind of biography, the *cofiant*, was a literary genre of its own in Wales and, at its best, can be a superb source.[24]

However, much of this one-time torrent of private-venture publishing has almost run into the sand in Wales. Admittedly, it has not entirely dried up. One commendably enterprising individual published at his own risk and expense over a period of some twenty years sixteen volumes of essays on local history by a variety of authors, not to mention a number of other associated volumes;[25] but he, let it be said, is an exception. Hardly less reduced than the role of the individual is that of the denominations and the religious bodies. The old big-scale denominational histories tended to go out with the antimacassar, although the Presbyterian Church of Wales has already produced two very substantial volumes on the history of the Calvinistic Methodists in Wales and there are more to follow.[26] More typical of contemporary circumstances are the latest history of the Independents and of the Baptists and a recent study of the Methodist Revival.[27] All are single-volume works, whereas two generations ago they would almost certainly have been three- or four-deckers of immense detail. Much of the denominational and religious history of Wales has become institutionalized, with each major denomination and the Church in Wales long having had an historical society publishing an annual historical journal.[28]

The institutionalization of historical study is indeed the most typical and possibly the most valuable development of the twentieth century. It has seen the founding of major national institutions, all of which have powerfully shaped the direction of historical studies. In 1907 the National Museum of Wales and the National Library of Wales were founded; both being the consummation of some of the most potent dreams and energies of Victorian Wales. The National Museum has gone a long way towards transforming our picture not only of the archaeology of prehistoric and early Wales but also of its industrial archaeology as well.[29] Its daughter institution, the National Folk Museum, is of more recent origin, but is already one of the leading institutions of its kind in the British Isles and its staff has been responsible for a number of important works of scholarship.[30] As well as being the major repository of books, manuscripts, maps and visual material relating to Wales, the National Library is itself responsible for many valuable publications in the form of bibliographies and calendars in addition to its *Journal*.[31] Another strategic institution is the Royal Commission on Ancient Monuments for Wales, the only positive gain to have emerged from the debris of various unsuccessful schemes to extend the Victoria County History to Wales. Since 1911 the Royal Commission has published inventories covering nine of the former Welsh counties, and although the earlier ones were somewhat sketchy and inadequate lists, the volumes on Caernarfonshire published since 1945 are models of thorough treatment.[32] Those on Glamorgan are even more detailed and comprehensive and represent the kind of investigation that the greatly enlarged staff of the Commission now find it possible to undertake. Still more recently, four Archaeological Trusts have been set up in Wales and have already signalled their presence with some highly promising publications.[33]

The most effective single force at work in fostering historical studies in Wales during this century has probably been the extension of the influence of the University of Wales. It would be idle to suggest that all the leading Welsh historians were to be found there, but a majority certainly have been. Nor is it an accident that the man who can properly be said to have revolutionized the study of Welsh history, John Edward Lloyd, was a professor at the University College of North Wales, Bangor, from 1899 to 1931. In the constituent colleges of the University the study of

Welsh history at undergraduate and postgraduate level has long been encouraged. Close co-operation between the colleges is maintained formally and informally by means of the University's Press Board and its Board of Celtic Studies.

The Press Board has a formidable record of publication, making it one of the leading university presses in Great Britain outside Oxford and Cambridge. It regards itself as having particular responsibility for the publication of works relating to the language, literature and history of Wales and the Celtic countries, and has discharged that responsibility honourably. In sixty years of existence it has published over 200 books on Welsh history. Its very existence has been an indispensable stimulus and support to Welsh historians, for many of whose books the backing of a commercial publisher would not have been easy to find — not on account of insufficient merit in them but because of fears of a limited market for them.

The other university board, the Board of Celtic Studies, has four committees, one of which is concerned chiefly with archaeology, another with history, a third with language and literature, and the newest with social studies. These committees bring together many practitioners of these subjects, from outside as well as inside the University, and they facilitate a great deal of formal and informal discussions and planning of programmes of work. Their budget enables them to be responsible for undertaking a series of publications and projects, e.g. the History and Law Committee has published thirty-one volumes of major Welsh historical records and others are at present on the stocks.[34] It is also responsible for the Studies in Welsh History series of monographs[35] and the *Welsh History Review*, and partly responsible for the *Bulletin of the Board of Celtic Studies*, founded in 1921 and now approaching its thirty-fifth volume. The Social Studies Committee, again, is responsible for the National Atlas of Wales, to be completed in 1988. Close contact is also maintained between the University and the Welsh Institutes of Higher Education, which pay serious attention to Welsh history.[36]

Finally, there exists in Wales a vigorous tradition of adult education, much of which is focused on local studies.[37] There has always been, and still survives in Wales, a powerful grass-roots attachment to the University, a deep awareness that it has been peculiarly a 'people's university'; the Welsh phrase *y Brifysgol a'r werin* has connotations which hardly begin to be conveyed by the English equivalent 'the University and the people'. In a whole variety of ways there is a remarkable degree of liaison between university and college teachers and all sorts of groups and societies which exist for the study of history. As tutors of external classes, public lecturers, broadcasters, advisers to societies, editors of local journals, unpaid consultants and readers of all kinds of manuscripts, university and college historians in Wales, especially those who are bilingual, tend to have their fingers more closely on the pulse of popular interest and activity than is usual elsewhere.

So much for a hasty and inevitably over-simplified survey of the antecedents and the formal structure of historical study in Wales. We might now profitably turn to look more closely at the substance of it at the present time.

Looking at the general state of local history in the country, it is difficult not to feel some cause for concern. Over large areas of Wales, and especially in the rural counties, population has declined sharply and is continuing to do so. This at its worst, as in Radnor District, for example, has actually left far fewer people than there were in old Radnorshire at the time of the first census of 1801 — 16,000 as compared with 21,000. Many of the rural areas are now relatively much poorer and markedly less diversified in their economic activity than they used to be. In some of them the number of the unemployed has reached alarming levels, numbering over 20 per cent of the adult population. That has necessarily increased still further the large numbers of their brightest and most enterprising school-leavers who have, for generations, been obliged to emigrate to find employment. This kind of demographic blood-letting has inevitably led to a fall in morale as well as in resources.

Moreover, the drop in population has tended to be most marked in the Welsh-speaking areas of Wales. There, the decline in the number of those speaking the Welsh language has been accentuated not only because of the steady emigration away from the rural areas of the north and the west but also because even in the Welsh-speaking areas fewer people have chosen to speak the language and more non-Welsh-speaking immigrants have arrived. Broadly speaking the result has been that whereas in 1901 three out of every five of the population spoke Welsh over the whole of Wales, now the proportion is about one in five, and they include among them a disproportionately larger number of the middle-aged and elderly. It would, of course, be misleading to suggest that it is only Welsh speakers who are interested in local history. This is far from being the case. Nevertheless, in those areas which were, for a large part of their history, Welsh-speaking, when a sizeable proportion of their inhabitants, possibly even the vast majority, cease to speak Welsh, it can seriously weaken their interest in the past of their own neighbourhood and cut them off from any interest in it or identification with it.

Furthermore, one has to add to this the effect of another feature of contemporary British life, indeed of twentieth-century life in any advanced industrial commu-nity — the greater mobility of the population as a whole in search of employment. At its most marked among professional and business classes, it produces, almost inevitably, a greater degree of rootlessness. As such it leaves its mark on local history no less than local government, making it more difficult to find recruits for either. Another consideration, not unconnected with this rootlessness, is the growing rarity of the gentleman-scholar of the old style. That he had his foibles and shortcomings, there is no question; yet it was his patronage, direct and indirect, which was often the key to live and active history in his locality. Some spirited observations on this subject came some years ago from the late W. J. Hemp, who himself produced some excellent studies of archaeology and architecture in Wales. He protested, and in print at that, against what he described as the 'universal decay of gentlemanly scholarship and learning' in the midst of 'herds of would-be scientific professors' and 'hordes of earnest specializing students'.[38] Hemp may have overdone it a bit in the heat of his not unrighteous indignation, but his comment brings us to what is a crucial consideration. In the last resort the health of local history will depend on the degree to which there is regular and informed exchange between amateurs and professionals. This is less easy than it sounds, and barriers exist on both sides. Professionals can be insufferably patronizing and pedantically exacting. Amateurs can suffer from an excess of misplaced zeal and ill-directed industry which fails to grasp the distinction between history and antiquarianism. Yet they are usually 'amateurs' in the literal and best sense of the term, and their diligence and devotion can put professionals to shame. Besides, they have an intimate local knowledge and an access to sources often denied to the professionals. The absolute need for regular and intimate communication between the two species of inquirer can never be overstressed.

These anxieties aired, we can take considerable encouragement from the many signs of health and virility that can readily be discerned in the local history scene. There is no mistaking the widespread interest in local history stimulated by many media of education, formal and informal. Even the very rapid change and rootlessness associated with modern life are themselves counter-productive and give rise not infrequently to curiosity about the past and an urge to find identification with it or to escape to it. There is a pressing and universal demand, whatever the origins of it, for classes, talks, courses, summer schools and books on local history. Much of this is channelled into purposeful activity by county and local history societies, branches of the Historical Association, adult education classes, and other local organizations. Some of these groups have an impressively large membership; Caernarvonshire History Society, for instance, has a membership of close on 1,000 in a total population within its area of 100,000. Those who aspire to give more permanent form to the results of their studies still contrive to do remarkably well, not only by means of essays in the local society's transactions but also in the shape of individual books and pamphlets. The writer may perhaps be forgiven for illustrating this from his own experience with authors' manuscripts on local history which have come his way over the past twenty or thirty years. Without taking account for this purpose of any books or theses by professionally-trained authors or of any articles intended for society transactions, there still remain an interesting range and diversity of manuscripts, all but one of which were published. They include the history of an abbey by a teacher who was not trained as an historian, the history of a coal-mining village by a miner who left school at twelve years of age, two histories of Swansea valley communities — the one by a retired mining engineer and another by a retired colliery clerk — essays on Gower history by an industrial chemist, the oral history of Gower by a teacher of modern languages, the history of a police force by a police superintendent, the history of Mechanics' Institutes by a tinplater turned librarian, the history of a parish by a clergyman, an account of local families by an estate agent, a town history by a solicitor, and the history of a leading football club by a professor of business administration.

The experience given above was cited not as being exceptional but rather as typical of the closer liaison between amateurs and professionals. It operates in two directions: the amateurs come to seek help, but the professionals have also been taking their expertise to a wider public. Some particularly valuable contributions are being made by the editors of local history journals, who have succeeded in setting a high standard. They aim at being scholarly without being dull, and yet at the same time seek to show that local history, no matter who is writing it, has to be susceptible to critical discipline if it is to be as productive as it could and should be. The editors have helped greatly by inducing amateurs and professionals to write for the same journals. The result has been to encourage a remarkably wide and varied range of authors to contribute.

Three other instances of fruitful co-operation may also be referred to here. The first is the annual summer school which the National Library used to organize for some years. Its sovereign advantage was that experts could not merely talk about sources and techniques but also that they could present at first hand to those attending the school the widest and most useful range of sources available to study Welsh local history. Another example of co-operation was provided by the sequence of events which led up to the publication of a book called *Merthyr Politics*.[39] There were a number of interesting aspects to this venture. Merthyr Tudful is a town which has none of those romantic associations regarded by many as the *sine qua non* of local history — not a tavern from which the Crusaders set out or where pilgrims rested, not a whiff of monastic sanctity or scandal, not a bed in which Elizabeth slept, not a Civil War battlefield, not even a church where Cromwell stabled his horses. What it does have is a fascinating tradition of radical working-class politics. This was the subject of four public lectures which the W.E.A. arranged for a popular audience that turned up in numbers which pleasantly surprised the organizers. The four historians who took part all made contributions that were refreshingly original in technique, analysis and presentation. Finally, the University of Wales was able to publish the lectures in an attractive volume sold at a bargain price because the Merthyr borough council made a substantial subvention towards its cost. The only disappointment was that the Merthyr precedent was not followed in other areas. The final instance that might be cited was that of the founding of the South Wales Miners Library which has attracted many working miners to its collections as well as professional historians. Moreover, out of that library and its activities has emerged the Society for Welsh Labour History, which has not only published an impressive annual volume of transactions, *Llafur*, but has deliberately aimed at as numerous and popular a membership as possible and has achieved it without sacrifice of scholarly standards.[40] It is in precisely this kind of close and continuing interchange between popular interest and professional expertise that the best hope for the future of local history lies.

Up to a point it would be perfectly feasible to argue that the history of Wales consists of the sum of its local histories. Such a thesis could, of course, be partly true of the history of any country, but it would be truer of Wales than of many other countries because the forces of its geography, economics and politics have always been centrifugal and not centripetal. None the less, it has always been believed — in Wales at least — that the whole of Welsh history was something more than the aggregate of its local parts. The people of Wales have always looked upon themselves, and still continue to do so, as being one of the separate nations of the British Isles. They see themselves and, in general, are seen by others to be as distinct an entity as the Scots or the Irish or the English. Even so, there was for a long time a nagging uncertainty about the validity of Welsh history as a field of study. It sprang chiefly from the intense focusing of scholarly history on the political development of the sovereign state. Nowhere was this more evident than in Great Britain because of the long history of centralized government in England and the incomparable richness of its archives preserved in the Record Office. As long as this approach remained enthroned as the official orthodoxy it was not easy to see how Welsh history could be said to exist after 1283–4, when political independence was extinguished. It could well be more than a coincidence that Sir John Edward Lloyd, the Welsh historian *sans pareil* but steeped to the eyebrows in nineteenth-century conceptions of the nature of history, ended his serious studies at 1283 and made only one major foray beyond that point — to chronicle the abortive attempt made by Owain Glyndŵr to restore an independent state in Wales. Looked at thus from the angle of conventional political history, the history of Wales was very different from, say, that of Scotland or Ireland. In Scotland, political independence was preserved much longer than in Wales, and even after union between England and Scotland had been achieved there remained major differences between the institutions of law, education, and religion in the two countries. Ireland, again, might not have been technically independent for long periods, but her disturbed and tragic history was so very different from that of England as to give it an unmistakable identity of its own. On the basis of this kind of comparison Wales might seem more akin to Cornwall; a region whose people were once of different origin, language, and culture from the English, but who had so long been merged into the English state that it did not make much sense to talk of Cornish history except as one of the local histories of England.

There certainly used to be a widespread assumption that Welsh history, if it existed, was a sort of local history to be relegated to an inferior status unworthy of the 'serious' historian. Even now, this supposition has not entirely disappeared; but it does seem to have become much weakened, and the whole argument has become increasingly unreal. This has come about partly because local history is no longer a kind of study at which an academic historian can cock a supercilious eyebrow. Even more to the point is that historians are now more willing than they used to be to recognize that the history of a people is not synonymous and coextensive with the history of its organization as a separate state or of its progress towards that condition. Few historians, if any, are now wedded to the notion that sovereign states are the supreme end-product of the historical process or that the evolution of these states and the relations between them are the only phenomena worthy of study. That does not mean denying the value of the history of the sovereign state, but simply to argue that the state is only one among a number of human collectivities that can properly engage an historian's attention. For that matter there is nothing sacrosanct about the history of a nation either. Yet it is a valid and rewarding subject, especially when it is possible to trace down the centuries the subtle and elusive process by which an ancient and distinctive set of cultural, social, and national values comes into being and is subsequently maintained, modified, or transformed within a wider political or economic framework. It is a theme which understandably has a strong appeal for those who were brought up as members of the community concerned. For them it is an essential quest for self-discovery. Nevertheless, the soundest justification for Welsh history, or any other history, is not that it bolsters patriotism or national consciousness. It is the simple historical fact that the Welsh have a history of their own which, despite its close links with the history of other European peoples and especially with that of the other British peoples, is in marked respects different. It is not possible properly to understand it if it is viewed as no more than a regional adjunct of the history of England. Its connecting-thread is not political or constitutional history but social development. Its field of study consists of that complex of features (some of which underwent drastic changes down the centuries) which made the Welsh different. In particular, it has to subject to careful scrutiny the interrelationships between the physical structure and climate of Wales, the economic, social, and religious institutions of the Welsh, their reaction to political authority, their language, literature, and cultural values, and their awareness of a separate past and a common identity. Such an examination must not fail to consider the similarities between the Welsh and other peoples as well as the differences between them; the one cannot be properly evaluated without the other.

The study of Welsh history has been greatly strengthened by the same changes of emphasis in historiography that have buttressed the study of local history during the past fifty years or so. The rapid strides made in economic history soon revealed that the appropriate unit for its study was rarely the sovereign state. It can hardly be a coincidence that some of the most striking advances in Welsh history in the generation immediately after the publication of Sir John Lloyd's *History of Wales* in 1911 took place in the field of economic history. Whatever might be said of the political history of Wales after 1283, it was plain that its economic circumstances were very different from those of England, as became evident from E. A. Lewis's *Medieval Boroughs of Snowdonia* (1912) and William Rees's *South Wales and the March, 1284–1415* (1924). Both were major pioneer works resulting from their authors' intensive exploitation of the rich veins of source material in the Record Office. William Rees went on 'mining' there assiduously for a long time subsequently and in 1967 published his huge two-volume survey, *Industry before the Industrial Revolution*. Only a short while after Lewis and Rees, came another seminal book, A. H. Dodd's *Industrial Revolution in North Wales* (1933), a splendidly clear and shapely study of a distinctive phase in more recent Welsh economic history. In the same generation a large-scale exploration of *Welsh Tribal Law and Custom* (1926) by T. P. Ellis showed the persistence after the Conquest of some highly distinctive legal and social arrangements in Wales. Since the publication of Ellis's two volumes historians have greatly refined his techniques and significantly modified his conclusions.[41] In doing so they have looked at the Welsh laws not simply in and for themselves but as part of the whole texture of subtly changing political and social conditions.

The way was therefore amply being prepared for the coming of the intensified interest in social history which has characterized the past thirty years or so. Its distinctive aim has been defined by a gifted practitioner among British historians, Professor Harold Perkin, in these terms: 'the social historian should take his society and try to see it whole'.[42] It is an approach which has been more familiar to Continental than British historians. The French have been particularly good at it, so it may not be surprising that the most accomplished example in Wales of this sort of historical writing should come from a scholar whose first researches were concerned with the French Revolution. When David Williams published his work on Chartism and, still more, his *Rebecca Riots* (1955), one of the outstanding studies of any aspects of British society in the nineteenth century, he set new standards of excellence for exhaustive and critical examination of Welsh society. Yet it ought not to be forgotten that social history had always been congenial to twentieth-century Welsh historians of many different kinds. Perhaps they had been writing social history all the time without calling it that, just as M. Jourdan had always spoken prose without knowing it. Certainly, J. E. Lloyd had a strong inclination in this direction, and it was even more marked in his very different but hardly less influential contemporary, Owen M. Edwards. Professor R. T. Jenkins's books on Wales in the eighteenth and nineteenth century are brilliant portraits of an age and a society.[43] The same sort of attraction was apparent in the studies of some literary historians, especially those of Griffith John Williams, whose volumes on the literary tradition of Glamorgan and Iolo Morganwg were penetrating essays in social history as well as being a *tour de force* of literary history.[44] This special interest in social history probably explains why there has been such a close and fruitful co-operation in Wales between historians and students of other disciplines like historical geography, anthropology and sociology. The studies emanating from such leading figures of the Aberystwyth School of geographers as Professors Emrys Bowen, Harold Carter and Glanville Jones, would in themselves be a sufficient reminder of that, not to mention the gifted geographers contributing to this volume.[45] Having said all this about the influence of social history it would not be inappropriate to remind ourselves that social history itself has a vast amount to learn. Its definitions, methods and techniques still need further refinement and precision. Some of the enthusiasts for it would suffer no harm from being a little more restrained about its pretensions and achievements, nor are they well advised in thinking that it can or should supersede all other kinds of history. Its general approach, however, is one which is particularly well adapted to the task of reconstructing the Welsh past and it ought probably to be the *forte* of historians in Wales.

Welsh history has also gained much from the emergence of exercises in comparative history and the search for inter-disciplinary co-operation. A great deal of new light has been shed, for instance, on early Wales as a result of the comparative study of Celtic countries by scholars like Professor Kenneth Jackson or Mrs Nora Chadwick and her associates.[46] Or, to take a very different example from a much later period, Professor Gwyn A. Williams has set the pioneer Welsh radicalism of the French Revolutionary era with his own inimitable flair and insight within the general framework of wider studies of European and transatlantic political ferment of the period.[47] The same sort of stimulus can be applied in more oblique fashion, for example, in relation to prophecy in medieval Wales. One of the most powerful literary and emotional responses of Wales in the Middle Ages is the persistence of a messianic and quasi-millennial motif, i.e. that there would appear, or reappear, a prince of Welsh descent who would lead the Welsh to victory and restore to them their right to rule over the whole island of Britain. The tradition has been explored, and with great distinction, within its own literary context.[48] More recently, however, all kinds of new facets are being opened up by looking at it afresh as part of a kaleidoscope of messianic and millenarian impulses in other times and places. Books as different as Norman Cohn's *Pursuit of the Millennium* (1957), Eric Hobsbawm's *Primitive Rebels* (1959), Vittorio Lanternari's *Religions of the Oppressed* (1963) or Sylvia Thrupp's symposium, *Millennial Dream in Action* (1962) say little or nothing about Wales, but they prompt all kinds of questions and analyses which can be applied to Wales. They do not, of course, supply ready-made answers, and conjectures based on them are no substitute for hard thinking about the surviving Welsh evidence. In revealing how universal this kind of response to the human predicament is, however, they enable us to isolate and explain the ways in which it particularly manifested itself in Wales.

Finally, among the other changes which have strengthened the study of Welsh history, not the least important has been the expansion of higher education. There are so many more openings now available in Wales and outside it for those whose researches are concerned with Wales. So much so that it seems worth reconsidering the formal arrangements which exist for the study of Welsh history in the University. A generation or two ago, when departments of Welsh history were first created there was every reason for taking such a course of action. At that time it was undeniably necessary to give academic recognition to the subject and to offer a reasonable prospect of advancement for those who were pursuing what was then, in terms of professional future, a risky study. At that point the nature of the structure of academic organization seems to have been such that a separate chair or an independent lectureship could not be established without the creation of a separate department. Nowadays, especially in view of the universities' financial stringencies, the structure needs to be much more flexible. Certainly, professors and lecturers should be appointed with a primary responsibility for studying and teaching the history of Wales; but they might well do it more effectively in schools or departments of history, alongside and in co-operation with other historians. Experience tends to confirm that Welsh historians enjoy and benefit from participating in the study and teaching of other aspects of history. To teach and study Welsh history too exclusively carry with them certain risks; the greatest, perhaps, being that they should appear to students, and others, as being a more limited and therefore, by implication, an inferior form of historical interest.

A second change of emphasis which appears equally necessary is to abandon the traditional division of Welsh history into a medieval and a modern period, with the watershed at the Act of Union of 1536. The major division which can best be justified is one between Wales before the Industrial Revolution and Wales since. Accepting this division carries with it the need to aim at dividing resources in people, money, books, and attention in a corresponding half-and-half apportionment between the period before, say, 1760 and the period since. Without such a policy commitment there is a danger that the study of the country's history will get seriously out of balance for a number of reasons. First, because the communities in which most Welsh people now live have been created by and since the Industrial Revolution. Moreover, the wealth of evidence available, especially for the detailed analysis of social change, is immeasurably greater than that which exists for earlier periods. Finally, in terms of the human society in general and of the tiny Welsh fragment of it in particular, the Industrial Revolution is one of the two or three great basic changes in the nature of human existence.

Looking forward to the future, it becomes difficult to discuss the prospects in anything but broad outline and in the sobering reflection that anyone who seeks to prescribe a proper course of conduct invites the rebuff, 'Physician heal thyself!'

In the first place, it is not to be expected for a moment that all historians of Welsh extraction should take Welsh history as their province. Why should they, any more than their fellow-historians elsewhere, be concerned solely with the history of their own country? Still, one may reasonably hope that many of them will become historians of Wales. What will determine that, in large measure, will be the quality of the teaching and research of those already committed to Welsh history. They have, therefore, a responsibility, more than ordinarily pressing, to be on their toes as teachers and active scholars. To the extent that they fall short, the point need hardly be laboured, they will fail to recruit to their ranks enough of the most promising and lively of the younger generation.

However, our understanding of Welsh history will also continue to depend on what might be described as the 'fall-out' from other historians' writings. Many of them will not be Welsh. Sir John Neale, we hope, was not the last to shed light on the parliamentary scene in Wales,[49] nor Dr Christopher Hill or Dr Geoffrey Nuttall to explore the Puritan elect,[50] Professor Alcock to illumine the Dark Ages,[51] or Dr David Walker or Dr Ian Jack to set the sources and events of the Middle Ages in context.[52] Many others may be Welsh but by no means exclusively or even primarily committed to Welsh history, though they may, like Dr Kenneth Morgan or Professor Ralph Griffiths, make quite outstanding contributions to the study of it.[53] In turn, one hopes, there will be a compensatory 'fall-out' from our own activity. Not merely because a reliable knowledge of conditions in Wales will add one more piece to the the jigsaws of British and European history, but also because we might conceivably bring to British historical studies new sources of evidence or novel ways of looking at them.

Yet, for the most part the health and vigour of Welsh history are necessarily going to depend on those who commit themselves wholly or chiefly to its study. One of the great risks, it hardly needs saying, is for a small group to become inbred and inward-looking. More than most historians, perhaps, they will need consciously to be alert to the results of other scholars and disciplines, seizing eagerly but not uncritically on what they have to offer. There has to be strong resistance to any assumption, overt or tacit, that Welsh historians must resign themselves to being engaged in a minor or inferior kind of history. They have to aim at measuring up to the criteria normally applied to any other historical writing published in the British Isles. Of course they ought to be ready to accept every opportunity of collaborating in co-operative ventures like the *Agrarian History of England and Wales*. (In parenthesis it is worth saying how refreshing it was to see H. P. R. Finberg giving substance to that 'England *and* Wales' and how admirably effect has been given to that policy in the volumes already published and those in preparation.)[54] The same principle should be applied to research pupils. Though they may be engaged on the history of Wales, they should warmly be encouraged to spend time in other institutions, mingling with other students, wherever this is appropriate. Seclusion and inbreeding are as bad for them as for their teachers.

Being a small group, however, has its advantages as well as its dangers. Welsh historians know each other well and are in close and frequent touch. This intimacy, together with the existence of institutions like Gregynog Hall, the University's residential centre for courses and symposia, and the Board of Celtic Studies, gives them the chance to aim at a rational programme of activity and distribution of responsibilities. They also enable historians based in Wales to keep in close contact with at least some of those Welsh historians of the *diaspora* in England and elsewhere. The latter ought not to be allowed to hang up their Welsh harps silent and neglected in exile. Students of the Welsh Laws have given an admirable lead in this direction by keeping in close and regular touch, organizing periodic symposia and publishing their results.[55]

There can be no question of any shortage of interesting questions on which the attention of Welsh historians can be fully engaged. This refers not simply to those necessarily limited subjects on which books and articles are written, but also to the bigger and broader themes around the study of which Welsh history is organized. No small part of the exercise is likely to consist of interpreting afresh from a contemporary angle a mass of information already in existence. For instance, the history of religion, which has rarely suffered from neglect in Wales, has nearly always in earlier generations been looked upon as a form of belief and activity conducted almost in a vacuum and bearing no very close relation to the condition of society at the time. In the last few years it has been refreshing to see it being viewed again in the light of religious allegiance as a social as well as an ecclesiastical or theological phenomenon. In the process, in addition to re-surveying a great deal of earlier information, much new evidence has been searched for and brought to light. Nothing could be more encouraging than to see an 'elder statesman' among historians and dedicated churchman like Canon E. T. Davies approach the task from precisely such a standpoint in his *Religion in the Industrial Revolution* (1965) and being joined by younger scholars like Dr F. G. Cowley and Dr G. H. Jenkins who have adopted a broadly similar approach to the study of other periods.[56]

Or we might take as another example the social implications of two characteristics which, more than any others, are peculiar to the Welsh — their language and their literature. We know very little about the social history of the Welsh language except for a few isolated episodes, and changes in the patterns of language use in Wales, and the reasons for them, are still largely uncharted with any degree of precision. Much the same could be said about Welsh literature. Devotedly though it has been studied by Welsh literary scholars, they have done so — and who shall blame them for it? — in response to a curiosity of an essentially literary, linguistic and bibliographical kind. There remain unanswered, even unasked, questions about Welsh poetry and prose, good and bad, who wrote it and why, who read it and with what effect, which are of the utmost importance to historians. Grateful as we are to the work of such splendid scholars as Professors Thomas Jones and Caerwyn Williams and others, there is much that remains to be done.[57]

When it comes to the nineteenth and twentieth centuries, where the kind of evidence they need exists for the first time in an abundance which is almost an embarrassment, historians of Wales and its localities ought to have a field day. For earlier centuries possibly the most interesting recurrent question is what happens to a small people living side by side with a larger neighbour, economically and politically more powerful, to whose sovereignty it gradually becomes subjected— as Professor Rees Davies has so illuminatingly revealed.[58] After the coming of industrial change we have to ask what happens to this same people, hitherto living in an isolated and rather static pastoral society, when it is subjected to a set of economic and social changes unparalleled in their force and speed? We have known a good deal about the economic consequences of the Industrial Revolution for some time,[59] but with the exception of the brilliant pioneer studies of Professors David Williams and Ieuan Gwynedd Jones and their pupils we have hardly as yet begun to examine its social repercussions.[60] How did the Welsh colonize their own country? How were the new industrial communities created? What happened to families, kin groups and class relations? What became of the mores and values of rural men and women when they migrated into industrial towns and villages? Did they create new cultural modes whose origins have been widely misunderstood? How did they organize themselves for work and security, for worship and politics, for leisure and culture? How did they transpose their attitudes to the thousands of English, Irish and Scots who came to Wales and how were they themselves influenced in turn? The questions could go on being multiplied indefinitely. What they underline is the urgency for a greater effort to be applied to the problems of the last century and the present one. They also emphasize once more the compelling need for the closest co-operation between local and national historians in Wales. In a memorable passage on the value of European history, Ranke recalled how

> in the course of the ages the human race has won for itself a sort of heirloom in the material and social advance which it has made, but still more in its religious development. One portion of this, the most precious jewel of the whole, consists of those immortal works of genius in poetry and literature, in science and art, which, while modified by the local conditions under which they were produced, yet represent what is common to all mankind. With this possession are inseparably combined the memories of events, of ancient institutions, and of great men who have passed away. One generation hands on this tradition to another, and it may from time to time be revived and recalled to the minds of men.[61]

Not to be aware of this heirloom is to be blind to the values of civilization. To the making of such a heritage many nations, great and small, have contributed. In the consideration of it we ought to beware of falling into the vulgar idolatry of the big battalions. The words of Thomas Crohan, in that beautiful and moving book which he wrote about his own tiny and now, alas, vanished community of Blasket Island fishermen off the south-west coast of Ireland, are worth remembering:

> I have written minutely of much that we did, for it was my wish that somewhere there should be a memorial of it all, and I have done my best to set down the character of the people . . . so that some record of us might live after us, for the like of us will never be again.[62]

Not to care for the claims of the little communities, whether local or national, is to be deaf to the still small voice of common humanity. That must be reckoned a cardinal sin in any historian.

NOTES

[1] J.M. Traherne (ed.), *The Stradling Correspondence* (1840), 167–8.

[2] Merrick's work survives in a number of manuscripts. An edition of it was published by Sir Thomas Phillipps (1825) and another by J.A. Corbett (1887; reprinted 1972). Neither can be regarded as

satisfactory and a new critical edition has appeared: Rice Merrick, *Morganiae Archaiographia, A Book of the Antiquities of Glamorganshire*, B.Ll. James (ed.), South Wales Record Society, 1 (Barry, 1983).

[3] George Owen, *The Description of Penbrockshire*, in H. Owen (ed.), Cymmrodorion Record Series, 4 vols. (1902–36); idem, E.M. Pritchard (ed.), *The taylors cussion* (1906); cf. also B.G. Charles, *George Owen of Henllys* (Aberystwyth, 1974).

[4] Thomas Kendrick, *British Antiquity* (1950); I.M. Williams, 'Ysgolheictod Hanesyddol yn yr Unfed Ganrif ar Bymtheg', *Llên Cymru*, II (1952–3).

[5] Prys T.J. Morgan, *The Eighteenth-Century Renaissance* (Swansea, 1982), 91.

[6] *History of the County of Brecknock* (2 vols. 1805, 1809). Other county surveys published about this time were David Williams, *History of Monmouthshire* (1796); S.R. Meyrick, *History and Antiquities of the County of Cardigan* (1808); Richard Fenton, *A Historical Tour through Pembrokeshire* (1811); Angharad Llwyd, *History of the Island of Anglesey* (Rhuthun, 1832); Jonathan Williams, *General History of the County of Radnor* (Tenby, 1859).

[7] P.T.J. Morgan, op. cit., 89–90.

[8] G.J. Williams, *Iolo Morganwg* (Cardiff, 1956); A. Lewis (ed.), *Agweddau ar Hanes Dysg Cymraeg, Detholiad o Ddarlithiau G.J. Williams* (Cardiff, 1969); cf. P.T.J. Morgan, *Iolo Morganwg* (Cardiff, 1975).

[9] Glanmor Williams, *Religion, Language and Nationality in Wales* (Cardiff, 1979), Chapters I and VI.

[10] A.H. Dodd, 'Welsh History and Historians', in Elwyn Davies (ed.), *Celtic Studies in Wales* (Cardiff, 1963); J.F. Rees, *Of Welsh History and Historians* (BBC, Cardiff, 1952); J.G. Edwards, 'Hanesyddiaeth Gymraeg yn yr Ugeinfed Ganrif', *T.C.S.* (1953)

[11] J. Ifano Jones, *A History of Printing and Printers in Wales and Monmouthshire* (Cardiff, 1925).

[12] Glanmor Williams, 'Wales — the Cultural Bases of Nationalism', in Rosalind Mitchison (ed.), *The Roots of Nationalism* (Edinburgh, 1980).

[13] Historical Manuscripts Commission. *Reports on MSS in the Welsh Language* 2 vols., 7 parts (1896–1910).

[14] Cambrian Archaeological Association. *A Hundred Years of Welsh Archaeology, 1846–1946* (Gloucester, 1946).

[15] R.T. Jenkins and Helen Ramage, *A History of the Honourable Society of Cymmrodorion 1751–1951* (1951); for details of its publications see *A Bibliography of the History of Wales* (Cardiff, 1962). A new, enlarged and much improved edition of the Bibliography is in preparation, under the editorship of Mr Philip Henry Jones, and should appear shortly.

[16] For details ibid., 22–3.

[17] J.A. Bradney, *A History of Monmouthshire*, 4 vols. (1904–33); A.H. Dodd, *A History of Caernarvonshire*, 1284–1900 (Caernarfon, 1968).

[18] J.E. Lloyd (ed.), *A History of Carmarthenshire*, 2 vols. (Cardiff, 1935, 1939).

[19] E.D. Jones (ed.), *History of Merioneth*, Vol. I (Dolgellau, 1967).

[20] *Glamorgan County History*: I *Natural History*, ed. W.M. Tattersall (Cardiff, 1936, 1971); II *Early Glamorgan*, ed. H.N. Savory (Cardiff, 1984); III *The Middle Ages*, ed. T.B. Pugh (Cardiff, 1971); IV *Early Modern Glamorgan*, ed. Glanmor Williams (Cardiff, 1974); V *Industrial Glamorgan*, ed. A.H. John and Glanmor Williams (Cardiff, 1980); VI *Glamorgan from 1780 to 1980*, ed. Prys T.J. Morgan is in preparation and is due to be published in 1988.

[21] Thomas Stephens, *The Literature of the Kymry* (Llandovery, 1849); *Madoc: an Essay on the Discovery of America* (written in 1858 and posthumously published in 1893).

[22] Originally published in 4 vols., but the better edition is the second, published in 6 vols. in 1910.

[23] Thomas Rees and John Thomas, *Hanes Eglwysi Annibynnol Cymru*, 5 vols. (Liverpool, Dolgellau 1871–91); J. Spinther James, *Hanes y Bedyddwyr yng Nghymru*, 4 vols. (Carmarthen, 1893–8); John Hughes, *Methodistiaeth Cymru*, 3 vols. (Wrexham, 1851–6); Hugh Jones, *Hanes Wesleyaeth yng Nghymru*, 4 vols. (Bangor, 1911–13).

[24] For instance, Owen Thomas, *Cofiant y Parch. John Jones, Talsarn* (Wrexham, 1874).

[25] Stewart Williams, *The Glamorgan Historian*, I–XII (1963–81), together with four other volumes on Glamorgan (1959–62) and a number of 'picture book' histories of towns and districts.

[26] Gomer M. Roberts (ed.), *Hanes Methodistiaeth Galfinaidd Cymru*, I (Caernarfon, 1974) and II (Caernarfon, 1978).

[27] R. Tudur Jones, *Hanes Annibynwyr Cymru* (Swansea, 1966); T.M. Bassett, *Bedyddwyr Cymru: The Welsh Baptists* (Swansea, 1966); D. Llwyd Morgan, *Y Diwygiad Mawr* (Llandysul, 1982).

[28] Details in *Bibliography*, 23.

[29] Among the more important books associated with the staff of NMW are R.E.M. Wheeler, *Prehistoric and Roman Wales* (Oxford, 1925); Cyril Fox, *The Personality of Britain* (Cardiff, 1959); W.F. Grimes, *The Prehistory of Wales* (Cardiff, 1951); G.C. Boon and J.M. Lewis (eds.), *Welsh Antiquity* (Cardiff, 1976); V.E. Nash-Williams, *Early Christian Monuments of Wales* (Cardiff, 1950); for modern industrial archaeology, F.J. North, *Coal and the Coalfields in Wales* (Cardiff, 1931) and *Mining for Metals in Wales* (Cardiff, 1962); D. Morgan Rees, *Mines, Mills and Furnaces* (Cardiff, 1969) and *The Industrial Archaeology of Wales* (Newton Abbott, 1975).

[30] For example, I.C. Peate, *The Welsh House* (Liverpool 1946); F.G. Payne, *Yr Aradr Gymreig* (Cardiff, 1954); Trefor Owen, *Welsh Folk Customs* (Cardiff, 1978); Geraint Jenkins, *The Welsh Woollen Industry* (Cardiff, 1969); W. Linnard, *Welsh Woods and Forests: History and Utilization* (Cardiff, 1982); and Eurwyn Wiliam, *Farm Buildings of North-East Wales, 1550–1900* (Cardiff, 1982).

[31] W.Ll. Davies, *The National Library of Wales* (Aberystwyth, 1937); for details of its publications, *Bibliography*, 1, 10, 24.

[32] Details in *Bibliography*, 27; cf. also Royal Commission on Ancient and Historical Monuments in Wales, *An Inventory of the Ancient Monuments in Glamorgan*, I, Parts 1, 2 and 3 (Cardiff, 1976), IV, Part 1 (Cardiff, 1981), III, Part 2 (Cardiff, 1982). See also the superb book by the Secretary of the Commission, Peter Smith, *Houses of the Welsh Countryside* (1975).

[33] E.G.T. James, *Carmarthen, An archaeological and topographical survey* (Carmarthen, 1980); D.M. Robinson, *Cowbridge: the archaeology and topography of a small market town in the Vale of Glamorgan* (Swansea, 1980).

[34] Details of the earlier volumes appear in *Bibliography*, 11–12; cf. also the University of Wales Press's catalogues (latest edition 1987) for details of this series and all other books published by the Press.

[35] F.G. Cowley, *The Monastic Order in South Wales, 1066–1349* (Cardiff, 1977); G.H. Jenkins, *Literature, Religion and Society in Wales, 1660–1730* (Cardiff, 1978); John Davies, *Cardiff and the Marquesses of Bute* (Cardiff, 1981); R.M. Jones, *The North Wales Quarrymen, 1874–1922* (Cardiff, 1981); David Stephenson, *The Governance of Gwynedd* (Cardiff, 1984).

[36] For example, the useful series of sources of Welsh history intended for schools edited by Hugh Thomas, *Llygad y Ffynnon* (Cardiff, 1972 ff.).

[37] The Department of Extra-mural Studies at University College, Cardiff published *The South-East Wales Local History Newsletter*, ed. P. Rider (47 issues, December 1977–July 1985).

[38] W.J. Hemp, 'The Tale of a Bucket', *Jnl. Mer. H.R.S.*, III (1957–60), 353.

[39] The four authors were Gwyn A. Williams, Ieuan Gwynedd Jones, Kenneth O. Morgan and Joseph W. England. Edited by Glanmor Williams, the volume was published in 1966.

[40] See also David B. Smith (ed.), *A People and a Proletariat* (1980), and David Smith and Hywel Francis, *The Fed: a History of South Wales Miners in the Twentieth Century* (1980), both of which books were closely associated with this venture.

[41] For example, J.G. Edwards's presidential lectures in *T.R.H.S.*, 5th series, XII–XIII; T. Jones Pierce, *Medieval Welsh Society*, ed. J. Beverley Smith (Cardiff, 1972); H.D. Emanuel, *The Latin Texts of the Welsh Laws* (Cardiff, 1967); Dafydd Jenkins, *Cyfraith Hywel* (Cardiff, 1970).

[42] H.P.R. Finberg (ed.), *Approaches to History* (1965), 51–82.

[43] *Hanes Cymru yn y Ddeunawfed Ganrif* (Cardiff, 1928); *Hanes Cymru yn y Bedwaredd Ganrif ar Bymtheg* (Cardiff, 1933).

[44] G.J. Williams, *Traddodiad Llenyddol Morgannwg* (Cardiff, 1948); idem, *Iolo Morganwg* (Cardiff, 1956).

[45] E.G. Bowen, *The Settlements of the Celtic Saints in Wales* (Cardiff, 1954); *Saints, Seaways and Settlements in the Celtic Lands* (Cardiff, 1977); Harold Carter, *The Towns of Wales* (Cardiff, 1965); *Merthyr Tydfil in 1851* (Cardiff, 1982); G.R.J. Jones, 'Post-Roman Britain', in H.P.R. Finberg (ed.), *The Agrarian History of England and Wales*, I (ii) (Cambridge, 1972) and many articles.

[46] K.H. Jackson, *Language and History in Early Britain* (Edinburgh, 1953); Nora Chadwick (ed.), *Studies in the Early British Church* (Cambridge, 1958); *Celt and Saxon* (Cambridge, 1963); Myles Dillon and Nora Chadwick, *The Celtic Realms* (1967).

[47] Gwyn A. Williams, *Artisans and Sansculottes* (1968); *Madoc* (1979); *The Search for Beulah Land* (1980).

[48] M.E. Griffith, *Early Vaticination in Welsh* (Cardiff, 1937); Ifor Williams, *Armes Prydein o Lyfr Taliesin* (Cardiff, 1955); Glanmor Williams, *Religion, Language and Nationality in Wales*, Chapter III.

[49] J.E. Neale, *The Elizabethan House of Common* (1949), Chapters III–V.

[50] Christopher Hill, 'Puritans and the "Dark Corners of the Land" ', *T.R.H.S.*, 5th series, XIII (1963); G.F. Nuttall, *The Welsh Saints, 1640–1660* (Cardiff, 1957).

[51] Leslie Alcock, *Dinas Powys* (Cardiff, 1963); *Arthur's Britain* (London, 1971).

[52] D.G. Walker (ed.), *A History of the Church in Wales* (Penarth, 1976); idem, *The Norman Conquest* (Swansea, 1977); R. Ian Jack, *Medieval Wales* (1972).

[53] Kenneth O. Morgan, *Wales in British Politics, 1868–1922* (Cardiff, 1980); idem, *Rebirth of a Nation: Wales 1880–1980* (Oxford, 1981); R.A. Griffiths, *The Principality of Wales in the Later Middle Ages* (Cardiff, 1972); idem (ed.), *The Boroughs of Medieval Wales* (Cardiff, 1978).

[54] *Agrarian History of England and Wales*, I (ii) (Cambridge, 1972); IV (Cambridge, 1967); V (Cambridge, 1984); VIII (Cambridge, 1978).

[55] The latest productions of this group are Dafydd Jenkins and Morfudd Owen (eds.), *The Welsh Law of Women* (Cardiff, 1980) and T. Charles-Edwards *et al.*, *Lawyers and Laymen* (Cardiff, 1986), together with a series of pamphlets. One historian who has kept in close touch with it is Dr Wendy Davies, whose distinctive researches on early medieval Wales have borne increasing fruit — *An Early Welsh Microcosm* (London, 1978); *The Llandaff Charters* (Aberystwyth, 1978); and *Wales in the Early Middle Ages* (Leicester, 1982).

[56] Above n.35.

[57] Professor Thomas Jones was responsible for immaculate editions of the Welsh chronicles: *Brut y Tywysogyon: Peniarth MS.20 version* (Cardiff, 1952); *Brut y Tywysogyon: Red Book of Hergest Version* (Cardiff, 1973); *Brenhinedd y Saesson* (Cardiff, 1971). A bibliography of Professor Caerwyn Williams's prolific writings is given in R.G. Gruffydd (ed.), *Bardos* (Cardiff, 1982). For a general bibliography of works on Welsh literary history, Thomas Parry and Merfyn Morgan, *Llyfryddiaeth Llenyddiaeth Gymraeg* (Cardiff, 1976).

[58] An unusually powerful exposition of this and other themes in the social history of medieval Wales will be found in Professor Rees Davies's, *Lordship and Society in the March of Wales, 1282–1400* (Oxford, 1978) and *Conquest, Coexistence and Change: Wales 1063–1415* (Oxford, 1987).

[59] E.g., A.H. John, *The Industrial Development of South Wales, 1750–1850* (Cardiff, 1950); B. Thomas (ed.), *The Welsh Economy* (Cardiff, 1962); J.H. Morris and L.J. Williams, *The South Wales Coal Industry, 1841–1875* (Cardiff, 1958); W.E. Minchinton, *Industrial South Wales, 1750–1914* (1969); A.H. John and Glanmor Williams (eds.), *Glamorgan County History V, Industrial Glamorgan* (Cardiff, 1980).

[60] Among the most important studies have been those by David Williams, *John Frost* (Cardiff, 1939); idem, *Rebecca Riots* (Cardiff, 1955); idem, *History of Modern Wales* (Cardiff, 1977); Ieuan Gwynedd Jones, *The Religious Census of 1851 in Wales* (Cardiff, 1976, 1980); idem, *Explorations and Explanations* (Llandysul, 1981); idem, *Communities* (Llandysul, 1987) Gwyn A. Williams, *The Merthyr Rising of 1831*

(1978) and n.47; Kenneth O. Morgan, n.53; Cyril Parry, *The Radical Tradition in Welsh Politics* (Hull, 1970); David Jenkins, *The Agricultural Community in South-West Wales* (Cardiff, 1971); D.J.V. Jones, *Before Rebecca* (1973) and *The Last Rising* (Oxford, 1985); David Smith, n.40; Hywel Francis, n.40; R.M. Jones, n.35; John Davies, n.35; D.W. Howell, *Land and People in Nineteenth-Century Wales* (1978) and *Patriarchs and Parasites* (Cardiff, 1986); Peter Stead, *Coleg Harlech: the First Fifty Years* (Cardiff, 1977); W.R. Lambert, *Drink and Sobriety in Victorian Wales* (Cardiff, 1984); G. H. Jenkins. *The Foundations of Modern Wales: Wales 1642–1780* (Oxford, 1987).

[61] Leopold von Ranke, *Universal History. The Oldest Historical Group of Nations . . .* translated by G.W. Protheroe (1884), 2.

[62] Tomás Ó Crohan, *The Islandman*, translated by Robin Flower (Oxford, 1951), 24.

[Ed: A striking, but understandable omission from the text of this chapter is a reference to the author's immense and unique contribution to Welsh historical studies. His publications listed in the Select Bibliography should therefore be added to those cited in this chapter.]

The Welsh Landform

D. Q. BOWEN

IN straightforward geological terms Wales, and in part adjacent areas, can be described as consisting of a core of Palaeozoic with some older rocks (Pre-Cambrian), surrounded on all sides by younger Mesozoic and Cenozoic rocks (see Fig. 1). Lower Palaeozoic rocks, with their characteristic NE–SW trend, swinging E–W in south-west Dyfed, impart a marked grain to the landscape, as well as to the shoreline of Cardigan Bay. Similarly the Upper Palaeozoic rocks of south Wales (WNW–ESE and W–E swinging NE approaching the Usk–Malvern axis and N–S in north-east Wales), influence geomorphic grain by their dominant alignments. Off shore, younger rocks are preserved in synclinal downwarps or in faulted basinal areas. These extend on land in the Vale of Clwyd, the Cheshire–Shropshire lowland, Tremadoc Bay (at Mochras near Harlech), and in the Vale of Glamorgan. Clear indications of their former landward extent occur in the Castlemartin Peninsula, Gower, around St David's, Gwynedd, and in north-east Clwyd. It seems likely, although not proven beyond reasonable doubt, that Mesozoic rocks formerly covered Wales, much as envisaged by O. T. Jones and E. H. Brown.[1] It seems less likely that their former extension had much to do with the development of the present Welsh landform.

Figure 1 summarizes the salient features of geological structure and the distribution of the major stratigraphical subdivisions of Welsh geology. This can be supplemented with reference to T. R. Owen and D. Q. Bowen.[2] Not shown on Figure 1 are the ubiquitous superficial deposits of Quaternary age.[2,3]

The principal landscape elements of Wales have been classified according to geomorphic character by Brown[4] (see Fig. 2). Truly mountainous areas are limited and are chiefly exemplified by the often rugged terrain in Gwynedd and adjacent areas. They owe their character to uplift during the Mid and possibly Late Tertiary, and also to deep and often spectacular glacial erosion. A correlation exists between elevation, inferred former precipitation (by analogy with the present), and the efficacy of such glacial erosion. This is demonstrated by three index landforms of glacial erosion, namely cirques, troughs and glacial moulding (roches moutonnées, streamlined hills and ridges, etc.), all of which decrease in incidence and intensity outwards from a core area focused on the Llanberis, Nant Ffrancon and Llyn Gwynant troughs.[5] Elevation also allows characterization of the Brecon Beacons (with moderate glacial erosional overprint), Black Mountains and Radnor Forest as mountain areas. These stand conspicuously above surrounding uplands which have been classified as dissected plateaux and hills.[6]

The dissected plateaux, as the term suggests, refer to the seemingly level and largely featureless inter-valley watershed areas displayed to advantage over much of mid Wales and in the uplands of the south Wales coalfield (Blaenau Morgannwg). They range in elevation between c.213m (700 ft.) OD and c.610m (2000 ft.) OD and

Fig. 1   Geology and structure of Wales and adjacent sea floors (from Bowen 1977). (Key on facing page.)

are largely, though not entirely, above the level of cultivation. A further unifying feature is the ubiquitous moorland, and the less extensive, though locally and regionally prominent, afforestation of recent times.[7] Visually, however, when contemplated in perspective view from points of exceptional vantage, they resemble plateau-like upland plains into which the Welsh valley system has been fashioned. But are the plateaux and valleys genetically related? Ever since Ramsay[8] first described the plateaux, debate has resounded on such issues. The plateaux have been ascribed to different origins by, among others, O. T. Jones, T. N. George and E. H. Brown.[9] These conflicts of interpretation are reviewed in Bowen[10] and a revised model based on new discoveries is outlined below.

Forming equally distinctive plateau-like surfaces below 210m (700 ft.) OD are the central plateaux.[11] In places they are spectacularly indifferent to the rocks and structures they cut across, for example in parts of Gower and on the Castlemartin Peninsula. By analogy with the intertidal shore platforms and the 'raised' similar platforms up to 15m (50 ft.) OD which carry on their surfaces 'raised beach' deposits, it could be argued that the coastal plateaux were similarly fashioned by marine processes; but they lack marine deposits and, in places — south-west Dyfed, Gower, and Môn (Anglesey) — are associated with younger (Permo-Triassic or Tertiary) rocks on their surfaces in a manner which could suggest their formation at those distant times, followed by their more recent exhumation from beneath formerly more extensive outcrops of such deposits.

Less debatable, although not entirely without some uncertainty about their genesis, are the characteristics of the Welsh valleys and coastlines. There is no doubt that a variety of geologically recent processes during Quaternary time (c. last 2·4 million years) have been responsible for these. However, distinction between the effects of processes operating today, which may also have operated in the past, and other past processes of different character or intensity, is difficult. For example, most

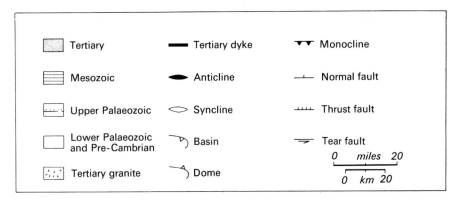

Key—A Tremadoc Bay basin; B Cardigan Bay basin; C St George's Channel graben; D St Tudwal's arch; E Cardigan coast shelf; F Bristol Channel syncline; G Lundy basin; H Irish Sea geanticline; I Central Irish Sea basin; J Holy Island shelf; K Liverpool Bay basin; L Cheshire basin
1 Port Dinorwic fault; 2 Bala fault; 3 Ystwyth fault; 4 Church Stretton fault; 5 Tawe fault; 6 Neath fault; 7 Llanbedr fault; 8 Teifi anticline; 9 Central Wales syncline; 10 Tywi anticline; 11 Clwyd graben; 12 Berwyn dome; 13 South Wales Coalfield basin; 14 Pumlumon; 15 Harlech dome

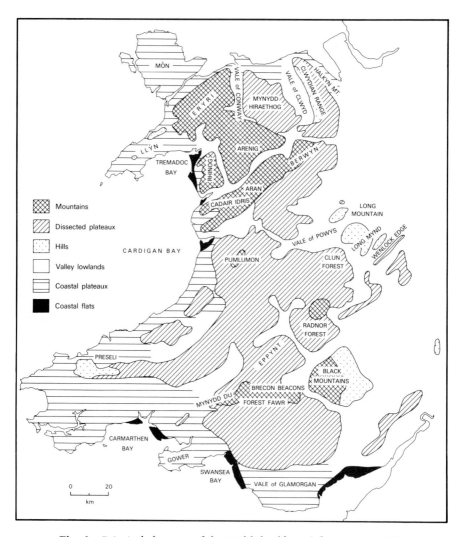

Fig. 2   Principal elements of the Welsh landform (after Brown 1960).

valley sides and floors are veneered and infilled respectively by superficial deposits, Ice Age glacial and periglacial deposits (the latter of frost-produced scree or fluvially-produced gravels), and Holocene (post-glacial) slope-deposits and alluvium. The distribution of superficial deposits is mapped in the National Atlas of Wales.[12] Glacial depositional landforms have also been mapped, and their distribution discussed and related to phases of glacial and deglacial activity.[13] The pattern of such deposits around the coast and their place in an evolutionary sequence is discussed by Bowen in the *Geological Journal*.[14]

On the coastline similar deposits mantle and, to varying degrees, bury a former line of cliffs fashioned in bedrock round much of Wales. Even in places such as the coast between Tenby and Linney Head where the sea today appears to be actively fashioning the cliffs, there is little doubt that these are ancient rather than contemporary. Exceptions occur: the softer rocks of the Vale of Glamorgan are clearly in active formation, as F. J. North showed in his demonstration of the bisection of Ice Age hill-forts by the landward retreating Lias cliffs.[15] The interpretative key appears to be rock hardness: on soft rocks the coastline is undergoing active fashioning today, but on hard rocks it carries an extensive inheritance from the past.[16]

Superimposed on both valley sides and valley floors and coastline are the often spectacular consequences of the most recent set of ongoing processes. These consist of slope-failure, for example, landslips, especially on glacially oversteepened slopes as in the main coalfield valleys;[17] historically significant changes in stream patterns on valley floors;[18] and on the coastline the soft sediments related to the post-glacial rise in sea-level on which the present dune systems, salt marshes and beaches of Wales lie. The consequences of this major rise in sea-level, described in a classic paper by H. Godwin on Swansea Bay[19] and with more modern techniques by M. J. Tooley in Clwyd,[20] are ubiquitous, and include among other phenomena the 'submerged forest' exposures and, less securely based, the 'folk-memory' recollections of lost drowned provinces. Such areas as 'Cantref-y-gwaelod' and 'Llys-Helyg', however, were undeniably dry-land as known to Late Upper Palaeolithic, Mesolithic and Neolithic peoples. On this the evidence provided by modern techniques is unequivocal.

When all is said and done, however, the outstanding characteristic of the Welsh landform is the high degree of correlation between rocks and relief both on regional and local scales. Many different processes, operating at varying intensities, have undeniably occurred, but their end-product has been a landscape displaying to an extraordinary degree of detail the effects of differential rock hardness and geological structure. To some this would confirm notions of long-continued subaerial erosion,[21] an approach partly explored by Challinor for the hinterland of Cardigan Bay,[22] and Bowen in the Talerddig district of Powys.[23] Such an approach has not yet been systematically explored throughout Wales, however evident its precepts on a larger scale.

THE ORIGIN OF THE LANDFORM AND DRAINAGE SYSTEMS

If a parental datum for the Welsh landform is sought, then it must be the inferred landscape of low relief which existed during Oligocene times (Table 1).[24] Such a low-lying landscape is inferred largely from the deep erosion evident in Llŷn and Tremadoc Bay during what must be the Early Tertiary. This is shown by Oligocene rocks of the Tremadoc basin lying unconformably across both Mesozoic and Palaeozoic ones, and also by the uniformly fine-grained nature of the Oligocene sediments which T. N. George took to imply a hinterland of low gradients and marked lack of energy. Today, correlative beds of Oligocene age lie off shore in St George's Channel and in the Bristol Channel, but also as outliers on the Castlemartin Peninsula at Flimston, at Treffynnon near St David's, and on Halkyn Mountain in Clwyd. Except for Treffynnon these are all preserved within solution subsidence hollows on Carboniferous Limestone where they have been protected

Table 1. Subdivisions of the Cenozoic Era and major events (direct and indirect) in the fashioning of the Welsh landform

Period	Epoch	Age (yrs) ka 10³ Ma 10⁶	Marine isotope stage	Major events in and relating to Wales
	Holocene (post-glacial)		1	Development of Mixed Oak Forest and its subsequent modification by prehistoric people from Mesolithic times. Operation of temperate, mid-latitude, fluvial, slope and marine processes on the Welsh landscape. Sea-level rises to present between 5000 and 2000 years ago
		10 ka		Loch Lomond Glaciation, with ice reoccupation of cirques in Eryri (Snowdonia), and the extensive operation of cold climate (periglacial) processes elsewhere.
		11 ka	2	Late Devensian Glaciation of most of Wales. Burial of the 'Red Lady' at Paviland Cave, 18 ka (Fig 4).
		24 ka	3	Some climatic amelioration. Possible occupation of Tremeirchion Caves, Clwyd
	Late	59 kg	4	Early Devensian glaciation in the mountains (extent of ice unknown)
		71 kg	5a–d	Cold (periglacial) events separated by times of climatic amelioration. Occupation of Coygan Cave, Carmarthen Bay.
		122 ka	5e	Relatively high sea-level of the 'last interglacial'. Reoccupation of the Welsh coastline; the last major modification of Welsh cliffs and shore-zone by marine abrasion; deposition of marine sands and gravels along the coast. Fossil evidence of a prolific interglacial fauna with hippopotamus, elephant, rhinoceros, hyena and deer in Gower and the Elwy Valley.
		128 ka		

			No.	Date	Description
Quaternary	Pleistocene		6	186 ka	Cold climate in Gower. Glaciation in upland Wales of unknown extent. Possible glaciation of the Irish Sea coastlines and coastal hinterland of north and west Wales.
			7	245 ka	Relatively high sea-level which reoccupied the Welsh coastline. Deposition of marine sands and gravels. Occupation of Bontnewydd Cave, Elwy Valley, Clwyd, (the earliest known 'Welsh' people).
				303ka	
			8		Glaciation of Wales. Maximum extent of ice in south Wales at the Paviland Moraine, Gower.
		Middle	9	339 ka	Relatively high sea-level and reoccupation of the coastline by the sea, with fossil remains of marine shells in Gower.
			10	362 ka	Glaciers possible on high ground. Elsewhere, cold climate (periglacial) modification of the landform.
			11		Inferred occupation of the coastline by a high sea-level. Possibly the earliest fashioning of the Welsh coastline as it exists today as cliffs, shore-platforms, estuaries, headlands and bays.
			12	423 ka	Massive glaciation of Wales and adjacent areas by Welsh and Irish Sea Ice Sheets (see Fig. 4).
				478 ka	Glaciation possible at several times, for example, between 524 and 565 ka, between 620 and 659 ka, between 689 and 726 ka. One of these, or earlier, included an extensive glaciation of Wales, when erratic rocks from the east of Snowdonia and from the Berwyn Hills, were transported by ice to the south-east (across the upper Severn Valley and across any Vale of Gloucester — if either existed at this time), at least as far as the then contemporary escarpment of the Cotswold Hills. Thereafter, these erratics were transported by streams of meltwater, through the Thames Valley to East Anglia.
				730ka	

Early	900 ka	'Glacial-interglacial' variability dominated by the 42,000 orbital cycle. Limited glaciation of upland Wales and cold climate (periglacial) processes elsewhere.
	2·4 Ma	
Neogene	Pliocene	Deep weathering. Some erosion, possibly in response to episodic pulsed uplift of Wales, or fault bounded blocks within Wales. Major climate change 3·1 million years ago when the Straits of Panama were closed by continental collision thereby setting up a meridional circulation of ocean water in the North Atlantic, the harbinger of moisture sources for subsequent ice-sheets, and the initiator of effective cold climate (periglacial) modification of Wales.
	7 Ma	
	Miocene	Uplift and dissection of 'Oligocene Wales' during the 'Alpine' earth movements which accompanied a steadily opening North Atlantic by sea-floor spreading and plate movement, and plate collision in southern Europe.
	23 Ma	
	Oligocene	'Oligocene Wales': a landform of low relief with plains, lakes and wide river valleys. Lake deposits survive at Halkyn Mountain, Flimston, Treffynnon and on the floor of Tremadoc Bay.
	33 Ma	
Palaeogene	Eocene	Uplift of Wales accompanying the opening of the North Atlantic Ocean by sea-floor spreading and plate movement. Igneous dykes injection in Gwynedd. Emplacement of the Lundy granite. Deep erosion and reduction of the landsurface by effective denudation before the evolution of the grasses for stabilizing the landform.
	Palaeocene	
	65 Ma	

from erosion. Collectively they show a deformation of the Oligocene landsurface on which they accumulated. This dislocation occurred primarily and principally during the Mid Tertiary ('Alpine') earth-movements, although not inconsiderable further flexure at the earth's crust, together with a pulsed vertical uplift, probably occurred during the Pliocene, continuing even into the Early Pleistocene (Table 1). During the Mid-Tertiary phase, dislocation of the pre-existing landsurface was locally severe. For example, vertical displacement on the Llanbedr Fault (Harlech) was at least 1350m (4430 ft.);[25] an elevational difference which far exceeds the present elevation of that part of Gwynedd. To what extent some of this movement occurred during post-Mid Tertiary times is indeterminate, but the possibility of fault-initiated landforms in the Welsh landscape exists: in this case the high coastal slope between Tremadoc Bay and the Rhinog upland, and by analogy, much of the coastal hinterland of Cardigan Bay, parts of Carmarthen Bay, and elsewhere. With either fault-initiated or erosionally modified fault zones, the clear imperative derived from an analysis of the Llanbedr Fault and the Mochras borehole into the Tremadoc Bay basin, is that the Welsh landform is geologically young. It has been suggested by Battiau-Queney[26] that the gross configuration of the Welsh landform approximates to a deformed Early Tertiary landsurface, and she has cited the evidence of deeply weathered (presumably during that time) surviving pockets of rock situated throughout Wales in topographic positions that correspond to the main lineaments of the landscape today. Such a view, however, ignores not only the unequivocal evidence from Llanbedr and Tremadoc Bay, but also all of Pliocene and Pleistocene time, when phases of deep and effective chemical weathering of rocks occurred, continuously at first, until about 2·4 million years ago, and episodically thereafter during the Pleistocene. Any elements of an Oligocene landsurface which may have survived the considerable erosion of later Cenozoic time are unlikely to be widespread. Regionally, any such Oligocene inheritance would be reduced to palimpsest faintness at best, and at worst it would have been completely erased.

The origin of the Welsh drainage system, and thus of its valleys, has long been controversial. Notwithstanding discoveries made in the past two decades regarding the geology of Welsh sea-floors, it still cannot be said that unequivocal evidence is to hand to show what happened. If the Chalk sea covered Wales entirely, then it is reasonable to assume that on Early Tertiary uplift, a drainage system was initiated.[27] To what extent this was erased or modified by Palaeogene erosion which culminated in a landscape of low relief (above), or by subsequent tectonics, is indeterminate. It seems not unreasonable to suppose that some, if not many, drainage lineaments would have survived the erosion and continued to drain Oligocene Wales. Established drainage lines could have survived subsequent uplift and dislocation of the Oligocene landsurface during the 'Alpine' earth-movements, although differential tectonic uplift, conditioned by major fault lines and fault blocks between, may have been influential. So much is indeterminate. Yet, if the simple device of examining the direction of rivers and valleys which lie discordant to geological structure (that is, do not run along lines of geological 'weakness') are examined and deemed to be relics of original streams, before their derangement by river capture and diversion, it may be possible to discern, however faintly, 'original'

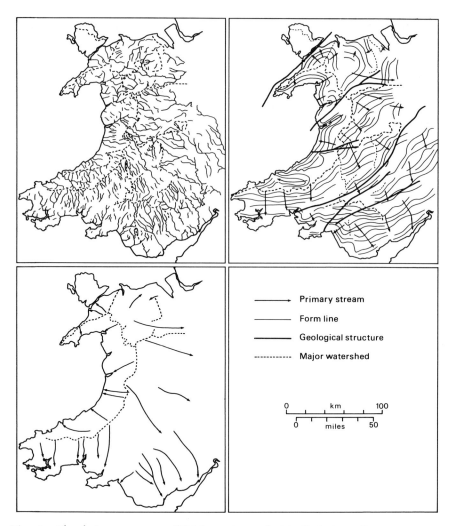

Fig. 3   The drainage systems of Wales: primary (original) drainage lineaments, now transverse to geological structure (top left); *form lines*, perpendicular to the primary drainage (top right); *centrifugal* 'original' (primary) drainage pattern of Wales (bottom left).

lineaments. Then, if 'form-lines' are drawn randomly, and normally, to such drainage lines, these may give clues about the 'original' regional slopes on which such rivers were initiated. The resultant pattern (Fig. 3) is centrifugal, rather than the radial pattern deduced from considerations of a chalk cover sloping south-eastwards from Snowdonia by O. T. Jones and E. H. Brown.[28] As such, a centrifugal pattern explains the hitherto anomalous valleys and streams draining westwards to Cardigan Bay, a pattern eminently compatible with the deep troughs of Mesozoic and Cenozoic deposits in and around St George's Channel, to which a regional slope must have long descended. Thus, for example, the Rheidol and Ystwyth streams must be regarded as original drainage lines, and the much cited and classical instance of 'river-captures' at Devil's Bridge and Cwmystwyth invalidated. Those who seek a unitary and universal generalization on the origin of the Welsh drainage system, however, are unlikely to be successful. It is almost certain that elements of immediately post-Cretaceous, Mid Tertiary and Pleistocene drainage developments have been inherited by the present system. The origin of the drainage is no less indeterminate in absolute terms than is the origin of the 'upland plains' (dissected and coastal plateaux of Fig. 2), and while the discoveries of recent years have constrained theory to some extent, they have, nevertheless, pointed to considerable complexity.

There seems little doubt that the widespread and effective phase of erosion which preceded and caused the development of the low-lying Oligocene landsurface and the initiation of the earliest drainage lines, was a response to uplift occasioned by the opening of the North Atlantic by sea-floor spreading (plate-tectonics/continental drift). The accompanying igneous activity, most spectacular in Ulster and Hebridean Scotland, also affected Wales, notably by dyke injection in north Wales where dykes are dated to 53 million years ago. Just as the early development of the Welsh landform is related to events in a wider, hemispheric, context, so also in its later development was it conditioned by events set in a global context. It is now abundantly clear that the global climate system, and the response by the oceans, ice-sheets and continents, have been controlled by variations in the earth's orbital system,[29] especially those with cycles of 100,000, 41,000 and 23,000 years.

THE LAST 2·4 MILLION YEARS

Analysis of climatic variability in and around the North Atlantic Ocean during the last 3 million years shows that more or less stable climatic conditions ended 2·4 million years ago.[30] Thereafter two climatic modes obtained: an earlier one with low amplitude fluctuations between 'glacial' and 'interglacial' conditions, when relatively low ice volumes occurred on the continents, and with a period dominated by the 41,000 year cycle; followed, after about 900,000 years ago, by larger amplitude changes in climate and ice volume, dominated by the 100,000-year cycle. The cause of the transition between the two modes is unknown, but one possibility is that the Himalayas and the Sierra Nevada were uplifted sufficiently at that time so as to modify the high-level circulation of the westerlies in the atmosphere. This caused large (Rossby) waves to develop, which had the effect of localizing storm tracks in mid-latitudes. The intensified precipitation that these brought became the nourishment essential for the rapid and extensive growth of the mid-latitude ice-sheets which shaped so much of North American and European relief. It seems probable that these large ice-sheets carried with them the seeds of their eventual destruction, not least because of instability and negative feedback effects, both of which imposed limiting factors on their growth. What is puzzling, however, is the dominance of the 100,000-year cycle, because it lacks the power to drive such major changes in climate. But the 23,000-year cycle is also strongly impressed on the sequence of climatic changes in middle and higher latitudes, and it is likely that the 100,000-year cycle evidence in the record is an artefact of interactions within the climate-ice-crustal system of the earth. The implications of these data for the development of the Welsh landform are considerable.

Just as the development of the main lineaments of the Welsh landform, its valley systems, the disposition of high and low ground, and the influence of earth-movements, must necessarily be related to and placed within the context of global tectonics, particularly those related to the steadily opening North Atlantic Ocean since the beginning of the Cenozoic, so too must its subsequent modification by processes driven by climatic change be related to a wider global and hemispheric context. The broad controls of orbital forcing of the climatic system have already been mentioned, and what follows outlines those responses within Wales and adjacent areas which have had significant effects on the landform. The principal events are shown in Table 1. These are based on the historical framework provided by oxygen isotope analysis of sediments throughout the global ocean, within which evidence from Wales can be assembled. This has been greatly assisted by new dating techniques such as amino acid dating, thermoluminescence dating and uranium-thorium dating.[31,32]

The earliest glaciation of Wales is inferred from erratic pebbles and boulders discovered in gravel deposits of an early River Thames in the upper and middle Thames Valley, but also along its former courses in East Anglia. These include igneous rocks from the eastern side of Snowdonia as well as from the Berwyns. The extent of the ice is not known, but must have been considerable if it was able to introduce such boulders into the drainage system of the Thames. In their carriage from north Wales to the Cotswolds, it seems not unreasonable to assume that the ice crossed what would be the upper Severn today, as well as any Vale of Gloucester which may have existed. It may be inferred from this that the geomorphology of Wales has changed since that time. Certainly during the last glaciation, some 18,000 years ago, ice in Wales was found in deep valley troughs, and whereas the total ice volume may well have been equal or similar to that for the earliest glaciation recognized, it was unable to 'escape' the valleys in which it lay. Thus the Welsh landform during the earliest glaciation, which probably occurred around about some 700,000 years ago, has been greatly modified by subsequent events.

There followed a considerable interval of time for which no evidence has been discovered. It has been argued that perhaps more than one similar glaciation occurred, each with much the same effects, including the transportation of Welsh rocks to south-east England. During this time the valley systems would have been progressively modified and overdeepened and by the time of the next clearly established glaciation, just after half a million years ago, it seems clear that the main elements of Welsh valleys, and indeed the Welsh coastline were established. Surviving glacial deposits at West Angle Bay, in the Bristol district, and in North Devon confirm this. This event involved glaciation by both Welsh and Irish Sea masses (Fig. 4), and corresponds with major glaciations in Europe and America.[33] It was followed by 'interglacials' when the Welsh coastline was further fashioned by marine processes (see Stages 11 and 9, in Table 1), although no evidence for the cold event (Stage 10) between them is known in Wales.

During Stage 8, however, a considerable expansion of Welsh ice, transported erratics from Mynydd-y-garreg, in Dyfed, across the Burry estuary to south-west

Gower, where the margin of the glaciation is marked by the Paviland Moraine.[34] In the succeeding 'interglacial' the sea rose to about its present position, or just above it, and reoccupied a Welsh coastline fundamentally identical with the present one on hard-rock coastlines. Beach deposits of this time, some 200,000 years ago, are found in Gower. Because the level of the global ocean at this time was probably below the present, and the raised beaches lie at elevations up to about 10m above OD, it seems likely that some uplift of Wales has occurred since then. Evidence from the Pontnewydd Cave, in the Elwy Valley, shows the earliest known occupation of Wales by prehistoric people, also about 200,000 years ago.[35] The following glaciation, time equivalent to Stage 6 of the global framework, cannot have been very extensive, because its evidence has been everywhere overridden, concealed or destroyed by later ice advances. In contrast to continental Europe, a limited extent to the ice-cover at this time has been adduced for all of the British Isles: it would seem that an explanation for this would lie in the pattern of precipitation during that time, with possibly the Rossby waves guiding greater westerlies precipitation over Scandinavia.

Oxygen isotope Substage 5e, some 125,000 years ago, is generally regarded as the 'last interglacial', that is, the last time before the present when global conditions resembled those of today. In Wales deep soil profiles developed and a prolific mammalian fauna roamed the countryside as is shown by excavations in Gower. Sea-level was marginally higher than at present and the hard-rock coastline of Wales was given an extensive and final marine modification. This event is marked by raised beaches at Llanwern, in Gower, Carmarthen Bay, south Pembrokeshire, Milford Haven, St Bride's Bay, Preseli and in Llŷn. Similar beaches almost certainly occur at the foot of abandoned cliffs now standing a short distance inland of the present shoreline at, for example, Aberaeron, Llan-non, Porth Neigwl, and numerous places along the coast of Clwyd; but all are buried by subsequent deposits of either, and or both, the Devensian cold stage and Holocene (post-glacial).

The repetitive pattern of later Pleistocene climatic fluctuations makes it likely that landform development was equally cyclical, if not entirely systematic in repetition. Given the relatively well-known consequences of the last major glacial cycle (120,000 to 10,000 years ago) it may be used to model earlier ones. Cumulatively, several such cycles would hold a key to the understanding of much of Welsh landform development.

The last glacial cycle commenced with disforestation of a well-wooded interglacial landscape with deep soil profiles. The ensuing soil erosion and colluvium, where deposited, heralded the onset of periglacial action on a largely vegetationless landsurface. Most of the cycle, even allowing for short-lived climatic amelioration (interstadials at c.105, 80, 60, 42 and 30 thousand years ago), was cold if not arctic throughout. Hill-slopes and coastal cliffs were denuded by frost and solifluction. Denudation and subsequent deposition often took on a cyclothemic aspect with initial frost action removing chemically prepared bedrock and resulting in basal blocky deposits: but subsequently frost action operated upon fresh unweathered rock, leading to upper finer calibre scree. The downslope mantle of periglacial waste debris merged with the fluvial system, probably of braided stream channels (because of prolific potential load and reduced stream discharge) during the

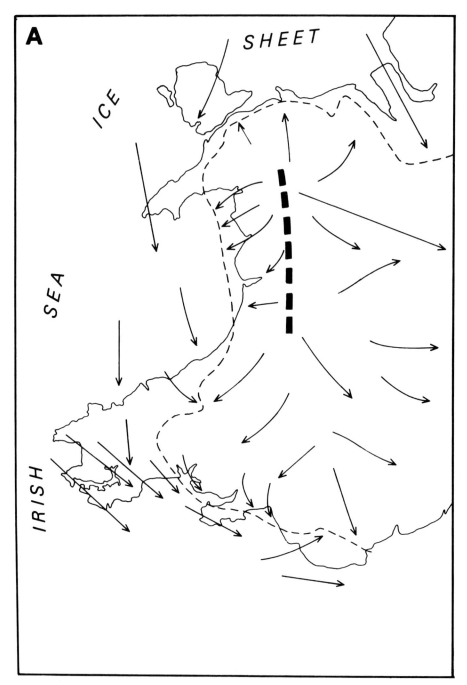

Fig. 4 **A,** Glaciation of Wales estimated at *c.* 450,000 years ago; **B,** Late Devensian glaciation of Wales, *c.* 20,000 years ago. On B, arcuate broken line in Gower shows extent of Welsh ice estimated at *c.* 260,000 years ago. Arrows show direction of ice-movement; heavy broken line indicates main Welsh ice-shed; thin broken line shows zone of contact between ice of Welsh and Irish Sea origin (modified from Bowen 1977)

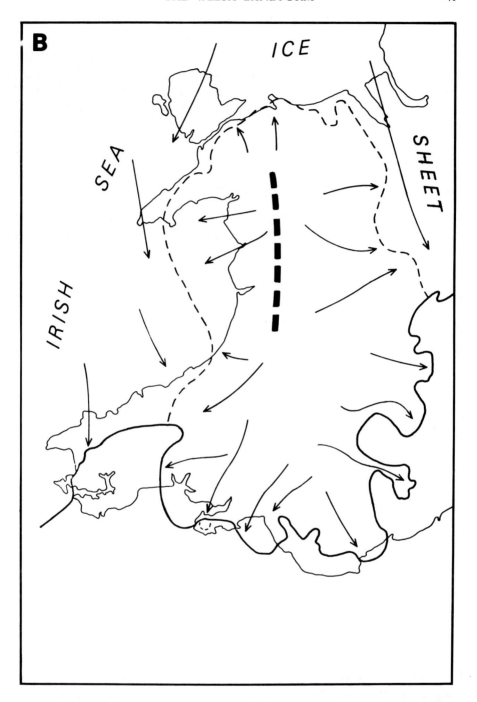

climatically cold and increasingly arid climatic regime. Such stream activity, however, sorted scree debris to form and deposit river gravels. The general events outlined, with due allowance for local variation caused by rock-type and general geomorphology, occurred repetitively and hold the key to a mode of landscape development.

It is still difficult to establish the character and timing of events between the 'last interglacial' (Substage 5e) and Late Devensian Glaciation (Stage 2). An early sequence of events, when the climate alternated between intense cold and temperate conditions, was followed by probable glaciation on the higher ground, but of unknown extent. Evidence is now to hand that extensive glaciation occurred at this time (Stage 4) in Ulster, parts of eastern Ireland, and Caithness and Orkney:[36] thus for Wales to have escaped glaciation of any kind at this time is improbable. The Late Devensian Glaciation of Wales (Fig. 4) occurred between 24,000 and 15,000 years ago and fashioned the great majority of landforms composed of till (boulder clay) sands and gravels. Its erosional effects, however, were limited, because the ice merely reoccupied glaciated valleys effectively fashioned by earlier glaciations. An important new development has been the reinterpretation of many Late Devensian Irish Sea drift deposits around Cardigan Bay. Some of these are now believed to have formed in glacio-marine environments: that is, they were deposited as muds or deltas in a full-glacial sea, while the earth's crust was still depressed as a result of the weight of the ice-sheets.

At the close of the Last Glaciation, between c.11,000 and 10,000 years ago, there occurred a brief but highly effective phase of geomorphic development triggered by climatic deterioration in an otherwise ameliorating climate after the disappearance of the last ice-sheet. Widespread permafrost obtained, evidenced by ground-ice depressions ('pingo'? scars) and ice-wedge casts, together with massive transference downslope of superficial materials, additional scree formation, and development of alluvial fans (as at Cardigan Bay) and low-level river terraces. All this was accompanied by the reoccupation of cirques by either glacier ice or, at lower elevations, by snow patches. The intensity and brevity of this episode probably holds a further key to the development of the landform and points to episodic erosion at times when optimal factors coincided, that is climatic deterioration after amelioration among other controls.

The onset of climatic amelioration about 10,000 years ago was rapid and a vegetational response leading to the development of a mixed oak forest association was complete by Neolithic times. The stabilization of the landsurface which this produced stands in great contrast to the events of the immediately previous 100,000 years which was dominated by cold climate processes. As described earlier, contemporary river, slope and coastal processes continue to operate against a rich variety of legacies from the 'ice ages'.

OVERVIEW

The geomorphology or shape of the Welsh landform is the result of the operation in time of external and internal variables. First, the external influence of plate tectonics relating to the opening of the North Atlantic Ocean over the past 65 million years, when structural lineaments initiated in earlier Mesozoic time (for example, the Mochras Basin, Bristol Channel, Cheshire–Shropshire and Worcestershire basins), were accentuated, leading to episodic and pulsed uplift of Wales throughout Cenozoic time, but reaching an intensity during the 'Alpine' movements of the Mid Tertiary. It would be a mistake, however, to assume that uplift at other times was insignificant. On the contrary, Pliocene and Early Pleistocene uplift was almost certainly important, while evidence from raised beaches, in Gower, and global sea-levels, show recent (neotectonic) uplift. Furthermore, evidence of considerable land-movements induced by ice-loading and unloading as recently as 17,000 years ago are well documented. Also, external forcing function of climatic change as driven by the earth's orbital variations, has conditioned the character and intensity of landforming processes for the past 2·4 million years. These are the interpretative keys for any analysis of the Welsh landform.

Internal variables are those of variations in the geology and structure and the way in which these have interacted with the external ones. A consideration of both shows that Wales cannot be conceived as 'a land of ancient mountains', nor as an unchanging timeless scene as evoked by the bard Ceiriog when he wrote that 'aros mae'r mynyddoedd mawr' (the great mountains are permanent). Instead, on geological and even prehistoric time-scales, rapid and major changes have occurred in recent geological time, a conclusion in accord with the broad philosophical judgement of W. D. Thornbury[37] who stated as much for global landscapes. It is a curious and novel circumstance that as more is learnt about such an evolutionary past, the evidence may be marshalled and modelled to look to future changes, not merely in terms of landform changes, but more importantly to the climatic changes which precede these. Much of the future will be predicted in terms of the past in the present. In this, the evidence from Wales is no less important than from elsewhere.

NOTES

[1] O.T. Jones, 'The Drainage Systems of Wales and the Adjacent Regions', *Quarterly Journal Geological Society*, 107 (1951), 201–25; E.H. Brown, *The Relief and Drainage of Wales* (Cardiff, 1960).

[2] T.R. Owen, *The Upper Palaeozoic and Post-Palaeozoic Rocks of Wales* (Cardiff, 1974); D.Q. Bowen, Sheet 1.1 'Geology', and Sheet 1.3 'Surface Morphology', *National Atlas of Wales* (Cardiff, 1982).

[3] Ibid.; J.A. Taylor, Sheet 1.6 'Vegetation', *National Atlas of Wales* (Cardiff, 1982).

[4] E.H. Brown, op. cit.

[5] D.Q. Bowen, 'The Land of Wales', in D. Thomas (ed.), *Wales: a New Study* (Newton Abbot, 1977), 11–35.

[6] E.H. Brown, op. cit.

[7] J.A. Taylor, op. cit.

[8] A.C. Ramsay, 'The Denudation of South Wales and the Adjacent English Counties', *Memoir Geological Survey* (1846).

[9] O.T. Jones, 'Some Episodes in the Geological History of the Bristol Channel region', *Report of the British Association for the Advancement of Science* (1931), 57–82; idem, *Quarterly Journal Geological Society*, 107 (1951), 201–25; T.N. George, 'The Welsh Landscape', *Science Progress*, 49 (1961), 242–64; idem, 'The Cenozoic Evolution of Wales', in T.R. Owen (ed.), *The Upper Palaeozoic and Post-Palaeozoic Rocks of Wales*, 341–71; E.H. Brown, op. cit; see also P.T. Walsh and E.H. Brown, 'Solution

Subsidence Outliers Containing Tertiary Sediment in North-east Wales', *Geological Journal*, 7 (1971), 299–320.

[10] D.Q. Bowen, *Wales: a New Study*; idem, *National Atlas of Wales*, Sheet 1.3.

[11] E.H. Brown, op. cit.

[12] D.Q. Bowen, *National Atlas of Wales*, Sheet 1.1; J.A. Taylor, ibid.

[13] D.Q. Bowen, *Wales: a New Study*; idem, *National Atlas of Wales*.

[14] Idem, 'The Coast of Wales' in 'The Quarternary History of the Irish Sea', *Geological Journal Special Issue No.* 7 (1977), 223–56.

[15] F.J. North, *The Evolution of the Bristol Channel* (Cardiff, 1929, and revised 1955).

[16] D.Q. Bowen, *Geological Journal Special Issue No.* 7 (1977), 223–56.

[17] A.W. Woodland and W.B. Evans, 'The Geology of the South Wales Coalfield. Part IV. The Country around Pontypridd and Maesteg', *Memoir Geological Survey* (1964).

[18] J. Lewin, Sheet 1.2 'Relief Hydrology', *National Atlas of Wales* (Cardiff, 1980).

[19] H. Godwin, 'A Boreal Transgression of the Sea in Swansea Bay: data for the study of post-glacial history', *New Phytologist*, 39 (1940), 308–21.

[20] M.J. Tooley, *Sea-level Changes: the coast of north-west England during the Flandrian Stage* (Oxford, 1977).

[21] J.T. Hack, 'Interpretation of Erosional Topography in Humid Temperate Regions', *American Journal of Science*, 258 (1960), 80–97.

[22] J. Challinor, 'The Hill-top Surface of North Cardiganshire', *Geography*, 15 (1930), 651–6.

[23] D.Q. Bowen, 'Y Tirffurf Cymreig', *Y Gwyddonydd*, 5 (1967), 14–22.

[24] T.N. George, in T.R. Owen (ed.), *The Upper Palaeozoic and Post-Palaeozoic Rocks of Wales*, 341–71.

[25] Ibid.

[26] Y. Battiau-Queney, *Contribution à l'étude Géomorphologique du Massif Gallois*. University de Bretagne Occidentale thesis (1980), 792pp. (published version distributed by Librairie Honore Champion, 7 Quai Malaquais, Paris).

[27] See note 1.

[28] See note 1.

[29] J.D. Hays, J. Imbrie, and N.J. Shackleton, 'Variations in the Earth's Orbit: pacemaker of the ice ages', *Science*, 194 (1976), 1121–32; A. Berger, J. Imbrie, J. Hays, G. Kukla, and B. Saltzman, *Milankovitch and Climate* 2 vols. (Dordrecht, 1984), 147–62.

[30] N.J. Shackleton, R.G. West, and D.Q. Bowen, 'The Past Three Million Years: Evolution of Climatic Variability in the North Atlantic Region', *Philosophical Transactions Royal Society of London, Series B.* (1988).

[31] D.Q. Bowen, G.A. Sykes, A. Reeves, G.H. Miller, J.T. Andrews, J.S. Brew, and P.E. Hare, 'Amino Acid Geochronology of Raised Beaches in South West Britain', *Quarternary Science Reviews*, 4 (1985), 279–318; D.Q. Bowen, J. Rose, A.M. McCabe, D.G. Sutherland, 'Correlation of Quarternary Glaciations in England, Ireland, Scotland and Wales', *Quarternary Science Reviews*, 5 (1986), 299–340.

[32] D.Q. Bowen and G.A. Sykes, 'Correlation of Marine Events and Glaciations on the North-east Atlantic Margin', *Philosophical Transactions Royal Society of London, Series B* 318, 6192635 (1988).

[33] V. Sibrava, D.Q. Bowen, and G.M. Richmond (eds.), 'Quaternary Glaciations in the Northern Hemisphere' *Quaternary Science Reviews*, 5 (1986), 511pp.

[34] D.Q. Bowen, D.G. Jenkins, A. Reid, and J.A. Catt, 'The Paviland Moraine: a Middle Pleistocene Ice margin in Gower', (submitted to *The Quarternary Newsletter*).

[35] H.S. Green, *Pontnewydd Cave: A Lower Palaeolithic Site in Wales* (Cardiff, 1984).

[36] See note 31.

[37] W.D. Thornbury, *Principles of Geomorphology* (New York, 1954).

Vegetation

WILLIAM LINNARD

THE general features of the development of the vegetation since the end of the last glacial (Devensian) period in the territory now known as Wales have been fairly accurately determined by examination of plant remains from archaeologically dated sites, and especially by pollen analyses carried out over the last fifty years, chiefly on samples of peat obtained from bogs at various places in upland and lowland sites.

Most of our native trees liberate into the air large amounts of pollen which is blown about by the wind, and some of this pollen 'rain' settles down on neighbouring lakes and pools or on the surface of peat bogs. The bog mosses, as they die back, do not decay completely but accumulate, forming deposits of wet peat which preserve the pollen grains. The species or at least the genera of the plants releasing pollen grains can be identified microscopically, the ratio of tree to non-tree pollen ascertained, and the relative proportions of individual species determined. By analysing samples of peat from various depths, the changes in the composition of the local flora over time can be followed.

The results of these pollen analyses may differ in local details, and in the later stages of the pollen record they often indicate divergent vegetation histories attributable in greater or lesser degree to the influence of man. However, taken together they reveal a great measure of agreement, and a fairly consistent picture of vegetation history emerges which conforms broadly to that shown by parallel studies carried out in other parts of Britain and Northern Europe.[1]

The general outline of vegetation development in relation to climatic phases, pollen zones, and human economic activity was summarized diagrammatically by Hyde over a quarter of a century ago.[2] This summary diagram remains substantially correct, though certain modifications have become necessary in the light of recent research which has revealed deviations from the established continental Holocene climatic periods in the maritime climates of the British Isles, and alterations have been made too in the chronologies of the culture periods of Neolithic, Bronze Age and Iron Age in the British Isles. As is explained in Chapter 6, radio-carbon dating corrected by dendrochronology has already caused modifications in the accepted picture, and future work will inevitably lead to further refinement. Fig. 5 attempts to update Hyde's diagram on the basis of the most recent data summarized and reviewed by Taylor.[3] This diagram summarizes the general situation for Wales as a whole, but it is necessary to distinguish three broad regional environments or zones having distinct bioclimates. The first, which may be termed the maritime or Atlantic zone, comprises Anglesey, coastal Gwynedd including Llŷn, coastal Dyfed and especially the extreme south-west peninsula, the lower vale of Towy, Gower, and the southern coastal fringe of Glamorgan. This zone merges rapidly inland into the second zone, the central mass of the Welsh uplands, an area of high rainfall and

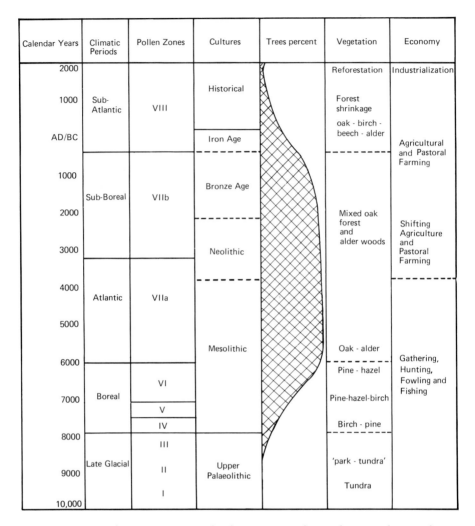

Calendar Years	Climatic Periods	Pollen Zones	Cultures	Trees percent	Vegetation	Economy
2000	Sub-Atlantic	VIII	Historical		Reforestation	Industrialization
1000					Forest shrinkage	
AD/BC			Iron Age		oak - birch - beech - alder	Agricultural and Pastoral Farming
1000	Sub-Boreal	VIIb	Bronze Age			
2000					Mixed oak forest and alder woods	Shifting Agriculture and Pastoral Farming
3000			Neolithic			
4000	Atlantic	VIIa				
5000						
6000		VI	Mesolithic		Oak - alder	Gathering, Hunting, Fowling and Fishing
					Pine - hazel	
7000	Boreal	V			Pine-hazel-birch	
		IV				
8000		III			Birch - pine	
9000	Late Glacial	II	Upper Palaeolithic		'park - tundra'	
		I			Tundra	
10,000						

Fig. 5 Diagram showing vegetation development in Wales in relation to climatic phases, pollen zones and human economic activity.

shorter growing season, which responds late to a warming but early to a cooling climate. The third zone is the Welsh borderland, with the least maritime climate, extending from the Dee estuary to the coast of Gwent and including the eastern parts of Clwyd, Powys and Gwent. Within these three major zones, local topography and soils impose further variation, in turn affecting the natural vegetation.

Natural vegetation itself is not static, and develops according to the climate and soil of the area. Bare ground is first occupied by pioneer plants, which are eventually displaced by a natural succession of species occupying the site more intensively, until finally the climax vegetation becomes established, this being the most highly developed form of plant community which the area can support. Over much of

Wales, and indeed the greater part of Britain and western Europe, the climax vegetation is broadleaved deciduous forest.

The last glacial period, the Devensian (Weichselian), drew to an end some 12,000 years ago, and in general, and in its simplest terms, the climatic picture since then has been one of gradual warming up for some three and a half thousand years until 6500 BC, followed by a period of 'optimum' climate of similar duration, until 3000 BC, and then a cooling period extending to the present. Of course, numerous shorter- and longer-term climatic fluctuations and cycles have occurred within these major periods.

Following the retreat of the ice at the end of the glacial period, a sparse tundra or 'park-tundra' vegetation of herbs and subshrubs gradually developed, similar to that observed in northern Scandinavia today. As the climate improved in the early Boreal period (Pollen Zone IV), the first trees to colonize large areas were the birches — light-seeded pioneer species, dispersed by the wind, capable of rapid spread and relatively undemanding as to site. The birches comprised the dwarf species (*Betula nana* L.), not now part of the Welsh flora, and the two common native species *Betula pendula* L. and *B. pubescens* Ehrh., which cannot be separated by pollen analyses. The pollen record shows that birch was for a time the sole tree present, but it was soon followed by the next invading species, another light-demanding tree, Scots pine (*Pinus sylvestris* L.), a conifer which has a very wide Eurasian distribution. Birch and pine continued to dominate the tree vegetation throughout the Pre-Boreal and early Boreal, apparently alternating in relative importance.

Pine continued to be an important element of the Welsh vegetation throughout the Boreal, with birch declining somewhat in importance and other broadleaved species such as hazel (*Corylus avellana* L.), elm (presumably only *Ulmus glabra* Huds., see below), and oak becoming established. Oak was soon to become the dominant native tree throughout Wales, and to remain so for seven millennia, up until the very recent period of extensive planting of exotic species, mainly conifers, in the nineteenth and twentieth centuries.[4] In Wales, oak is represented by two species, the pedunculate oak (*Quercus robur* L.) and the sessile oak (*Q. petraea* (Matt.) Liebl.), but these are indistinguishable in pollen analyses or by examination of the wood. *Q. robur* is the main species in the lowlands and on the heavier soils of the borderland, while *Q. petraea* is the main species in the uplands in areas of high rainfall and on the older siliceous rocks. Natural hybrids between the two native oak species are frequent.

In Taylor's ecosystem model for the Early Mesolithic,[5] Pollen Zone VI is divided into VIa with a hazel maximum in both uplands and lowlands, birch declining in favour of oak, elm and pine in the lowlands and promoting a major expansion of pine in the uplands. Thus, early Mesolithic man would have found mixed broadleaved forests in the lowlands, and birch/pine in the uplands. In Zone VIb, hazel became reduced everywhere, surviving as an understorey beneath oak and elm; pine survived especially in the uplands, where birch declined. In Zone VIc, oak and pine expanded, especially in the uplands, with the pine increasing particularly at higher altitudes; hazel decreased in the lowlands, the relatively thermophilous small-leaved lime (*Tilia cordata* Mill.) arrived, as did the common or black alder (*Alnus glutinosa* Gaertn.). The latter, a nitrogen-fixing species, spread rapidly everywhere.

During the Boreal, with rising sea levels and submergence, the land links with Ireland were broken, and somewhat later the British Isles became detached from continental Europe. Forest probably reached its greatest altitudinal extent during the climatic optimum of the Atlantic period, but conditions in the preceding Boreal and in the succeeding Sub-Boreal may also have enabled trees to colonize land at high altitudes. At the time of maximum forest expansion, forest would have covered most of the land area of Wales apart from the very highest mountains. Subfossil tree roots and stems, commonly known as bog-wood and identified as pine, oak and birch, are found in peat at many places at altitudes up to about 2000 ft., which coincidentally is the general upper limit of planting by the Forestry Commission in Wales today. Only 1 per cent of the land area of Wales lies above 2000 ft., i.e. above the probable upper forest limit, and some 6 per cent of the land area lies between 1500 and 2000 ft., at altitudes where tree growth is possible, though rates of increment would not be rapid. Naturally, areas of marine sands, lakes, rock and scree, and special sites such as salt marsh or very exposed areas would not have carried forest vegetation. Wind too is a limiting factor of great importance, especially on west- and north-facing slopes.

After the Boreal, the climate became wetter during the Atlantic period, with a warmth maximum. Mixed deciduous woodland is generally believed to have attained its maximum expansion and vigour, except at higher altitudes and in exposed locations. The proportion of alder increased substantially, and that of pine decreased quite sharply to a very low but fairly steady level, persisting in the uplands where competition with other tree species was least. During this climatic optimum, small-leaved lime formed a small but important element of mixed oak forests, especially on lower and warmer sites. Alder was dominant on wet marshy sites, and occurred with oak in valleys, plains and slopes. Some elm was present at all altitudes, but oak forest became the characteristic and major vegetation of the lowlands in the Atlantic and later periods, and of the highland zone too in the later Sub-Boreal period.

Tycanol Wood, on the north slope of the Preseli range, is today an area of primary sessile oak/ash/hazel with a rich bryophyte flora, where there has almost certainly been some woodland cover since Atlantic times.[6] Other fragments of ancient woodlands with a particularly rich flora of epiphytic lichens occur in the Gwaun Valley and Coed Rheidol in Dyfed, and in Coed Cymerau, Coed Ganllwyd and Coed y Rhygen in Gwynedd (now National Nature Reserves).

During the Atlantic period, with its wetter and windier climate, peat mosses gradually invaded the plateaux and upper slopes. The effect of the small Mesolithic population of food-gatherers, hunters and fishers on the vegetation in this period has been generally thought to be slight, but recent research suggests that human influence was more important and, in conjunction with climatic change, could have brought about significant modification of forest, at least locally. The ability of small numbers of men with hand-axes and the deliberate use of fire to modify or destroy forests can be considerable.

Towards the end of the Atlantic period, with a cooler and then drier climate, Mesolithic nomadism was replaced by the more settled Neolithic system. Areas of heath and upland peats spread, but extensive mixed deciduous woodlands dominated by oak persisted at lower altitudes and on steep slopes. Ash (*Fraxinus excelsior* L.) arrived *c*.3000 BC and spread locally. Heath and bog expansion favoured birch and pine, especially on drying sites.

Though extrapolated from fragmentary evidence, the pollen maps produced by Birks *et al*.[7] for pine, birch, oak, elm, alder, hazel and lime in Wales at 3000 BC, just before the start of marked decline in elm pollen and before the most extensive of the Neolithic clearances, show that pine was by then very rare everywhere, and not an important element in the Welsh forests; oak was the principal component of the forests; birch was not a major forest species, though occasional high pollen values are recorded in south Wales; elm was moderately important in parts of south Wales but very rare in the north; alder was frequent in north, mid and south Wales, but not the south-west; hazel was common everywhere except Snowdonia; and lime was important only in mid Wales. At this time the first weeds of grazing and cultivation appear in the pollen record, and also cereal pollen. Scrub and forest-margin species such as bracken also become more prominent, reflecting the increasing clearance of forest.

The question of elm decline associated with the advent of Neolithic farmers is still unresolved. The timing and extent of the decline varied, apparently being less dramatic in Wales than in Ireland and lowland England, and being accompanied by the appearance of typical weed species such as plantains and nettles. Though the possibility of a catastrophic epidemic such as occurred during the 1970s cannot be dismissed, the decline of elm is generally ascribed to the selective influence of man, in felling or lopping trees particularly suitable for leaf fodder for pounded livestock during winter, and seems to have restricted what was previously a quite widely distributed tree to certain favoured areas, in particular the middle stretches of the larger rivers in eastern Wales, and some small regions in the south, west, and north of the country. Lime and perhaps also ash are believed to have been affected in the same way.

Early in the Sub-Boreal (early VIIb) the ecological equilibrium of the Mesolithic begins to be lost, and Neolithic and later Bronze Age people with metal tools and more sophisticated use of fire caused selective and locally massive deforestation. Peat growth continued on the higher, wetter plateaux, but pine and birch reasserted themselves somewhat. Elm disappeared from many areas, as did lime.

All the native broadleaved species of Wales are capable of regenerating more or less vigorously by coppice sprouting from the stump after felling. The vigour depends on tree species, age and light, and the subsequent survival and growth of the coppice shoots depend on freedom from browsing and other damage. The procedures of clearance of natural woodland by shifting cultivation or slash-and-burn agriculture of Neolithic and later farmers are recalled succinctly in the Mabinogion tale of Culhwch and Olwen, where Ysbaddaden sets his first task for Culhwch: 'Dost see the great thicket yonder? . . . I must have it uprooted out of the earth and burnt on the face of the ground so that the cinders and ashes thereof be its manure, and that it be ploughed and sown . . .'.[8]

In practice, initial site selection was a skilled job, to avoid frost hollows, stony terrain and areas prone to seasonal waterlogging. Open woodland rather than dense hardwood forest would obviously be preferred for ease of clearance. Trees were dealt with in two ways: the large trees, especially hard-wooded species such as oak, were killed by girdling the bark and chopping away some of the sapwood, while smaller trees were felled. Large stumps would probably be left *in situ*, as complete clearance of the site by uprooting would be excessively laborious for only short-term agricultural utilization. The forests cleared were often open upland woodlands of oak and/or birch, as for example on sites studied in Powys,[9] and in the lower Conwy valley.[10] The felled material would be spread over the area and left to dry out, for burning to be done in one operation, probably in spring, and repeated if necessary. Crops would be sown under dead standing trees. Each slash-and-burn site, perhaps a few acres in size, would be cropped for only a few years before its fertility was exhausted and another site would have to be used. This would result in a regular programme of tree girdling and felling, drying out and burning, and then cultivation. Felling would have to be done at least a year before crop sowing took place. Some of the root suckers and coppice regeneration from stumps in and around the cleared areas would be destroyed by grazing animals, while surviving sprouts from successive clearings would tend to form an age sequence similar to managed coppice. Excavations in the Somerset Levels have revealed numerous wooden trackways of Neolithic age, and of various types, the evidence indicating quite sophisticated methods of production and utilization of the local woody species, with ample evidence of coppiced hazel stands. The understanding of coppicing and its systematic application has probably been a regular form of woodland management ever since Neolithic times, and in the mixed arable and livestock husbandry of the Neolithic farmers, sheep were an ideal means of exploiting open oakwoods, and would have had a significant effect in eliminating tree regeneration around settlements.

During the Middle and Later Bronze Age, the climatic and anthropogenic effects on the forests continued, with peat accumulation, and the spread of heath, moorland grasses, bracken and scrub. The plateau woodlands were mainly birch/hazel/pine, with alder prominent in wet habitats at low and intermediate altitudes. Oak forest still occupied large areas on slopes and lower lands.

The abandonment of small areas used for shifting cultivation would often be followed by natural succession back to secondary forest. This process of alternating clearance and natural forest regrowth is also described in the tale of Culhwch and Olwen, by the Owl of Cwm Cawlwyd: 'the great valley you can see was a wooded glen, and a race of men came thereto and it was laid waste. And the second wood grew up therein, and this wood is the third . . .'.[11]

With the cooler and wetter climate of the Sub-Atlantic (at the start of Zone VIII) during the Iron Age the tree-line and agricultural and settlement limits were all reduced in altitude. Peat formation increased in the uplands, especially on deforested areas and wet soils, with the development of extensive *Sphagnum* moss and *Eriophorum* (cotton grass) communities, which Leland later described so graphically as 'wilde pastures . . . sogges and quikke'.[12] The improved tools and more settled mode of life at lower altitudes marked the start of major clearance of the dense low-altitude forests in Wales.

This period also saw the immigration into Wales of beech (*Fagus sylvatica* L.) and probably hornbeam (*Carpinus betulus* L.), the last tree species to form part of the native flora before the period of proven introduction by man. Beech is native in Wales only in south-east Powys, Gwent and east Glamorgan, where numerous relict beech woods and place-names incorporating the Welsh name for beech (*ffawydd, ffawydden, ffawyddog*) are found within or immediately outside the eastern fringe of the coalfield.[13] The pollen evidence for the presence of beech in Wales before the Roman invasion is not conclusive, but the discovery of quantities of beech charcoal in an Iron Age hearth at Radyr (Glamorgan) dated at or before the first century AD proves the nativity of beech in Wales.[14] The charcoal in this hearth was in the form of short thick sticks, some evidently cut with an axe, and indicated that the forest environment there was ash/oak/beech woodland, with elm (probably *Ulmus glabra*) an important accessory species, and also occasional birch, field maple (*Acer campestre*) and holly, with hazel the main shrub. Apart from birch, all these species still occur in the present-day woodlands at the hearth site, together with sycamore and lime (Plate 1).

The natural area of beech in south-east Wales apparently remained relatively stable for nearly 2000 years. Numerous documentary references and place-names attest to beech as a timber species in south-eastern Wales from the thirteenth century onward, but it remained confined to the south-east corner, its failure to spread further northward and westward naturally being apparently attributable to its intolerance of the wetter and cooler conditions prevailing there.

Jury evidence for a general survey of the estates of the Earl of Pembroke in 1570 gives a clear statement of the local geographical distribution of beech in Glamorgan at that time: 'within the said Foreste called Forreste Keven y Vyd and Forest Keven Onn there ys for the most parte Beache of sundry sortes and no oeke or Tymber at all'; 'Forest Maes yr allt . . . in which there ys oeke and beaches'; 'Llowyd Koyd is replenyshed most with oke, glyn Kynon moste with beache and some with okes, glyn Tave with bothe and Koed Marchan all with okes'[15]. The natural distribution of beech in Wales, which was not obscured by planting in the west and north until the eighteenth century, was noted at the end of the seventeenth century by Edward Lhuyd in correspondence; 'In noe part of Northwales is found any flint or chalk, nor beech trees' (1 July 1690), and again: 'In South Wales I found several plants common which I had never seen in North Wales, such as . . . Fagus' (24 November 1696).[16]

The post-Boreal status of Scots pine (*Pinus sylvestris* L.) in Wales is much more doubtful.[17] Pollen records from north and south Wales show pine present at all levels from the Pre-Boreal onwards, but from the end of the Atlantic period (*c.*3000 BC) at levels so low that the pollen may have been carried in by the wind from far away, for example Ireland. Hyde concludes that pine died out 'almost if not quite completely' in Wales. Remains of pine trees in submerged forests off the coast between Penmaen-mawr and Priestholm were recorded by John Ray in 1662, and pines have also been identified off the coast at Borth and Ynys-las. Godwin believed that a relict stock of native pine might have persisted in Wales in special bog and mountain sites, for example, at Borth Bog near the pine trees found in the submerged forest. Pine charcoal found in a Neolithic cairn at Bryn Celli Ddu (Anglesey) was dated at *c.*1500 BC. Pine trunks and stumps have frequently been found in peat beds in various parts of Wales, for example at Llyn Llwydiart in

Plate 1   The Iron Age hearth at Radyr, with an old beech tree growing on the edge of the hearth.

Anglesey, in Cwm Bychan (Merioneth), and 'in the deeps of Monmouth, where turfe is digged'. This subfossilized resinous bog-wood was used by Welsh peasants in later centuries for splints and torches.

Significantly, the earliest Welsh literary reference to pine, in the form of torches or fires of pine, comes not from Wales itself but from the country of Gododdin, between the Forth and the Tyne, in a sixth-century poem by Aneirin.[18] Other early literary references to pine (*ffenitwydd, ffinydwydd*) occur in the thirteenth-century manuscripts of the *Kat Godeu* (*Cad Goddau*) and Mabinogion (White and Red Books), but although the original sources of the surviving manuscripts are from even earlier periods, they cannot be regarded as providing definite evidence of the existence of living pine in Wales. The same applies to later poetical references to pine, e.g. by Madog Benfras in the fourteenth century.[19] Place-name evidence is even more uncertain, and there are no early place-names that incorporate a pine/fir element, though it has been suggested that names such as Coed Du or Coed Duon (=black wood) may refer to former pine-dominated woodland. The absence of pine from the lists of tree values in the Welsh Laws attributed to Hywel Dda is strong evidence that it had completely died out; such a uniquely useful species would surely have been mentioned in lists reflecting relative usefulness to man. Scots pine was planted widely in Wales from the seventeenth century onward, but there is no positive evidence of the existence of living pine in Wales before then. Therefore, the possibility of the uninterrupted survival of the species in Wales since Boreal times must remain open and doubtful.

Using sophisticated biometrical methods of analysis, Richens has made a detailed study of the variation and distribution of elms throughout England, and discusses their history in relation to man.[20] He argues that in England the earliest introduction of elms by man may be of Later Bronze Age date, and that thereafter the elm in the pollen profiles is not necessarily *U. glabra*. In a further special study devoted to Wales, Richens and Jeffers[21] show that elm of any sort is now rare over much of Wales, and that the only elm certainly native is the wych elm, *U. glabra*, which is now frequent in nineteen regions, the largest of these lying along the English border in the basins of the Dee, Severn, Usk and middle Wye. The other regions of *U. glabra* in the south, west and north are much smaller.

In Wales the English elm (*U. minor* var. *vulgaris*) occurs in no natural communities, is normally sterile, and must be an introduction. It occurs in several distinct localities in southern Wales, coexisting in high frequency with *U. glabra* in areas west of Cardiff and near Monmouth. In posing the questions as to when and from where the English elm was introduced into Wales, Richens and Jeffers argue that where no direct historical evidence is available, recourse must be had to the implications of the distribution pattern. Here a useful working hypothesis is that the date of introduction of a plant brought in by man is unlikely to be later than the latest archaeological or historical distribution corresponding with that of the plant. On this basis they show that the modern distribution of English elm in south-east Wales corresponds closely to the former boundary of English speech in 1750, as indicated, for example, by the language used in church services, and the facts at present available suggest that the English elm was introduced into south-east Wales by immigrants from Somerset, perhaps even before the Norman invasion.

The Dutch elm (*U. × hollandica* var. *hollandica*), the principal landscape elm of western Wales, was introduced in the eighteenth century and widely planted thereafter, especially on exposed sites near the sea.

Most of the native trees of Wales in the period before large-scale introduction by man are listed in the Welsh Laws, and accorded cash values which reflect their relative usefulness to man: alder, apple, ash, beech, crabapple, elm, hazel, oak, thorn, willow, and yew. Other native trees, such as aspen, birch, holly, lime, maple and poplar, are not specifically mentioned in the Laws but were covered in the category of trees not bearing edible fruit.[22] As already noted for pine, the absence from the Laws of valuable or distinctive trees such as sycamore is strong evidence that the species was not present in Wales when the Laws were compiled. Sycamore (*Acer pseudoplatanus* L.) was introduced perhaps by the Normans, though probably even later. Originally associated exclusively with human settlement, it has been widely planted since at least the seventeenth century, has spread naturally and is now a common naturalized species in many parts of Wales.

The relatively poor native flora formed only few natural forest types. Oak, the most valuable and most extensive tree, formed two main vegetation types, viz. pedunculate oakwood dominated by *Quercus robur*, and sessile oakwood dominated by *Quercus petraea*. The two oaks produce pollen that is not distinguishable, and readily interbreed to produce a number of hybrid forms intermediate between the two parent species. The pedunculate oakwood occurs in the lowlands, with associate species including wych elm, small-leaved lime, field maple, cherry, aspen, holly and yew, and often hazel underwood; only remnants of this type of woodland now exist, as the soils on which it developed are well suited to agricultural use. The ground flora includes dog's mercury, wood sanicle or primrose on the heavier soils, and bluebell and wood anemone on the lighter ones. The sessile oakwood, for millennia the typical native woodland over the large part of upland Wales, with older acidic rocks and higher rainfall, still covers quite considerable areas on steeper slopes. Birch and rowan are the typical associates, the birch forming pure stands in places, especially at higher altitudes. Bracken commonly dominates the field layer, persisting after the woods are felled, and bluebell, bramble and foxglove are frequent.

On particular sites, other forest types predominated, and some fragments still persist today. Alder woods, dominated by common alder (*Alnus glutinosa*) together with various willows (especially *Salix caprea* and *S. cinerea*), occupy marshy valley-bottom sites. On gentle slopes alder also forms woods with ash and oak.

Ash woods, dominated by common ash (*Fraxinus excelsior*), and mixed ash/oak woods occur on Carboniferous Limestone in south Wales, on steep slopes, with aspen and wych elm as associated species. Shrubs such as dogwood, spindle and wayfaring tree are a particular feature of limestone woodlands. The field layer may comprise ramsons (*Allium ursinum*), dog's mercury or hart's-tongue fern. Ashwoods also occur on basic igneous rocks in Gwynedd, and some residual ash/oak/field-maple woods are found on the Lias limestone in Glamorgan.

Beechwoods, dominated by beech (*Fagus sylvatica*) and with some associated oak, ash and wych elm, occur in south-east Wales. The ground flora is very thin, and in the densest woods the soil may be quite bare (*Fagetum nudum*), but with more light the ground flora includes ramsons, bluebell, dog's mercury and bramble. Two of the best remaining semi-natural beechwoods are in the Cwm Clydach National Nature Reserve, south-west of Abergavenny.

At the time of the Roman invasion, the general vegetational pattern was one of small areas of settlement and cleared agricultural land in a matrix of broadleaved woodlands, mainly oak, extending up to altitudes of *c.*1250 ft., or higher in sheltered valleys, with heaths, moorlands and bogs at higher altitudes. Around settlements, with their temporary or semi-permanent clearings for agriculture, were areas of grazed forests or open woodlands where occasional individual trees were selectively felled for particular purposes, and probably areas of woodland regularly coppiced. Further away from areas of settlement, the structure of primeval forest unmodified by man's activity is a matter of conjecture, for no completely natural virgin broadleaved forest exists in Britain. By analogy with areas of presumed virgin forest in Europe, such woods in Wales would have consisted of a relatively high proportion of very old and large trees with little underwood, and large quantities of rotten stems and other fallen debris on the ground.[23] As individual over-mature large trees died or fell from natural causes, allowing light to reach the forest floor, regeneration of light-demanding species would be able to develop naturally from seedlings, root suckers or stump sprouts, with shade-tolerant species beneath.

The historically recorded clearances of the natural woodlands of Wales, and the modification of the vegetation and landscape by planting have been fully chronicled elsewhere,[24] and lie outside the scope of this paper, as does the development of agriculture. Suffice it to say by way of summary that climatic change and human intervention have been responsible, during the course of a few millennia, for completely transforming the natural vegetation, reducing the percentage of woodland from a maximum of some 90 per cent of the land area of Wales to about 10 per cent, all broadleaved, by the sixteenth century. During this period human intervention mainly took the form of clearance — both deliberate and as a result of ignorance and neglect — for arable and livestock agriculture. Strategic military fellings during the twelfth and thirteenth centuries were also an important contributory factor.

Welsh woodlands have long been valued as much for livestock grazing as for their wood resources. This is graphically illustrated by one of the very rare early technical descriptions of multiple land-use in a Welsh wood, namely the forest of Pencelli (Eglwyswrw) in 1594:

> 'the same contyneth . . . aboute 500 acres of woodde and is enclosed with quicksett and pale rownde about and under lock, and doth contyne in compasse . . . about 4 myles and thre quarters. . . . Yt is all growne with greate okes of 200 yeres growth and more and some younge woodde of 60 yeres growth, and most of it well growen with underwoode as orle, hazell, thornes, willowse and other sortes . . . the herbage whereof . . . will somer 30 breedinge mares and winter 300 sheepe and 200 cattell well and sufficiently, beside swyne which may be kepte there. Allso there is in the said woodde 14 cockshottes wherein is greate store of woodcockes taken . . . Allso there breedeth in the said woodde sparrhawkes . . . Also the panage of hogges, bees and hony . . . The herbage of the said woode is very good for cattell, horses, mares, sheepe and swyne, and there is store of faire fresh ryvers and springes in the same woodde . . .'.[25]

From the sixteenth century, human intervention has taken the form of further clearance for agriculture, together with careless over-exploitation for commercial purposes, notably for charcoal, ship-building, tan-bark, and mining timber. This, coupled with the increasing introduction of exotic species, mainly conifers, in mixtures or pure plantations from the mid eighteenth century onwards, further reduced the percentage of woodland to only some 5 per cent of the land area of Wales, while simultaneously altering its composition to approximately equal proportions of conifers and broadleaves by the end of the nineteenth century. The latest forest census figures (1982) reveal that a further considerable change has taken place during the twentieth century: woods and forests now make up nearly 12 per cent of the land area of Wales, 58 per cent of this being state-owned, and conifers accounting for 70 per cent. (For comparison, the corresponding figures for England are 7·3 per cent total forest cover, 27 per cent in state ownership, and conifers accounting for 43 per cent.)

Of course, the story of the interrelationship of human settlement and vegetation is a continuing one, and it would be instructive as well as diverting to trace recent settlement patterns by naturalized escapes and changing fashions in planting: sycamores for windbreaks on old farm sites, rhododendrons growing as weeds, pairs of giant wellingtonias before great country houses, pretentious monkey-puzzles in small gardens in industrial valleys in the nineteenth century, and more recently a rash of fast-growing Lawson and Leyland cypresses following the spread of post-war suburbia.

NOTES

[1] References to the methodology of pollen analysis and the various published studies for Wales are too numerous to list here. Readers are referred to the syntheses and extensive bibliographies to be found in the following works: H.J.B. Birks & H.H. Birks, *Quaternary Palaeoecology* (1980); H. Godwin, *The History of the British Flora* (Cambridge, 1975); H.A. Hyde & S.G. Harrison, *Welsh Timber Trees* (Cardiff, 1977); W. Linnard, *Welsh Woods and Forests: History and Utilization* (Cardiff, 1982); W. Pennington, *The History of British Vegetation* (1974); O. Rackham, *Ancient Woodland* (1980); J.P. Savidge, 'The Effects of Climate, Past and Present, on Plant Distribution in Wales' in R.G. Ellis (ed.), *Flowering Plants of Wales* (Cardiff, 1983); A.G. Tansley, *Britain's Green Mantle* (revised by M.C.F. Proctor; London, 1968); J.A. Taylor (ed.), *Culture and Environment in Prehistoric Wales* (BAR British Series 76, 1980); and D. Walker & R.G. West (eds.), *Studies in the Vegetational History of the British Isles* (Cambridge, 1970).

[2] H.A. Hyde, *Welsh Timber Trees* (Cardiff, 1961 ed.), 11.

[3] The editor's 'Environmental Changes in Wales during the Holocene Period' in J.A. Taylor (ed.), *Culture and Environment*.

[4] W. Linnard, op. cit.

[5] J.A. Taylor, *Culture and Environment*, 113.

[6] F. Rose, 'The Vegetation and Flora of Tycanol Wood', *Nature in Wales*, 14 (1975), 178–85.

[7] H.J.B. Birks *et al.*, 'Pollen Maps for the British Isles 5000 Years Ago', *Proceedings of the Royal Society of London* (B), 189 (1975), 87–105.

[8] Gwyn Jones and Thomas Jones (eds.), *The Mabinogion* (Everyman, 1966), 113.

[9] C.B. Crampton, 'A History of Land-use at Aberduhonw, near Builth Wells', *Brycheiniog*, 14 (1970), 41–52.

[10] R.E. Hughes, 'Environment and Human Settlement in the Commote of Arllechwedd Isaf', *T.C.H.S.*, 2 (1940), 1–25.

[11] Gwyn Jones & Thomas Jones, op. cit., 125.

[12] John Leland, *The Itinerary in Wales in or about the years 1536–9* (ed. L. Toulmin-Smith, 1964), III, 122–4.

[13] W. Linnard, 'Historical distribution of beech in Wales', *Nature in Wales*, 16(3) (1979), 154–9.

[14] W.F. Grimes & H.A. Hyde, 'A Prehistoric Hearth at Radyr, Glam.' *Trans. Cardiff Naturalists' Society*, 68 (1935), 46–54.

[15] N.L.W. Bute Box 104, MS. 1, 96, 163.

[16] R.T. Gunther, *Early Science in Oxford. Vol. XIV. Life and Letters of Edward Lhuyd* (Oxford, 1945), 106, 315.

[17] For discussion and references, see e.g. H.A. Hyde, *Welsh Timber Trees*, 59; and Linnard, *Welsh Woods and Forests*, 8.

[18] Ifor Williams (ed.), *Canu Aneirin* (Cardiff, 1938), 26, 233.

[19] Ifor Williams & T. Roberts (eds.), *Cywyddau Dafydd ap Gwilym a'i Gyfoeswyr* (Cardiff, 1935), 124.

[20] R.H. Richens, *Elm* (Cambridge, 1983).

[21] R.H. Richens & J.N.R. Jeffers, 'The Elms of Wales', *Forestry*, 58 (1985), 9–25; see also R.H. Richens, 'The History of the Elms of Wales', *Nature in Wales*, 5 (1986), 3–11.

[22] W. Linnard, *Trees in the Law of Hywel* (Pamphlets on Welsh Law, Aberystwyth 1979).

[23] O. Rackham, op. cit.

[24] W. Linnard, *Welsh Woods and Forests*.

[25] 'The Extent of Cemais, 1594', *Pembrokeshire Records Series*, 3 (1977), 63.

The Landscape

FRANK EMERY

FEW books can have exerted such a profound influence upon recent generations of local historians as W. G. Hoskins's seminal volume on *The Making of the English Landscape*, first published in 1955.[1] By opening our eyes to the historical evidence enshrined in the landscapes about us, Hoskins pioneered a new dimension of study that has broken many an inter-disciplinary barrier by involving not only historians of the economic and social variety but also archaeologists of all periods, ecologists, historical geographers, philologists and many others. The first study of the Welsh landscape along these lines appeared in 1969, and south Wales has been treated in the series edited by Hoskins.[2] Landscape history has become a vigorous and popular field for research, as we see from the most recent introductory survey by Clive Knowles.[3]

Several questions of general intellectual interest are prompted by the meanings of 'landscape'. It is perhaps more necessary in Wales than for England, though difficult to do so, to draw a distinction between landscape and scenery. After all, Wales is regarded as being highly scenic: most of those who braved the rigours of the 'Cambrian Tour' in the eighteenth and nineteenth centuries did so in search of picturesque scenery, and if we are to believe all they wrote they seem to have found it in abundance. Hoskins suggests a measure of difference when he says of the Cornish coastline 'this is scenery rather than landscape. In fact it is rather like looking at a pretty woman who has no intelligence. I expect a landscape to speak to me and to ask questions — or rather pose problems, which merely pretty scenery does not'. Let us agree, then, that landscape possesses much more than the superficial and passive qualities of scenery.

It does so if we then accept it as a unique kind of document, 'the richest historical record we possess', in Hoskins's words: other historians have believed that, for instance John Richard Green a century ago. Of course, this is very much the historian's viewpoint. Others, such as geomorphologists or plant ecologists, may think differently. Man, they would argue, has arrogantly believed himself to be the creator of landscapes; in reality he can, at best, only add human artefacts to the enduring totality of the natural landscape. Such a viewpoint is conditioned partly by the perspective of a semi-geological time-scale, and an unwillingness to accept man's full impact on a changing environment. Here we shall accept landscape as the imprint of past communities as they went about their business of using the land and its resources. Nor should this preclude their intangibles, whether social, artistic or technological.

It is not as easy as it may seem, however, to identify the formative phases we should know if we wish to comprehend the making of the Welsh landscape. To begin with it is difficult to know what the Welsh landscape looked like in earlier times, even a century ago, let alone to try to grasp how it was made and to evaluate man's share in its design. The nature of the evidence that has to be used is exceedingly varied, and may even condition our methods of study. At different times, in this brief survey, we shall reconstruct the salient patterns in a past landscape; we shall identify man-made landscape; and we shall reconstitute those themes of human action that made and remade the Welsh landscape.

Nowadays, more than ever before, it is possible to reach close to the natural elements that are inherent in the Welsh landscape. Beneath and within most of the accretion of man-made or man-induced detail in any piece of landscape there is the natural order of altitude, rock, soil, water, slope, flora and fauna, always tempered by the prevailing climate. Such basic foundations and lineaments are now well to the fore and within reach of our understanding in the National Nature Reserves. Their distribution through the country reflects, in a rough-and-ready way, the impact of man's activities in the landscape. They are most abundant in those parts of Wales where the natural environment has inhibited large-scale transformations, and least abundant where dense populations of relatively intensive farmers and urbanized communities have made a deeper impression on the landscape. Hence, of the thirty-three NNRs in Wales (August 1981), no fewer than eighteen are located in north Wales; eleven in the largest region of Dyfed–Powys; and only four in south Wales.

To illustrate the general principle being advanced here we shall look at three contrasting reserves. They all share the advantages of protecting some plant and animal communities, as well as guarding 'the survival of a tract of countryside that typifies a particular form of habitat'.[4] In addition, they represent natural landscapes that are under particularly severe pressures elsewhere in the countryside. The first is a broadleaved woodland, Coedydd Maentwrog NNR in Gwynedd. Originally part of the extensive property of the Plas Tan-y-bwlch estate, it was declared a reserve in 1966. Although conditions are somewhat ameliorated on these valley slopes, the background conditions of acidic soils developed on the Upper Cambrian Shales and a mean annual rainfall of some 180cm. are typical of much of upland north Wales. This mature woodland, broken by open areas of bracken, small areas of tree regeneration and rocky outcrops, is largely comprised of sessile oaks (chiefly Q. petraea) with some scattered birch and rowan trees. Most of the established trees are well over 100 years old, and the age-structure pattern reflects the planting and felling policies followed in past times by the management of Tan-y-bwlch estate. The bracken-covered glades are the result of selective felling of the more valuable timber, so even here in the recesses of Gwynedd it is necessary to take into account the positive and negative agencies of human action in the landscape.

Again, the western parts of Coedydd Maentwrog still bear the traces of a dense undergrowth of Rhododendron ponticum, the flowering exotic shrubs that were so extensively planted on many estates in Victorian Wales. They thrived in the mountainous north, but now in the reserve the alien rhododendrons are being removed, and the bare ground is recolonized slowly with mosses preparing the way. Here again we see the controlling hand of scientific man; the spread of rhododendron is checked as an 'artificial influence', part of the ecological objective of managing the reserve so as to allow 'natural' development to take place. Heavy grazing in sheep is another intrusion that is to be combated. The flocks remind us of one of the most powerful agencies of all that have made their mark on the Welsh landscape — the sheep and cattle that were the backbone of Welsh hillfarmers for countless generations. Here they are suggested by the small, walled fields that occur in the easternmost reserve, now invaded with bracken and wind-pruned oaks. Sheep-grazing now counts as trespass within the reserve, and has been discouraged also by the forestry management that surrounds its periphery. Sheep-proof fences have been set around the entire reserve, and this means a new lease of life for tree regeneration. Mixed groups of oak, birch and hazel saplings now flourish in some of the clearings. As part of the rich wildlife within the reserve, a small herd of feral goats again reminds us of the role played by this omnivorous creature in keeping open and grassy so much of the upland landscape of Wales.

Reclaimed riverine or coastal marshes — known collectively as 'wetlands' — are very much at risk in Britain today because of the weight of technology behind those farmers who wish to drain them and convert them into productive fields. The landscape of the Fens shows the way for such development, and Wales is fortunate in having several wetlands where the risks are slight. One of the best known of these used to be called Tregaron Bog (Cors Tregaron), in Dyfed, but the National Nature Reserve established there since 1955 is now known as Cors Caron. Technically speaking, it is 'an extensive raised mire system', bisected by the Afon Teifi. Its palaeo-botanical physical history has been studied in depth, showing that it came into being over a lake that occupied the open valley of the Teifi in Late-Glacial times. A distinctive zonation of 'wetland' plants includes grasses, rushes, sphagnum or peat, and heather, while the 'flashes' of open water support many species of wildfowl.

Even in this unpromising environment of Cors Caron man has taken advantage of such resources as it offers. Until approximately twenty years ago people went into the bogs to cut peat for fuel, and their waterlogged cuttings are being recolonized by willow and bogplants. More important, farmers living on its margins enjoyed rights of grazing their sheep and ponies over Cors Caron. This traditional mode of pasturage is continued under existing tenancies and licences with the Nature Conservancy Council. Another ancient practice is that farmers burn their rough pastures in the spring so as to encourage an earlier and better 'bite' of fresh grass. Measures are now taken to safeguard the reserve from fires that go out of control.

The third National Nature Reserve takes us to Oxwich Bay on the south coast of the Gower peninsula, scenically one of the most beautiful landscapes in Wales, and well known for its attractiveness both within the Principality and far beyond its boundaries. Gower was the first Area of Outstanding Natural Beauty to be designated in Britain, in 1956, and we shall return to examine its landscape from various standpoints in due course. The Oxwich NNR is a mixed habitat of sand dunes, freshwater marsh and saltmarsh, sheltered by the encircling woodlands of ash, oak and sycamore that clothe the limestone cliffs. It all looks comparatively untouched, and indeed its wildlife is extraordinarily rich: 600 or so flowering plants flourish there, including varieties like the dune gentian or bloody cranesbill, representing almost a third of the British flora.

Nevertheless there again we have to acknowledge the effects of fluctuating human agencies in what appears superficially to be a natural landscape, more indirectly and surreptitiously, perhaps, but still a factor in fully understanding the landscape. Estate papers reveal that in the sixteenth and seventeenth centuries the Oxwich sand dunes were sufficiently vegetated with marram and other grasses to make them a used asset for rough grazing in common by the manorial tenants. Stock grazing of the dunes was discontinued some fifty years ago and this, together with the demise of the rabbit, has changed the plant succession towards a mixed deciduous woodland. Likewise in the past the mixed fen near Penrice was far drier than it is today, and four manors shared its resources for pasture and meadow hay. Perhaps due to a clogging of the natural drainage by silting and blown sand, the land here became waterlogged by about 1700; thus, to improve and restore its quality, Thomas Mansel Talbot (who lived at Penrice Castle) began, in 1770, an ambitious scheme of local engineering in the landscape.

Besides the utilitarian motive, Talbot also wished to enhance the parkland surrounding his mansion by creating a 'lake' between it and the beech dunes — a piece of landscape design or landscape gardening, which reveals how the landscape has been used as a medium for the expression of aesthetic taste, by those who had the land and means to do so. Talbot built an embankment along the lower part of the old channel of the main river-outlet, Nicholaston Pill. A new channel was cut to the north of the sea wall, connected with a dredged outlet, thus draining the salt marsh to provide 200 acres of sheep grazing; regulation of the levels also provided him with his serpentine ornamental lake. In our own time this Georgian system has broken down, and a freshwater marsh has come into being. Management of the NNR at Oxwich is aimed at controlling the scrub that tends to invade the reed swamp and fen (as well as the dunes), and preventing the silting up of the open channels and freshwater marsh. Conservation of the character of the varied wetland habitats is thus the modern imperative in this unique landscape, against the known background of natural and man-induced changes in the plant successions. The need for such informed conservation is increasingly acute, as witness the hundreds of thousands of holiday-makers who throng the Gower beaches within a stone's throw of Oxwich NNR.

We find, therefore, the naturalists' interest in the Welsh landscape stressing not only its wildlife (the living things that would populate it, perhaps, had human communities never appeared on the scene), but also its arrangement into diverse habitats. This structure appears in the excellent survey by William Condry, where the Welsh coastlands are given detailed treatment, for instance, divided into peatlands, polders, beaches, dunes and estuaries on the one hand, cliffs, headlands and islands on the other. This is done 'not only for their beauty but also for their special ecology and their unique populations of seabirds, seals and other wildlife'.[5] Such considerations are a necessary starting-point for studying the historic landscape, but clearly they have to be subordinated to a different focus, that of the cumulative impact of human settlement and use of the land. In Wales an initial problem is to establish the prolonged time-scale within which the humanized (or 'cultural' as Americans, Germans and others prefer to term it) landscape has evolved. It is so prolonged, in fact, that the prehistoric phases have to be given full scope, even if the material evidence for their effectiveness is so fragmentary that much has to be merely inferred about them. In thinking about this earliest formative dimension of the Welsh landscape we should be mindful of the results of recent research on the making of the English landscape. When the great pioneer of landscape history, W. G. Hoskins, first delineated the story in 1955 he urged as one of his guiding principles that we should always accept that the landscape is generally far older than we might expect it to be. Since then it has been found that prehistoric and Romano-British influences are far more persistent in the modern landscape than Hoskins suspected. Much more landscape-making was accomplished by the Neolithic, Bronze and Iron Age communities than was once thought possible. Christopher Taylor has gone so far as to claim that there were more people in the landscape, more farmed land, and less woodland in 1000 BC than there were in England in 1000 AD. Such exciting re-calculations have yet to be substantiated for Wales.[6]

It is not easy to come to grips with these inescapable foundation layers in the landscape, taking us back some six millenia before the present day. One straightforward approach is to regard the surviving structures of prehistoric people as relict features still with us in the present landscape. Wales is rich in a complex range of relict burial chambers of the Neolithic period, standing stones and stone circles of the Bronze Age, hill-forts of the Iron Ages. Their local groupings, densities and distributions have been studied with scientific zeal that has gained increasing heights of precision since Sir Cyril Fox's classic synthesis of *The Personality of Britain*.[7] It is still heady stuff: Glyn Daniel described recently how the Neolithic sites of Barclodiad y Gawres and Bryn Celli Ddu 'are apparented to the passage graves of Brittany and Portugal; so those shy traffickers, the dark Iberians whom Matthew Arnold spoke of in *The Scholar Gypsy*, are facts of archaeology'. Referring again to the carriage of some of the stones of Stonehenge from the Preseli Hills, 'this remarkable transfer of stones must have meant the change of a cultural centre from south-west Wales to Salisbury Plain'.

Within a comfortable walking radius of the Oxwich NNR in Gower, for instance, we find ample evidence of relict prehistory of the landscape. Neolithic burial sites, built by the earliest sedentary agriculturists to utilize the land, range from King Arthur's Stone, rearing itself boldly on the crest of Cefn Bryn, to the more discreet and ruined chamber among the sand dunes of Penmaen Burrows. Most widespread and noticeable of all, perhaps, are the Iron Age fortifications built on promontories, such as 'Maiden Castle' (surely so christened by an antiquarian Talbot) on Oxwich Point; or on hills, their ramparts and ditches encircling the summits of Cil Ifor or Llanmadoc Down. These hill-forts provide a helpful interpretive link between the more distant aeons of landscape-making, and features of all kinds that we hold in our more familiar perception of Welsh history. They are symbols, perhaps, of continuities and persistences that run up to the present.

At a material level, the hill-fort builders farmed the land in a mixed system both for field-crops (wheat, barley, flax) and for livestock (sheep, cattle, pigs). They may have spread into eastern Wales and the Borderlands as early as about 1000 BC, during the onset of the Late Bronze Age. At first, the hill-forts were little more than single homesteads surrounded by a simple rampart and ditch. But as the subsequent incursions of new settlers built up, so did the hill-forts grow and diversify into many forms, some of them commanding structures of three or four sets of defences, with skilfully-designed entrances. 'The individual hill-forts we see today', writes Emrys Bowen, 'reflect only the final stages of this development, each fort reaching back in some cases to the Late Bronze Age, and surviving into the Roman occupation'.[8] At the non-material level, too, they are symbols of continuity in matters of Welsh culture. Hill-fort builders introduced the forms of Celtic speech which are ancestral to modern Welsh: from them derives the cumulative process by which Wales became fully Celtic. Again, the Iron Age B newcomers of the fourth and third centuries BC imposed themselves as conquerors and free tribesmen on the people who occupied the land before them. These were grouped into bond-vills, rendering services and dues to their overlords. Here we have the seeds of traditional Welsh society as it first appears, much later, from the earliest written records.

Nor is it possible to interpret Christian churches as artefacts in the landscape without tracing their origins to such distant times. Christianity first brought its message during the Romano-British period, when many hill-forts were still in everyday use, and it was splendidly reinforced from the fifth century AD by the evangelizing travels of the Celtic saints. Their ecclesiastical settlements or *llannau* often retain the name of their original founder or their founder's patron, and served as nuclei for villages that also perpetuated the saint's name. The church itself was reshaped and rebuilt many times over in succeeding centuries, but its dedication remains as a token of its proto-historic foundation. At Oxwich the church bears the name of St Illtud, one of the earliest of the Celtic saints who was active in the Romanized regions of south-eastern Wales. The churches of another three villages in Gower are also dedicated to him.[9]

Finally, close by Oxwich we find in the landscape a remarkably fine illustration of the significant role of the castle, another relict feature with which Wales is abundantly provided. The castle has its roots in the Anglo-Norman conquest that began to unroll in the late eleventh century, symbolizing a new order of political, social and economic organization — just as the hill-forts symbolized a much older order of things. Eastern and southern Wales quite quickly became the acquired territory of Anglo-Norman magnates, who exercised their power and control from the secure base of a castle. At Penrice in Gower, just inland from Oxwich Bay, we see the juxtaposition of three sites that summarize with vivid clarity the sequence over time of land acquisition and landownership. The oldest of the three is now a hummocky strongpoint overgrown with trees and bushes, but it was an earth-and-timber castle (of the motte-and-bailey type) that marked the first Anglo-Norman foothold in South Gower, perhaps as early as 1099. This 'Mounty Brough' (to use its ancient local name) was succeeded in the fullness of time by the stone edifice of Penrice Castle, now a spectacular ruin perched on its limestone outcrop. It began as a round keep some time before 1250, the curtain wall, towers and gatehouse being completed by 1300. Third in line, below the medieval ruin stands Penrice Castle in the modern sense, the country house built by Thomas Mansel Talbot in the 1770s, purely domestic and decorative in character.

Clearly a major task confronting anyone who attempts a thorough analysis of the making of any fragment of the Welsh landscape is to assess the relative weight that must be given to the earliest formative phases of a primeval landscape. Given the drift of current research in studies of the English landscape, where the prehistoric and proto-historic weight of evidence is assuming much more significance than in the past, at the expense of formerly influential documents like the Domesday survey of 1086, this assessment is unavoidable. As to the primeval landscapes, one guideline is that some regions of Wales were settled persistently and repeatedly in prehistoric times. Here we must look to the coastal margins, mostly lowlands, and especially to those regions of well-drained intermediate soils (intermediate that is, between heavy clay and light sands) in Anglesey, Llŷn, Eifionydd, Ardudwy, much of Pembrokeshire and southern Carmarthenshire, peninsular Gower, the Vale of Glamorgan, and the plains of Gwent. In these landscapes the weight of man's influence was felt in their repeated occupation by Neolithic settlers, followed in turn by users of bronze and iron, and into the more intensive phase of Romano-British occupance.

We cannot overlook the fact, therefore, that long before the familiar unrolling of recorded history a far-reaching measure of change was initiated in these peripheral, lowland regions of Wales. It followed the efforts of communities to secure shelter, food, and fuel by means of the material technology known to them, and in accordance with their beliefs and experience. To a series of lesser degrees this was true of the whole of Wales, from the well-endowed inland environments such as the middle valleys of the Usk and Dee, through to the more grudging habitats offered by the more extreme upland regions. Besides the various relict and monumental inheritances from these remote times, a basic contribution to the evolution of landscapes was the disappearance of much of the virgin forest or climax vegetation of mixed deciduous woodland. Wherever prehistoric man cleared the trees, deliberately or incidentally, to secure open ground for his shifting fields, and grazings, the forest retreated and made way for heathland and the broad expanses of treeless waste that extends over so much of Wales. Pollen analysis has shown that as early as the Neolithic period weeds of cultivation (e.g. the plantain) make their appearance, as the transition for clearance to cultivation, grazing, burning, and thence on to soil impoverishment and podzolization went ahead. Eventually this produced an environment suited for the first entry of thorny species with which we are familiar today — gorse (that beautifies in springtime with its rich yellowness many a defunct coal-tip), holly and the bramble. So much deforestation has to be traced to the primeval landscapes, indeed, that what the medieval historian has been tempted to describe as 'native original forest' was at best a kind of secondary, regenerative growth.

Nevertheless, in the light of the certitude of historic, documentary evidence, we may suggest that the broad lineaments of the Welsh countryside were determined between the twelfth and sixteenth centuries. In other words, there have been little more than cosmetic changes or additions to the rural landscape since about 1600. The essential patterns of rural settlement and agrarian systems were as well known to the Elizabethan Welshman as they are to us today. This proposition puts Wales on par with the upland regions of northern or western England. Whereas much of midland or southern England was radically remodelled by the enclosure of common fields and common wastes after 1600, by private agreement or the wholesale process of enclosure by Act of Parliament, such events were unknown in Wales. Nor did Wales share in the making of landscaped parks and gardens in the grand style of England. As shared experiences we can identify little more than the enclosing of open pasturage on the uplands by parliamentary act after 1800, and the wholesale, even indiscriminate, planting of trees (often on the same hill enclosures) by the Forestry Commission during the last sixty years. To comprehend fully the Welsh countryside in its twin major expressions of uplands and lowlands we are forced to return to the territorial divisions of Wales as they stood in the twelfth century. There is no need here to explain the full differences of kind that existed between *Pura Wallia*, 'Wales Proper' in the north and west of the country, and *Marchia Wallie*, the 'March of Wales' that surrounded it to the east and south. But the distinction is real enough to justify the separate identification of structural themes in the Welsh countryside to this day.

In the Welsh uplands two elements are outstanding because they recur throughout the rural landscape. One is the dominance of single farms, with occasional loose clusters of houses, standing separately from each other in a compact mosaic of small fields. The other is the intimate and integral presence of open moorland on the hills and mountains. To understand the history of the landscape, therefore, we should explore the circumstances in which the web of scattered farmsteads, with their appendant fields and open pastures came into being. Historically the setting is *Pura Wallia*, 'inner Wales' or 'proper Wales'. The evolution of this pattern is more complex than we might think. It may be expressed as a series of stages, each reflecting a phase in the destruction of the medieval tribal order by new and powerful social and economic forces.

Stage one began in the twelfth century when, far from being predominantly scattered, the structure of rural habitation was substantially grouped or nucleated. Such was the case in Anglesey, Llŷn and throughout the coastal lowlands of northern and western Wales. Here the townships were small, and the better-quality expanses of arable and meadow were set out as open sharelands with intermixed holdings. The unit of settlement was the *rhandir*, 'open field made up of irregular-shaped parcels of varying size and engirdled with a cluster of homesteads set in small enclosures'.[10] The lands were subject to partible inheritance, the splitting up of a holding between all the sons at their father's death. Fragmentation was clearly a potential problem, but was offset by the scope for bringing in fresh land from the abundant waste. Kinship was the basis of landholding, and primary settlements (*hendrefi*) emerged in the twelfth century in townships over which one family had sole control.

From the partition of each *hendref* the nuclei of clanlands or *gwelyau* grew among the first generation of co-heirs. Thus the nucleated settlements of each free clan sprang from the appropriation of arable land in the *hendref*, giving rise at each partition to a new girdle of clustered homesteads around the sharelands. By contrast, in the true hill country townships were larger: some nucleated settlements were found, as in the *maerdref* where the lord had his courthouse, or in villages where bondmen cultivated his demensne or personal farm, but generally speaking here the habitat was more scattered. Each farm or *tyddyn* had the option of pioneering fresh land from the common waste, especially easily done from the *gafael* or grazing land over which a particular clan enjoyed exclusive rights. Thus seasonal dwellings on the higher pastures (*hafod, lluest*) could become permanent settlements, especially as population pressure grew due to the enfranchisement of bondmen and to general increases in numbers. More single farms were brought into the landscape, as happened with the intermediate dispersion of medieval colonists in Devon and Cornwall.

The earliest signs of a second stage, marking the disruption of the old tribal order and an acceleration in the establishment of scattered farms, were clear by about 1300. After the Edwardian conquest of 1284, in north Wales a series of legal and institutional changes began to undermine the status of *gwely* and *gafael* as units of communal landownership. One outcome was that tribal lands of bond and free origin passed to the open market, to be bought or leased by those who were better placed than their neighbours. Some of the well-known landed estates, such as Peniarth, Nannau, and Hengwrt, had become pieced together by such means before the close of the fifteenth century. Another reflection of all this ferment in the landscape was the enclosure of the old open sharelands and *ffridd* pastures. Rationalization of the *tyddynnod* yielded single farms now standing on their consolidated land, surrounded by their small hedged fields. The traditional groups of dwellings in clusters, such as the *maerdref*, became a thing of the past.

A third stage followed after the Acts of Union (1536–42) when by law the inheritor of land was to be the eldest son, not all the male heirs equally as in the past. Estate-building and other individual initiatives were greatly helped by this, leading to 'purchased exchanges and hedging and enclosures'. A special feature at this stage was the seizing and encroachment of common pastures by expansionist landowners and tenants. The most spectacular manifestation of this process lay with those who leased the upland granges and sheepwalks of the monastic houses, after their dissolution in the 1530s. Many of these were changed into large walled enclosures that may still be traced in the present landscape, as with the former Cymer Abbey lands in Trawsfynydd.[11] A fresh layer of scattered farmsteads likewise appeared, some of them in Snowdonia reaching far into the high summer pastures at altitudes of 400m. More typical of this colonization of the waste was a Denbighshire farm described in 1693: 'though not so steep and woody on the eastern side, yet it appears that it has been as woody before they rid the ground for ploughing. The owners have carried away most of the stones to make their walls and indeed to clear the ground. It was but a wild place, and this is but the eighth heir of that house, since it was built or any of that land cultivated.'[12] This rare glimpse of how the landscape was made would put the origins of this farmstead in the middle of the sixteenth century: Clegyr Mawr still stands on its site near Melin-y-wig, in broken country to the south of Clocaenog Forest. Nor does the story of how scattered dwellings appeared end there, because a final stage was to come when common pastures were enclosed by parliamentary act, especially between the General Inclosure Acts of 1801 and 1845.

All this holds true principally for the regions of northern and western Wales where native institutions were not seriously assailed by Anglicization until the late thirteenth century. What of the landscapes of *Marchia Wallie*, the 'March of Wales' that lay to the south and east? The transition is more easily made in these more complex territories because many of the great Marcher lordships were subdivided into two distinct systems, and their landscapes mirrored different patterns in accordance with them. 'The fundamental division of a lordship into Englishry and Welshry', says William Rees in his classic study of the subject, 'though nominally based on racial grounds, had a more significant economic origin. Rents and services characterized the one, and tribute the other'.[13] The economic character of the early conquest of Wales by Anglo-Normans is strongly reflected in the coincidence of lowland and Englishry in the lordships of the March. The Anglo-Norman potentates introduced a series of new institutions that had an impact on the landscape: feudal methods of land tenure, manorialized agriculture, towns, and organized trading.

Ideally, the Marcher lord's castle housed his exchequer and courts; from its security he maintained control over the lordship. His personal estate or demesne land was ploughed, harrowed and harvested for him by unfree tenants, who thus also held their small shares in the open, unhedged arable fields. Burgesses enjoyed the right to trade in the towns, which were granted charters by the lord and where markets and fairs were held. This form of land settlement was most pronounced in the coastlands and open valleys within the marcher and royal lordships. There they found, above all, a physical environment and resources that favoured the cultivation of field crops, the grains that yielded bread and drink, as a basis of manorial life. The Englishries were attractive to colonists from outside Wales: a Flemish community was introduced to southern Pembrokeshire by Henry I by 1108, and an English settlement flourished in peninsular Gower under the earls of Warwick, so that by about 1170 Earl William could address the Swansea charter 'to all barons, burgesses, and men, English and Welsh'.

The effects of all this were thoroughly well evident in a survey of the lordship of Gower made in the 1690s. The low-lying coastal plateau of West Gower was almost all corn ground. On its level tracts of tillage all the field crops were cultivated — wheat, barley, oats, rye, peas, vetches, even clover. It had 'stores of limestones', some of which, together with corn and livestock, were shipped to the West Country. The well-drained loams were 'plain, all corn ground, very good and profitable', with saltings, common pastures, and some meadow in addition. Gower was Anglicized, as 'in former times all people both high and low did talk the old English'. Such wealth of farming resources stood out sharply against the neighbouring 'mountain country' of Blaen Gŵyr, the Welshry of the Marcher lordship. That was a more difficult terrain, where the land was naturally better suited to support sheep than cattle, or to feed cattle than to bear corn, its main crops being oats and barley. In this respect Gower, with its two faces of diversified lowland and restricted hill country, stood as a microcosm of all Wales.[14]

How had the detail of landscape evolved in the Gower Englishry? From the outset it contained compact villages of various sizes and shapes, together with small groupings of farms, all interspersed with some single dwellings. The pattern of rural settlement was a far cry from the scattered single farms of upland Wales — 'several and lone houses' as George Owen called them in Elizabethan times, though such were found in the Welshry landscape. In Gower the nucleus of English settlement lay in a group of thirteen manors which pre-dated the death of Henry I in 1135. Around their central villages stretched the common fields, in which the strip holdings lay open, separated only by turf banks. Most of these were enclosed with hedges or walls by 1500, but at different scales that still show in the Gower landscape. Near the villages we see small but long, narrow fields enclosed from the *landshares* of former open fields; elsewhere the lord's demesnes were enclosed on a grander scale of large, square fields, sometimes subdivided again in more recent times. Medieval deer parks are quite frequently found in Gower: Park le Breos was carved out by about 1300, each of its four ditched walls running for a mile in length still visible on the ground. By 1650 it has 'a long time been disparked and divided into three parts', in each of which a large single farm had been built, but in which 'much wild and woody ground' still persisted.

This takes us to the critical theme of trying to measure the varying extent of forests and woodlands, their nature, usefulness and the way in which they have contracted and expanded through time in the historic landscapes of Wales. In his pioneer study of the problem, William Linnard argues that 'the continuing story of how man has used, destroyed and modified the woodlands of Wales, and of his changing attitudes to woods, is important for appreciating many aspects of history and for understanding much of the Welsh landscape today. As such it should also provide a basis for considering the future role of woodlands in Wales'.[15] Certainly we cannot simply presume that the process was one of the slow but surely inexorable reduction of a forested wilderness. It is unlikely that the whole countryside was equally well wooded at the close of the first millenium AD. Some of the Welsh uplands and more of the coastal lowlands were devoid of tree cover at that time. In any case, timber and underwood had a positive economic value in their own right. Only when they failed to hold it in a competitive economy, however rudimentary, would they yield to other uses of the land; given sufficient demand and proper management, trees were valuable and might even be replanted after earlier clearances. There were many such gains within the last 200 years, some of them long before the massive tree-plantings of the Forestry Commission.

Evidence of a greater abundance of native woodland comes from a number of sources within the last few centuries. John Leland, writing in the 1530s, described many localities 'as it were a forest ground', or 'much wood', such as the valleys cut into the coalfield uplands of Glamorgan, or again near Llandovery and Whitland, 'standing in a vast wood as in a wilderness'. Thomas Pennant, the naturalist, provides similar evidence in the 1760s and 1770s, describing parts of the Dee, Severn and Vyrnwy valleys well clothed with timber. But both Leland and Pennant, with other writers, give the overall impression of the coastal and border lowlands of Wales as being thinly wooded by about 1800. Similarly the uplands above about 300m were bare of trees: woods survived best on intermediate valley slopes. Leland, indeed, also gives us a pointer, clear in his own day, as to what sort of pressures had worked towards clearing the landscape of woodland. There were several interconnected and overlapping causes of deforestation: 'the wood cut down was never coppiced, and this had been a great cause of destruction of wood through Wales'; 'after cutting down of woods the goats have so bitten the young spring (i.e. new growth) that it never grew but like shrubs'; 'men destroyed the great woods that they should not harbour thieves'; and, a sign of things to come with mounting force in the future, the smelting of lead ore on Pumlumon 'has destroyed the woods that sometimes grew plentifully thereabouts'.[16]

Most fundamental of all these was the basic need for clearing the waste, including expendable woodland, for fields in which crops could be cultivated and livestock pastured. Early pioneers whose activities are well documented were the Cistercians, who had thirteen Welsh abbeys on whose property they assarted or colonized the waste. Their medieval granges experienced a great deal of deforestation. Linked perhaps to the known upsurges of population again in the sixteenth century, fresh onslaughts led George Owen to regret the disappearance of a number of great woodlands in Pembrokeshire, replaced with cornfields. Closely associated with such endeavours was the destructive effect of grazing by sheep, cattle, and goats. As agrarian development went ahead, the growing flocks and herds checked the regeneration of trees on cleared ground as well as inhibiting natural growth. They achieved this by direct feeding, or indirectly when the pastoralists who kept them burned their rough grazings in the spring season, so as to encourage the growth of new grass. Sheep were easily the most numerous of the farmers' stock from about 1500 onwards, and they have been the most influential of all the depredators. Lewis Morris saw it happen in the hills of Cardiganshire in the 1750s: wealthy men had flocks of 15,000 sheep and above ('which is more than Job had'), demolishing all before them so that 'the whole country is open, almost like a common field'.[17]

Mining and smelting and all the varied processes of industrial manufacture were to prove a source of destruction for woodland in Wales. In themselves there was no inevitable risk of destruction, so long as the pace of demand for trees was matched by sensible management of the timber resources. Iron-masters who demanded charcoal for their furnaces in the early modern period could be supplied from properly regulated felling of coppices that were then encouraged to grow again for another twenty years, thus avoiding the total destruction of this vital source of industrial fuel. Unfortunately some of the industrialists were indifferent to conservation, as demand outran local supply, while some landowners were only too willing to sell their timber outright to the shipbuilders or timber merchants, often to pay pressing debts. Nor should we forget, at this point, the other side of the coin whereby estate-owners undertook massive schemes of afforestation. For instance, Thomas Johnes of Hafod in Cardiganshire planted 4 million trees between 1769 and 1813. This also raises the question of wholesale landscape gardening in Wales, whereby men of wealth created around their country houses the sort of landscape they wished to see. Such 'picturesque' schemes are rare by comparison with England, because there were few really extensive landed estates with resident owners, and because the professional landscape designers felt the naturally scenic settings were so dominant and attractive in themselves. Ornamental parks thus tend to be on a modest scale, as at Rhug on the upper Dee, or Gloddaeth in Caernarfonshire, or at Penrice Castle in Gower.

Nowadays the pendulum of tree-planting has swung much farther and the Welsh landscape is replete with the handiwork of the Forestry Commission. Since 1919 the new state forests have revolutionized the appearance of huge stretches of countryside. Not only their quantity but also their quality are quite unique. The conifer rules supreme on a scale that would amaze its early champions like Johnes of Hafod: quick-growing exotic trees by the million, Sitka spruce, Norway spruce, Lodgepole pine, Japanese larch. Nothing else in modern times compares with the scale of landownership enjoyed by the Forestry Commission, and the potential for influencing the appearance of the landscape. To find a parallel we have to go back in time before 1530 when so much land was owned by the monastic houses. Plantations now clothe approximately ten per cent of the land of Wales, occupying sites that were in the main at the moorland margin when the parliamentary surveyors for enclosure walked over it a century ago. There has been criticism of the dark ranks of conifers, on aesthetic grounds, but more recently attempts have been made to design the plantations in a sensitive fashion. Each forest should be 'developed into a good landscape attuned to its locality', to quote the landscape architect Sylvia Crowe. Otherwise there is a risk that upland Wales will look more like Finland, especially with the man-made reservoirs that have been added to the 'Welsh Lakeland' over the last hundred years — the Elan Valley, Nant y Moch, Llyn Clywedog and Llyn Brianne.

The new lakes are reflective of the need for regulated water supplies to the industrial complexes and urban communities of Wales. For the last two centuries there has been an expanding wave of industrial landscapes, and these are now being studied and interpreted more intensively than ever before. Revealing guide-lines to the Welsh experience may be found in Barry Trinder's excellent introduction, *The Making of the Industrial Landscape*.[18] The scope for local history research in this direction is very great, whether on the artefacts of the Industrial Revolution ('industrial archaeology' of the mines, works, tramways, canals, workers' dwellings), or on the newly urbanized societies that spring up so rapidly, to serve the labour needs of collieries, furnaces, foundries and mills. Merthyr Tudful, the cradle of Welsh industry, as much as Ironbridge was in England, is a fertile scene of such research. The exploration of industrial landscapes is helped immeasurably by the volume of documentary and other sources that become available after about 1800. Of particular value are the decennial censuses of population published from 1801, permitting the numerical analysis of how quickly these landscapes became filled, even to the point of congestion, with people. Their communities also appear with greater accuracy on the maps and plans produced by the Ordnance Survey through the nineteenth century. The growth (or contraction) of settlements can be pictured from the larger-scale series of maps. Then as the social and economic problems inherent in the industrial communities became so evident — signified by infant mortality, or cholera epidemics, or lack of schools — official reports and surveys and commissions all add their special insights to what was happening in industrial Wales.

Visually, there are two or three distinctively Welsh forms of industrial landscape. In Gwynedd the extraction of slate has made its special mark, accentuating the natural ruggedness of the terrain with its huge tips and dumps of rock-rubbish. This man-made scree was generated both by the mines of Blaenau Ffestiniog and by the massive open quarries of Penrhyn or Dinorwic, which flourished throughout the nineteenth century. In south Wales the many rivers that cut themselves into the coalfield plateau have sponsored the 'Valleys', where collieries were sunk from the Ebbw in the east to the Gwendraeth in the west. Their landscape reflects two phases of economic life: coal-mining enjoyed more than fifty years of steady expansion and prosperity down to the time of the 1914–18 war; then in the twenties and thirties the Valleys floundered in the Depression, with poverty, unemployment, and misery as many collieries were closed. Their recovery from that trauma has been uneven. As the mining townships grew on sites often cramped by the physique of the narrow valleys, they appear like ribbons or strings of beads, some of which coalesce to form larger units, as in the Rhondda. Within each township the elongated patterns were emphasized by the long rows of terraced houses built along the steep slopes. In the past the landscape was cluttered with a jumble of old colliery buildings and gear, chimneys, sprawling coal-tips, ponds and tramroads. Nowadays, in favoured localities, this has been successfully tidied up and is succeeded by industrial estates or even by plantations of conifers. Much harder (but not impossibly so) to redeem, are the industrial wastelands that were the legacy of smelting iron, copper, zinc, lead and nickel. George Borrow in 1854 was startled to see the 'burning mountain' at Dowlais and the copperworks at Swansea: 'immense stacks of chimneys surrounded by grimy diabolical-looking buildings, in the neighbourhood of which were huge heaps of cinders and black rubbish. So strange a scene I had never beheld in nature.' The work of rehabilitating derelict land still goes on there.

Ideally the historian should study the Welsh past in its totality; as Glanmor Williams sees it, 'Whatever survives from the past — its written and printed records, yes certainly — but also its landscape, its material remains of every kind, its language, dialects and oral traditions; whatever has escaped the annihilation of time is grist to the mill.'[19] Perhaps the landscape is of special value in this sense because it shows a capacity to absorb and retain so many indelible marks of what has happened, as it builds up its layers through time. Certainly for this reason, too, it lends itself peculiarly well to detailed studies of localities, although a full understanding also demands a comparative framework within which work must be structured. There is much still to be discovered in this way. 'Wales is so little different from England', Doctor Johnson told Boswell, 'that it offers nothing to the speculation of the traveller'. Had he confined his viewing to the landscape of one or two Englishries there may have been a grain of truth in what he says, but it remains a hopelessly superficial comment.

NOTES

[1] W.G. Hoskins, *The Making of the English Landscape* (1955).

[2] F.V. Emery, *Wales* (The World's Landscapes series), (1969); Moelwyn I. Williams, *The South Wales Landscape* (1975).

[3] C.H. Knowles, *Landscape History* (Historical Association General Series, 107, 1983).

[4] *Nature in Wales*, New Series, 1, Part 2 (1982), (Cardiff, 1983), 17–33.

[5] W. Condry, *The Natural History of Wales* (The New Naturalists Series, 66), (1981), 254.

[6] Glyn Daniel, *The National Museum as a mirror of ancient Wales*, A 75th Anniversary Lecture (Cardiff, 1983), 24.

[7] C. Fox, *The Personality of Britain* (1952).

[8] E.G. Bowen, 'Early Settlement', chapter 3 of D. Thomas (ed.), *Wales: New Study* (Newton Abbot, 1977), 72.

[9] E.G. Bowen, *Saints, Seaways and Settlements in Wales* (Cardiff, 1977).

[10] T. Jones Pierce, 'Landlords in Wales: the nobility and gentry' in Joan Thirsk (ed.), *The Agrarian History of England and Wales* IV (Cambridge, 1967), 357–80

[11] C. Thomas, 'Enclosure and the Rural Landscape of Merioneth in the Sixteenth Century', *T. Inst. Brit. Geog.*, 42 (1967), 153–62.

[12] Bodleian Library, Oxford: MS Ashmole 1829, 171; B. F. Roberts, 'Llythyrau John Lloyd at Edward Lhuyd', *N.L.W. Jnl.*, XVII (1971), 108.

[13] W. Rees, *South Wales and the March* (Oxford, 1924), 28–31.

[14] F.V. Emery, 'Edward Lhuyd and Some of his Glamorgan Correspondents: A view of Gower in the 1690s', *T.C.S.* (1965), Part 1, 59–114.

[15] W. Linnard, *Welsh Woods and Forests: History and Utilization* (Cardiff, 1982), xx.

[16] John Leland, *The Itinerary in Wales in or about the years 1536–9*, in L. Toulmin Smith (ed.) (1906); J. Rhys (ed.), *Tours in Wales by Thomas Pennant* (Caernarvon, 1883).

[17] F.R. Lewis, 'Lewis Morris and the Parish of Llanbadarn Fawr, Cardiganshire', *A.C.*, XVIII (1938), 15–30.

[18] B. Trinder, *The Making of the Industrial Landscape* (1983).

[19] Glanmor Williams, *Wales and the past: a consort of voices*, A 75th Anniversary Lecture (Cardiff, 1983), 19.

Place-Names

GWYNEDD PIERCE

> Some to the fascination of a name
> Surrender judgment hoodwinked.

WHETHER the eighteenth-century English poet who fashioned that rather prosaic couplet had place-names specifically in mind may, perhaps, be open to question.[1] Had this been so, however, he could hardly have expressed what is very nearly a universal truth more aptly. That place-names have an intrinsic fascination is undeniable. Literature, from the earliest times and in many languages, is liberally sprinkled with onomastic tales. The homespun interpretations, often fanciful, of innumerable contributors to journals and local newspapers have been a godsend to hard-pressed editors faced by imminent publishing deadlines. Popular interpretation, likewise, has resulted occasionally in what has amounted to the creation of a local industry based on the exploitation of names like *Beddgelert* or *Caerfyrddin*. The artful construction of *Llanfairpwllgwyngyllgogerychwyrndrobwll-llandysiliogogogoch* out of two adjoining parish names with all the trimmings added, but of no real antiquity, has been a source of considerable additional revenue to railway companies as well as proving to be a lucrative attraction to credulous but hard-headed business operatives.

The possibilities are legion, but such considerations, on the other hand, have hardly been conducive to the realization that the proper interpretation of place-names is an academic discipline of a peculiarly complex nature. It is only in comparatively recent times, the last sixty years or so, that this fact has slowly gained acceptance. The day of the dilettante in this specialized field is almost over. Almost, because it is still a matter of concern that many who would rightly hesitate to express judgement on an historical issue without paying due regard to the evidence of their sources, written or material, are prone to make assumptions about the meaning of place-names in historical contexts, to reach false conclusions on the basis of these assumptions and to be susceptible to inaccuracy in the matter of identification, to mention a few of the more obvious disaster areas. The evidence of place-names, therefore, tested by means of an established method of investigation, can be as valuable to the historian as the contribution of the archaeologist with his expertise in the evaluation and recognition of material evidence. As the late F. T. Wainwright argued cogently some years ago, this does not mean that place-name study and archaeology 'exist only to serve the historian. They exist in their own right, with objectives and methods proper to themselves. They are not mere ancillary aids to the study of history.' Being separate disciplines, this is true enough, the former being essentially linguistic. Wainwright's plea was for an effective co-ordination between them in order further to build up a reliable picture, even some measure of interpretation, of the past. He cites the examples of the Anglo-Saxon settlements in

Britain or the Scandinavian impact on the British Isles which could scarcely have been comprehended at all, and less accurately, were it not for the collaboration which he advocates. It is true that the examples given occur in early periods of history which are lacking in trustworthy historical sources and documentation, but the point he makes is the crucial one that in respect of those early periods archaeology and the interpretation of place-names can amplify the historical record, 'not infrequently mitigating its deficiencies and repairing its omissions'.[2] It has been proved that in some particulars this can also apply to later periods.

The need for co-ordination for which Wainwright called has largely been fulfilled during the course of time through co-operation because it is patently obvious that his ideal of a scholar who is a consummate master of the three disciplines is an academic mirage. In a further, more recent, and by far the most perceptive discussion of place-names and history, Margaret Gelling acknowledges this and accepts that 'the disciplines of history, archaeology and philology must remain to some extent distinct. There will continue to be demarcation problems'. However, one is still left with the impression that the archaeological contribution is more acceptable to the historian than that of the philologist, indeed, 'that the philologists operate a sort of closed shop'.[3] It may be that because the archaeologist is concerned primarily with the material remains of the past (notwithstanding the fact that his techniques are highly specialized — his closed shop) and that he has to contend with problems and difficulties pertaining to his discipline, there is a tendency to regard his interpretations as having more tangible attributes and being in some ways more convincing than those of the philologist who offers the evidence of language, or that aspect of linguistic development which is incorporated in place-names. The study of language has wider implications in popular estimation and a mystique which seems less directly adaptable for use as a means of interpreting the past. This is reinforced to some extent by the undeniable fact that the only direct information that place-names can provide is linguistic information, so that what is being attempted is the use of such evidence to supply information of a non-linguistic character, for the historian is not primarily interested in lexicography, phonology, word-formation and the like for its own sake. He does not have to be a philologist, neither does the archaeologist, but the student of place-names has to be something of a historian, to have a knowledge and understanding of the techniques of interpretation employed by both the historian and the archaeologist and of their sources (which are often his sources), though formerly tending to be regarded by them with a kind of benign tolerance and not, strictly, being totally 'accepted' within their élite circle.

It may be as well, therefore, to recall the basic method of place-name study and to emphasize and illustrate certain aspects which are especially relevant to the local historian in terms of what it can offer him in the way of information and how far he can participate in the work of recovering and recording that information, even if he does not feel sufficiently qualified to deal with the philological and semantic problems involved. No more succinctly effective outline of that method can be found than that provided by Gelling, that it is,

> . . . a philological discipline which is based mainly on written evidence. This evidence
> consists of early spellings of names, and these have to be extracted from sources ranging

in date from the earliest Greek and Latin texts which make reference to the British Isles to the first edition of the Ordnance Survey one-inch maps produced in the nineteenth century. The spellings are identified when possible with modern place-names, and the series of spellings for each item is presented in a manner which illustrates the development of the sounds in the spoken name, so that the philologist can study this development and reach conclusions about the original form and meaning.[4]

The two stages are quite clear, recovery and recognition on the one hand, interpretation on the other, with the second stage being almost completely dependent upon the evidence produced by the first. If that evidence is not available, it is better to leave a problem unresolved for the time being than to resort to fanciful interpretation, for it is not inconceivable that further evidence may be discovered which could make a mockery of a conclusion based on uncertain evidence and perhaps lend some credence to the well-known, but mischievous observation attributed to Sir John Morris-Jones that only fools concern themselves with the interpretation of place-names.[5]

Several points call for emphasis where the first stage is concerned. The range of sources from which the evidence is extracted is, indeed, as wide chronologically as is indicated by Gelling. As Wales is particularly susceptible to the influence of an increasing modern non-Welsh-speaking presence, it is often necessary to extend the chronology of sources consulted to a later date than that of the first edition of the OS maps. The solution of one stubborn problem came to the present writer from the evidence of the form of a name which occurred in the address at the head of a tradesman's bill in the middle years of the nineteenth century. Documents of every conceivable kind relating to the area which is being investigated, ranging from national or state documents to the humblest farmer's correspondence or account-books should be diligently searched where available. This presumes the ability to read handwriting of all periods with accuracy and to have a knowledge of local historical associations. In particular, a close acquaintance with the topography of the area is essential, for how else could initial doubt be cast on the interpretation of the second element of the name of a holding which takes the form *Rydhill* in 1566 as the common word *hill* unless the topography of the location is known to be the flat and featureless moorland near Dinas Powys in the Vale of Glamorgan? Further investigation reveals that the 1566 form is an attempt to give some meaning to the otherwise forgotten surname of the holder of that land at one time, the surname being *Riddle* and having been adopted as the name of that holding, *Riddle Farm* 1783-6.[6] The fact that *Riddle* is also a well-attested English surname in the south-west counties of England on the other side of the Severn estuary, Somerset in particular, provokes thoughts about the nature and origin of settlement in the Dinas Powys area,[7] and the further realization that the name is now lost but is 'hidden' in a literal Welsh translation of the English common noun *riddle* 'a sieve', namely W *rhidyll*, in the extant *Pont-y-rhidyll* as the name of a small bridge in the vicinity, has its own contribution to make to the cultural and linguistic history of the area.[8]

There is no doubting the fact that the task of collecting place-name forms is laborious and time-consuming, even tedious at times, save for the occasional moment of exhilaration when significant forms appear to shed new light on a long-standing problem or to support a suspected derivation, for it involves the recording of field-names and minor names as well as major names. Electronic devices may well improve the method of recording the collected evidence in time, but the well-tried card- or slip-index method is reliable, reasonably permanent and a good deal cheaper. Forms of individual names are then rearranged in chronological order according to the dates of the sources, thus providing the basis on which the work of interpretation can begin. It is best tackled on a territorial basis, ultimately with the view of producing a national survey, the administrative county being the largest unit which is within manageable proportions if there are assistants available to share the work. Again, in Wales, mainly because documentation is predominantly related to them, this means the historical counties as constituted before the 1972 Local Government Act. Otherwise, smaller units, contemporary or historical, are within the capabilities of individuals, the parish or a number of parishes being particularly suitable for the local historian. Unfortunately, Wales has never seen the inauguration of a project for surveying the place-names of its historical counties on the admirable pattern and scale of that produced in England, since 1924, by the English Place-Name Society. This is not to deny the existence of superlative work produced by Welsh scholars, past and present, on individual names or select categories of names taken more or less at random from all over the country, either when a particular need arose or when investigation was called for largely in expositions and notes relating to textual contexts and historical documentation.[9]

Such a limitation in detailed territorial coverage, however, deprives the toponymist of much of one of his most useful aids, namely the provision of comparative material concerning the nomenclature of localities in broadly similar topographical situations elsewhere or, indeed, the use of similar elements in different situations, as well as confirmation of certain colloquial changes in the forms of names in other areas which are identifiable in his own area of investigation. For example, the known fact that a name like *Ystrad Wrell*, Carms., assumes the form *Ystrad Wrallt* confirms the possibility that the suffix *-ell* is capable of modification in the vernacular > *-all*, and that in addition there occurs the growth of an excrescent *-t* > *-allt* (not uncommon after final *-ll* in Welsh), as in a word like *anystywell* > *anys-tywallt* (GPC s.v.) or the stream-name *Ariannell*, Denbs., > *Eirianallt* by vowel affection,[10] the suffix having a diminutive function and not to be connected with W *allt* (*gallt*) 'slope, ascent'. Consequently a stream-name in the vicinity of Port Talbot, Glam., which appears on early editions of OS maps as *Arnallt Brook*, and in the modern street-name *Rhanallt Street*, can be suspected of having been an original Welsh form in *-ell*. This is confirmed by collected evidence to have been W *Arannell* > **Ar(a)nnell* > **Arnall* > *Arnallt*. Moreover, still further investigation reveals two more facts, the one relating to the form of the name *Arannell*, the other concerning its function and meaning. In the first place, because of another colloquial change known to occur in the southern areas of Wales, it can be established that the southern *Arannell* is the counterpart of the Denbs. *Ariannell* by reference to the well-attested process of dropping the consonantal *-i̯-* in the vernacular, thereby making it possible to identify the name as a stream-name in at least a dozen other locations. However, secondly, what emerges from comparative work is that this form also occurs in early texts as a personal-name, both male and female, so that it is perfectly possible that coupled with a common noun like *tref*, or *tir* etc., this personal name could appear in conjunction with such a noun as an element in a place-name to signify possession or tenure. Such, in outline, is the basis of reasoning which has led to the positive identification of a location referred to in a Margam Abbey document of 1518 as *treranell*, i.e. a contraction of *Tref Arannell*. The name is no longer current, but the additional evidence of collected forms establishes beyond reasonable doubt that it is enshrined in the unlikely-looking Anglicized form *Angelton*, near Bridgend, Glam., through an intermediate form, *Tre Angel* 1618 (pronounced in the Welsh manner), which is not a 'corrupt' form as some might be led to suppose but a normal consequence of nasalization in the spoken Welsh language of the district which, again, is exemplified elsewhere as in *Yrannell* > *Yrangell* in Pembs.[11]

The example quoted above also serves to illustrate another consideration which is of prime importance to the toponymist. He is interested not only in the original form and meaning of a name but also in the various phases of its development and the influences that have transformed it, when this has occurred, over the years. This could well be thought of as part of the process of interpretation, but only in one sense is this true because the development must be understood before the original form can be ascertained with confidence. This is essentially an historical approach to which linguistic appreciation is superadded. The result may well be to add to a knowledge of the nature and development of a language in any given area, but historical inferences, direct and indirect, can be drawn from such conclusions and these may throw light on a particular period, the nature and extent of settlement, movements of people, their relationship to each other, aspects of their organization and the like. What is noteworthy in the case of *Trerannell/Angelton*, over and above matters pertaining to meaning and function, is the substitution of the English suffix *-ton*, OE *tūn* 'farmstead, homestead' for an original W *tref*, and that at a comparatively late date, the first half of the eighteenth century, as the collected forms show quite clearly.[12] In an area like the Vale of Glamorgan this kind of substitution is not particularly well evidenced, the reverse is far more common, namely the substitution of *tref* for *-ton* and more often than not at much earlier dates, a fact which is not without its significance for the social historian.

The whole question of the interchange of *tref* and *-ton* in the toponymy of Wales is a matter which poses a number of problems which are as yet far from being satisfactorily resolved, if only because of the lack of county-by-county place-name surveys which could provide much-needed comparative information. Both elements are representative of the English/Welsh linguistic confrontation which is such a feature of post-Norman Wales and possibly, had we the data to prove this, of pre-Norman Wales, since a number of names in *-ton* in Welsh border areas are recorded in Domesday Book (1086), which may indicate their existence before the composition of that well-known compilation. In such cases we could be dealing with examples of the direct provenance of OE *tūn* 'enclosure', of which *-ton* is the derived suffix element and, perhaps, more than any other almost a symbol of the influx of Anglo-Norman and later English settlement in a manorial context in those areas in which it is mostly to be found, such as Pembs., south Glam. and Gower, Gwent and the north-east. Both *tref* and *-ton*, however, have a range of semantic development which makes precision in ascertaining their exact original meaning in place-names sometimes difficult to achieve. If we take the exemplary work of Dr B.

G. Charles on non–Celtic names as a sample, where over 340 -*ton* names in Wales are recorded, and judging from the dates at which the forms are first evidenced by him, the highest incidence occurs in the late thirteenth and fourteenth centuries rather than the twelfth. This may well be because the documentary sources are more plentiful in the later period, it is true, but it is also pertinent to note that on the other hand quite a number are not first evidenced until the sixteenth century.[13] This is a wide time-span, so that considerable semantic variation, analogical formations etc. can be expected as the assimilation of English elements of the population into Welsh communities increased in intensity. In most immediate post-Norman names it is likely that -*ton* indicates 'farmstead, homestead', but that it can also mean 'hamlet, village' in others is not improbable, either directly so named or bearing the name of an original farmstead around which such a settlement developed. Further, it can mean 'estate, manor, vill' at a comparatively early date, as has been argued in the case of *Knighton*, Rads., which occurs in Domesday Book as *Chenisteton*, and subsequently *Cnichteton* 1193 etc.,[14] as well as 'fee, small lordship'.[15] Furthermore, that there is an affinity between the use of -*ton* and W *tref* in place-nomenclature is reasonably clear, the latter being a native word extensively in use in pre-Norman times. At least *tref*, almost invariably reduced to *tre* in common speech, would appear to be the Welsh element that approximates most closely in meaning to the English element (or vice versa). Originally this probably meant 'habitation, dwelling-place, homestead' including the land held with the homestead, before developing the popular sense 'hamlet, village', but, at first technically 'the group of villein homesteads clustered together for the purpose of common cultivation of the surrounding land',[16] an administrative unit, the so-called 'township' of varying status which, in the opinion of T. Jones Pierce, 'to men familiar with the social structure of the border and northern shires of England . . . could have presented few peculiar features'.[17] But it is evident, if we are to judge from the forms of various compounds in which *tref* is coupled with other elements to indicate specific functions or location and which occur in place-names either as simplex forms or as elements in larger compounds, that the element might vary in its popular connotation. In *maerdre(f)* (W *maer* 'reeve, royal bailiff or official') the social and organizational function of *tref* would seem to remain the dominant idea, the unit having evolved its particular function of an economic unit providing customary services at a comparatively early stage.[18] Less clear, in some cases, is the specific meaning of *tref* in compounds like *coetre(f)* (W *coed* 'wood, woodland', *y goetre*, which becomes *goytre* at the hands of non-Welsh scribes and cartographers), or *melindre(f)* (W *melin* 'mill', which could be confused with W *bileindref*<*bilain* 'villein', i.e., 'villein township' or 'farm held in villeinage', GPC s.v.), i.e. whether *tref* is a collective unit or a single homestead.[19] The latter would certainly seem to be indicated in combinations that were well-known terms connected with the practice of transhumance, the best known being *hendre(f)* (W *hen* 'old') which Jones Pierce maintains was also used 'to distinguish the site of the original settlement or *tref* from the later administrative *tref*' by the later Middle Ages,[20] although it is to be noted that not every *hendref* was so named. Similarly *hafdre(f)* (W *haf* 'summer', 'summer homestead', cf. *hafod, hafoty, hafdy* GPC s.v.) which appears in some areas as *hawdre(f)* and forms the second element of *Ynysawdre* in Glam.,[21] and *cynhaefdre(f)* (*cynaeafdref*, W *cynhaeaf* 'harvest-time, autumn') sometimes assuming spurious forms like *Cefnhafdre*, *Gwenhafdre*, and possibly by analogy with *hawdre(f)*, *Y Gynhawdre* in Lledrod, Cards., but more regularly in local parlance as *Cynheidre*.[22] Both these terms survive as farm-names in Glam. and Carms. in the Neath–Port Talbot area and north of Llanelli, with the qualifying adjectives *mawr*, *bach*, *isaf* 'lower', *uchaf* 'higher' and *canol* 'middle' which imply the later subdivision of a primary single holding. Much later, of course, W *tref* developed the modern meaning of 'town', and it is not without significance that the etymological source of E *town* is OE *tūn*.

Evidence for an early post-Norman substitution of E *-ton* for an original W *tref* in place-nomenclature is so scarce as to be virtually non-existent or subject to conjecture on uncertain grounds, as in the case of *Allington*, Denbs., which occurs in Domesday Book as *Alentune*, because the first element is the river-name *Alun* and the fact that the Welsh alternative *Trefalun* exists, although not evidenced until 1561.[23] The main weight of existing evidence supports the view that in this period *-ton* is used to denote settlements of direct Anglo-Norman, or even earlier provenance, and the degree of intensity of such settlement is, indeed, often reflected in a preponderance of surviving English place-names in localities. Where there was a Welsh 'recovery' and changes in local administration took place, what resulted was 'the mingling of English and Welsh elements with consequent confusion in nomenclature'.[24] Some, particularly in the north-east, fell into disuse at an early stage while others came under Welsh influence to such an extent that their English origin tended to become obscured,[25] but the great majority show Welsh influence in the development of their forms in the later medieval period, particularly from about the late thirteenth century onwards.

In the case of names in *-ton*, two main tendencies are apparent. The first shows no outright attempt at replacement or substitution of elements, merely, in some cases, a modification of the existing form of the defining English element by Welsh speakers (nearly always a personal name or family surname to denote possession, or a common noun to signify location or association) and a similar modification of *-ton* to *-tyn* in the north-east and border areas, as in *Mertyn* for *Mereton* 1086 (OE (*ge*)*mǣre* 'mere, boundary' or OE *mere* 'pool'), *Mostyn* for *Mostone* 1086 (OE *mos* 'moss, bog'), or *Prestatyn* for *Prestetone* 1086 (OE *preost* 'priest', additional interest being given to this form in that the Welsh propensity for accentuation on the penult preserved the medial *-e-*, from the OE genitive plural ending *-a*, which would otherwise have disappeared, to give the more usual English form *Preston*) among others in Flints.[26] In south and west Wales this kind of modification shows *-ton* > *-twn*, as in the Glam. *Wrinstwn* (*Wrenchiston* 1216–72), *Nyrstwn* (*Nurston*), *Crostwn* (*Crosstown*), *Nortwn*, *Silstwn* (*Gileston*), *Britwn* (*Burton*, the present English name having a metathesized form of OE *brycg* 'bridge' as first element, *Britoun* 1536–9, which is better preserved in the Cymricized form), but it is to be noted that not all of these examples are evidenced in medieval documents, many are colloquial forms preserved in the popular oral Welsh verse-form of Glamorgan, the *triban*, and therefore of uncertain date.[27]

More plentiful evidence exists for the replacement of *-ton* by W *tref*. It is difficult, even so, in the present unsatisfactory circumstances concerning the availability of comparative evidence to find a consistent norm by which to judge the significance of this process. It would seem, in many cases, that it can be attributed to a tacit acceptance of the broad affinity in meaning between the two elements among the native Welsh population and not, necessarily, a full comprehension of the finer shades of meaning which either could have had at any given time. Also the fact that no doubt the persistence of -*ton* as a name-forming element may be the consequence of modelling comparatively new place-names on older names which contain the element, without due regard to the full significance of its meaning — something which is undoubtedly true of many later *tref* forms — is a point which should not be overlooked. It is not always possible, therefore, to determine the precise meaning of -*ton* in the original forms where substitution has occurred, and the recorded evidence for the *tref-* forms, particularly in Glamorgan, is late in comparison, often not earlier than the sixteenth century or in later sources which are more consciously literary or have a strong oral basis like the popular rhymes referred to above. Rarely is a name like *Clementiston* 1332, Pembs., first evidenced almost contemporaneously with a Welsh form, *Trefclemens* 1326, but an element of uncertainty still remains concerning this example, for although it is the colloquial Welsh form *Treglemais* which has prevailed, which suggests the possibility of an original form in *tref-*, the personal-name or surname which it also contains does not provide strong support for such an assumption.[28] The majority of such names for which evidence is available clearly indicates that the forms in -*ton* are the earlier and constitute a category of names which is by now reasonably well known, such as the Pembs. *Letterston/Treletert*, *Jordanston/Trewrdan*, *Cadygan(i)ston* 1326–63/*Trecadwgan*[29], or the Glam. *Laleston/Trelales*, *Bonvilston/Tresimwn* (Simon de Bonville), *Flemingston/Trefflemin*, *Candleston/Tregawntlo*, to note a few examples.[30] This is consistent with the evidence which is now emerging, on less impressionistic grounds than formerly, concerning the social structure of communities in an area like the Vale of Glamorgan during the sixteenth century.[31] It points to a considerable resettlement by the Welsh of former predominantly English-held land and property which had suffered the ravages of pestilence and disturbance up to the beginning of the fifteenth century.[32] But the categorization of the place-name evidence on a systematic scale has still to be accomplished. There are anomalies and inconsistencies, some of which are as yet not satisfactorily explained.

Not all -*ton* forms are what they seem to be, some being original forms with OE *dūn* 'a hill', mainly as ME *doun* in the suffix form -*don* 'a hill, an expanse of open hill country', as in *Blackton*, *Cornton* (*Corntown*) Glam. or *Minerton*, *Sodston* and possibly *Orielton*, Pembs.[33] There are also -*ton* forms which have Welsh personal names or common nouns as first elements which are not sufficiently well evidenced to convince us that they could be English renderings of Welsh originals, like *Leason*, Gower, *Leysanteston* 1304, with W *Lleision*, a masculine Christian name, a Welsh form *Treleison* occurring late, in 1641; *Crickton*, also in Gower, *Crytton* 1583 (which Charles prefers to read as *Crycton*) with, possibly, W *crug* as first element but with no Welsh equivalent either recorded or current.[34] Other -*ton* names occur in ecclesiastical contexts and merit the toponymist's careful attention before conclusions are attempted. Perhaps A. H. Smith's reference to the use of -*ton* to refer to secular establishments 'having Christian connections' is more easily understood when the first elements in the names are common nouns like *church*, *monk* or *priest*, as in *Carew Cheriton*, Pembs. (*Churcheton* 1346), a lost *Wenvoe Church(e)ton* 1540 in Glam. and probably *Cheriton*, Gower; *Moncton*, Glam., *Monkton*, Pembs. (two examples), *Mounton*, Pembs. (*Monketon* 1326) and Gwent (*Monketowne* 1535, a possession of Chepstow Priory); and *Prestatyn*, Flints. (*supra*).[35] As in the majority of cases in England, where *bishop* occurs with *-ton* it signifies a farmstead unit belonging to a see,[36] as in *Bishopston*, Gower (*villa Episcopi c*.1230), and Gwent (possessions of the Bishop of Llandaf, the syncopated form *Bishton* being used generally for the latter, but recorded for the former in 1535), notwithstanding the fact that the church foundations in both these places have their own earlier Welsh names, *Llandeilo Ferwallt*, Gower, and *Llangadwaladr*, Gwent, so that *-ton* here cannot be construed as having been used as an alternative for W *llan*. They are, rather, establishments at the places previously so named. Even in the case of *Kennexton(e)*, Gower (*Kenithstoane* 1642), where it would appear that the first element of the name is that of the saint, *Cenydd*, to whom the neighbouring church of *Llangynydd*, or *Llangenydd* (*Llangennith*) is dedicated, no direct connection between *-ton* and *llan* in the name can be assumed though there may have been a connection in the secular sense of attached property.[37]

But what of other names where *-ton* does, indeed, appear to be the equivalent of W *llan*? These need careful interpretation, and the evidence for the evaluation of current forms is critical. *Tythegston*, Glam., would appear to be for W *Llanduddwg* > *Llandudwg* (although the Welsh name is not, at present, evidenced before *c*.1566), but the collected evidence for the modern form shows that the terminal *-ston* (including the genitival *-s* which is attached to the personal name) has developed by analogy from an original E *stow(e)*, *Tethegestow* 1258 etc., OE *stōw* 'place, place of assembly' (cf. *Chepstow*, Gwent, OE *cēap* 'market' + *stōw*, 'market-place')[38] having acquired the sense of 'holy place' (of assembly) in a Christian context.[39] Its use in this sense as a later equivalent for W *llan* is logical and can be seen in *Dingestow*, Gwent, for W *Llanddingad* (earlier *Merthyr Dingad*, *merthir dincat* LL 31), or *Wonastow* (*Won(e)warestowe* 1293 etc.) for *Llanwynwarwy* (locally *Llanwarw*, *Lanngunguarui* LL 201) among others.[40] Similarly, two examples of *Michaelston* near Cardiff were originally *Michaelstow(e)*, namely *Michaelston-le-pit* and *Michaelston-super-Ely*,[41] both having Welsh equivalents, *Llanfihangel-y-pwll* and *Llanfihangel-ar-Elái*, with the possibility that the original form of the former (though not proven) was *Llanfihangel*, whatever may be said for the latter.[42]

What is more difficult to explain is an apparent direct rendering of W *llan* by *-ton* where there is no evidence of an intervening *-stow(e)* stage. Two further examples of *Michaelston* in Glam., Cwmafan, and Gwent, *Michaelston-y-fedw*, are in this category, and so is *Peterston-super-Ely*, W *Llanbedr-ar-fro*, near Cardiff,[43] as are two places named *Cadoxton* (with the saint's name *Cadog*) in Glam., the confusion being compounded here by the fact that the one (near Neath) is W *Llangatwg*[44] and the other (near Barry) *Tregatwg*.[45] In *Ilston*, Gower, *-ton* occurs with the saint's name *Illtud* (*Ilewitteston c*.1396, *ecclesie Sci Iltuti de Illiston* 1490), the Welsh form *Llanilltud Gŵyr* being known as an alternative form of the name, and *Dixton*, Gwent (*Dukeston* 1291, probably for a form resembling **Tydiwg's-ton*) would appear without question to be a direct rendering of W *Llandydiwg* (*Lann tydiuc*, LL 276).[46]

Whether there is some kind of analogical development in such cases or not, it is difficult to say, as is a possible reference to an attached community or 'village', for it would seem that the combination of a saint's name with -ton in a purely ecclesiastical sense is not evidenced in English place-names.[47] Here is an instance where a substantial body of evidence from as wide a field as possible is necessary before a firm conclusion can be deduced.

Later evidence of the interchange of W tref and E -ton in an area like the Vale of Glamorgan is not such as to suggest firm regional patterns, as far as can be judged at present. It seems to be intermittent, depending perhaps on changing circumstances in particular localities although there appears to be a pronounced period of Cymricization overall which reached a peak by the eighteenth century.[48] It is in such a context that Trerannell > Angelton must be placed. This is noteworthy because it does not conform with the general trend, whereas in the neighbouring parish of Llangan an astonishing example of Cymricization by the introduction of a form in tre- for an original -ton can be dated to the beginning of the sixteenth century. The name is that of the hamlet of Goston (first evidenced in that form in 1536), so named, it is reasonable to assume, from an original farmstead. The first element is clearly the ME form of OE gōs 'goose', giving the sense 'goose farm' i.e. 'frequented by wild geese'.[49] By 1596–1600 the form Tress appears in one MS source as an alternative name for the hamlet which later sources indicate should be read as Treos[50] (Velin Treos o. Treos Mill 1679, Treose 1825 etc.) and the name appears on the first edition of the OS map (1833) as Treôs or Goston. What makes the Welsh form of the name remarkable is that it not only has the substitution of tre(f) for -ton but that it also adopts the English element gos- with no attempt at translation and, further, that it displays the normal Welsh process of lenition of the initial consonant in a genitival relationship after tre- > Tre-os. The strong Welsh influence here continued into another phase of development in the eighteenth century seen, perhaps significantly, in Griffith Jones of Llanddowror's annual reports, Welch Piety, 1748–50 where the name appears as Tre Oes,[51] this being an obvious attempt to make some sense of an otherwise meaningless (in Welsh terms) Tre-os, because of the known tendency in the local Welsh dialect to reduce and lengthen the dipthong -oe- to -ō- (cf. W coed > cōd, troed > trōd etc.) The long -ō- in Tre-os was thus misinterpreted as being originally for W -oe- and the spurious form Treoes (equally meaningless in its context) was thus introduced. This form has persisted in print and has some currency in modern times on maps and road-signs but should not be perpetuated.

To have dwelt at such length on aspects of the interchange of two elements only in Welsh place-nomenclature may appear wildly extravagant of space within the permitted limits of a short chapter, but such a constraint demands a high degree of selectivity and it is hoped that some principles will have become apparent — namely, that the approach, because of the nature of the material evidence, is primarily linguistic, and that an appreciation of phonological changes and morphological variations as well as an awareness of the operation of influences to which place-names have been subjected over the years are essential. It may be deemed that much of the derived information is not precise enough and therefore of diminished value, but in very early periods when written evidence is scarce, how much entirely trustworthy evidence does the historian have at his disposal? The place-name investigator has one advantage here. He can at least appeal to a body of established rules that have what approximates to the force of a 'law' in their general application to linguistic development.[52] This will indicate the significance of why the river-name *Taf* takes the form that it does as the second element of the name *Caerdyf* as opposed to the nearby *Llandaf*, and for that matter why the original form of the name is better preserved in the 'English' form *Cardiff* than the current Welsh form *Caerdydd*;[53] or why the English form *Pembroke* (earlier, *Penbroc*) retains the unlenited form of the medial *-b-* in comparison with the Welsh *Penfro*.[54]

On the other hand, the employment of such techniques in the elucidation of the form and meaning of a name may lead some to suppose that the process of name-giving itself in the first place was a complicated matter. The place-name investigator is not, by and large, attempting to solve clues in some kind of jumbo-size *Times* crossword puzzle set by a professional compiler. The act of name-giving was not, and is not, an academic exercise carried out by experts conscious of the need to bequeath to succeeding generations, like the historical chronicler, a record of settlement which can be categorized and tabulated. It is, rather, the spontaneous application of a distinguishing label or tag to a location, descriptive or otherwise, by ordinary folk for the purpose of identification. The relatively simple and uncomplicated solution is always to be preferred to that which is so involved as to imply motives on the part of the original name-givers which are unrealistic and erudite.

This can be illustrated by reference to the popular naming of visible remains of the past, reaching back to prehistoric times, which must have existed as features of the landscape from post-Roman times onwards. Comparatively speaking, the names given to such remains are late, some very late, but certainly not by people who were able to distinguish, let us say, between multivallate or univallate Iron Age hill-forts and Bronze Age round cairns. Consequently, consistency in the use of particular words to signify particular types of monuments, such as W *caer* or *dinas*, is not to be expected. If a broad distinction can be made between the corresponding *car* or *ker* and *dynas* in Cornwall, in that the latter refers to a larger fortification than the former, such a proposition is hardly tenable in Wales.[55] Almost a century ago Sir John Edward Lloyd suggested that wherever *dinas* (a derivative of *din*, cf. Corn. *din*, Irish *dún* 'stronghold, fortress', Br. **dūno-*, Celt. **dounon*) is found in Welsh place-names of some antiquity it relates to the site of a hill-fort (with no resort to classification of types).[56] The occurrence of the basic form *din* is indicative of an earlier phase of name-giving, as a prefix in *Dinorwig*, *Dinlleu*, *Dinbych*, *Dinorben* etc. or as a suffix in *Gorddin(og)*, *Breiddin*, *Myrddin* etc., and proof that it had lost its significance even by early medieval times is the existence of a tautologous form like *Dinas Dinlleu* in the Mabinogi tales, or the addition of *Caer* in *Caerfyrddin* (*Carmarthen*) for *Myrddin* < *Moridunum* (not the ubiquitous Merlin of legend), unless *caer* in that instance specifically refers to the Roman settlement.[57] But evidence points to the fact that a later native population applied the term *dinas* indiscriminately to structures that were to them visible remains having the appearance of fortifications, whether they were open settlements or defended settlements in reality. It is as well to note also that *dinas* does not necessarily, at all times, even refer to a 'fortification' but to prominent elevated natural features which look like suitable locations for defensive positions although there are no visible structural remains.[58] *Dinas*, Rhondda, which takes its name from *Mynydd Dinas* which rises above the modern urban settlement may well be of this type.

A further point to note is that many known hill-fort sites and man-made structures which might have been designated *dinas* with equal propriety in the popular view are, in fact, termed *caer* generally in Wales; in Glamorgan more are so named than are called *dinas*. In general, *caer*, and not *dinas*, was certainly used to indicate the sites of Roman towns and forts like *Caerwent, Caerllion, Caerhun, Caersws* etc., although this cannot be regarded as a hard-and-fast rule.[59] This must have influenced the view held at one time that W *caer* was a derivative of the Lat. *castra*, though untenable on etymological grounds, together with the use of OE *ceaster*, which *is* a loan-word from *castra*, as in English place-names ending in -*chester*, *Chester* itself, and others like *Caistor, Caister* etc.[60] But W *caer* is a native word < Br. **kagro-*, which developed the basic sense of 'enclosure' and has the same root-form as the noun *cae*, now 'field', but earlier 'a hedge, a barrier' (cf. W *cae drain* 'thorn hedge') i.e. that which encloses, and subsequently the land thus enclosed to form a field. It is cognate with E *hedge*, OE *hecge*, so that its use in Welsh to signify hill-forts and the like which are themselves essentially enclosures seems rational. Furthermore, lack of popular discrimination in the use of these terms is heightened by the use of the plural form *caerau* to designate individual hill-forts, the two best known in Glam. being *Caerau* near Ely, Cardiff, and near Llantrisant. One can only conjecture that this occurs when structures present a complicated visible arrangement of defences. The site near Ely is particularly noticeable for its additional medieval ringwork in the north-east corner as well as being the site of a parish church, the Llantrisant example being multivallate. In both, the ordinary observer might easily have assumed the presence of more than one structure.[61] Though the site of *Pencaerau* (noted as *Caerau, Mynydd y Caerau* in an early nineteenth-century source) south of Neath,[62] is now classed as univallate, it may have had a more complicated appearance as it has hollows in it and the possible remains of a round hut,[63] while the name of a modern settlement north of Nantyffyllon in the Llynfi Valley, *Caerau*, derives either from a stream-name, a nearby farm being *Blaencaerau* (W *blaen* 'source, upper reaches', suggesting a lost *Nant-y-caerau*) or another *Mynydd Caerau* in the vicinity (from which the stream may have been so named) which has no more substantial remains upon it than a number of cairns, some of which appear to be natural features, but still enough, apparently, to attract the appellation.[64]

A similar use is made of W *castell* 'castle' and the plural forms *cestyll* and *castellau* in their application to early sites, with which may be compared the use of *castle* in England, as in the well-known *Maiden Castle*, Dorset,[65] such names being almost invariably late and possibly arising from a time when *castell* or *castle* became a general term for 'fortress'. Both the Welsh and English words are well evidenced in Glam. in this and the specific medieval sense,[66] the name of the Traherne family's residence in Llantrisant, *Castellau*, being derived from that of the holding of land in the vicinity which was *Tir-y-castellau* (*Tir kystylle* 1630, *Tir y kistille* 1696, *Tir y Cystylle* 1698 etc.) on which stood the properties of *Kystylle Ycha, Higheste Kystylle, Loweste kystylle* 1570, to be followed by the modern farmsteads of *Castellau-fach*, *-ganol*, and *-uchaf* on the south-western slopes of rising ground on which the remains of a hill-fort are situated marked by the name *Lle'r Gaer* on the OS map.[67]

The main pitfalls to avoid when handling recorded place-name forms containing *caer* or *castell* are, in the case of the former, to assume the presence of *caer* when in reality it may well by W *cae* 'field' + 'r, the apostrophied contraction of the Welsh definite article *yr*. It is infrequently that any differentiation is made between the two in documents and the difficulty is increased when the second element is obscure as, for instance, in the difficult name *Caer Dynnaf*, Llanbleddian, Glam., the large and impressive multivallate fort south-east of Cowbridge, or *Caer Gwanaf* (*kaer gwanar* 1631) south of Meisgyn (Miskin) a farm-name at present but marking the location of an enclosure regarded by the RCAHM as being of doubtful authenticity.[68] In the case of *castell*, allowance must also be made for its late use as a 'mocking' term, as in *Castell-y-dryw* (*Wren Castle*), Llantriddyd,[69] *Castell-corryn*, Llantrisant (W *corryn* 'spider'), or *Castell-y-mwnws*, Llantrisant (W *mwnws* 'dust-heap, mound, debris, ashes'), all referring to ruined remains but probably not of early origin.

Numerous further examples of common nouns used by a native population to name sites and structures of bygone ages could be quoted, of which the following are examples: W *twmpath* 'tump, hillock, mound' (with its possible variant form, especially in Glam., *dimbath*, *dinbath*); W *gwersyll* 'camp, encampment' and *gwersyllfa* (with *-fa* < *-ma* 'place'); W *disgwylfa* 'a place of observation, look-out, watch-tower' in elevated situations; W *carn*, pl. *carnau*, *cernydd*, *cerni* 'cairn, mound, barrow' and the derived *carnedd*, pl. *carneddau*, *carneddi*, probably the most common of all; W *crug* 'heap, knoll, cairn'; W *bedd* and the pl. *beddau*, often used in the belief that prehistoric remains such as mounds, cairns, standing stones and the like are either themselves the 'graves' of specifically named heroes, giants or groups of people, legendary or otherwise, or that they mark such graves, as with the E *grave* in *Giant's Grave*, Briton Ferry, etc., also W *mynwent* 'cemetery'; W *pebyll* 'tent, pavilion' (a singular noun of masculine gender < Lat. *papilio*, pl. *pebyllau*, the modern feminine singular form *pabell* being a more recent creation) used as the name of a Bronze Age ring-cairn in Glam., its almost circular bank perhaps having suggested a former tent-like structure, possibly having a military significance in the popular view (cf. the use of *gwersyll* noted above), but in the parish and place-name *Cilybebyll* possibly referring to 'a dwelling, a cottage'; E *beacon*, OE (*ge*)*bēcon* 'a sign, signal, a beacon' used for round cairns which could have served as beacon platforms, and borrowed in the Welsh form *begwn*, *began* in minor names; W *clawdd*, pl. *cloddiau*, both 'wall, dyke, hedge, fence' and the antithesis 'ditch, trench, fosse', etc.[70]

Words used also to denote early lines of communication, tracks and roads more particularly, are not especially clear-cut in their specific designation and cannot always be interpreted as reliable indicators of type. In general, terms like W *heol* and *ffordd* are comparatively late, while W *sarn*, and *ôl* appear to be earlier. The use of *sarn* to indicate Roman roads is prevalent throughout Wales,[71] and it is a word derived by Sir Ifor Williams from a root-form **ster-*, which gave Lat. *sterno*, and would seem to have a meaning which is connected with the sense of treading or trampling.[72] Melville Richards points out, however, that 'as Roman roads were characterized by their hard surface *sarn* has, in the past, been taken to be an infallible testimony to the presence of a Roman road. This was particularly the case with names like *Sarn* (*H*)*elen*, . . . *sarn* does, no doubt, sometimes indicate the course of a Roman road, but it certainly does not in all, nor even in the majority of cases'. In Cardigan Bay and on the north Wales coast it is also used for natural rock formations in shallow water, as in *Sarn Wallog, Sarn Badrig, Sarn Mellteyrn* etc., and it is often used for a causeway, raised or otherwise, across moorland or marshy ground. In the combination *Sarn Helen* is found the most characteristic consequence of antiquarian 'Helenomania' in Wales resulting from the legendary fusion of Elen Luyddog, reputed wife of Magnus Maximus, and Helen, mother of Constantine the Great, and Richards notes twelve examples of this name used for roads and tracks in north and south Wales. He also notes that some of them may well contain W *halen* 'salt', as in *Sarn-yr-halen* recorded from the sixteenth century in Worthenbury, Flints., because *sarn* is also commonly used with elements which indicate the commodity or produce most frequently transported along such tracks. It is only a detailed survey of such names in relation to their localities which will establish the significance and the antiquity of *sarn* in them.

The use of *ôl* 'imprint, track' which appears in territorial boundaries in the *Liber Landavensis* may well have more significance in indicating the antiquity of the routes in the vicinity of places where it forms an element in their names. In that source it is usually compounded with the names of domesticated animals to denote well-worn tracks or paths along local boundaries, as in *ol huch* (W *hwch* 'sow') 'the sow's track', or *oligabr, ol ygabr* (W *gafr* 'goat') 'the goat's track',[73] and the plural form *olau*, of similar meaning, is found as an element in place-names. Five examples have been noted in Glam., four of these having as first element the significant W adj. *uchel* 'high' which suggests tracks or ways in elevated situations, possibly ridgeways or minor lines or communication over high ground. A farmstead named *Uchelolau* (*Eghelloley* 1611, *Ychylola* 1799, *Highlight* 1846, *Uchel-Oleu* 1886) existed on the ridge between the Ewenni and Ogwr rivers not too far removed from a 200 m length of *agger* which is regarded as the only structural vestige of the Roman road from Neath to Cardiff. It will be noted that in 1846 the name is erroneously rendered *Highlight* in English, the element *olau* being misunderstood as the lenited form of W *golau* 'light', and is identical with *Highlight* near Barry, another *uchel-olau* first evidenced earlier, in the thirteenth century.[74] Two other farmsteads which no longer stand, though their sites are discernible, were subdivisions of a property named *Ychylola* 1799, *Lecholola* 1801, *Uwchalola* 1846, and stood on each side of an important line of communication, the only track across a considerable extent of high ground over the eastern spur of Mynydd-y-gaer north of Rhiw'rceiliog, near Pencoed, being named on the first edition of the one-inch OS map *Uchel Olaf Isaf* and *Uchel Olaf Uchaf* respectively.[75] The remaining example, where the evidence of collected forms of the name is essential in its interpretation, is the name *Rheola* in the Neath Valley. This was *Hirrole* 1295, *Hyrolle* 1295–6, *Hirolle* 1376, *hirole* 1598, etc., *Rheola* 1763, *Rhyola Farm* 1812, where the W adj. *hir* 'long' forms the first element and *olau > ole > ola* in common speech locally, 'the long track, way', which assumed its modern form by the second half of the eighteenth century.[76] The location is below the ridge of Hirfynydd along which runs a known straight 3 km. extent of a so-called Sarn Helen, the Roman road running north-east to Coelbren.[77] It cannot be proved that the *hir-olau* of the place-name refers to this road, but the coincidence of position is noteworthy, and the fact that the name is evidenced in the thirteenth century implies strongly that the reference is not to some comparatively modern construction which may well have been called *Heol-hir* (of common provenance).

That *ôl*, *olau*, precedes *heol* in usage is highly probable and, therefore, to be noted, as is suggested by a name in the parish of Welsh St Donat's, now *Heol-y-march*, where *heol* has been substituted for an earlier *ôl*, *Ollmarch* 1603, 1659, *Olemarch* 1612, 1665, 1751, *Olmarch* mid 17c, *Olmargh* 1637–8, 1658, *Oldmarch* 1659, *Oelmarch* 1659, etc., with W *march* 'horse, steed' as second element, 'the horse's track', and may have had significance as a boundary line.[78]

It should also be noted that another hazard in the identification and interpretation of recorded forms of place-names which needs to be dealt with in a rational manner, particularly in Wales, is that which presents itself in the guise of what are all too often regarded as 'corrupt' forms. This term is rarely merited and betrays a failure to make allowance for the imperfections of oral and scribal transmission which are well nigh inevitable when perpetrated by scribes and speakers unversed in the language of the place-names themselves. This is as true, for example, of an Anglo-Norman scribe's attempt to record Welsh place-names as it is of his Welsh counterpart's efforts to convey non-Welsh place-names. The problem is well illustrated in the compilation of Domesday Book, which was the earliest written source of scores of Anglo-Saxon village and parish names in England but in which the Norman scribes tended 'to represent English sounds by the nearest equivalent in their own language. As a result the spellings of Domesday Book have often to be treated with considerable caution'.[79] Much of the historical documentation of Wales was susceptible to this treatment because it was so often the product of non-Welsh scriptoria and such imperfections proliferated in the normal course of copying and transcription. The emphasis here should be on the representation of sounds, for that is essentially what a scribe attempted to do in the first place, and that at a time when there was no orthographic standardization. Clerks in courts and departments of state, later in estate offices and those of local administration and the like, merely attempted to express in writing what they *heard* and did so in terms of their own language medium. Visual distortion is a relatively recent and literate phenomenon but may well have been influenced by earlier distortion, it is true, ultimately to have a permanent effect on the forms of some names. But such forms should not be dismissed as being worthless by the toponymist. They have their value, even as an aid to interpreting meanings, if the investigator constantly bears in mind the need to be aware of the native language of the scribe, and in the case of Welsh names recorded by English scribes (by far the most common cause of 'corrupt' forms in Welsh nomenclature) to work back to those Welsh forms through the medium of English sounds.[80]

One brief example only will be given here which, however, also brings in an additional consideration, namely, that some forms which could be taken as English distortions in reality preserve, during the period in which they are recorded, the contemporary Welsh pronunciation in a dialect of which hardly any vestige remains except in such so-called 'corrupt' place-names forms. In the virtually extinct Gwentian Welsh dialect of Glamorgan the dipthong *ae* became a full long *ā* vowel sound, then the *ā* was narrowed to *ǣ*, thus *cae* 'field' > *cā* > *cǣ*, a sound for which an English scribe's equivalent in his own orthography could only be *kay*, and this is precisely the form which occurs for *cae* in scores of field-names in estate documents and surveys from the sixteenth century onwards, with *ka* or *ca* as an alternative. This is the vowel quality which is represented in the second element of *Pentrebane*, near St Fagans, this second element being the Anglo-Norman surname *Pain* or *Payn* (Lat. *Paganus*) borrowed into Welsh as *Paen*. The original form of the name was *Cefn-tre-baen*, becoming *Pentre-baen* > *Pentrebān* > *Pentre-bān*, the second element of which was represented as *-bane* by non-Welsh scribes. Similar examples are *Llys-faen* 'stone court (house)' > *Lys-fān* > *Lys-fǣn* > *Lisvane*, to the north of Cardiff; *Trevrane* for *Tre'rfrân*; *Nant Brane* for *Nant Brân* in more than one location, the mill on a stream of that name becoming *Brane's Mill* in Llansamlet; *(Y)Gare* for *(Y)Gaer*, several examples[81] (the place-name *Gelligaer* being still pronounced *Gelligare*, and although the original spelling has been carefully preserved here, documentary forms in *-gare* abound). This is why *Aberdare* is so spelt, being locally *Aberdǟr*, *'Berdǟr* for *Aberdâr*, and the much maligned and misunderstood local 'English' pronunciation of *Cardiff* as *Cǟrdiff* astonishingly preserves a trace of the same sound reaching back to the original form *Caerdyf* and possibly represented in documentary forms as early as the twelfth century as *Kairdif, Kerdif, Keyrdif* etc.[82] Evidence of this kind is plentiful in recorded forms of minor names and field-names, such as *Heol Lace* for *Heol-las* 'green way', *Maysycoed* for *Maes-y-coed*, *Bryn y Vrane* for *Bryn-y-frân* etc.[83]

However, the emphasis laid up to this point on influences that have affected the forms of place-names should not be understood as being in any way an attempt to make a case for this aspect as the prime reason for place-name study. Clearly, the toponymist must endeavour to establish the original form and meaning of a name, and to determine whether it falls within either of the two major divisions of place-name types, the topographical or the habitative, many of the former having become habitative by virtue of settlement at or near topographical features or the need to define a settlement by reference to its topographical location. In Wales, despite what has already been achieved, and for reasons which have been noted earlier, this basic work on a national territorial scale is still in its early stages. We cannot yet move confidently into a second stage of place-name study as is now being done in England, that is a reconsideration of the collected data based on EPNS county surveys in order to establish regional semantic and morphological variations in the use of very common elements like OE *feld, land, hyll, dūn* etc., and to quantify such elements in order to add to their value as historical evidence for settlement.[84] The most valuable work of this kind attempted in Wales to date is that contained in Melville Richards's lists of the occurrence of certain selected place-name elements, but these lists must have some limitations in territorial coverage, based as they are on one individual's collection of place-name forms, unique and remarkable pioneer work though this is.[85]

If we take early ecclesiastical settlement as an example, and the very common W *llan* as an element in names of that category, the toponymist has in the first place to establish, as far as this is possible, whether a name which appears to contain *llan* in modern forms, often in medieval forms, does so in reality. Because of its overwhelming preponderance in Welsh place-names, popular influence has resulted in the substitution of *llan* for other elements of one syllable which bear a resemblance to it, phonological resemblance in particular, and especially where that substitution is not entirely devoid of significance because of the existence of a known early monastic or ecclesiastical foundation at the location denoted by the original element. *Llancarfan*, Glam. was originally *Nantcarfan*, with W *nant* 'valley, glen' rather than its later meaning of 'stream, brook', despite the location there of the early Cadog foundation.[86] Similarly the neighbouring *Llantriddyd* for an original *Nantrhirid* (the W pers. name *Rhirid*) in all probability, the medial -*t*- of the modern form being apparently the vestigial final -*t* of the original first element.[87] A considerable number of *llan*- forms in Wales are already known to have evolved in this manner, such as *Llanboidy/Nantboudy*, Carms., *Llangwnnadl/Nant Gwnnadl*, Caerns., *Llantarnam/Nant Teyrnon* (*Llanfihangel Nant Teyrnon*) and *Llantoni* (*Llanthony*)/*Llanddewi Nant Hoddni*, Gwent etc. What appears to be the tautologous *Llaneglwys*, Brecs., was originally *Nanteglwys*, and can be compared with the Cornish *Lanteglos* for *Nanteglos*, this substitution being well-evidenced in the peninsula in names like *Lancarrow*, *Lanhaduon*, *Lansant* etc.[88] Another possibility is that in some modern *llan* names the element may be a substitute for W *glan* 'bank, shore' in riverside locations because of the 'restoration' of lenited forms in *lan* after prepositions in common speech under the erroneous impression that they were original *llan*- forms, as in *Llanbradach*, *Llancaeach*, *Llanmorlais*, Glam., among many other examples.[89] Further, *llan* may have been substituted for an original W *llwyn* 'grove, bush, copse' as in *Llwyneliddon*, Glam., becoming *Llanlidan* 1545–53, *ll.liddan* c.1566, *Llan Leiddan* 1590–1, the Anglicized form being *St Lythans*,[90] and cf. *Llangwaran*, Pembs., *Llanhywel*, Rads.[91] Yet again, *llan* can appear for an original W *llain* 'strip of land' as in *Llangawsai*, Cards., *Llan-y-crwth*, *Llan-y-delyn*, Pembs.,[92] or for W *llyn* 'pool' as in *Pontllanfraith*, Gwent.[93]

Such is the nature of much basic groundwork which remains to be done on a nationwide scale in Wales before refinements in interpretation can be undertaken with confidence. In the case of early Christian foundations, although archaeology has thus far yet to reveal as much as it has about the secular, much has been learnt from textual analysis, particularly of hagiological literature, analogies from other Celtic areas and the evidence of inscribed and decorated stone monuments. Place-name evidence is on the whole corroborative, and it has at least begun to identify a vocabulary, largely but not exclusively archaic, which was employed to denote Christian settlement. Some elements are, significantly, borrowings from Latin into Welsh, such as *merthyr*, Lat. *martyrium* 'a martyr's burial place' but more probably in Welsh examples 'a sanctified burial place, or cemetery' rather than the scene or location of a martyrdom;[94] *eglwys*, Lat. *ecclēsia* 'church', and *capel* Lat. *capella* 'chapel' (probably later in its application and not to be confused with locations of modern Nonconformist chapels). Such terms also become interchangeable for reasons which are not quite clear at this juncture, except that the use of the native *llan* for *eglwys* (yet another substitution) as in *Llangeinwyr* (*Llangeinor*), Glam., first evidenced by the present writer in 1466, for an earlier *Egluskeynor*, *Egliskeinwir*, *Egluskeinwir*, *Egleskeynwyr* etc. in the twelfth and thirteenth centuries, may have occurred as finer shades of meaning became blurred. On the other hand, *merthyr* precedes *eglwys* in *Eglwysilan*, Glam., which was *merthir ilan* (LL 32, 44), and one or two Latin terms are notable for their rarity, such as Lat. *oratorium* 'oratory' which seems to provide a more logical etymology than has occasionally been suggested for *Radur* (*Radyr*) near Cardiff, Glam. and north-west of the town of Usk, Gwent,[95] and Lat. *basilica* in *Basaleg* (*Baseleg*) Gwent.[96] Far more common in use for 'oratory', or simply 'chapel of ease', is W *betws*, a borrowing of OE *bede-hūs*, but here again the toponymist must establish its exact meaning for it could be a form of W *bedwos*, *bedwes* (cf. *Bedwas*) < W *bedw* 'birch tree' + a collective plural suffix -*os* giving the sense of 'birch grove' > *betwos* by provection of -*d*- to -*t*- before -*w*-, and then *betws* by analogy with the ecclesiastical *betws*.[97] Other terms are beginning to be more positively identified as place-name elements of this *genre* which are not recorded in dictionaries, such as a derivative of Lat. *monastērium*, in the Vulgar Lat. form *mon'stērium*, which is W *mystwyr* and develops colloquial forms like *mystwr* and *mwstwr*; while others which are reasonably well known as common nouns still await an evaluation of their significance in place-names, in varying circumstances, such as the religious significance of W *cil*, normally 'nook, corner, retreat', as compared with Irish *cill* 'enclosed cemetery'; W *ystafell* 'chamber, room', Lat. *stabellum*, in view of the fact that the Welsh laws refer to hermits as *gwŷr ystafellog*; W *allor* 'altar', Lat. *altare*, where popular etymology in identifying stone monuments as 'Druidical' sacrificial altars is not suspected; or W *llodre* 'place, site building' cognate with Irish *láthrach* of unknown etymology, as in *hen lotre elidon* in LL 157, included in the bounds of St Lythans, and sometimes disguised in modern forms like *Llandremor*, Llandeilotalybont, Glam., which is *Lladremor* a.1568, *Llodremor* 1584, or *Llety Brongu* near Betws, Glam., which is *Llodre Brangye* 1570, *Llodre Brangig* 1584, and its variant form *lontre* in the unidentified *lontre Tunbulch* LL 183, near Bishton (Llangadwaladr) in Gwent, to mention a few examples.[98]

No more has been attempted in this chapter than to give an impression of the usefulness of place-name evidence to the social historian together with some account of the methods and techniques employed in their interpretation and in adapting the information which may be gleaned from such evidence. Whole categories of place-name types have had to be excluded. This includes minor names and field-names, but the general principles discussed apply also to such categories. It has been argued that the original process of name-giving was probably spontaneous rather than contrived, for the purposes of identification rather than those of 'record'. If place-names record anything, however, they are a record of settlement, except for purely descriptive topographical statements concerning features of the landscape like the names of hills and mountains. But even in the case of the latter, the vocabulary employed and the linguistic features of the forms of such names have their historical value. In gathering what is evidently going to be a formidable mass of evidence in each county in Wales before it becomes possible to reach conclusions in national terms, the local historian can fulfil a critical role. Even if he does not feel capable of dealing with the linguistic problems involved, he can record forms of names from documentation and oral testimony, he can identify locations, and in particular he can determine the topographical setting of names in order to establish regional variation in the use of common place-name elements.

NOTES

[1] William Cowper (1731–1800), *The Task*, Bk. VI. 7, 101–2.

[2] F.T. Wainwright, *Archaeology and Place-Names and History* (1962).

[3] Margaret Gelling, *Signposts to the Past. Place-Names and the History of England* (1978).

[4] Ibid., 11.

[5] Ifor Williams, *Enwau Lleoedd* (Liverpool, 1945), 1.

[6] It is the accepted form in place-name studies, when evidence is quoted, to give the form of a name, its date of attestation and a reference to the source. Since this chapter is not, strictly, a survey of place-names presented in the normal way, only the dates of quoted forms are given. It should be understood that such dated forms are either taken from the author's own collection (mainly of Glamorgan names) or from printed evidence appearing in the work of other scholars. In the case of the latter, or of the former if available in print, reference will be made to the sources throughout.

[7] R.A. Griffiths, 'Medieval Severnside: the Welsh Connection' in *Welsh Society and Nationhood*, essays presented to Glanmor Williams (Cardiff, 1984), 70–89.

[8] Gwynedd O. Pierce, *The Place-Names of Dinas Powys Hundred* [*P.N.D.P.*] (Cardiff, 1968), 233–4.

[9] Pre-eminent among scholars whose work is indispensable are Sir Ifor Williams, Professor J. Lloyd-Jones, Kenneth Jackson, Melville Richards, Dr B.G. Charles and R.J. Thomas. Their notes, and those of others, have appeared widely scattered in learned journals and publications, and no attempt is made here to provide an exhaustive bibliography. Reference will be made to relevant articles where necessary. In general terms, however, notice should be taken of available standard works of reference. Such are, Ifor Williams, *Enwau Lleoedd* (Liverpool, 1945) and Sir Ifor's notes in I.A., Richmond and O.G.S. Crawford, 'The British Section of the Ravenna Cosmography' in *Archaeologia*, XCIII (1949). His notes to edited texts such as *Canu Aneirin* (Cardiff, 1935), *Canu Llywarch Hen* (Cardiff, 1933) and *Pedeir Keinc y Mabinogi* (Cardiff, 1930), among others, contain a wealth of lexicographical information; J. Lloyd-Jones, *Enwau Lleoedd Sir Gaernarfon* (Cardiff, 1928), a pioneer study of place-names in Caernarfonshire; Kenneth Jackson, *Language and History in Early Britain* (Edinburgh, 1953); Ellis Davies, *Flintshire Place-Names* (Cardiff, 1959), not always reliable and limited in its range and presentation of evidence; Melville Richards's notes on some Welsh town-names in Margaret Gelling, W.F.H. Nicolaisen and Melville Richards, *The Names of Towns and Cities in Britain* (1970) [*N.T.C.B.*]; R.J. Thomas, *Enwau Afonydd a Nentydd Cymru* (Cardiff, 1938) [*E.A.N.C.*] is well nigh indispensable; B.G. Charles, *Old Norse Relations with Wales* (Cardiff, 1934); idem, *Non-Celtic Place-Names in Wales* (Cardiff, 1938) [*N.C.P.N.*], the latter being the standard authoritative survey of non-Welsh names in Wales, to which should be added the English Place-Name Society's county volumes since 1924 (in progress) for comparative purposes, especially A.H. Smith's *English Place-Name Elements* (two vols. 1956) [*E.P.N.E.*] and Kenneth Cameron, *English Place-Names* (1961–82). Particularly useful for purposes of identification is Melville Richards, *Welsh Administrative and Territorial Units* (Cardiff, 1969), whilst Elwyn Davies (ed.), *A Gazetteer of Welsh Place-Names* (Cardiff, 1957–75) provides a list of major modern name-forms standardized according to the recommendations of the Language and Literature Committee of the University of Wales Board of Celtic Studies. The University's *Dictionary of the Welsh Language. Geiriadur Prifysgol Cymru* [*G.P.C.*] has many references to Welsh place-names under words which are reliably known to occur as elements in such names.

[10] *E.A.N.C.*, 94.

[11] *E.A.N.C.*, 94–5. For a full discussion see G.O. Pierce, 'Trerannell: Angelton' in *Morgannwg*, 27 (1983), 59–65.

[12] Ibid.

[13] For a tabulation of this information, see G.O. Pierce, 'Enwau-Lleoedd Anghyfiaith yng Nghymru', *B.B.C.S.*, XVIII (1959), 255.

[14] Ibid., 257–8.

[15] For a further discussion of *-ton* in place-names in Wales, see G.O. Pierce, 'Some Aspects of English Influence on Place-names in Wales' in *Onoma*, XVII (1972–3), 176–81.

[16] J.E. Lloyd, *A History of Wales* (3rd edn. 1948), 295.

[17] T. Jones Pierce, *Medieval Welsh Society*, edited by J. Beverley Smith, (Cardiff, 1972), 40–56, 105–6.

[18] Ibid., 343; William Rees, *South Wales and the March 1284–1415* (Oxford, 1924), 13–14.

[19] *G.P.C.* defines *coetref* specifically as a singular 'woodland homestead or dwelling'.

[20] Jones Pierce, *Medieval Welsh Society*, 222, n.68.

[21] There is no entry under this form in *G.P.C.* but see Melville Richards, '*Hafod* and *hafoty* in Welsh Place-Names', *Mont. Coll.*, LVI(1) (1959), 7.

[22] Melville Richards, '*Meifod, lluest, cynaeafdy* and *hendre* in Welsh Place-Names', *Mont. Coll.*, LVI (2) (1960), 180, and *G.P.C.* see under *cynaeafdy, cynhaefdy*.

[23] *N.C.P.N.*, xxiv, 194.

[24] W. Rees, op. cit., 69.

[25] *N.C.P.N.*, xxii, xxiv.

[26] *N.C.P.N.*, xxiv, xxxix, 228, 230–1; Ellis Davies, *Flintshire Place-Names* (1959), 108, 113–14, 140.

[27] *P.N.D.P.*, 323, 188, 76, 172–3, 171.

[28] *N.C.P.N.*, 31.

[29] Ibid., 30, 35.

[30] Ibid., 135–6, 145, 149, 153; *P.N.D.P.*, 12–13.

[31] M.Griffiths, 'The Vale of Glamorgan in the 1543 Lay Subsidy Returns', *B.B.C.S.*, XXIX (1982), 709–47.

[32] For some evidence for a Welsh recovery in the fourteenth century see B.Ll. James, 'The Welsh Language in the Vale of Glamorgan', *Morgannwg*, XVI (1972), 19, and cf. *Glamorgan County History* III, 298–302, 310; also D. Elwyn Williams, 'A Short Enquiry into Surnames in Glamorgan from the Thirteenth to the Eighteenth Centuries', *T.C.S.*, (1961) II, 46–7.

[33] *P.N.D.P.*, 172; *N.C.P.N.*, 143, 21, 101, 12.

[34] Ibid., 121–2.

[35] Ibid., 92, 158, 116, 146, 16, 64, 99, 250; *P.N.D.P.*, 301.

[36] K. Cameron, *English Place-Names*, 134.

[37] *N.C.P.N.*, 114, 241, 120.

[38] Ibid., 243.

[39] *E.P.N.E.*, ii, 159; K. Cameron, op. cit., 126–7.

[40] *N.C.P.N.*, 267, 265.

[41] Ibid., 155–6.

[42] *P.N.D.P.*, 146–52.

[43] *N.C.P.N.*, 133, 239, 156.

[44] Ibid., 132.

[45] *P.N.D.P.*, 21–3.

[46] *N.C.P.N.*, 262.

[47] See *E.P.N.E.*, ii, 188–98; K. Cameron, op. cit., 126–7.

[48] B.Ll. James, *Morgannwg*, XVI (1972), 23 ff; *P.N.D.P.*, xvii–xviii.

[49] Cf. *Goose Green*, Pembs., which is *Gossegrene* 1435, *N.C.P.N.*, 75.

[50] See William Rees's transcription, *S.W.M.R.S.*, Publication No. 3 (1954), 130.

[51] *G.C.H.* IV, 463.

[52] See F.T. Wainwright, *Archaeology and Place-Names and History*, 47–55, for a useful discussion of this point.

[53] G.O. Pierce, *G.C.H.* II, 459; also *N.T.C.B.*, 67.

[54] Ibid., 149.

[55] M. Gelling, *Signposts to the Past*, 130.

[56] J.E. Lloyd, 'Welsh Place-names', *Y Cymmrodor*, XI (1890), 15–16.

[57] *N.T.C.B.*, 68.

[58] Egerton Phillimore, *Y Cymmrodor*, XI (1890), 42.

[59] *G.C.H.* II, 468–9.

[60] M. Gelling, *Signposts to the Past*, 151–3.

[61] Royal Commission on Ancient and Historical Monuments in Wales, *An Inventory of the Ancient Monuments in Glamorgan* [*Glam. Inv.*] I, Pt. 2, 44–5 (673) and Fig. 23; Pt. 2, 43–4 (672) and Fig. 22.

[62] D.R. Phillips, *The History of the Vale of Neath* (Swansea, 1925), 21.

[63] *Glam. Inv.* I, Pt. 2, 24 (626).

[64] Ibid., I, Pt. 1, 86–7 (286–94).

[65] K. Cameron, op. cit., 115–16; *P.N.D.P.*, 72, 82–3 for *Castle Ditches* and *Castell Moel* (*Liege Castle*), Llancarfan.

[66] *G.C.H.* II, 471–2.

[67] *Glam. Inv.* I, Pt. 2, 30 (639).

[68] Ibid., I, Pt. 2, 40–1 (670), 72 (iii); *G.C.H.* II, 471.

[69] *P.N.D.P.*, 125; *Glam. Inv.* III, Pt. 2, 96–8.

[70] For a summary, with examples, of the use of these elements in Glamorgan, see *G.C.H.* II, 472–8.

[71] The standard work on this element is Melville Richards, 'Welsh *sarn* "road, causeway" in Place-names', *Études Celtiques*, XI (1964), 383–408.

[72] *B.B.C.S.*, XI, 148–9.

[73] J. Gwenogvryn Evans and John Rhys (eds.), *Liber Landavensis, The text of the Book of Llan Dav* (Oxford, 1893), 166, 42, 134.

[74] *P.N.D.P.*, 311–14.

[75] *Glam. Inv.* I, Pt. 3, 4–5, the track being noted as T10 or T11.

[76] See Melville Richards, *B.B.C.S.*, XXV, 422, and my own collection of forms.

[77] *Glam. Inv.* I, Pt. 2, 109.

[78] *G.C.H.* II, 462–3.

[79] K. Cameron, op. cit., 21.

[80] For a further introduction to this topic see G.O. Pierce, *Onoma*, XVII (1972–3), 182–91.

[81] *P.N.D.P.*, 268, 283.

[82] *G.C.H.* II, 469.

[83] *P.N.D.P.*, 80, 279.

[84] The most recent statement is the study of topographical place-names in England by Margaret Gelling, *Place-Names in the Landscape* (London, 1984).

[85] For example: 'The Irish Settlements in South-West Wales', *Jnl. Royal Soc. of Antiquaries of Ireland*, XC (1960), 133–62 (*cnwc, cnwch, loch*); 'Welsh *meid(i)r, moydir*, Irish *bóthar* "lane, road" ', *Lochlann*, 2 (1962), 128–34; 'Welsh *rhyd* 'ford' in Place-names', *Études Celtiques*, X (1963), 210–37; 'The Distribution of some Welsh Place-names', *Lochlann*, (1965), 404–14 (*clogwyn*), 4 (1969), 179–225 (*ton, twyn, tyle*); '*Ffridd/Ffrith* as a Welsh Place-name', *Studia Celtica*, II (1967), 29–90; 'Ecclesiastical and Secular in Medieval Welsh Settlement', ibid., III (1968), 9–18; 'Places and Persons in the Early Welsh Church', *W.H.R.*, 5 (1971), 333–49; 'The Supernatural in Welsh Place-names' in Geraint Jenkins (ed.), *Studies in Folk Life* (Cardiff, 1969), 304–13; 'Welsh *dryll* as a Place-name element' in *Indo-Celtica*, Gedächnisschrift für Alf Sommerfelt (München, 1972), 150–94, 219; and nos. 20, 21 and 71 *supra*.

[86] *E.A.N.C.*, 47–50; *P.N.D.P.*, 67–70.

[87] *P.N.D.P.*, 121–4.

[88] *E.A.N.C.*, 49–50; M. Richards, *Studia Celtica*, 3 (1968), 16; T.F.G. Dexter, *Cornish Names* (1926), 34.

[89] *E.A.N.C. passim*, for numerous examples of this substitution.

[90] *P.N.D.P.*, 260–2.

[91] *E.A.N.C.*, 50.

[92] Ibid., 213.

[93] *N.T.C.B.*, 152; see also *G.C.H.* II, 483–5 for a fuller discussion of *llan* substitutions.

[94] J.W. James, *T.C.S.* (1961) (2), 178; Wendy Davies, *Wales in the Early Middle Ages* (Leicester, 1982), 180–2.

[95] *N.T.C.B.*, 157.

[96] *B.B.C.S.*, VII, 277.

[97] Ifor Williams, *Enwau Lleoedd*, 51–2, and *G.P.C.*, see under *bedwos*.

[98] See further, *G.C.H.*, II, 486–7.

Houses and Building Styles*

PETER SMITH

THE HISTORICAL AND GEOGRAPHICAL CONTEXT

IT is essential when trying to understand a building first to understand its social position. Houses like society, whether historic or contemporary, may be divided into three classes — upper, middle, and lower. In a late medieval and early modern context *upper class* indicates the houses of the feudal and manorial lords; *middle class* means the yeoman tenants of the *upper class* who paid the rents and worked the farms with the help of the *lower class*, who formed the labouring poor. The earliest houses to survive are those of the upper class, whose dwellings can in Wales be traced back as a continuous story to defensive structures built during the Norman invasions. Next, in order of survival, are the houses of the middle class — the yeoman farmers, whose dwellings can be traced back to the period just before the Reformation, but no further. Of houses of the labouring poor, however, none survives from earlier than the late seventeenth century and very few from before the end of the eighteenth century. It is true that there is archaeological evidence for humble dwellings from long before the Industrial Revolution, such as the round huts of the Iron Age Celts, and the long huts, platform houses and deserted villages of later date. But these can only be seen as disconnected, isolated (and often localized) episodes out of which it is not possible to construct a continuous story.

The beginnings of *domestic architecture* in the strict sense of *both* words can be seen in terms of the demilitarization of the houses of the upper classes — the replacement of the castle by the manor house — and the appearance of the first durable houses of the yeoman class — the replacement of the hut by the farmhouse. Both processes were interrelated and took place at different times in different regions. The great increase in the power of the central government at the expense of the local territorial lords, a feature associated with the establishment of the Tudor monarchy, was felt first in southern Britain and only very much later in parts distant from the capital, in the far north and west. It was thus in southern Britain that the demilitarization of the houses of the upper classes began and it is in the south that the earliest durable farmhouses are found. There is thus by the sixteenth century a primary distinction (i) between the south, where the upper classes preferred the hall to the tower, and the north-west where they preferred the tower to the hall, and (ii) between the south where the durable peasant house began to appear at an early date and the north-west where it did not appear until much later. In this analysis Wales belongs to the south (Figs. 7, 8–9).

* I am grateful to the Royal Commission on Ancient and Historical Monuments in Wales and Her Majesty's Stationery Office for permission to reproduce here figures and plates previously published in *Houses of the Welsh Countryside*. All plates are from the National Monuments Record Collection and mainly the work of the Commission's staff photographers.

Main
Building Regions
(a) wall construction
17th century

Stone 2

Stone 2

Stone 2

Stone 2

Half-timber 2

Stone 2

Stone 1

Half-timber 1

Stone 2

Fig. 6 Main building regions of the British Isles as determined by walling materials common in the seventeenth century. At this time there were two main areas of half-timbered building and two of stone. In the half-timbered area, brick was already making inroads as supplies of timber became exhausted, while the stone area included localities where earth wall (cob) was common.

Note how north-eastern Wales falls clearly into the half-timbered area. Had the map attempted to represent the situation in the mid-sixteenth rather than the mid-seventeenth century, the whole of the Welsh borderland would have fallen into this area.

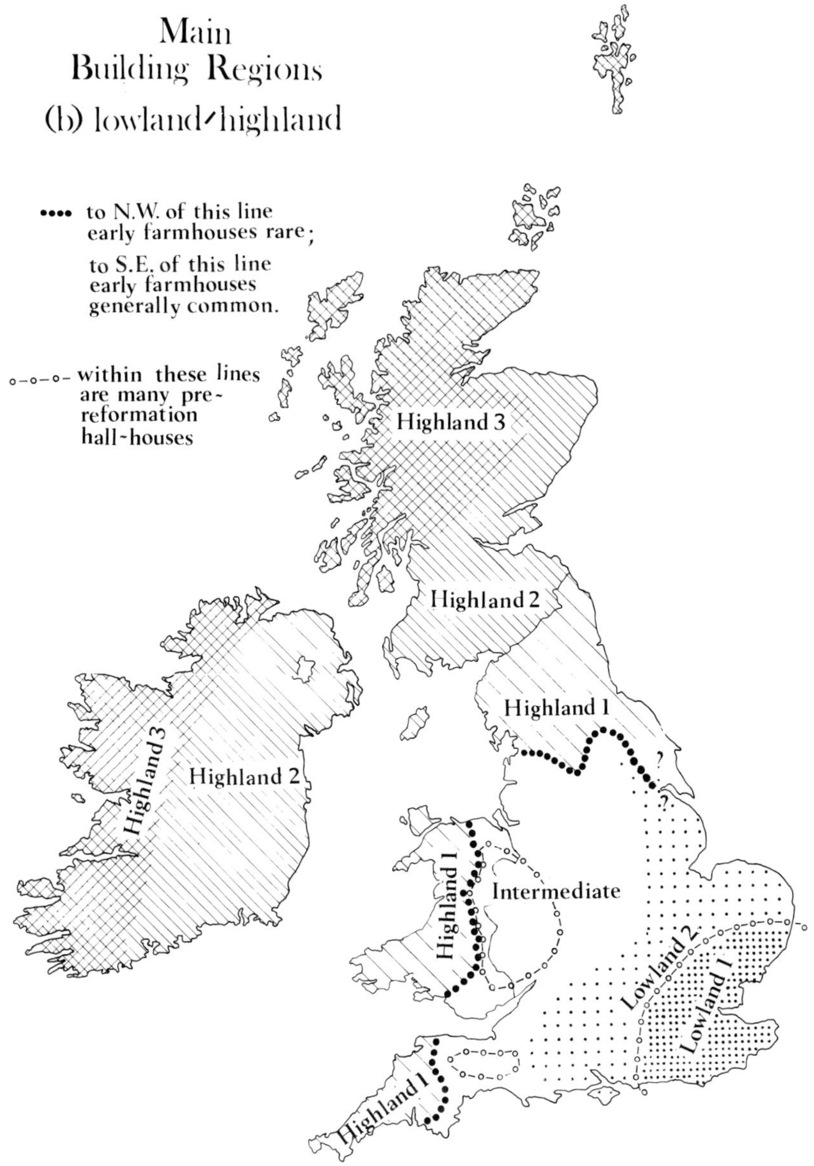

Main
Building Regions
(b) lowland-highland

•••• to N.W. of this line
early farmhouses rare;

to S.E. of this line
early farmhouses
generally common.

o−o−o− within these lines
are many pre-
reformation
hall-houses

Highland 3

Highland 2

Highland 1

Highland 3

Highland 2

Highland 1

Intermediate

Lowland 2

Lowland 1

Highland 1

Fig. 7 The main building regions of the British Isles as indicated by lowland or highland characteristics, showing the important intermediate zone (which includes eastern Wales) incorporating both. In general, farmsteads become poorer (and more recent) as the scene moves north-west. Pre-Commonwealth, sub-medieval farmhouses are relatively numerous in most of the lowland and intermediate zones. However, the much rarer pre-Reformation hall-houses seem to be most in evidence in three distinct concentrations separated from each other by the limestone belt and the sea. Of these two, the south-east and the west Midlands, are associated with areas of timber building (see Fig. 6).

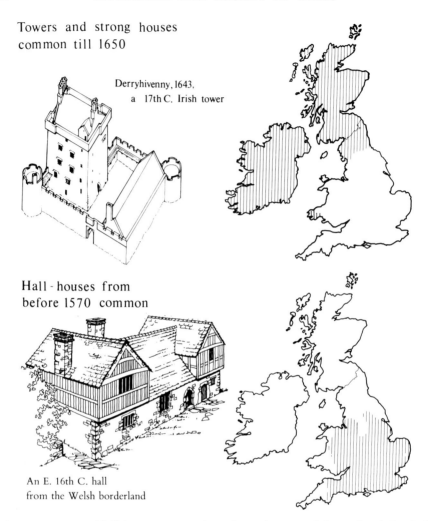

Towers and strong houses
common till 1650

Derryhivenny, 1643,
a 17th C. Irish tower

Hall - houses from
before 1570 common

An E. 16th C. hall
from the Welsh borderland

Fig. 8   Towers and hall-houses. During the early modern period the medieval, fortified, upper-class house fought a stubborn rearguard action in the north-west of the British Isles, the last Scottish towers being built late in the seventeenth century, while the houses of the Scottish magnates reflected the influence of the tower long afterwards. In the southern Britain in contrast the non-defensive hall-house was dominant well before the Reformation. It provided shelter for both landlord and tenant, until displaced by sub-medieval, storeyed derivatives from about 1560 onwards.

Note that in Wales, only Pembrokeshire can claim much in the way of tower-houses. However, it is clear that here and in Glamorgan the hall-house, whether at gentry or peasant level, is poorly represented.

Single-storeyed houses common until 1850

Two-storeyed houses common after 1570

Fig. 9 Late single-storeyed houses and early storeyed houses. The large-scale replacement of the hall by the storeyed house appears to have began in south-eastern Britain about the accession of Elizabeth I, and soon spread over the lowland and intermediate zones. The sub-medieval storeyed peasant house does not seem to have appeared in strength in the inner highland zone until rather later — in the far north of England not until the Commonwealth, and it hardly reached Ireland or Scotland at all. Here most farmhouses remained single-storeyed until the nineteenth century and even in west Wales where storeyed, sub-medieval houses were certainly being built in the late sixteenth century, the single-storeyed cottage still houses a large proportion of the rural population.

But such a simple duality needs to be much further elaborated. This is best achieved in terms of the theory of successive rebuilding. Some years ago, in an essay that made a considerable impact, Professor W. G. Hoskins wrote of 'The Great Rebuilding' which took place between 1570 and 1640 when the medieval hall-house was replaced by the sub-medieval storeyed house. But Sir Cyril Fox and Lord Raglan had already shown in *Monmouthshire Houses* that there was a great rebuilding earlier than Hoskins's rebuilding, a rebuilding which produced the hall-houses themselves. In fact we should rather think not of one but of four great rebuildings, each associated with a particular type of house, and each taking place in different parts of the British Isles at different times, each phase overlapping its successor. These rebuildings might be likened to the ripples from a stone dropped in a pond, the point of impact being London. The first great rebuilding was the rebuilding in which the durable medieval hall-house replaced its impermanent predecessors. This rebuilding began in the fifteenth century, and is discernible mainly in the lowland and intermediate zone of southern Britain (Fig. 7). In the second rebuilding — Hoskins's rebuilding — the storeyed sub-medieval house replaced the durable hall-house. In the lowland and intermediate zones this rebuilding began about 1560, but it did not reach the inner highland regions *in strength*, particularly the northern counties of England, until 1650, when it replaced not the durable hall, as in the south, but the impermanent single-storeyed house (Fig. 9). It did not reach the outer highland regions at all. The third rebuilding, the rebuilding which produced the symmetrical, centrally-planned house of the Renaissance, most typically exemplified in the Victorian farmhouse, began about 1650 in the lowland and intermediate zones. It reached the inner highland zones not long afterwards, and in the late nineteenth century provided all highland zones with their commonest house-type. In the western coastlands of Scotland and Ireland it replaced not the substantial hall nor even the sub-medieval storeyed house, but rather the single-storeyed impermanent peasant dwellings which in the south-east had been superseded as early as the fifteenth century. We are now in the throes of the fourth great rebuilding in which the symmetrical, centrally-planned house of the Renaissance which flourished from c.1650 up to 4 August 1914 is itself being replaced by houses whose design is not dictated by the axial straitjacket of Renaissance aesthetics but by a rational analysis of need — the 'freely planned' houses of the twentieth century. The spread of the last development has been very fast indeed. It has become the countrywide basis of house layout in far less than the century it took the sub-medieval storeyed house to travel from Kent to Cumberland. Indeed, a salient characteristic of our age is the extraordinary speed at which developments take place, and at which new ideas are transmitted, while the salient feature of earlier ages was the slowness of change, resulting in that great ancient regional variety which constitutes the fascination of our study.[1]

THE WANING OF THE MIDDLE AGES — CASTLES, TOWERS AND HALLS — THE FIRST GREAT REBUILDING

It is not proposed here to trace in detail the development of the castle in Wales — a specialist study in itself. The earthworks, mottes, and ring-works of the Norman period gave way to stone structures in various patterns of plan, culminating in the great concentric fortresses of the thirteenth century. In such buildings, defensive strength was the overriding consideration. Defence continued to be a major factor in later castle building, but domestic needs come to play an increasingly important role. In the sixteenth century and later, several of the greater castles such as Chirk and Powys, St Donat's and Raglan, continued to be occupied by their lords who adapted them as best they could to later needs. Others, conspicuously those of royal foundation, were deserted and fell into decay as Wales ceased to be regarded as a hostile country requiring an army of occupation but instead came to be looked upon as an integral part of the Tudor kingdom, regulated by its own magistrates and represented in parliament.

The fortified tradition is also represented by much smaller strongholds, the tower-houses, and grouped with them, first-floor halls. Many were built with stone vaults and are better represented in Pembrokeshire than any other Welsh county (Pl. IIa). Remote from London, its material culture closely resembled that of Ireland and Scotland where the tower and first-floor hall also reigned supreme. Both tower and first-floor hall are distinguished by having the primary accommodation on the first floor. Glamorgan is the only other Welsh county where the tower and first-floor hall tradition is reasonably well represented, a county even better endowed with castles than Pembrokeshire, and like Pembrokeshire ill provided with hall-houses (Fig. 10, Pl. II b, c, d). But in all other Welsh counties houses in the first-floor hall and tower tradition are insignificant in their numbers, an indication that early Tudor Wales was well on the way to becoming a peaceful society in which the upper classes could build non-defensive residences and the yeomen could begin to think of building durable homes.[2]

In contrast with the tower and first-floor hall is the hall-house which not only housed the *uchelwyr* in most parts of Wales (Fig. 11, Pl. III a), certainly in the north and east, but also the peasantry, the first of whose surviving houses, the dwellings of an emerging class of yeomen, are by the beginning of the sixteenth century clearly discernible in the borderland (Fig. 12, Pl. III b, IV). While a handful of upper-class halls, notably Tretower Court, have defensive features such as gatehouses and enclosure walls, the character of the hall-house group as a whole was not determined by defensive considerations. Also in contrast with the towers and first-floor halls of Pembrokeshire, whose main parallels lay in Ireland and Scotland, the Welsh hall-house was linked with the hall-house of the English west Midland counties and an emerging Severn Valley culture.

Indeed there appear to be three regions of southern Britain where the substantial late medieval peasant hall-house is found in exceptional quantity. It is significant that two lie within the half-timbered zones (Figs. 6–7). The first is the region south-east of the limestone belt and pre-eminently the counties of Kent, Sussex, Essex and Suffolk; the second is the west Midland area, particularly the counties of Worcestershire, Herefordshire and Shropshire. This last region takes us right up to the Welsh border and indeed crosses it. The result is that not only does eastern Wales possess vastly more early peasant houses than western Wales; in this respect it also compares favourably with some parts of England.[3]

The central feature of the hall-houses is the hall itself, the large room open to the roof which constituted the 'living room' of the dwelling (Pl. IV). At the 'upper' end was the 'high-table' where sat the householder and his family; in the middle was the open hearth which provided the heating; at the 'lower' end was the cross-passage providing the means of entry. Such a hierarchical layout (reflecting the arrangement in the halls of the nobility), was common form irrespective of how the secondary rooms might be arranged. Another common characteristic was the decorative treatment of the roof. This ornamentation is to be found not only among the crown-post roofs of the south-east but also among the different decorative systems developed amongst the cruck and side-purlin roofs of the west Midlands and Wales (Figs. 12–15, Pl. IV).

The hall-house is the starting-point of all studies of peasant building in the British Isles. It is worthwhile to consider whether a layout taken for granted here is common to the rest of northern Europe. It is significant that it is impossible to translate the word 'hall' in its primary historic sense of a large living-room into either French or German with any precision. This alone suggests that the evolution of domestic architecture on the Continent has been somehow different. Indeed it is impossible to see in most of the various forms of German farmhouse anything closely resembling either the primary British hall-house form or its derivatives. It is equally significant that Professor G. I. Meirion-Jones's pioneering studies in Brittany have uncovered no hall-houses in our sense of the word. An important factor in both France and Germany is the very early use of the entire roof space for storage, a development which precluded the ornamentation of the roof structure in the English and Welsh fashion. Another factor may have been the preference of many of the continental gentry (like their Irish and Scottish counterparts) for the tower-house, a preference which would have inhibited the full development of the hall-house form by confining it to the lower orders of society.[4]

The earliest form of heating was the open hearth. In eastern and central Europe this was superseded by the enclosed stove, and in western Europe by the wall fireplace. It is of interest to note that while the open hearth phase can easily be detected in existing English and Welsh hall-houses Professor Meirion-Jones failed to uncover a single open-hearth house in Brittany. It is uncertain whether this means that the walled fireplace was adopted later in England and Wales than in Brittany, or (as seems more likely) that the surviving peasant houses in England and Wales are older than the oldest in Brittany.

Beyond their central feature, the hall itself, hall-houses usually had various ancillary rooms. While it might be assumed that the hall represent the original house before the development of secondary accommodation, it appears that by the time the earliest surviving hall-houses were built, the house had progressed beyond a simple, single-cell building. Although Sir Cyril Fox and Lord Raglan thought that they had discovered such primary single-room, hall-houses, a re-examination of their material on the ground suggests that what they had uncovered were mostly the cores of originally larger buildings whose secondary rooms had been lost or replaced.[5] However, the problem of whether secondary structure is to be seen as a simple enlargement — the provision of new accommodation or merely a replacement of what had been before — recurs constantly in our studies (see also p. 130). Related to it is the problem of whether a layout is the result of subdivision and rearrangement within the original envelope, or the result of additions to it. It is of interest to note that while the peasant houses of northern Germany are seen as the result of the first process, those of middle and southern Germany are seen as the result of the second.

The secondary rooms of the Welsh hall-house were related to the hall itself in various ways. Amongst the upper-class houses L. T. U. or H plans occur, the central hall flanked by wings at right angles to it (Fig. 11, Pl. III *a*). But much more commonly the whole layout was contained within a single rectangle and covered by a continuation of the hall roof (Fig. 12, Pl. III *b*). Amongst houses of this latter plan a primary distinction should be made between these halls, where the unit at the passage end (henceforward described as the outer room) contained a byre, and those where it was purely domestic. Although the long-house (with byre at the passage end) is generally associated with the yeoman class (e.g. Fig. 12) not only is it clear that not all peasant houses (e.g. Pl. III *b*) were long-houses, but it is also becoming increasingly apparent that some upper-class houses may have been (Fig. 13). Thus although there is a tendency in some circles to assume that the long-house is the primary form of peasant house, it is evident that there are regions both on the Continent and in the British Isles where it does not occur and where the combination of house with farm buildings in any form is a late and secondary development. The long-house is totally absent from south-eastern England and even within the highland zone it is far from universal. In Wales there is late-medieval evidence for the long-house in the borderland, with later versions in most of the southern counties (Fig. 26, Pl. VIII *a*), but in Anglesey, Caernarfonshire and the coastal area of Merioneth, long-houses of any date (at least within the usual definition of the word of a house and byre combined and intercommunicating at the point of entry) have yet to be discovered.[6]

In later years the byre of the long-house was often converted to other purposes, but the basic form of a hall between one or a pair of small rooms at the dais end, and a large room at the passage, suggests that a house may originally have been a long-house. Conversely where the outer room is small and the inner room is large, a long-house is improbable. The passage partition (if it survives) provides another useful indication. Where this incorporates a plain doorway, and long open panel alongside (for feeding the cattle) then a long-house is likely (Figs. 12, 13). Conversely, ornate doorways and the absence of such a panel precludes a long-house (Figs. 14–15). As suggested earlier, indications of the long-house may be found in houses of high status while some houses of much lower status may be without them. This suggests that the problem of the long-house is complex, and does not merely depend on rank or on regional backwardness.[7]

The presence or absence of the byre as an integral part of the house greatly influenced the rest of the house plan. Those houses with a byre at the passage end had to have all the purely domestic ground floor accommodation at the dais end, while those houses without the byre could arrange this accommodation at each end of the hall. In the first, the parlour and store room were behind the dais partition; in the second, the parlour might be at either end. The secondary rooms might be open to the roof like the hall or were floored over and carried small chambers above which were reached by makeshift ladder-stairs.

Fig. 10   Garn-llwyd (Llancarfan, Glam.) is a good example of a proprietor's house, in the 'vertical', tower-house tradition, even if not actually fortified. The hall is on the first floor standing over what was probably a kitchen. A projecting turret contains secondary accommodation including a parlour. The mural stair rising through two floors to a gallery is a remarkable feature. The roof is a comparatively rare example of an ornate open roof in a Glamorgan house. Although the collar-purlin occurs in a number of churches the cusping on the windbraces does not occur elsewhere in the country.

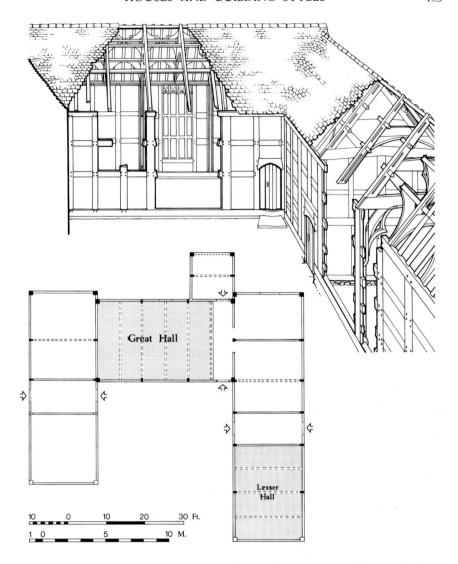

Fig. 11 Bryndraenog (Bugeildy, Rads.). This is also a proprietor's house, but in a completely different building tradition, for it is a very large hall-house, incorporating two halls within its ambitious H plan. It is entirely of timber construction and contains some of the finest structural carpentry in Wales. The base crucks which frame the main hall incorporate some most elaborate carving, including fretwork.

Fig. 12   An early sixteenth-century hall-house from the Welsh borderland based on Rhos-fawr (Llanfyllin, Mont.). Virtually unaltered since it was built, it perfectly preserves the early form of the hall-house without fireplace. The construction is a mixture of cruck (highland) and box-frame (lowland) supporting a (highland) ridge-beam and through-purlin roof. The house has six rooms, four on the ground floor and two on the first. At the dais end of the hall (nearest the viewer) are two small rooms, probably dairy and a small parlour. At the passage end is a single large room which the long open panels of the partition suggest may have been a byre. It is, nevertheless, no mean building for the standard of craftsmanship is high. It and its generally less perfectly preserved fellows indicate the rise in the Welsh borderland of a rich peasant class which it seems reasonable to call yeomen. The class was clearly in existence before the Reformation by which time it was housed in durable buildings of sound quality. Once it had begun, the rise in the standard of housing was rapid. Within a generation such cruck-framed, hall-houses were being replaced by box-framed, storeyed houses with enclosed fireplaces instead of open hearths, while glazed windows were being added to their amenities before the end of the sixteenth century.

Fig. 13 Tŷ-mawr (Castell Caereinion, Mont.) illustrates the use of aisled construction found in a number of the more important halls in north-eastern Wales. In this case every truss apart from the central base-cruck to the hall is aisled. Of considerable interest is the design of the passage partition with its open panels (compare Rhos-fawr Fig. 12). This suggests that this evidently upper-class house may have been a long-house, and if so, indicates that the long-house form reached much higher levels of society than has previously been supposed.

Fig. 14   Cochwillan (Llanllechid, Caerns.). This illustrates the hammer-beam roof which had developed out of the aisle-truss roof, and which followed it as a means of conferring splendour on houses of ambition. Unlike its open-hearth, aisle-truss predecessor (Fig. 13) this hall had an enclosed (lateral) fireplace from the time of building. The view is taken looking towards the passage-partition constructed in a way which makes it clear that the rooms at this end (in contrast with Figs. 12 and 13) were purely domestic. The ornate doorhead probably led to a parlour, while the high door alongside was probably to provide headroom for a stairway. Cochwillan was probably built for William Gruffydd, who in reward for his services at Bosworth, was made High Sheriff of Caernarfonshire for life.

Fig. 15 Gloddaeth (Penrhyn, Caerns.) is another hammer-beam roofed hall likewise with a lateral fireplace. The view is taken looking from the opposed doors of the 'passage' towards the dais behind which is the dais partition which is embellished by a painted canopy. It is important to remember that the idea of social precedence implicit in the layout of these landowners' halls with their 'high table' at one end and 'passage' at the other was mirrored in the halls of their tenants, in some cases even to the extent of their making a simple copy of the ornate dais canopy illustrated here.

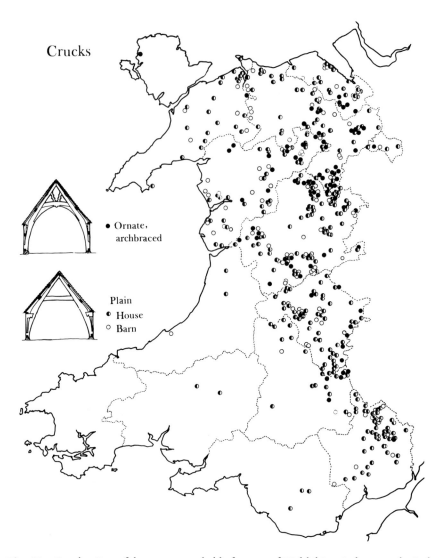

Crucks

Ornate,
archbraced

Plain
House
Barn

Fig. 16 Crucks. One of the most remarkable features of Welsh historical geography is the way in which only half the country was dominated by the true cruck, where the blade is made of a single piece of timber. It is unlikely that this method of construction was used much for houses after 1560, but it is probable that it was still used for farm buildings. The one-piece cruck, like the half-timbered house, links northern and eastern Wales with the west Midlands of England, and its western boundary established a diagonal line across the country, which can be seen in a number of other distribution patterns.

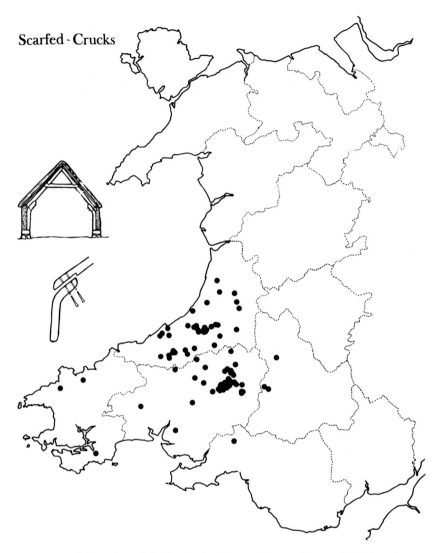

Fig. 17 Scarfed-crucks. While the single-piece cruck was characteristic of north-eastern Wales, in much of south-western Wales a scarfed-cruck made up of two pieces of wood was the dominating type of frame. These scarfed-crucks are also common in Somerset, Dorset, and Devon. However, while most of the west of England's scarfed-crucks are thought to be pre-Elizabethan and are reinforced by side pegs through a mortise, most of the scarfed-crucks of south-west Wales are probably later, and are secured by face pegs without the use of a mortise. An instance is Llwyncelyn (Talley, Carms.) dated 1739. A feature common to both the English and the Welsh scarfed-cruck regions is the extensive use of earth wall as an infilling between the frames after these had been erected.

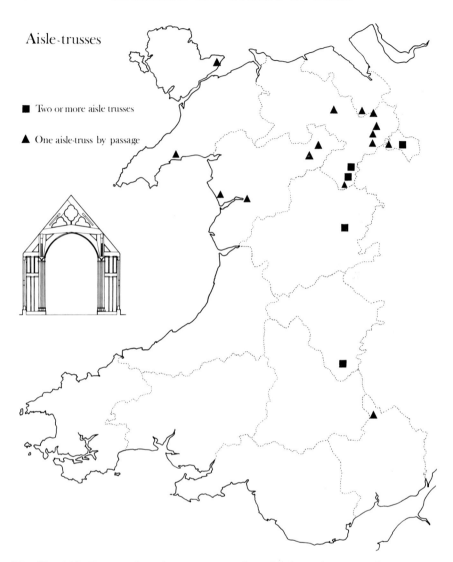

Aisle-trusses

■ Two or more aisle trusses

▲ One aisle-truss by passage

Fig. 18   Aisle-Trusses. The aisle-truss in a number of different designs is a form of ornate roof which embellished a relatively small number of houses but which is found in much the same area as the major cruck concentration (Fig. 16). A link with the west Midlands is again evident.

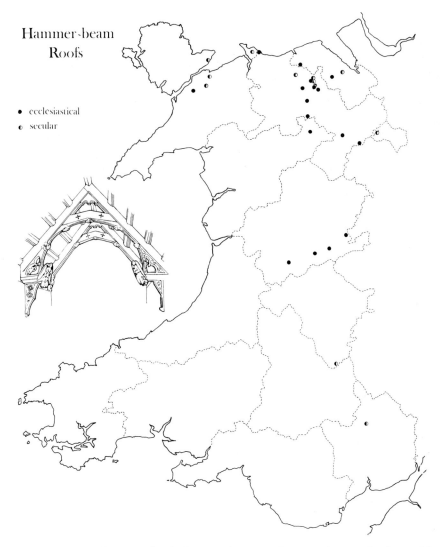

Hammer-beam
Roofs

• ecclesiastical
○ secular

Fig. 19 Hammer-beam roofs. The hammer-beam roof seems to have evolved out of the aisle-truss roof, and represents the culmination of the ornate open-roof tradition which is such a feature of the architecture, both domestic and ecclesiastical, of southern Britain in the late Middle Ages and Early Modern times. The map above illustrates both domestic and ecclesiastical examples which are again confined to that part of Wales north-east of a line drawn from Newport to Machynlleth.

However, one familiar element in the modern house — the kitchen — is usually not easily identified in the hall-house or in its sub-medieval descendants. Indeed, it is far from certain where meals were prepared. According to one view this was done in outbuildings, the assumption being that the nineteenth-century outside bakehouse merely replaces an earlier outside kitchen. According to another view the hall itself served as a kitchen. This interpretation harmonizes with the present use of the large middle room as a 'living-room/kitchen' in an otherwise kitchenless house.

A distinctive feature of most hall-houses, and one which again was retained in the later sub-medieval phase, was the siting of the house down rather than across the slope, probably to facilitate drainage both internal and external. When the layout incorporated a byre this was usually, but by no means inevitably, downhill. The siting was also adapted in the storeyed phase of building to achieve a boarded floor or even a cellar under a downhill parlour. When a house so sited is abandoned and falls into ruin it leaves a platform whose grass-grown remains form a characteristic feature of the countryside. Some such platforms have been dated to as early as the fourteenth century, but clearly many could be much later.

The medieval hall had either stone or half-timbered containing walls. In the north-western countryside the few surviving halls, nearly all of high social status, are stone-walled, although it is clear that in the same region early town-houses were half-timbered. In the south-west the few surviving halls were also of stone. But in the east, half-timbered construction predominated in town and countryside alike. Here, before the Reformation, only a handful of houses were stone-walled. Interior partitions were mainly of some form of timber construction. All-timber, post-and-panel construction was generally used for the dais partition, while for the remaining partitions 'half-timbered' close studding or squares were preferred, in each case the timber frames infilled with wattle-and-daub.

The more important doorways had shaped heads in the perpendicular style, the four-centred profile being only occasionally varied with the two-centred or ogee. In a handful of houses of very high status glazed windows were to be found, but most windows were provided with shutters only, and consisted of diagonally-set wooden mullions.

The main frames of the medieval Welsh house were most often of cruck construction where pairs of monoxylous timbers cut from the trunk and branch of large oaks carried both roof and wall (Figs. 12, 13, 16, Pl. IV). This form of frame is common throughout the borderland counties as it is in the adjoining west Midlands. It also extends into Snowdonia although the crucks of the north-west are generally less well finished and probably later than those of the borderland. Elsewhere in Wales the pure cruck form is rare but roofs clearly related to it are general. These include the A-frame where the blades rise from the wall tops and the scarfed (two-piece) crucks of Carmarthenshire and Cardiganshire (Figs. 17, 26). These roofs (mostly post-medieval) are bayed like the cruck and carry the rafters by means of side purlins.[8]

The alternative to the cruck frame is the box-frame, the dominant form in south-eastern England. Here the roof and wall are (unlike the cruck) of two distinct elements. The wall frame consisted of two upright posts connected by a tie. Above the tie the roof frame varied. In south-eastern England it was usually a trussed rafter roof often stiffened with crown-posts and collar purlins. Alternatively it might support a bayed A-frame roof carrying side purlins. This latter combination had penetrated the half-timbered borderland of Wales before the Reformation. But the trussed rafter type of superstructure, in contrast, is hardly known in Welsh domestic work, though found extensively in Welsh churches particularly in south Wales.[9]

The factors determining the distribution of these various roof and frame patterns are a great mystery, but it does appear that the basically south-easterly distribution of the box-frame and the trussed rafter roof mirrors a similar distribution in lower Germany whereas the basically northerly and westerly distribution of the bayed, side-purlin roof mirrors a similar distribution in north-western France. Nevertheless, it is clear that before the end of the Middle Ages forms of roof originating outside the cruck system were well established in Wales, the trussed rafter in church work, the aisled truss in domestic work (Fig. 13) and the hammer-beam in both ecclesiastical and secular building (Figs. 14, 15, 19).[10]

The aisled-truss and hammer-beam houses form a most remarkable series of pre-Reformation buildings in Wales (Figs. 13–15, 18–19). The aisled system of building was widespread in south-eastern England, a system probably related, however distantly, to a very ancient tradition of aisled building in lower Germany. Aisled building in south-eastern England is found at two levels: first to provide a framework for houses of ambition and second to provide corn-barns of vast capacity. In its first role it was displaced by other forms of roof in the fourteenth century: in its second it has survived to modern times. In its first role — as the framework for an upper-class house — it achieved fashionable acclaim in Wales at the moment it was going out of fashion in south-eastern England — as good an illustration as any of 'the ripples in the pond'. In its second, agricultural, role it was never imitated in the Principality.

Like its successor, the hammer-beam roof, the aisle-truss is only found in the north-eastern half of Wales. Indeed the major concentration of ornamental roof forms in the north-east, compared with the much plainer roofs in the south-west is one of the most remarkable aspects of Welsh historical geography. For not only are hammer-beams and aisle-trusses confined to this region but other ornamentally developed features of the bayed side-purlin roof such as arch-braces, cusping, and windbraces are much more numerous here than in south-west Wales. It is evident that this cleavage in the Welsh scene (comparable to the diagonal resultant of the parallelogram of forces) can be related to the adjoining English regions: the north-east with its crucks and elaborate bayed roofs both domestic and ecclesiastical relates to the west Midlands; the south-west with its scarfed-crucks, its simple bayed domestic roofs and its trussed-rafter church roofs relates to the Dumnonian peninsula. The division may also have been influenced by the Edwardian invasions, although these took place a century or so before the earliest surviving roofs were built. Dr A. J. Taylor has shown that most of the craftsmen who built the royal castles of north Wales were recruited from across Offa's Dyke while most of those working in south Wales were recruited from across the Bristol channel.[11] Even more ancient evidence for the twin directions of cultural drift is to be found in the scatter of English place-names, one along the border, the other along the Severn Sea.

THE SECOND GREAT REBUILDING —
THE SUB-MEDIEVAL STOREYED HOUSE

The most important architectural development of the early modern period was the beginning of the replacement of the medieval hall-house by the sub-medieval storeyed house as the dwelling of the squires and the yeomen. This revolution coincides in southern Britain with the Reformation and a period of rapid inflation, of rising population, and of increasing prosperity. It is likely that these all helped to enrich the farming class. The extensive replacement of ecclesiastical by lay landowners probably made it easier for tenants to obtain favourable leases, while rising prices and fixed rents obviously favoured primary producers. However, by the time the housing revolution reached the north of England a century later many of these factors had ceased to operate. But while the period of rapid inflation had come to an end by 1640, prices began to move in favour of pastoral farming, thus helping the mountain areas. There is reason to think that in Glamorgan, for example, the major rebuilding in the mainly pastoral *blaenau* was substantially later than in the corn-exporting *bro*, and that many of the sub-medieval houses of northern Glamorgan are late seventeenth century. But more than anything else the change is to be attributed to that spirit of technical innovation leading to a rising standard of housing which first appeared in the south-east and then spread northwards and westwards.

At the beginning of the sixteenth century the core of a typical farmhouse was a draughty smoky open hall (Figs. 12–13, Pl. IV). At the end of it the farmhouse had become a storeyed building fitted with fireplaces, chimneys and stairs and lighted by glazed windows. Houses of this type appear not only in those eastern areas of Wales which had pioneered the durable hall-house but also in those western regions where surviving early sixteenth-century yeoman halls are either rare or non-existent. The change from the hall to the storeyed house can be charted by inscriptions beginning in the 1570s. These early inscriptions occur in strength, first in the north-east, then in the borderland generally and finally in the south-west.[12]

One factor influencing the form of the sub-medieval plan was the layout of the preceding hall-house; a second was the position favoured for the main fireplace and its relationship with the entry. Most of the alternative positions should best be understood as stages in an evolutionary sequence (Figs. 20–1). The earliest is the lateral fireplace. This had appeared in the last phase of the hall-house (Pl. III *a*, V *a*, Fig. 22). The laterally-sited fireplace affected the basics of the medieval plan very little and permitted the retention of those time-honoured features, the cross-passage and the dais partition. The next position was the fireplace placed internally at the lower end of the hall, backing on the passage and facing the dais (Fig. 23, Pl. VI). The third, which developed out of the second, is the lobby-entry pattern where the fireplace was built not against the passage, but in the passage itself thus blocking it and creating a lobby-entry (Fig. 24, Pl. VII). These three can be seen as a series of developments moving progressively away from the medieval conception. The second type resulted in a great reduction in the size of the hall, while the third eliminated that fundamental feature, the passage. There remain two other patterns which fit less clearly into the evolutionary pattern. Both involve the placing of the fireplace at the dais end of the hall so that the traditional hierarchical arrangement of this room was destroyed as the fireplace replaced the 'high table' as its focus. This displacement occurs both in three-unit and in two-unit houses. In the first, the fireplace backs on to a room behind the dais partition, usually a parlour, and indeed is associated with types of plan retaining a large parlour at this end of the house. But it is not a common Welsh pattern. In the second, the fireplace is sited against the end wall of a two-unit house, that is there is no room beyond the fireplace (Fig. 28, Pl. V *b*). This became a very common type of plan in west Wales, particularly in Gwynedd, where an end-chimney house consisting on the ground floor of hall, passage and two secondary rooms alongside the passage, became the standard form of storeyed house.

The remarkable fact has emerged that the numbers of these different patterns of plan vary considerably from region to region in a way that harmonizes quite well with their distribution in other parts of southern Britain (Fig. 20). The typologically early lateral chimney house occurs peripherally in Wales, matching a marked westerly concentration observable in south-western England. The second type, having the fireplace backing on the entry, occurs mainly in south-eastern Wales, evidently a continuation of the same pattern in the Cotswold–Bristol region. The third and latest in the series, the lobby-entry type, is most strongly represented in north-eastern Wales, above all in the Severn and Dee valleys, a distribution which mirrors a similar concentration in the north-west Midlands and the southern Pennines. The end-chimney type has a very wide distribution, but is clearly predominant in several remote regions such as south-western Cumbria which, like Gwynedd, stands at the furthermost limits of the area within the British Isles within which the sub-medieval storeyed house is commonly to be found.[13]

But nowhere does the locally favoured type achieve an absolute predominance. The alternatives occur, though in small numbers. The fact, for example, that there are a handful of lateral-chimney houses in western Montgomeryshire, and a rather larger number of chimney-backing-on-the-entry houses scattered across the county, most of which were later converted into lobby-entrance houses, suggests not only that we are looking at a sequence, that each area went through a similar evolution, but that the speed of this evolution varied greatly. In the Severn Valley the lobby-entry house stage was reached early, and lasted long, whereas in Monmouthshire, for example, it may be assumed that it superseded the chimney-backing-on-the-entry house only very belatedly, as there are very few instances of the type in this county.

It is also evident that there is a broad distinction east and west (Fig. 20). In the east, some form of internal-chimney houses or types closely related to the internal-chimney pattern prevail, whereas in the west the fireplaces are nearly always sited on the outside wall whether lateral or gable. It is also worthy of note that the western pattern is typologically early in the sense that many of these houses retain the cross-passage, whereas in Powysland in the north-east it is the typologically most recent sub-medieval house, incorporating the lobby-entry, which preponderates.

Besides the larger, three-unit houses there is the problem of the smaller two, or occasional one-unit houses. These fall into patterns, which when analysed on the basis of the relationship between entry and fireplace, clearly relate to the main large

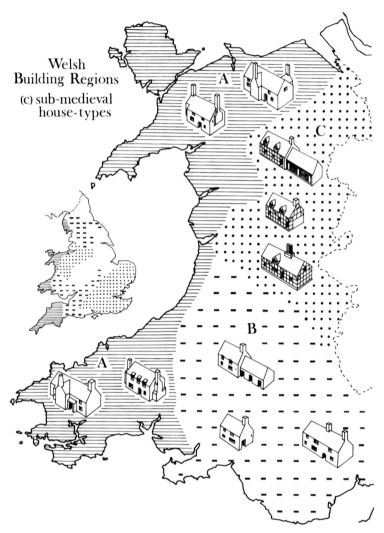

Fig. 20 Welsh sub-medieval house types. This map of the main Welsh sub-medieval house types (admittedly very much simplified) points to contrasts of some significance. The first is between the western regions, where the chimney on the outside wall predominates, and the east, where internal chimneys are more numerous. Within the eastern area there is a further significant contrast between the south-east, where the chimney is placed backing-on-the-entry (and thus retaining the cross-passage), and the north-east, where the chimney is placed in what historically was the cross-passage, creating the lobby entry. Parts of England, particularly the south, show a clear progression of the types from east to west, lobby entry, chimney backing-on-the-entry, and chimney on the outside wall, but the existence of three major concentrations of lobby-entry houses, one in the south-east and one in the southern Pennine area linked with north-east Wales, and one in eastern Ireland poses certain problems. The Irish examples are mainly single storeyed.

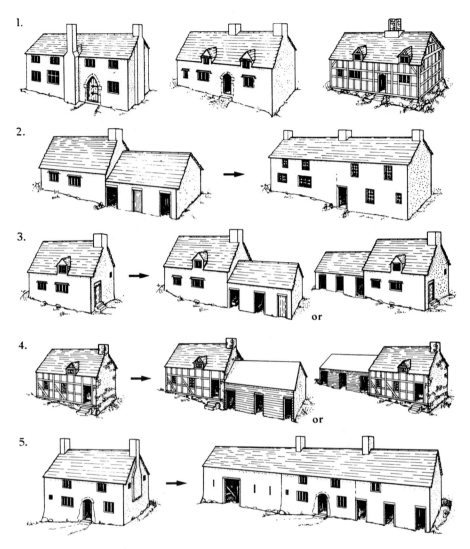

Fig. 21 The main types of sub-medieval house:

(1) Classic three-unit houses, each showing different ways of siting of the main chimney, but each having the great parlour at the entry end and the service room at the dais end.
(2) The long-house with byre as outer room, also showing later redevelopment.
(3) The two-unit, end-entry house, showing farm extensions.
(4) The two-unit, end-chimney and lobby entry house, showing farm extensions.
(5) The two-unit, end-chimney and cross-passage house, showing farm extensions.

Note 2, 3 and 4 are related to 1 *above*, but 5 stands apart from all the others in having the secondary rooms at the entry end only.

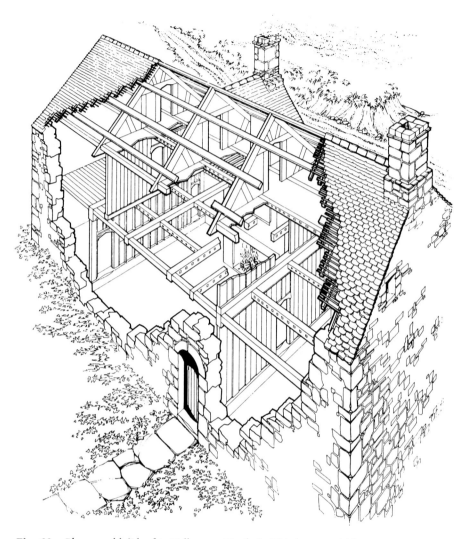

Fig. 22   Plasnewydd (Llanfair Talhaearn, Denbs.). This house, which retains its interior arrangements and partitions little altered since it was built in 1585, illustrates the lateral chimney plan, the most conservative of the sub-medieval plan patterns, as it was possible to retain the arrangements of the hall as they were in the Middle Ages, that is to say keep it as a hierarchically organized space in which the dais partition and 'high table' stood as the focus of a room which was entered from the socially inferior cross-passage end. Behind the dais partition were two small rooms, an unheated parlour and a dairy. It is not clear whether the room at the passage end was intended to be a heated parlour or a kitchen.

Fig. 23   Trewalter (Llan-gors, Brecs.) built in 1653 illustrates what is probably the next step in the development of the sub-medieval house. In this case the fireplace is so placed that it backed onto the cross-passage with the result that it effectively halved the size of the hall. The fact that the hall had lost some of its importance is perhaps also indicated by the use of the 'outer room' beyond the passage. This is clearly a large parlour heated by a gable fireplace, and lighted by large mullioned and transomed windows. Possibly the hall now served as a kitchen though retaining the dais partition which would argue that it was still a room of status.

Fig. 24   Talgarth (Trefeglwys, Mont.) built some time between 1660 and 1670 exemplifies the third and final phase of the large, three-unit, sub-medieval house. In this case the hall fireplace stands on the site of the passage, the parlour fireplace backing onto it. The passage, that time-honoured feature of the medieval house, has finally disappeared to be replaced by the lobby-entry, giving access to the hall on one side and a heated parlour on the other. This pattern of plan emerged as the favoured layout in the upper Severn Valley as in the north Midlands and south-east of England where there are scores of examples, but seems to have been much slower in gaining acceptance in other parts of Wales. It is also very rare in the west of England as well as in the four northern counties of England.

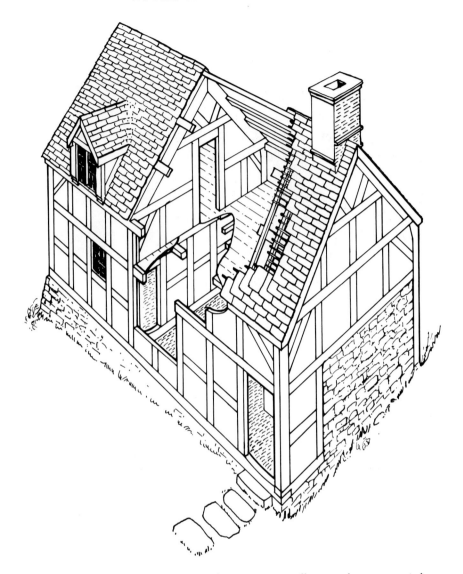

Fig. 25 Bron Rhys (Tregynon, Mont.) must serve to illustrate those two-unit houses which appear as 'cut-down' versions of the various types of three-unit house. While this may appear to have been a house such as Talgarth (Fig. 24) which has somewhow lost its third room, houses of this form are so numerous as to make it inconceivable that it was not a house-type in its own right, even though it may be difficult to discover medieval prototypes for the form. A possible explanation is that the development of the storeyed house, offering much more space on the first floor, provided enough floor space to render a further unit — the outer room — unnecessary. The two-unit, end-entry house (see Figs. 20, 21) is another instance, in this case a modification of the three-unit, fireplace backing on to the cross-passage house illustrated by Fig. 23.

Fig. 26   Tŷ'r celyn (Llandeilo Rural, Carms.) illustrates the combination of house and byre in a single range, so planned that the entry to the house is off the cross-passage feeding walk in the byre. This is clearly a version of the fireplace backing-on-the-entry plan illustrated in Fig. 23, and might also be regarded as an up-dated version of the medieval long-house illustrated in Fig. 12. The two-unit, house and byre, are structurally distinct, the byre being built against the previously built house which was of the two-unit, end-entry type. This form of combined house and byre was common in the uplands of south Wales.

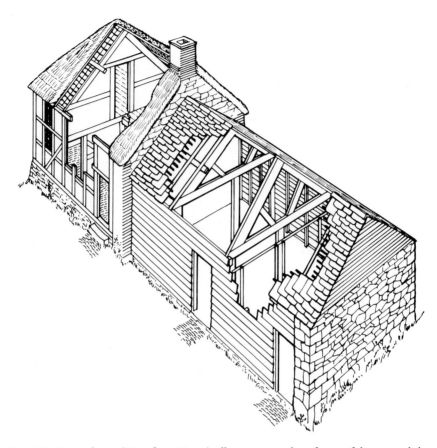

Fig. 27 Pen-y-bont (Manafon, Mont.) illustrates another form of house and byre homestead, showing how the different entry arrangements arising from different (and probably successive) forms of the sub-medieval plan affected eclectically the relationship between the house and the adjoining byre. In this case, the house (which as in Fig. 26 preceded the byre in the building sequence) followed the same two-unit, lobby-entry, end-chimney pattern as Fig. 25. Against the entry end (but not intercommunicating with it) was placed the byre. Thus the house and byre had each their own entry, unlike the house in Fig. 26 where the house was entered through the byre. This combination of house and byre in the same range was common in the uplands of mid Wales.

Fig. 28   An end–chimney, cross–passage house, based on various houses in north–west Wales. This house differs fundamentally from the various sub–medieval houses (Figs 22–27) previously illustrated, in several ways. First is the fact that though retaining the medieval cross–passage it has no 'dais end'. In place of the dais partition stands a fireplace and this is the focal point of the hall. Hence it is clear that the ideas of a social hierarchy, implicit in the medieval hall and most of its sub–medieval derivatives, are not present here. Second is the fact that it is a two–unit house in its own right and not, as it were, a cut down version of a three–unit house. Finally, there is no link with the long–house. The passage divides the hall from dairy and parlour and not from the byre. If a byre were added to the end wall (as often happened), no intercommunication between house and byre resulted. Although, unlike the other sub–medieval houses, it is difficult to establish any medieval precursor for the type, it is clear that houses were being built to this type of design in west Wales as early as the late sixteenth century (the earliest firmly dated example yet known being Uwchlaw'r Coed (Llanenddwyn, Mer.) 1585. It is also evident that the majority of houses in both the north–west and the south–west of the Principality, whether on two floors or one (as in Fig. 29) are closely related to it.

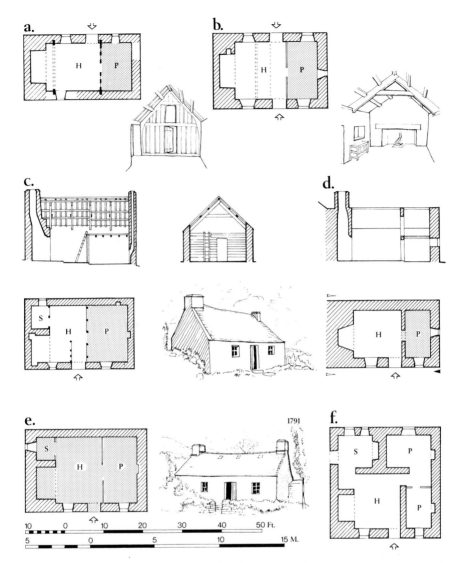

Fig. 29 End–chimney cottages. Long after the gentry and the yeomen had adopted the storeyed house in place of the hall for their homes, the poor continued building impermanent, single-storey dwellings. Their quality, however, began slowly to improve, probably from the late seventeenth century, and very rapidly after the agricultural and industrial revolutions began to raise the standard of living of all classes. The durable single-storey cottage preceded the cottage on two floors, and in west Wales single-storeyed cottages still survive in vast quantities. They might be regarded as belated hall-houses built generations after the middle class had abandoned the hall-house for the storeyed house. They differ, however, from the medieval, yeoman hall-house in that they all seem to have been provided with fireplaces and chimneys from the time of building. These fireplaces are most commonly sited on the end wall resulting in a basic similarity of plan to the end–chimney, storeyed house in Fig. 28, found extensively in the same region. The 'hearth' and not the 'high table' was the focal point of the room.

    a Tyddyncynnal (Llechwedd, Caerns.); *b* Cae-lloi (Beddgelert, Caerns.); *c* Llain-wen-isaf (Llanychâr, Pembs.); *d* Hafodygelyn (Aber, Caerns.); *e* Pen-y-bont (Beddgelert, Caerns.).

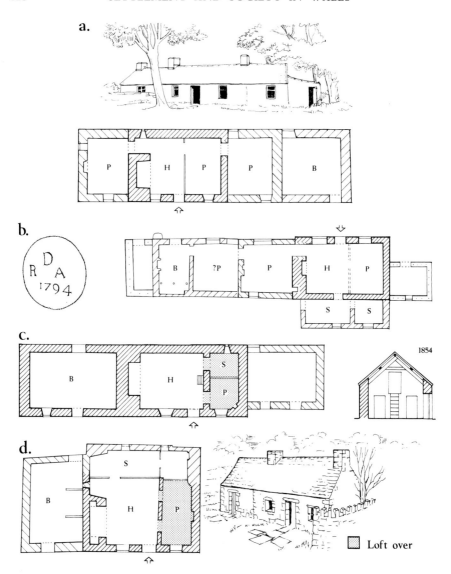

Fig. 30   End-chimney cottages (*contd.*). These cottages were often the nucleus of small holdings whose occupiers farmed on a small scale on their own account, but supplementing the income won from their holdings by labouring for their richer neighbours or working in nearby mines and quarries. Such people, half peasant, half artisan, are portrayed in the novels of Dr Kate Roberts. It is significant to note that when byres and other farm buildings were tacked on to the cottage, there was no link at the point of entry for these cottages (in contrast, for example, with the contemporary 'black-houses' of the Hebrides) are not in the long-house tradition.

   a Groeslon-newydd (Llanrug, Caerns.); *b* Brynhedydd (Llanasa, Flints.); *c* Rowlyn-uchaf (Caerhun, Caerns.); *d* Cae'r-gors (Llanwnda, Caerns.).

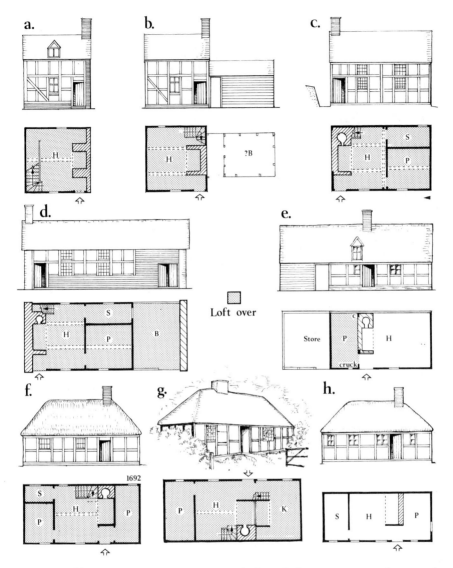

Fig. 31 Lobby-entry cottages. In contrast with the end-chimney cottages of west Wales illustrated in Fig. 30, are the lobby-entry cottages of the Severn Valley, the older examples of which do suggest a direct link with the three-unit, late-medieval hall-house. The progression of the earlier type, either single storeyed or fitted with a very low loft (illustrated at the bottom of the page), to the later, fully two-storeyed type (at the top of the page) is most interesting, for it makes it clear that as the cottage gained in height it lost in length. The existence of a sizeable room on the first floor made the third unit (the outer room) unnecessary.

a Cottage, Pool St. (Berriew); *b* Cottage (Berriew); *c* Cymeryr-bach (Llanidloes); *d* Glan'rafon (Llangurig); *e* Cottage at Pont-dol-goch (Llanwnnog); *f* Little House (Llandinam); *g* Pencopi (Trefeglwys); *h* Gwern Cottage (Llanfechain).

house groupings. Thus the two-unit house entered by a doorway in the end wall (Pl. VI *b*, *c*) clearly relates to the three-unit house with its hall fireplace backing on the passage (Pl. VI *a*). Similarly a two-unit house with a lobby-entry alongside an end fireplace, clearly relates to the three-unit, lobby-entry, central fireplace (Pl. VII). Not only are such 'mini' houses found in this condition, they also occur seemingly as the original nucleus of what are now three-unit houses in which the third unit is structurally secondary to the remainder. Such 'mini' houses can be variously interpreted. According to one view (when found without additions) they are fragments of once larger houses which have lost their third room. This line of reasoning also argues that when found as the nucleus of an otherwise later house, the later structure represents not so much an addition to a primary house, as a replacement of a pre-existing structure usually presumed to have been a byre (see also p. 102). The alternative view argues that there are so many of these 'mini' sub-medieval houses as to create a strong presumption that they are a house form in their own right without necessarily assuming the loss or the replacement of the original third unit. In this analysis many of the three-unit houses have been formed by a simple process of addition. The debate has a bearing on the development of the house-and-byre homestead in its broadest sense, or the long-house in its narrowest. Were farm units added to houses by a simple process of addition, as the structural joints would suggest, or were such seeming additions simply replacements of earlier buildings which were contemporary with the house part? Our view is that the 'mini' houses (particularly the lobby-entry, end-chimney type) are so numerous by the seventeenth century as to leave little room to doubt that they are a house type in their own right even if it may be difficult to find their medieval hall-house precursors, and that when found as the nucleus of larger houses (long-house and others) such houses are as likely to have been formed by process of addition as by 'alternative rebuilding', although in the nature of the evidence absolute proof either way is not possible.

While many sub-medieval houses of the lateral-chimney, chimney-backing-on-the-entry, and lobby-entry pattern can be related to medieval long-house forms, particularly in the retention of the smaller inner, and large outer rooms, it is equally clear that the various patterns of fireplace and entry position assumed a life of their own as it were, irrespective of room use. In houses which retained the byre as the outer room there developed an important difference between those houses retaining the passage which also served as a feeding-walk in the strict long-house tradition — (a type mainly found in the south), (Fig. 26, Pl. VIII *a*) — and those where the passage had been superseded by the lobby-entry where intercommunication between house and byre ceased, as was generally the case in the Severn and Dee valleys (Fig. 27, Pl. VIII *b*). In other houses the outer room might be a parlour, a pattern that again occurs in all the fireplace situations, but most characteristically in houses of the lobby-entry pattern as the central stack was able to warm the parlour as well as the hall (Fig. 24, Pl. VII *a*). Standing rather apart from the others is the end-chimney house of Gwynedd which is difficult to relate to an earlier long-house type of plan but also could not be made into a long-house even when combined with a byre, as domestic rooms stood between the passage and the byre (Fig. 28, Pl. V *b*).

While the storeyed house had become established by the seventeenth century as the house of the squires and the richer yeomen it must be assumed that the poor continued to live in impermanent single-storeyed buildings. The first durable houses of the poor, still in the single-storeyed form, begin to emerge in the borderland in the late seventeenth century as three-unit hall-houses (Fig. 31, *f*, *g*, *h*). But there are very few of them as in this region the poor soon went over to the storeyed house and in so doing changed from the three-unit to the two-unit plan, as they now had sufficient space on the first floor (Fig. 31, *a*–*d*). In the west, however, the durable poor man's house did not emerge in strength until well on in the eighteenth century and here it retained the single-storeyed form until about 1850 (Figs. 29–30). Such houses may also be regarded as belated survivors of the hall-house tradition. In Pembrokeshire, Caernarfonshire and above all in Anglesey there are hundreds if not thousands of these belated halls. In the developing slate-quarrying and lead-mining areas they formed the houses not only of poor peasants and labourers, but also of miners and quarrymen. There are scattered hamlets of single-storeyed miners' houses as far east as Flintshire.

Unlike the medieval yeoman hall, all of these later cottage-halls had a wall fireplace as part of their original structure, nearly always on an end wall, and giving the cottage a plan basically similar to the end-chimney, sub-medieval house of Gwynedd save that there was no overall upper floor. These late poor men's halls of the west are thus clearly not long-houses or of long-house derivation, a fact which distinguishes them from the 'black-houses' of western Scotland, and the single-storeyed cabins of western Ireland.

The sub-medieval rebuilding coincided with a number of developments of structure and changes in decorative fashion. Some of these arose from changes in the form of the house itself while others arose independently. The changeover from the hall to the storeyed houses led to the abandonment of the cruck frame and its replacement by the box-frame in half-timbered areas, while in the mass wall regions various forms of A frame in which the trusses rested on or close to the wall tops became the norm. In the south-west, scarfed-crucks in which the cruck form was made out of two pieces of wood became common amongst earth-walled buildings (Fig. 17).

As the roof was no longer visible from the main room, the embellishment of the trusses with arch-braces and other decorative features declined although lasting as long as the 1670s in north Wales. The ornament which had been applied to the roof tended to be applied to the ceilings. The ornately carved wooden ceiling like all other forms of ornate woodwork is more extensively to be found in the north-eastern than the south-western half of Wales. In the former the joists were usually exposed; in the latter they were often hidden under plaster.

Other features associated with the adoption of the storeyed house was the universal installation of the enclosed fireplace and chimney while some sort of fixed stair became general. Fireplace and chimney construction varied from region to region. In addition to the common stone-walled fireplaces there should be noted the half-timbered fireplace of the Severn Valley built of the same black-and-white framework as the house walls themselves. In contrast with such were the wickerwork fireplaces of the Teifi and Aeron valleys. Both seem to have been reasonably incombustible in the days of the slow-burning peat fire.

Stair forms also showed considerable local variation. The commonest form was a winding stair between the fireplace jamb and the return wall, usually constructed of solid stonework but sometimes capped with wooden treads. In the half-timber areas such winding stairs were framed of wood, but again nearly always sited next to the fireplace. Winding stairs of one sort or the other occur commonly in all Welsh counties except Pembrokeshire, Anglesey, Flintshire and Denbighshire. It must be admitted that how the first floor was reached in these counties before the arrival of the framed well, and dogleg stairs of the Renaissance remains a mystery.

The most evident outward change unrelated to changes in form of plan was the rapid contraction of the area in which in late-medieval times half-timbered building had been the norm (Fig. 6). Half-timbered building which had been common in Monmouthshire, and which in north Wales had reached as far west as the Conwy was now restricted to the north-eastern towns and the north-eastern lowlands, that is the southern part of the Vale of Clwyd, the Wrecsam area, the Severn Valley and eastern Radnorshire. Within this heartland, however, there continued to be built some of the finest timber buildings in Wales, some of it as late as the first half of the eighteenth century. While stone replaced timber along the fringes of the old timber zone, in the heartland it was eventually replaced by brick. This gives this part of north-eastern Wales the black-and-white/brick look reminiscent of the west Midlands of England and in contrast with the stone and stucco look of the rest of the Principality.

The general adoption of the glazed window with widely spaced mullions in succession to the unglazed window with narrowly spaced mullions was perhaps the greatest contribution to human comfort since the invention of the house itself. Sir Cyril Fox and Lord Raglan considered that the glazed window had become general amongst the yeomen of Monmouthshire during the last decade of the sixteenth century, though unglazed windows were retained for secondary rooms for long afterwards. South-eastern Wales is fortunate in possessing many examples of both window types, and is to be noted in particular for large numbers of windows incorporating the sunk chamfered moulding — in wood in Monmouthshire, in stone in Glamorgan — a highly localized feature which is a reminder of how provincial were so many building traditions at this time.[14]

In the realms of decoration a distinction should be made between forms derived from late Gothic architecture and those of classical inspiration. The Gothic derivatives are often markedly localized, and show much variation in their incidence between north, mid and south Wales. Characteristic of the north is the retention of decorative forms of open roof, the 'Cyclopean' doorway, the crow-stepped gable, while the south-east has the ornate doorhead and the pentice. Previously noted is the fact that the north has many more inscriptions dating before 1600 than the south, and also more shields of arms, features which would seem to be associated with the intellectual primacy of the north during the sixteenth century.[15]

The substantial storeyed sub-medieval house is one of the keys to Welsh history, and helps to explain why the Welsh language survived much better than Scottish or Irish Gaelic. It is common to explain this survival in terms of religious history, and the great emphasis the Welsh Protestants placed on Bible teaching and religious instruction in the native tongue. But *most* of Gaelic Scotland was more Protestant and Puritan than Wales, and yet Gaelic has practically disappeared from the Scottish mainland. However, Protestant Wales possessed what Protestant Scotland lacked — a relatively wealthy and independent yeoman class living since the middle of the sixteenth century in substantial storeyed houses. It was surely this class that preserved for so long the native language and culture, a class much better equipped for the task than the much poorer and certainly much worse housed peasants of Scotland and Ireland.

THE THIRD GREAT REBUILDING — THE RENAISSANCE AND THE DEVELOPMENT OF THE CENTRALIZED PLAN

About 1650 there emerged the third of the great changes in house design, the appearance of the centrally-planned house, the house also inspired by the aesthetic principles of the Renaissance. In such houses the staircase now occupied the central position in the design. In the sub-medieval houses — metaphorically speaking — the house was built first and the staircase fitted in somehow afterwards; in the houses of the new plan, also metaphorically speaking, the stair was erected first and the house was constructed around it. Such a plan provided a central circulation which connected every room in the house directly with the entry. At the same time it avoided the passage room inherent in the medieval and sub-medieval plan, where one room could only be reached through another. The new plan made each room self-contained, thus greatly raising standards of privacy.

The centralized plan also harmonized well with the search for that symmetry which was the hallmark of Renaissance aesthetics (Pl. IX). There had, of course, been symmetrical elements in medieval design, but most of such symmetrical conceptions had been based on the long axis of the house. The new symmetry was based on the short axis, and the entrance around which the whole building was now devised. Axial planning became the foundation stone of a whole school of design.

Many elements of the 'new look' had been discernible for three-quarters of a century before 1650, particularly the ornamental details arising from the orders of classical architecture. Earlier modifications of the sub-medieval plan included the double-pile plan, that is the provision of two ranges of accommodation backing on to each other, the T-shaped or cruciform plan in which a kitchen projecting at the rear replaced the third unit, the service-room in the main range (Figs. 32–3). This then consisted of two units rather than three. Alternatively the service-room might be moved from the end to the middle of the house, thus creating a more symmetrical plan. In each case a room clearly recognizable as a kitchen became for the first time a common feature. A storeyed porch enclosing the front door became a favoured embellishment from the late sixteenth to the early eighteenth centuries. This could be used not only to give some 'punch' to the main front, but also to mask asymmetrical elements in the elevation arising from the retention of the traditional forms of plan (Figs. 34–5).

An essential prerequisite of the new plan was a revolution in the design of the stair. In the sub-medieval house the winding stair was usually constructed in a recess alongside the fireplace. Although such steps were awkward in use, they had the merit of taking up but little space. In the early seventeenth century much more

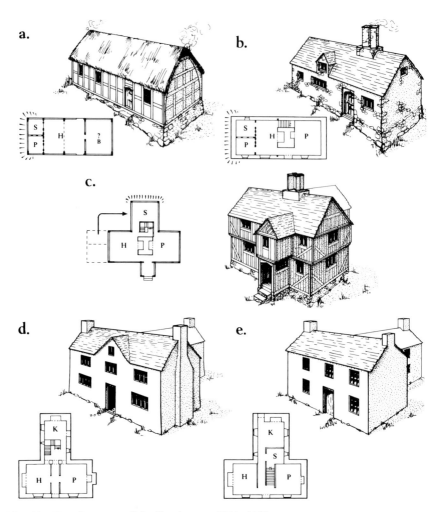

Fig. 32   Development of the farmhouse *c.*1500–1850.

*a c.*1500. Half-timbered, downhill-sited hall, outer room use uncertain, ? byre.

*b c.*1560. Hall rebuilt as storeyed house; fireplace and chimney replace gable-vents; stone walls replace timber, outer room now a parlour.

*c c.*1630. Early Renaissance cruciform house sited across the slope; porch to front, service-room to rear.

*d c.*1680. Early centrally-planned house, rear kitchen, and well stair, gable fireplaces.

*e c.*1850. Late centrally-planned house, rear kitchen, central stair passage, gable fireplaces.

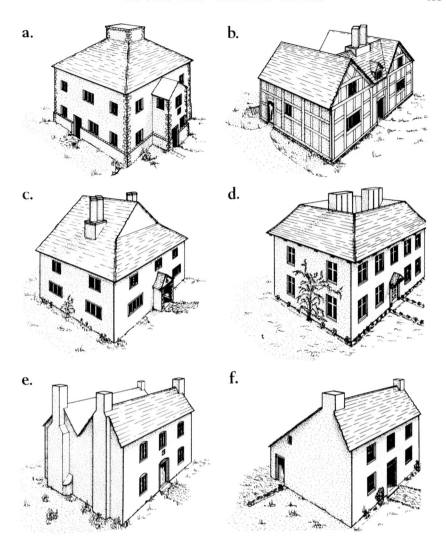

Fig. 33 Different types of Renaissance 'double-pile' designs.

*a c.*1650. The square house with central stack.

*b c.*1670. The U plan.

*c c.*1670. Square plan with spine wall, overall roof.

*d c.*1670. Square plan with spine wall, double roof.

*e c.*1720. The double-pile plan with double roof, gable chimneys.

*f c.*1800. Single-pile main unit with lean-to and gable chimneys.

Fig. 34   Perspective view of Henblas (Llanasa, Flints.) built in 1645. The house illustrates an aspect of the early Renaissance design before the realization of the full centralized plan of the later Renaissance. The fireplace stands opposite the entrance and the hall is a passage-room. However, there is a rear stair projection for a spacious framed stair and a rear kitchen. Likewise the house is tall and compact unlike the long low sub-medieval house. The ashlar detailing is unusually fine. The storeyed porch giving an emphasis to the front is characteristic of the period, though the oriel and heraldic panel indicate a house of exceptional ambition.

Fig. 35   Plasauduon (Llanwnnog, Mont.) is another good example of an early Renaissance house embracing several characteristic features: the siting across rather than down the slope so that the main front faces downhill, the storeyed porch, the rear projection containing stair and kitchen, and as Henblas (Fig. 34), windows in the end walls. The removal of the kitchen to the rear gives a central block of two units (hall nearest the viewer, and parlour beyond the stack) instead of the three units (parlour, hall and inner rooms) of the sub-medieval house. However, the hall is still a passage room giving access to parlour, kitchen and chambers on the first floor.

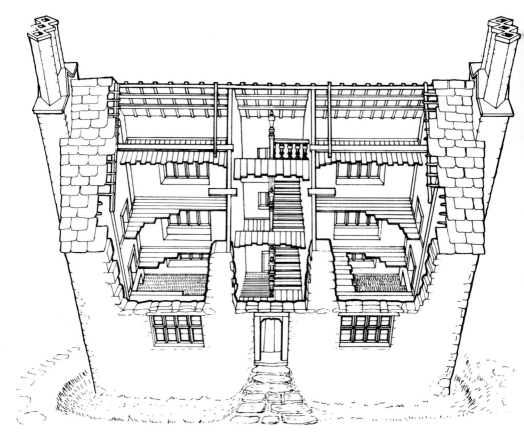

Fig. 36   Tŷ-faenor (Abbey Cwm-hir, Rads.) exemplifies the arrival of the late Renaissance plan, and may well be the first house in Wales to do so. It appears to have been built by Richard Fowler, possibly at the time of his nomination as High Sheriff of Radnorshire in 1656. The salient feature is the placing of a dogleg stair in a central stair-passage. On each side of the stair and passage the rooms are arranged so that each can be reached independently of the others. These are thus no passage-rooms. Such a plan requires the siting of the fireplaces on the end walls in order to clear the middle of the house for the stair. Another feature is the fact that there is no dominant room (the ancient hall) and all rooms are of similar size. This plan harmonized very well with the search for external symmetry — the placing of the entrance exactly in the centre of the front — which became the main basis of the aesthetics of house design in the eighteenth and nineteenth centuries. A characteristic, not universally adopted however, was facing the house uphill and siting the kitchen and service-rooms in the basement. This arrangement represents a refinement of an already highly satisfactory system of circulation, as the gentry could enter the house at the front at the level of the 'reception rooms' where they were insulated from the servants who would no doubt enter at the back at the level of the kitchen.

Fig. 37 Plasnewydd (Llanwnnog, Mont.), is another good illustration of the late Renaissance plan. Probably built somewhat later than Tŷ-faenor (Fig. 36), it combines all its salient features with a 'double-pile' layout. The central stair-passage thus provides a separate access to four rooms (two at the front and two at the back) on each of the main floors. Like Tŷ-faenor the house faces uphill, so that advantage can be taken of the sloping ground to provide a kitchen, servants' hall and store-rooms in the basement. Curiously, although the plan would have permitted a completely symmetrical elevation, this was not achieved in its entirety. For reasons that are not clear the room to the left of the entrance was provided with two small windows rather than the one large window lighting the room on the right.

The basic elements of the Tŷ-faenor plan — the central stair, the gable chimneys (thought not commonly the basement) — were increasingly adopted for the smaller manor-houses, and the Plasnewydd plan for the larger during the eighteenth century, while during the nineteenth century they provided the model for most rural housing larger than a cottage.

spacious structures altogether began to make their appearance. These framed wooden stairs, in the form of a well or a dogleg, required a great deal more room. Originally such stairs were housed in projecting turrets specially provided. It was the placing of the new framed stair in the body of the house and opposite the entry which eventually revolutionized the whole layout.

The earliest houses incorporating this final development appear quite suddenly in widely separated parts of Britain about the middle of the seventeenth century. Although the idea has been attributed to Sir Roger Pratt and his designs for Coleshill, there are other houses seemingly as early, and if spread by diffusion from a single site, such diffusion must have been very rapid. In social terms the type seems to have its origin, as did the earlier sub-medieval house, amongst the upper-middle class. Just as the open hall long survived amongst the grandees, and the court, so also did the passage-room.

It is notable that the earliest Welsh example of the new central stair passage plan, Tŷ-faenor (Abbey Cwm-hir, Rads.) unlike Coleshill, is completely bereft of conventional classical ornament (Fig. 36). The central dogleg stair has massive newel posts, almost Jacobean in conception, while the front door opening on to the stair has the ornate rather than classical frame. Tŷ-faenor was built only one room deep, but another early example of the new look, Plasnewydd (Llanwnnog, Mont.) was built in two ranges, front and back. This handsome half-timbered building is again without a single detail of Greco-Roman descent (Fig. 37, Pl. IX a). The windows are of the horizontal mullioned type, and even these are not arranged symmetrically about the front elevation. This omission suggests that outward symmetry and centralized circulation were distinct if converging ideas.

The durable hall-house of the tenant farmer had become established about the same time as the Tudor dynasty; the adoption of the sub-medieval storeyed house coincided with the triumph of the Reformation; the centrally-planned Renaissance house gained acceptance during the Commonwealth and is a type to be associated with the rise to supreme power of the Parliament of Squires which was the final outcome of the Civil War and Restoration. As a squire's house it began, but gradually it spread to most classes of rural society so that by the end of the nineteenth century the symmetrical box built around its entrance and stairway, in greater or smaller versions, housed the greater part of the rural community. Such houses tended more and more to be built apart from their farm buildings so that there was little difference in basic layout between the house of squire, parson and peasant. This standardization of the 'villa' plan for several social groups did not take place universally in Western Europe. Even in nineteenth-century Germany a farmhouse could never be confused with a parson's house or a squire's house. In Britain it could, and the fact that it could is an indication of the headlong development of the British State following the establishment in 1660 of the crowned republic, carrying it at least for a period far ahead of its nearest continental rivals and competitors.

EPILOGUE — THE FOURTH GREAT REBUILDING —
THE FREELY-PLANNED HOUSE

The First World War not only altered the map of Europe but also marked a great watershed in the history of housing. It heralded the end of the dominance of the axially-planned symmetrical, central stair-passage house which, making its first appearance during the Commonwealth, had dominated the house plan throughout the nineteenth century. In the great housing drive of the post-war years much freer layouts came into use. Experiments with forms of plan continued after the Second World War, but in spite of the almost total cessation of house building during the conflict, this war cannot be associated with the radical break in a long established tradition of domestic architecture associated with the first. The later developments in house design — experimentation with the 'open plan' in which self-contained circulation was sacrificed to gain as spacious as possible an interior — were merely carrying pre-war experiments to their logical conclusions.

In the new post-1918 houses, fashionable decorative treatments have followed each other in a bewildering succession of tastes. Historical styles, Georgian or 'Mock Tudor', have alternated with self-conscious modernism. Thus the underlying brickwork might alternatively be disguised by applied half-timbering or designed to look as if it were poured concrete. At the time of writing a vernacular revival is sweeping south-eastern England, an inevitable reaction to a quarter of a century of functionalism and formalism. It is to be expected that this movement which is now making the market-towns and villages of southern England look more picturesque than they have looked since the end of the seventeenth century will soon reach Wales, as by the laws of historical development propounded here it surely must.

More fundamentally important has been the development of new means of heating resulting in the reduction of fireplaces in the house or sometimes their total elimination. Thus for the first time since the sixteenth century has the placing of the fire ceased to be a critical factor in determining the plan.

The development of road transport helped to complete the revolution in the use of materials, the replacement of locally produced stone by transported brick. The replacement of the solid by the cavity wall made it possible for the first time to achieve completely dry interiors. Another conspicuous development was the abandonment of the vertically-proportioned, sliding sash window worked by counter weights which had been introduced not long after the Restoration, and which had become the hallmark of the centrally-planned house. Fashion reverted to the horizontally proportioned window and the hinged, outward-opening light, which had been the norm in the later sub-medieval phase. The outward opening casement like the sliding window appears to be a British peculiarity. The continental window normally opens inwards, because of the need to close the external shutters against the heat of the sun and at the same time maintain ventilation.

None of these developments have until recently made much impact on the Welsh countryside where the great stock of centrally-planned Victorian farmhouses has proved quite adequate for a still declining farming population, and the farmscape of western Wales, in particular, still remains a great architectural monument to the Victorian age, with farmhouses of this period still far outnumbering all built before or since. In eastern Wales, because the housing stock was generally older, more new houses are to be seen, many replacing medieval or sub-medieval houses, rightly or wrongly deemed to have reached the end of their useful life.

If the impact of new housing has been relatively gradual the same cannot be said of the farm buildings. Until recently the greater part of the buildings on a Welsh farm would have dated from the nineteenth century. Only a handful would have survived from before the golden years of the mid nineteenth century, and relatively few could have been built since. However, since the Second World War the changes in agricultural technology have been rapid and with it a transformation in the buildings required. The result is that even if the farmhouses themselves remain, the traditional farm-buildings, timber-framed, stone or brick, are rapidly being replaced by much larger structures of steel or concrete giving each farm the look of a small-scale factory rather than the custodian of the time-honoured traditions of peasant life.

NOTES

[1] Sir Cyril Fox and Lord Raglan, *Monmouthshire Houses* I (1951), II (Cardiff, 1953), III (Cardiff, 1954); W.G. Hoskins 'The rebuilding of rural England, 1570–1640', *Past and Present*, 4 (1953) 44–89; R.W. Brunskill, *Vernacular Architecture of the Lake Counties* (1974).

[2] For Glamorgan see Glam. Inv. III Pt. 2 (1981), IV Pt. 1 (1982) and Pt. 2 (1988).

[3] M.W. Barley, *Houses and History* (1986), 148.

[4] K. Baumgarten, *Das deutsche Bauernhaus* (Berlin, 1980); G.I. Meirion-Jones, *The Vernacular Architecture of Brittany (Edinburgh, 1982)*. Recent *Cahiers de l'Inventaire*, e.g. *Millevaches en Limousin* (1987), indicate that up to the end of the seventeenth century the French *noblesse* lived in tower-houses.

[5] Sir Cyril Fox and Lord Raglan, *Monmouthshire Houses*, particularly Vol. I.

[6] R.C.A.M. Inv. *Anglesey* (1937) and *Caerns.* (1956–64).

[7] I.C. Peate, *The Welsh House: a study of folk culture* (Liverpool, 1944); J.T. Smith 'The long-house in Monmouthshire: a re-appraisal' in I.Ll. Foster and L. Alcock (eds.), *Culture and Environment, essays in honour of Sir Cyril Fox* (1963), 389–414.

[8] N.W. Alcock, *Cruck Construction: an introduction and catalogue* (1981).

[9] R.A. Cordingley, 'British historical roof-types and their members', *Trans. Ancient Monts. Soc.*, (1961), 73–118.

[10] P. Smith, 'Hall Tower and Church, Some Themes and Sites Reconsidered', in R.R. Davies (ed.) *et al. Welsh Society and Nationhood* (Cardiff, 1984), 122–60.

[11] A.J. Taylor 'Castle-building in Wales in the later thirteenth century', in E.M. Jope (ed.), *Studies in Building History*, 107, 111.

[12] P. Smith, *Houses of the Welsh Countryside* (1988, 2nd edition), 651–5.

[13] P. Smith, 'The Architectural Personality of the British Isles', *A.C.*, (1980), 1–36.

[14] Sir Cyril Fox and Lord Raglan, *Monmouthshire Houses* III, 43.

[15] P. Smith, *Houses of the Welsh Countryside* (1975), Maps 47–8.

Plate II Tower-houses and first-floor halls: the tower-houses, *a* The Old Rectory (Angle, Pembs.) and *b* Candleston Castle (Merthyr Mawr, Glam.) were buildings with a clear defensive intention as evidenced by the machicolations of *a* and the barmkin wall visible to the left of the tower at *b*. The first-floor halls *c* Garn-llwyd (Llancarfan, Glam.) and *d* Llanfihangel Place (Llanfihangel, Glam.) are related to them in that the primary accommodation is on the first floor. In all there is a marked vertical emphasis.

Plate III   Hall-houses: *a* Ciliau (Llandeilo Graban, Rads.), *b* Pit Cottage (Llan-arth, Mon.). These in contrast with the first-floor halls and towers illustrate the much more widespread hall tradition as exemplified by the H plan *a*, evidently the house of a proprietor, as well as the simple rectangular cruck-framed hall *b* presumably the house of a yeoman farmer.

Plate IV Hall-houses contd.: the interior of Tŷ-draw (Llanarmon Mynydd Mawr, Denbs.). Although long abandoned and used as a farm building this picture gives some idea of the structural elegance of many cruck-framed halls. These, the homes of an emerging yeoman class, survive in large numbers in the marches of Wales, and make the borderland a rewarding quarry for students of early peasant architecture.

Plate V Sub-medieval storeyed houses: *a* Plas-ucha (Llanfair D.C., Denbs.) and *b* Dyffryn-gwyn (Tywyn, Mer.) 1640, illustrate patterns of plan having the fireplaces on the containing walls, lateral or gable. Internal evidence proves that Plas-ucha is a modified hall-house, originally without fireplaces, where an open hearth was ventilated by a louver, the supporting truss of which still survives. Dyffryn-gwyn was clearly built as a new storeyed house in 1640. Its descent from earlier hall-houses is not very clear.

Plate VI Sub-medieval houses: *a* Y Fro (Llanbedr Ystrad Yw, Brecs.) exemplifies a large family of houses whose hall fireplace (in contrast with Plas-ucha and Dyffryn-gwyn), (Pl. V) is sited internally so that it backs on to the cross-passage. Both *b* Bridge Cottage and *c* Pont Yspig Cottage (both Llanfihangel Crucornau, Mon.) seem to be diminutive members of the same family. Were that part to the left of the middle chimney to be removed from *a* a house similar to *b* or *c* would result. Similarly if a further unit were to be added to *b* or *c* a house similar to *a* would be created. However *b* and *c* are house forms in their own right. The small gable window lighting the fireplace stair proves that no third room has been removed, nor was any such room intended to be added.

Plate VII   Sub-medieval storeyed houses: *a* Aston Hall (Churchstoke, Mont.)? 1692, is an exceptionally impressive example of a three-unit, lobby-entry house in which the hall fireplace is set not backing on to the passage, but actually in the passage, blocking it and thus creating a lobby-entry. Such a plan, which seems typologically later than the fireplace-backing-on-the-passage group illustrated on the previous page, made it possible for the hall fireplace to provide background heating for an adjacent parlour, or for a stack which both hall and parlour fireplaces backing on to each other could share. At *b* Bron Rhys (Tregynon, Mont.) and *b* Tŷ-cerrig (Llanfor, Mer.) are houses which seem to relate to the larger lobby-entry house in the same way that the small gable-entry houses on the previous page relate to the larger cross-passage house.

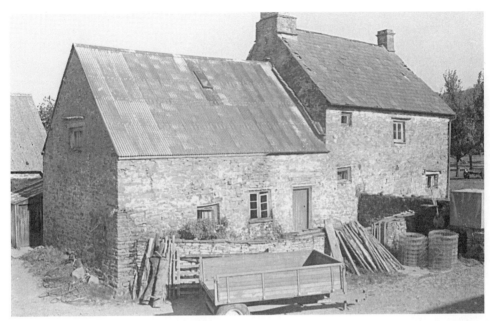

Plate VIII   Sub-medieval houses illustrating types of plan in which byre and dwelling were combined. The long-house *a* Pen-y-bryn (Llangatwg, Brecs.) is evidently related to the fireplace-backing-on-the-entry house (Plate V) as it too has a passage (serving also as a feeding-walk) running behind the fireplace, while the house-and-byre homestead *b* Garnedd (Llanwyddelan, Mont.) is clearly related to the lobby-entrance houses (Pl. VII) as a lobby-entry, not a passage, stands between house and byre. Both can be conceived as being derived from the medieval long-house but eclectically influenced by a local preference for either the cross-passage or the lobby-entry plan.

Plate IX   Early central stair-passage houses: *a* Plasnewydd, (Llanwnnog, Mont.) *b* The Old Rectory (Llanbedr, Denbs.). Such houses were the late seventeenth-century precursors successively of the standard eighteenth-century manor-house and the standard nineteenth-century farmhouse. Note the contrast here with all the houses on the previous pages — the centrally-placed doorway behind which the entrance hall gives on to the stair and around which the rooms are arranged. No longer is there one room of overriding size and importance — the hall — but four rooms on each floor of much the same size as each other. Note the 'traditional' mullioned and transomed window is here still retained to be replaced by the counter-weighted sliding sash window early in the eighteenth century.

Archaeology

H. N. SAVORY

INTRODUCTION

B RITISH archaeology has been slow to mature as a scientific discipline.[1] It has, of course, deep roots in the pioneering labours of the great sixteenth, seventeenth and eighteenth-century antiquaries, who laid the foundations of a distinctive British tradition of field archaeology, or amassed collections of 'curiosities' which were the starting-point for modern museum collections. They were followed, particularly in the nineteenth century, by more specialized amateurs, some of whom dug into prehistoric burial mounds and earthworks or Roman forts and 'villas' with varying standards of care, while others, including the great John Evans, collected, classified and recorded stone and bronze implements. Towards the end of the last century, a more responsible attitude towards excavation was gaining ground among amateurs, led by General Pitt-Rivers, though few had the means to rival his thoroughness. With the growing realization that objects found during excavation need to be assigned to particular phases of human occupation or construction on a given site, and related to accurately drawn plans and sections, a distinctive British school of excavation technique developed early in the present century, with an application to sites of all periods, irrespective of the existence or otherwise of written records. With the modern growth of professionalism the two traditions of field archaeology and excavation technique have been steadily upheld in Britain.

On the other hand, until early in the present century and particularly in the field of prehistory, British archaeology was lagging behind that of some continental countries in the development of an intellectual system for interpreting the data assembled by the collector and the excavator, largely owing to the slowness with which the subject gained academic status. Hence the acceptance, at least in part, of continental systems based upon the theoretical 'Three Ages of Stone, Bronze and Iron' and 'Type Sites'. Museum curators, indeed, needed such systems for the classification and display of many of their specimens. Thus they were very willing to adapt the typological techniques developed on the Continent for working out evolutionary sequences for these specimens. This was done with the help of associations in hoards or grave-groups, or the evidence from stratification on carefully excavated sites. Such techniques had their application to Romano–British and medieval, as well as prehistoric material.

It has long been evident, however, that the purely archaeological methods just described are insufficient for understanding and presenting the results of prehistoric research and what these reveal of a complex process of cultural diffusion and local adaptation in Britain. This difficulty should be seen against a chronological framework based upon highly subjective inferences from supposed emanations from, or parallels with, distant but relatively well-dated cultures in southern Europe or the Near East. It has been handled, in different ways, by a growing number of specialists[2], aided by an ever-increasing body of scientific applications, coming to join the long-established collaboration of the physical anthropologist, botanist and zoologist. First came the geographical and geological applications, which pointed to the variable conditions affecting settlement, and the specialist studies of ancient soils, climate and botany, which began to offer an alternative chronological framework for early man.[3]

More recently, ecological studies have brought the relevant scientific and archaeological disciplines together to show more clearly the changing environments within which human settlement took place locally.[4] Most dramatic of all, however, has been the arrival of scientific dating methods, especially those based on radio-carbon ('C 14'), to provide an independent and objective (if not very precise) chronology, which has transformed our perspectives, especially in earlier periods, and clarified the relationships between cultural groups.[5] This dating process has been particularly valuable to students of the Old and New Stone Ages. However, beneficial results will undoubtedly be derived from research in all periods or areas, even as late as the early Middle Ages in Wales, where there is a scarcity of finds which can be given a close date archaeologically.

It is very easy, at the present time, to lose sight of the inescapable limitations of archaeology, especially prehistory, imposed by our dependence upon what, from its nature, has been capable of survival, especially from remote ages, and the small proportion of this which has become available for study, or could be revealed by the increasingly expensive process of excavation. Nowhere is this more apparent than in our chosen field, that of settlement and land use, and the types of society thereby represented. The British tradition of field archaeology has ensured that much remaining from ancient man-made landscapes has been recorded, in maps or otherwise, that has since been destroyed by agriculture or industrial or urban development, and the Royal Commissions on Ancient Monuments have steadily raised their standards in this respect over the past seventy years.

Field archaeology, indeed, received a powerful stimulus from air-photography after the First World War, and the scope of this technique has increased since the Second.[6] The result is that we can now see, especially through crop-marks, how much once existed, in certain areas, which was not visible to the field archaeologist on the ground — how much, indeed, that we can never hope to explore by excavation before it is finally obliterated. Among these fading vestiges are field systems, agricultural or pastoral, of various dates, with the associated settlements — prehistoric, Romano-British or medieval. But we cannot hope to make a complete map of land use in any area, in any particular period, from this evidence, because of what has been erased by subsequent use, and because of the limitations which local variations of soil, climate and crops impose (especially in Wales) upon the patterns that may be visible on an air photograph. We are still left with a fragmentary palimpsest which modern techniques may help us to interpret to some degree, where opportunity and finance occur, and help us, with caution, to draw more general conclusions. But we are still dealing, as John Aubrey, the founder of British field archaeology, said with 'scattered planks from a shipwreck'.

Plate X   Aerial reconnaissance in Wales: 'Henge' sites at Llandygái.

ARCHAEOLOGY IN WALES

Archaeology in Wales has naturally gone through the same stages of development as the rest of Britain, and since 1975 the work of University, Museum and Royal Commission staffs has been supplemented by the creation of four government-funded Rescue Archaeology Trusts which are often able to carry out excavations on a far larger scale than was hitherto normally possible. The fact that these excavations have arisen from the need to anticipate destruction of archaeological sites, rather than as part of a programme of research on sites selected to throw light on particular problems, has not reduced unduly their cumulative value from a research point of view, because it has become clear that the nature and sequence of activity on many sites cannot be understood without total excavation.

Old Stone Age Hunters, c.250,000(?)–8000 BC

The first problem for the prehistorian — when man first appeared in Wales? — has been a difficult one and still awaits a definite answer. Successive periods of glaciation have placed the greater part of the evidence wholly out of reach; its survival, locally, has largely depended upon deposits remaining in some caves which are present in the Carboniferous Limestone areas of south and north-east Wales. However, a few hand-axes of Middle Palaeolithic date have been picked up from surface deposits in south-east Wales and its borders, and others have been found very recently in the cave at Pontnewydd, Cefn (Denbs.) in association with fragmentary human remains of hominid type. It is likely, therefore, that from at least a quarter of a million years ago parts of Wales were being visited, when climatic conditions permitted, by small parties of primitive hunters. During the Upper Palaeolithic, evidence from caves suggests a somewhat greater frequentation of parts of Wales during periods of relatively favourable climate between c.36000 and 25000 radio-carbon years bc and again around the 10th millennium BC, before the final Pleistocene climate deterioration which ended c.8000 BC.[7]

Mesolithic Food-gatherers, c.8000–4000 BC

With the end of the Pleistocene and the beginning of the Holocene, the onset of rapidly warming 'Boreal' climatic conditions soon opened up the whole of the British Isles to man the hunter, fisher and food-gatherer, returning across the land-bridge which still connected Britain to the Continent and settling in Scotland and Ireland for the first time. As the sea-level rose, following deglaciation, the land-bridges were submerged, but man, possessed by now of small boats, could still explore the coasts and cross narrow seas. Equally rapidly, the plants and animals of the tundra were reinforced or replaced by an ever more varied flora and fauna, and tundra was replaced by forest in all but the highest and rockiest districts. The Mesolithic is the time when the natural environment could develop, in response to favourable climatic conditions, without being disturbed by man, except perhaps towards the end. He was certainly penetrating the inland forests in pursuit of their denizens — notably red deer, aurochs and wild boar. However, it was the coastal tracts of Wales, extending far out over areas which are now submerged, that saw the primary settlement by Mesolithic man; until recently, indeed, it was solely along the coasts that evidence for his presence had been found: but that evidence has now come to light, even on the high uplands of the interior, hidden under the blanket peat that formed long after its deposition.[8]

Until recently the concept of Highland and Lowland Zones, developed particularly by Fox,[9] profoundly affected our ideas on the chronology and quality of prehistoric human settlement in Wales from the beginning of the Holocene onwards. Now, in the light of radio-carbon datings as well as environmental studies, it is clear that the idea of Highland Zone retardation is irrelevant before the climate deterioration of the later Bronze Age, and that the coastal areas of Wales, in particular, provided a distinctly favourable habitat in Neolithic and early Bronze Age times, with an abundance of wildfowl, fish and shellfish, and a forest-cover steadily spreading inland which encouraged the formation of a fertile 'brown earth' which, after forest clearance, offered possibilities of cultivation and stock-raising on all but the highest and roughest ground.

The Neolithic Farmers, c.4500–2500 BC

The arrival in Wales of the earliest domesticated plants and animals, and the inception there of forest clearance can now, as a result of C 14 dating, be seen to have taken place very little later, if at all, than in other parts of Britain. Here, too, it was the favourable environment of some coastal areas and of the main river valleys of the Marches which attracted the first farmers, but the archaeological evidence shows that the new settlers arrived by different routes and soon developed regional cultural traits which reflect different contacts with the outside world. Their culture in its primary form represented a synthesis of elements derived from the Atlantic coastal areas of the Continent on the one hand and the interior of central and eastern Europe on the other; from the first came a tradition of mass communal burial, often in megalithic chambers set in elaborately constructed 'long' or 'round' cairns, while from the second came the tradition of oblong or trapezoidal timber-framed houses, contrasting with the round or oval huts of the Mesolithic hunters and the round-houses of the creators of the megalithic tradition in south-west Europe.

The regional differences which soon developed reflect a geographical determinism arising from the central position of Wales within the British Isles. Settlers or 'influences' arriving by Atlantic coastal routes particularly affected the Irish Channel areas and laid the foundations of an enduring link between north-west and south-west Wales and Ireland. The simple form of 'Passage Grave' set in a circular cairn belongs to the earliest phase of megalithic construction in these areas, as it does in parts of western France and Iberia, about the turn of the fifth and fourth millennia BC. On the other hand the 'Severn–Cotswold' group of chambered long cairns, centred on south-east Wales, reflects settlement about the same time from neighbouring parts of England.[10]

It has become clear that the bones found in Welsh megalithic tombs of the Early and Middle Neolithic, some of which remained in use for several centuries, can only represent a very small proportion of the people who lived near them and would have been needed for such engineering tasks as the lifting of a capstone weighing forty tons on to the megalithic chamber at Tinkinswood (Glam.). The basis for the selection which took place is a matter for speculation of the kind which often lies on the margin of serious prehistory. Moreover, isolated finds of stone axe-heads and other characteristic artefacts of the Neolithic have a far wider distribution, especially in mid Wales, than surviving or recorded megalithic tombs, and yet it has been shown that cereals were being cultivated far up the Wye Valley at this time. In spite of this, there are no ancient field systems in Wales, which can as yet confidently be assigned to the early Neolithic, although such have been revealed by the removal of blanket peat in various parts of Ireland. Although a few apparently isolated dwellings of this period with the typical oblong, ridge-roofed layout, have been found in Wales, nothing comparable to the large settlements represented by the 'causewayed camps' of Lowland Britain and the fortified sites recently discovered in Cornwall and on the Cotswold escarpment have so far come to light in Wales — unless, of course, the earliest of the two 'Henges' at Llandygái (Caerns.) can be seen in this light (p. 157 and Pl. X).

The process by which the Mesolithic hunter-fishers were absorbed into the early farming communities remains obscure, though it may have been a lengthy, and sometimes a violent one. Certainly the Neolithic people were themselves hunters as well as farmers, to judge by the quantities of their distinctive leaf arrowheads which have been found in some areas, and the powerful bows which we know from the Somerset Levels could be used to propel them in warfare as well as the chase, as we know from recent excavations at Crickley Hill (Glos.)[11] It has, indeed, been suspected that the indigenous food-gatherers may have contributed to certain Neolithic traits, like the development of stone-axe factories exploiting suitable rocks in north-west and south-west Wales.[12] Indeed, their footloose mode of life, in pursuit of game or of alternative materials for their implements, might readily have adapted to seasonal transhumance with domesticated cattle, or trade in implements derived from axe factories such as those of Penmaen-mawr.

Whatever the causes, it is clear that from the latter part of the fourth millennium BC regional groups were emerging, in various parts of the British Isles, including Wales, which can be differentiated by burial practices and artefacts, notably in the infinitely variable field of ceramics, and which tended to distance themselves in these respects from contemporary groups in neighbouring parts of the Continent. The most striking aspect of this insular originality is the appearance of what seems to be an almost exclusively British ceremonial tradition of 'Henge' monuments and stone circles and the replacement of inhumation by cremation and, to a large extent, oblong dwellings by round ones in some communities.[13] By this time we can suspect the emergence of centres of population and power (with spiritual and temporal perhaps combined, as in early Egypt) around the great monuments of Avebury, Silbury Hill and elsewhere in Wessex, sometimes involving great circular, timber-framed buildings. Another great centre of activity was developing around the great Passage Grave concentration centring on New Grange in Ireland. Clearly a large and well-organized labour force was required to carry out these great public works and those who controlled it must have exercised power over a large area, but for us, unlike Egypt, an impenetrable veil is drawn over their names, and the language they spoke. The question, of course, arises as to what reflection these developments had in Wales.

At present one can only say that the two successive 'Henges' with associated 'Cursus' at Llandygái (Caerns.) constitute the only site in Wales which is at all comparable to those of Wessex. Apart from a few possible connecting links in the central Marches and an unexplored site in Gower, the 'Henge' and stone-circle tradition in Wales seems to express itself through small monuments of late, apparently mostly Bronze Age date. This and other evidence seems to point to relatively small and poor communities in the third millennium, and it is possible that the effect upon soils, especially in upland areas affected by heavy rainfall and exposure to wind, after more than a millennium of forest clearance and primitive agriculture may have led to conversion to rough pasture in some areas, and forest regeneration in others: there is even some evidence that blanket peat was already beginning to form in some upland districts. But it is towards the end of the third millennium, during the long transitional period between the conventional Neolithic and Early Bronze Age, that we can now point to the earliest surviving traces of field systems linked to settlements in Wales.

Early and Middle Bronze Age, c.2500–1200 BC

The central compartment of the Three Age System and its conventional chronology has suffered particularly from the effects of the new radio-carbon-based chronology, both at its beginning and at its end. The earliest implements of copper or of bronze have long been loth to appear in significant associations with other artefacts, and the arrival of the 'Beaker Folk', who did very occasionally place a copper or bronze weapon in a grave, has tended to be used to mark a dividing line between the Neolithic and the Bronze Age, conventionally set near the beginning of the second millennium BC. Now, however, the overlap between the earlier 'Beakers' and characteristic phenomena of the later Neolithic is seen to extend over several centuries towards the end of the third millennium and it is by no means certain that the 'Beaker Folk' played the only, or even the first, part in the introduction of the earliest metal technology into the British Isles.[14]

There can be no doubt that a new racial type — robust and broad-skulled — makes its appearance in many of the inhumation burials accompanied by 'Beakers' in most parts of Britain, as in neighbouring parts of the Continent, and there is no real evidence that this type had evolved locally in Britain before the introduction of 'Beakers'. But we are probably dealing with the movements of small groups of people pursuing a semi-nomadic mode of life and able to make their way into thinly populated regions without threatening the existence of locally established communities, especially at a time when, as it appears, pastoralism had become the dominant form of land use.[15] 'Beaker' pottery is well represented at 'Henge' sites in Britain, including Llandygái (Pl. 10, p. 153) and one must suppose that the newcomers, if such they were, had something to offer to the important people there — whether it was gold ornaments, copper daggers or succulent joints of lamb. It is also clear that the local people did not lose their identity, because their ceramic traditions, 'Henge' and stone-circle building, and practice of cremation burial, sometimes now in round barrows and cairns, continued, though they readily acknowledged the superiority of the barbed and tanged arrowheads which the Beaker Folk undoubtedly introduced from the Continent. Within a century or two after the beginning of the second millennium Beaker pottery and the associated practice of inhumation had gone out of use.

Study of the round barrows and cairns which can still be seen in large numbers on the uplands of Wales, as well as in what are now the well-cultivated main river valleys and coastal plains, has revealed evidence of social stratification and of continuing agriculture, and hints, where barrows occur in groups, that settlements may have existed not far away. Indeed, in a few cases, the traces of round or oval timber-framed huts have been preserved underneath the mounds. There is still, however, no trace in Wales of any great centre of wealth and power having arisen, such as that which existed for a time around Stonehenge and had its reflection in the richly equipped chieftain burials which have been brought to light in nearby round barrows. It is to this phase, however, near the end of the third and the early part of the second millennium, that it now seems possible to assign some of the ancient field systems, associated with scattered round huts, traces of which survive in north-west Wales. This at any rate seems to be indicated by radio-carbon dates obtained at Tŷ-mawr, Holyhead by Dr C. Smith,[16] and this evidence may apply to certain sites in Caernarfonshire (p. 166 below and Fig. 38a).

Study of the copper and bronze implements, which all too rarely come to light on Welsh burial or settlement sites of the earlier Bronze Age, has been given a new direction by a project recently undertaken by Dr P. Northover for the Board of Celtic Studies. The results of metallurgical analysis of a very large number of implements found in Wales and the Marches have served to emphasize the importance of local mineral resources in north and mid Wales, alongside a diversity of imports of raw material or finished products which, at various time, came from Ireland, other parts of Britain, and even the Continent.[17] These show that, after an initial dependence upon the early Irish production of copper implements, Wales was supplied to a considerable extent from local resources, supplemented in the south-east by imports from southern England. The northern Welsh production of bronze implements reached its apogee c.1500–1200 BC, with a precocious use of local lead resources for the alloying of bronze used in the manufacture, chiefly, of palstaves, which were exported as far as the Continent.

The Later Bronze Age and Early Iron Age, c.1200 BC–AD 75

With the later Bronze Age the nature of archaeological evidence changes in most parts of Britain, and there is much to suggest that political and social upheaval was taking place in parts of the island. The old world of barrow burial, stone circles and power centred on Salisbury Plain fades, and there is an increasing resort to hilltop settlements in which the population appears to be concentrated for safety and which were sooner or later defended by palisades or ramparts which begin the long history of many sites which were formerly supposed to be Early Iron Age hill-forts. Even in Wales the old burial customs disappear, the earlier Bronze Age ceramic tradition is replaced by one in which continental influences appear, and the metallurgical industry based on north or mid Wales copper declines and is replaced, at least in south Wales, by the 'Penard' industry of continental origin (c.1200–1000 BC), which spread to Ireland. The extent to which the changes reflect actual immigration from the Continent, rather than the effects of climatic change, awaits further discovery and research. There can be no doubt that the onset of colder and wetter conditions, by more than one stage, at the end of the second millennium and the beginning of the first, to inaugurate the 'sub-Atlantic' climate phase, finally reduced the Welsh uplands to their present relatively inhospitable condition, with widespread blanket peat.[18] From now on it is appropriate to speak of a sharp contrast between a Highland and a Lowland Zone in Britain. The effects are clearly seen in the contrast between the distributions of Early Bronze Age burial and ceremonial sites, which are abundant on the Welsh uplands and later Bronze Age and Early Iron Age embanked enclosures as shown, for example, on the Ordnance Survey *Map of Southern Britain in the Early Iron Age*.[19] The latter have a marginal distribution around the main moorland areas of the interior, although many of them are on high ground and in a suitable position for the exploitation of upland pasture as well as the cultivation of neighbouring valley floors and sides. As there is reason to think that by this time sheep had grown in importance at the expense of the cattle and pigs favoured by Neolithic man,[20] one can understand that the moorland still had some economic value; indeed, it is in this context that we may ultimately be able to understand the scattered huts and paddocks of upland Breconshire and Glamorgan (p. 166 below and Fig. 39).

A further contrast which the map reveals is that between the very large hill-forts of the Marches, the Cotswolds and Wessex and those of most parts of Wales, where the hill-forts of major size are very few in comparison with the numerous small earthworks, many of which are hardly of any military significance at all. Of course, further analysis shows that there are many local differences which are likely to relate to a long and varied local history.[21] Unfortunately, the large-scale excavation needed to understand these differences has so far told us much more about the Marches than regions further west, although the imbalance is now being corrected in Carmarthenshire and Pembrokeshire by the work of the Dyfed Archaeological Trust and, to some extent, in Gwynedd, by the Gwynedd Archaeological Trust, while unfortunately least progress has been made in south-east Wales (p. 166).

Excavations at Croft Ambrey (Heref.),[22] the Breiddin in Montgomeryshire[23] and Moel y Gaer in Flintshire[24] have shown that many of the large hill-forts of the Marches were first built at some time during the later Bronze Age and already at that time contained large villages, with numerous round-houses and 'four-poster' structures which have generally been interpreted as supports for buildings in which grain or winter feed were kept. The lavish use of timber at these sites suggests that forest was now being cleared extensively in their neighbourhood, presumably in the first place for agricultural or pastoral purposes, although the related field systems have not been identified.[25] On the other hand, although a promontory fort at Llansteffan in Carmarthenshire has been shown to have been built during the later Bronze Age,[26] most of the small earthworks of west Wales seem to belong to the Early Iron Age, after the sixth century BC or an even later date.[27] None the less, some of them contained a small number of round-houses and 'four-posters', as did the great Iron Age hill-fort of Danebury (Hants.) though in much greater profusion, and one must look upon this type of internal layout as an old-established and long-enduring feature of later Bronze Age and Early Iron Age culture in southern Britain.[28] Moreover, the distribution of small enclosures of farmstead size in mid Wales has now been shown by air-photography to extend far into large hill-fort territory in Shropshire, and an example recently excavated by the Clwyd-Powys Archaeological Trust at Collfryn near Welshpool has proved to have the features — round-houses and 'four-posters' — found elsewhere, and quite strong defences, including the widely-spaced outer banks long thought to be characteristic of a 'south-western' group in Wales and the West Country, no doubt related to an economy in which stock-raising was particularly important.[29] The hill-forts of north-west Wales, however, still present a distinct problem (p. 166).

Until recently the question of cultural groups in Wales during the first half of the first millennium BC was approached chiefly from the study of bronze implements. This reveals a marked difference between the characteristic types of the Marches, north-west and south-west Wales, and those of the south-east. Most strikingly, the 'Wilburton' industry, characteristic of lowland England and the Marches in the early part of the first millennium, is replaced in south-east Wales and south-west England by that which produced the 'south Wales' socketed axes, while north-west Wales depended on its own production, with some help from Ireland, and the south-west has its own type of socketed axe. These contrasts seemed to relate to the possible predecessors of the tribes which occupied these areas on the eve of the Roman conquest.[30]

Although one should not lose sight of the hint of retardation towards the west, as provided by the bronze implements, it now seems that the process by which the Celtic tribes of the Ordovices, Cornovii, Silures and Demetae developed, each in its own natural region, will not become clearer until some of the larger hill-forts in north-west, mid and south Wales, which were probably seats of local political power, have been explored as extensively as certain sites in the Marches have been. The formula 'cumulative Celticity' is no doubt a helpful one,[31] and one must bear in mind the evidence for a later phase of widespread disturbance represented in most parts of Wales by the refortification of many sites, large and small, with multiple 'dump' ramparts.[32] The cumulative process, however, is not likely to have begun earlier than the earlier upheavals, towards the end of the second millennium, because it seems to have been set in motion, as far as any new element in the population is concerned, by the expansion of central European cultural groups towards the north-west during the later Bronze Age, while the Neolithic and Early Bronze Age cultures of Britain have their roots mainly in the Atlantic seaboard areas of Europe, which can hardly have been Celtic in the fourth and third millennia BC.

The Roman Period, c. AD 75–450

With the arrival of the Roman armies in Wales one might seem to be moving from the uncertainties of archaeology into the clear light of history. In fact, however, history only provides us with brief details of some Roman campaigns in Wales during the first century. These include the names and approximate locations of the tribes which confronted the Romans there, and the names of a few places or Roman generals. What we now know of the Roman period in Wales, as in other parts of Britain, still largely depends on the archaeological research of the past century. As a result of numerous excavations, we know a great deal about both the Roman military occupation of Wales over a period of more than three centuries[33] and the development of urban life on the southern seaboard,[34] but a great deal less about life in the countryside, apart from limited areas in the south-east and north-west.[35]

We know that the Silures, in due course, became a *civitas* governed by an *ordo* and that the Demetae had a town, Moridunum, though there is no evidence for its exact status.[36] In north and mid Wales no town is known, and it was probably the *vici* attached to certain Roman forts which were more or less continuously occupied down to the late fourth century — Segontium in the north-west and Caersws, Forden and Llandrindod in mid Wales — which came nearest to providing urban facilities for their neighbourhoods. We have no direct evidence for the civic status of the Ordovices after pacification apart from the hints given by Dark Age inscriptions.[37] It might seem that the evidence for continued or renewed occupation at certain hill-forts in north Wales relates to the lack of urbanization and betokens a certain resistance to Roman authority, but from the third century onwards the insecurity caused by parties of Irish raiders is more likely to have been the reason.[38]

It seems that the existence of towns along the southern seaboard of Wales had the effect, found in most parts of lowland Britain, of encouraging the development of 'villas' — buildings approaching, to some degree, the architectural standards found in Romano-British towns, and in some cases those of *villae urbanae*, representing possibly the estates of local grandees. But this degree of sophistication was only reached in the south-east, and to some extent, in the Usk and Tywi valleys, while further afield in west Wales simple rectangular buildings, without mosaics or bath-suites, are normally the only concession to Romanization. However, a large proportion of these sites merely represent the continuation, under Roman rule, of Early Iron Age homesteads. Many of these only abandoned their original layout, with round-houses, after a long delay, while others never did so. It is therefore hardly surprising that even further away from urbanization in mid and north Wales, the Early Iron Age type of homestead, with a small number of round-houses and other traditional structures, sometimes with enclosing earthworks, seems to have remained in use throughout the period of Roman rule, This holds true even in the neighbourhood of Roman forts in the Severn Valley, and one such, close to the hill-fort on the Breiddin, provides one of the rare examples of an attached cultivation system of this period to be seen outside north-west Wales.[39] Elsewhere there are certainly traces of such systems, but because of the continuity of the tradition represented by the homesteads to which they may have been attached, it is difficult to establish from superficial study whether these were established in later prehistoric or Roman times.[40] The place of the major villas of south-east Wales seems to have been taken in north Wales by certain exceptionally large and well-built homesteads of native tradition, like Dinllugwy in Anglesey and the well-to-do establishment, native in its architectural tradition but evidently the centre of an agricultural estate, at Dinorben hill-fort in Denbighshire, and it is perhaps significant that this site, like some of the major villas in the south-east, should have suffered a decline during the third quarter of the fourth century.[41]

The Dark Ages, c. AD 450–1100

In the centuries following the collapse of the Roman province, archaeologists find themselves in a difficulty which is as great as that which confronts them in some prehistoric periods. Burials, because they are Christian, do not provide much evidence individually, except in so far as they may be radio-carbon dated; inscribed stones, though they provide useful information, have often been removed from their original position;[42] settlements are hard to find because their architecture reverted to prehistoric methods of construction which leave only indeterminate traces above ground, or none at all; artefacts, especially ceramic, which can be approximately dated rarely appear in useful associations; and the linear earthworks which are characteristic of the period are particularly difficult to date by archaeological methods. So far, no definite evidence of large-scale reoccupation and refortification of Early Iron Age hill-forts, such as occurred in Somerset, has come to light in Wales,[43] and evidence for prolonged activity on Romano-British sites, urban, military or rural, apart from Caerwent, is hard to find.[44] It does now begin to appear that the tradition of the round-house, which had survived in much of Wales under Roman rule, died out fairly soon after its collapse, to be replaced by the crude beginnings of the 'long-house' tradition of the later Middle Ages (p. 171).

It may be said, of course, that written sources, of a sort, are abundant, especially for the earlier Dark Ages, but it is precisely the poor quality of these which increases the darkness. Much of this evidence, of course, relates to the early Church, and it is, for the most part, far from contemporary; unfortunately, though the traditions point to many sites, exploration on sites which have been occupied in later periods, has not produced very much of interest, and it is curious that what may well have been an early monastic site, containing many 'long-houses', on Gateholm, Pembrokeshire, appears not to be mentioned in the early literature.[45] The interesting suggestions which Dr Wendy Davies has made concerning possible continuity between Romano-British estates and early medieval ones mentioned in Llandaff and Llancarfan charters cannot as yet be substantiated archaeologically.[46] It must be confessed, in fact, that the archaeological study of early medieval settlement in Wales is really still in its infancy. Baulked by the difficulties, archaeologists have hitherto paid most attention either to the inscribed or sculptured stones, or to typological studies of 'Dark Age Import Wares' and metalwork, the finds of which in Wales are rare but throw interesting light on contacts with the Mediterranean and Atlantic coasts of Europe as well as with Ireland and Scotland.[47]

The Later Middle Ages, c. AD 1100–1500

With the coming of the Normans, the task of the archaeologist is transformed once more. Sites and contemporary records abound and Wales presents ample material for the specialists in the international field of medieval military and ecclesiastical architecture. But there remains a more humble field in which the techniques which archaeologists find useful for earlier periods still have a place, alongside the new ones of the vernacular architecture specialist (see Peter Smith's chapter in this volume): the study of deserted or shrunken medieval villages and field systems, often helped by air photography.

A COMPARISON OF GLAMORGAN AND CAERNARFONSHIRE

Old Stone Age (Palaeolithic), c.250,000–8000 BC

While parts of Gower and the Vale of Glamorgan escaped the worst effects of the last glaciations, north-west Wales did not. Accordingly, two hand-axes of Middle Palaeolithic type have been picked up from surface deposits at Rhosili and Pen-y-lan, Cardiff,[48] but none in north-west Wales. Upper Palaeolithic man frequented caves, so that here again he is relatively well represented by finds in Gower caves (notably Paviland) during the phases of favourable climate, but the caves on Orme's Head, Llandudno have so far only produced a little material.[49]

Mesolithic, c.8000–4000 BC

An improved environment brought hunter-fishers to the coasts of Glamorgan and Caernarfonshire equally quickly, but whereas relatively abundant traces of such activities have been found on the uplands as well as the coasts of Glamorgan,[50] none have so far been reported from the interior of Caernarfonshire. It remains to be seen how far this merely reflects the chances of discovery, but the move inland, mainly towards the end of the Mesolithic, seems to indicate adaptation to a different environment and may even relate to some forest clearance connected with the beginnings of animal domestication.[51]

Neolithic, c.4500–2500 BC

With the arrival of the first agriculturalists in Wales the apparent disparity between our two regions disappears. In fact Caernarfonshire has rather more surviving or recorded megalithic tombs than Glamorgan and can claim two important centres for the production of stone axe-heads, thus beginning a lead in extractive industry which lasted until iron ore and coal rose to prominence in Glamorgan in the early modern period. On the other hand, the apparent preference of the first farmers for the upland interior of Glamorgan rather than that of Caernarfonshire may relate to transhumance by early pastoralists who used old clearings in the forest seasonally.[52]

The megalithic tombs of Caernarfonshire have not been excavated with modern techniques, but superficial study suggests that they represent types derived from sea contacts with Ireland, west Wales and the Atlantic seaboard of Europe in the first place, followed by some influence from the Severn–Cotswold group carried, no doubt, by traffic up the Severn itself. An obvious context for such traffic would be the trade in stone axe-heads. In Glamorgan the sequence appears to be reversed, with influence from west Wales and perhaps ultimately from Ireland.[53]

The most striking feature of the Neolithic in Caernarfonshire is the development there of 'axe-factories' at Graig Lwyd (Penmaen-mawr) and Mynydd Rhiw in Llŷn. The products of Graig Lwyd, notably, made their way to many parts of England,[54] and the importance which this conferred on the neighbourhood is reflected in a group of ceremonial sites — two 'Henges' and 'Cursus',[55] revealed by an air photograph at Llandygái. Emergency excavation of some of these sites has shown that the earliest of the 'Henges' must have been built before the end of the fourth millennium and have been one of the earliest of its type in Britain, and the ceremonial burial in it of a stone axe-head underlines the significance of the traffic in such implements for this particular 'Henge'. In spite of the eastward orientation of this traffic, the early appearance of cremation at Llandygái and the presence of pottery of Irish affinity at an early stage there creates a suspicion that the contacts with the 'Boyne' megalithic group in Ireland may have played a part in the origin of the earlier type of 'Henge' in Britain.

The Earlier Bronze Age, *c*.2500–1200 BC

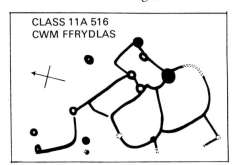
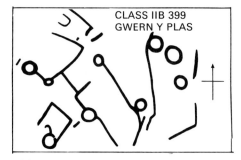

CLASS 11A 516
CWM FFRYDLAS

CLASS IIB 399
GWERN Y PLAS

Fig. 38a   Earlier types of round huts in Caernarfonshire.

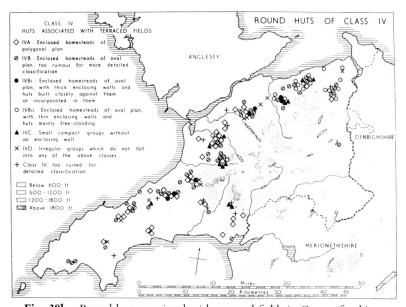

Fig. 38b   Round huts associated with terraced fields in Caernarfonshire.

During the transitional phase towards the end of the third millennium Glamorgan seems to have led the way at least in the transmission of the new types which were spreading from the Continent to Ireland, to judge by the Beaker bowl of early type deposited in the Tinkinswood megalithic chamber and the rare copper axe-head from Aberpennar (Mountain Ash),[56] and it may well be that more evidence of these early coastal links with Ireland is deposited in those low-lying tracts which are now submerged beyond the present coastline. Similar contacts along the northern seaboard of Wales may not have begun much later, although no Beaker pottery or metalwork of the earliest phase has so far been found in Caernarfonshire. However, evidence for the smelting of copper, presumably derived either from Anglesey or Orme's Head, at some date in Early Bronze Age, has been found near Llandygái.[57] The construction of a new 'Henge', of later type, at Llandygái[58] towards the end of the third millennium reflects the continuing importance of this area, but its conservatism is also suggested by the persistence of the stone-circle tradition nearby on Penmaen-mawr mountain far into the second millennium.[59]

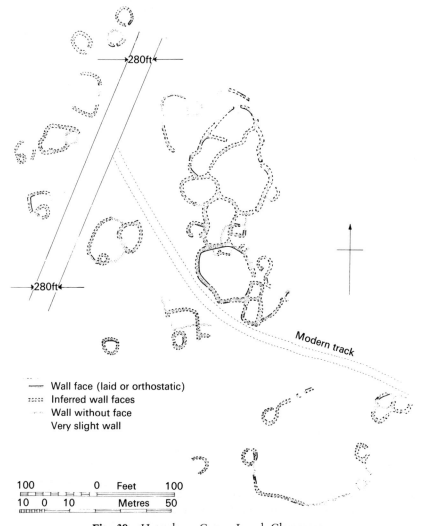

Fig. 39 Huts above Garreg Lwyd, Glamorgan.

In both our areas the location of so many Early Bronze Age burial mounds or cairns on what is now high moorland — even on mountain tops in Caernarfon-shire — suggests that in the favourable climatic conditions then prevailing, a mobile, largely pastoral population could benefit from earlier forest clearance, but as before location of actual settlements and attached field systems is difficult. In Caernarfonshire the evidence from Tŷ-mawr suggests that some of the scattered groups of round huts, associated with stone-walled enclosures of variable shape and size, which survive in the county, often on high ground (Fig. 38a) may belong to this period, though no evidence of date has so far been found in them, and broadly similar sites on the Glamorgan uplands, also undated, may have originated about the same time (Fig. 39).[60] Unfortunately, the field systems which may have been related to the round huts, or groups of such found at Saint-y-nyll, St Brides-super-Ely in the Vale of Glamorgan and near Oystermouth in Gower,[61] have not survived, although we know from a find at the Pond Cairn, Coety, that wheat and barley were being grown in the Vale in the Early Bronze Age.[62]

Towards the middle of the second millennium some large groups of round barrows in or near the Vale of Glamorgan may indicate the approximate position of settlements, and the contents of some of them, notably the Breach Farm barrow, Llanfleiddan,[63] seem to suggest the emergence of a chieftain class. But whereas Glamorgan at this time was dependent for its metalwork upon imports from mid or north Wales, Ireland or southern England, Carnarfonshire could of course draw on the flourishing local 'Acton Park' industry (p. 158).

The Later Bronze Age and Early Iron Age, c.1200 BC–AD 75

In Glamorgan the general trend during the later Bronze Age is represented by pottery from caves,[64] and a hill settlement which was in due course fortified at Coed-y-cymdda, Gwenfô.[65] How common this type of settlement was in Glamorgan in the first part of the first millennium BC, while the area was served by the 'south Wales' axe industry,[66] and whether any of the larger hill-forts of the area go back to this time, are questions that must await further excavation, but the famous hoard of transitional Late Bronze Age–Early Iron Age metalwork from Llyn Fawr can be interpreted as loot from further east and a large single-ramparted hill-fort at Llancarfan has been shown to replace a small walled enclosure which itself appears to be Early Iron Age.[67] Small defended settlements are, indeed, common in the Vale and Gower, as they are further west, but the uplands of Glamorgan show very little sign of habitation, apart from the enclosures already mentioned above which may or may not have still been in use in this period.

In Caernarfonshire, on the other hand, there is a remarkable series of defended hilltop settlements, some of them very large, along the north coast, often on very high ground.[68] It might seem that these represent an extension of the culture which built the large, later Bronze Age hill-forts of the Marches, but closer examination reveals a number of distinctive features: wall-ramparts without ditches and other features of construction which link them rather with hill-forts in south-west Wales, Ireland and the Atlantic and Mediterranean coasts of the Continent. They have not yielded many datable finds, but a small group of embanked settlements in south

Llŷn which have a layout recalling the sites in west Wales with widely-spaced banks, appear to have originated in the Late Bronze Age–Early Iron Age transition.[69] It is difficult at present to relate to these sites the great series of enclosed hut-groups, often linked to terraced fields, which seem to be prehistoric in tradition although the finds so far made in them are of Roman date (p. 168 and Fig. 41, p. 170 below).

The maritime contacts, which in Caernarfonshire are chiefly reflected in military architecture, brought to Glamorgan pottery of Breton origin found in the Bacon Hole cave, Gower and on Merthyr Mawr Warren and the Early La Tène metalworker's mould found on Worm's Head.[70] But the lead anchor-stock of Hellenistic type found in the sea off Porth Felen in Llŷn hints that small exploratory vessels from the Mediterranean world were reaching Caernarfonshire long before Agricola's time.[71] Glamorgan naturally differs from Caernarfonshire in that its contacts with lands across the Severn estuary at the time that multiple 'dump' ramparts were being built are amply demonstrated by pottery and metalwork,[72] while the Llyn Cerrig Bach hoard shows that the contacts with Ireland were still being maintained in north-west Wales at this time.[73]

The Roman Period, c. AD 75–450

It might seem that the Roman period presents us with two comparable distributions of settlements directly related to land use, but it must be stressed that the picture in both areas is in fact far from complete. In lowland Glamorgan probably many more 'villas' of one kind or another remain to be discovered, while in Caernarfonshire it is probable that surface traces of many homesteads have been destroyed in fertile areas near the coast which have been cultivated in recent times.

In the Vale of Glamorgan it now seems that a small town at Cowbridge[74] served the numerous villas of the region, apparently having developed from the industrial suburb of a Roman fort, in which iron-working was carried on, exploiting, no doubt, the ores on the southern edge of the coal basin, as the Early Iron Age inhabitants of Mynydd Bychan fortified homestead had done earlier.[75] The villas (Fig. 40a and 40b) ranged from the *villa urbana* at Llantwit Major to modest establishments like Whitton which evolved slowly from a pre-Roman embanked farmstead with round-houses to one with simple stone-built rectangular buildings, while at Mynydd Bychan a similar settlement was abandoned early in the second century before being rebuilt in this way. Field systems related to the villas have not survived, apart from traces related to partially explored farmsteads within the great hill-fort near Llanfleiddan and at Dinas Powys. The sites are concentrated on the fertile, well-drained limestone-based soils south of the Roman road from Cardiff to Neath.[76]

In Caernarfonshire the contrasting picture probably depends not only on environmental conditions but the fact recorded by Tacitus, that the Ordovices were severely punished for their resistance to Agricola,[77] and the presence of permanent garrisons at Segontium and Kanovium.[78] The enclosed hut groups, of which several have been explored, seem in most cases to have been built no earlier than the second century AD. Although some small examples associated with walled fields which may have been largely pastoral in use could be prehistoric (though there is no associated find to support this),[79] the enclosures which contain up to five or six round huts suitable for an extended family group might be adaptations to local building materials of an Early Iron Age type. This type was commonly built of earth and timber in other parts of Wales, where it persisted into the Roman period (p. 167) and it may have been introduced to Caernarfonshire by peasants imported by the Romans. The word 'peasants' is used advisedly, for the attached fields (Fig. 41), in cases where a rough estimate can be made of their extent, cover from ten to twenty acres, like the holdings of many medieval villeins. Mixed farming seems to have been the normal activity at these homesteads, but the location of the terraced field systems seems to be definitely related to the most fertile and well-drained ('brown earth') land.[80]

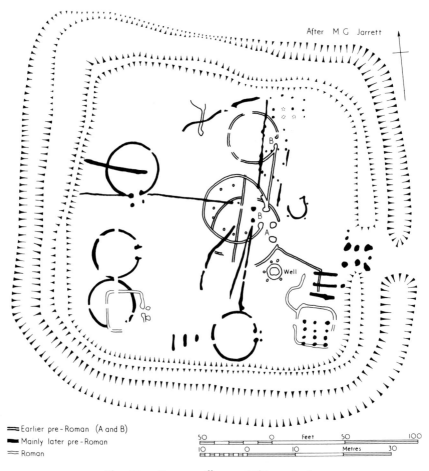

After M G Jarrett

Well

Earlier pre-Roman (A and B)
Mainly later pre-Roman
Roman

50   0   Feet   50   100
10   0   10   Metres   30

Fig. 40a   Roman villa near Whitton Lodge.

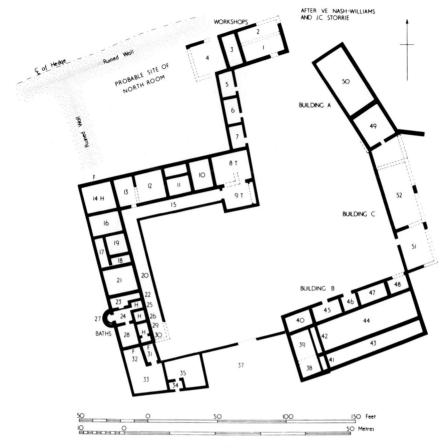

Fig. 40b Roman villa at Llantwit Major.

The Dark Ages, *c.* AD 450–1100

One difficulty in establishing the survival of Romano-British estates in the Dark Ages by archaeological means is that in Glamorgan, at least, it seems that most of the villas so far explored were abandoned soon after the middle of the fourth century,[81] possibly as a result of the severe raids made by the Picts and Scots at this time.[82] Similarly there is really very little evidence for activity at the enclosed hut groups of Caernarfonshire after the late fourth century, and the fort at Segontium seems to have needed repair as a consequence of the raids.[83] It is of course possible that activity on some Glamorgan villa estates was resumed in new, very likely wooden, buildings nearby, and there is more than a hint that this may have happened at Llantwit Major.[84] The fact remains, however, that the type of site which can definitely be dated by finds in the sixth or seventh century, in both areas, is a small chieftain's stronghold, in a remote or well-fortified position. It is at such sites — Dinas Powys in Glamorgan[85] and at Dinas Emrys and Degannwy in Caernarfonshire[86] that

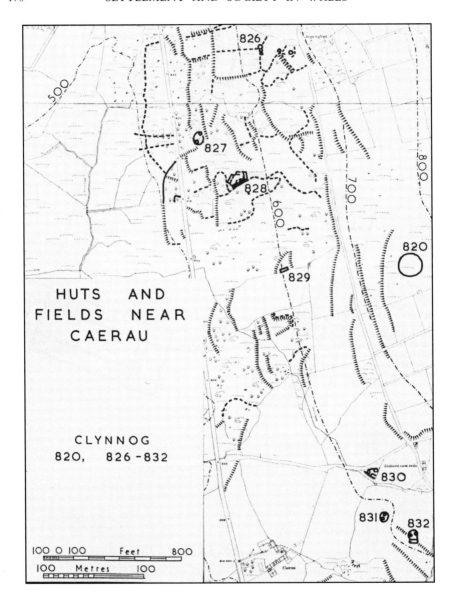

Fig. 41   Huts and fields near Caerau, Caernarfonshire.

'import ware' and ornamental metalwork of Irish or local manufacture appear and at Dinas Powys there is a hint that large numbers of succulent young pigs were being exacted from the local country folk.

The chieftains at Dinas Powys lived in timber-framed, rectangular and ridge-roofed buildings, of which only slight traces remained, and this seems to be in line with what happened elsewhere in sub-Roman Britain. What was really an ordinary Romano-British form of simple building, rendered no doubt in ordinary rough rural carpentry, finally replaced the round-house of ancient Celtic tradition. Even small peasant dwellings, like the one recently found at Glan-y-môr, Barry and dated by radio-carbon to the eighth or ninth century, seem to follow this pattern and to anticipate the long-houses with oblong plan and rounded corners found in Glamorgan at Mynydd Bychan, Barry and Rhosili.[87] In Caernarfonshire, too, it is likely that the long-house has its roots in the Dark Ages, even though many of the remains of simple dwellings of this type, the traces of which survive here and there on higher gound, sometimes with fields attached, are thought to be of much more recent date. In general, they represent scattered farms with holdings not very different in size from those of their predecessors, the Romano-British enclosed hut-groups.[88]

The Later Middle Ages, c. AD 1100–1500

The Norman manorialization of the most fertile parts of Glamorgan naturally has its reflection in open field systems which still survive, and can be studied in air photographs, notably at Rhosili in Gower;[89] others can be studied in old manorial maps.[90] In this area, too, the dwellings of the Welsh on the uplands stand out as a distinctive type — the 'platform dwelling', scattered singly or in pairs, occasionally in threes,[91] and in the lowlands a number of deserted or shrunken villages, sometimes with traces of field systems attached, have recently been studied.[92]

NOTES

[1] G.E. Daniel, *A Hundred Years of Archaeology* (1950).

[2] V.G. Childe, *Prehistoric Communities of the British Isles* (Edinburgh, 1940); T.D. Kendrick and C.F.C. Hawkes, *Archaeology in England and Wales, 1914–31* (1932); J.G.D. Clark, *Prehistoric England* (London, 1940); S. Piggott, *Neolithic Cultures of the British Isles* (Cambridge, 1954).

[3] C.F. Fox, *The Personality of Britain*, fourth ed. (reimp.) (Cardiff, 1959); F. Zeuner, *Dating the Past: an Introduction to Geochronology* (1958); P.J. Ucko and G.W. Dimbleby (eds.), *The Domestication and Exploitation of Plants and Animals* (1969); J.M. Renfrew, *Palaeoethnobotany* (1973).

[4] J.G. Evans, *The Environment of Early Man in the British Isles* (1975); M. Shackley, *Environmental Archaeology* (1981).

[5] M.J. Aitken, *Physics and Archaeology* (1961).

[6] O.G.S. Crawford and A. Keiller, *Wessex from the Air* (Oxford, 1928); P.J. Fowler (ed.), *Recent Work in Rural Archaeology* (1975); H.C. Bowen and P.J. Fowler (eds.), *Early Land Allotment*, B.A.R., 48 (Oxford, 1978); J.G. Evans, S. Limbrey and H. Cleere (eds.), *The Effect of Man on the Landscape in the Highland Zone*, C.B.A. Research Report, II, (1975).

[7] D.Q. Bowen, 'The Pleistocene Scenario of Palaeolithic Wales', and R.M. Jacobi, 'The Upper Palaeolithic in Britain, with Special Reference to Wales', in J.A. Taylor (ed.), *Culture and Environment in Prehistoric Wales*, B.A.R., British Series, 76, (Oxford, 1980), 1–14 and 15–59 respectively. For a preliminary report on the excavations by Dr H.S. Green in the Cefn (Clwyd) caves, see H.S. Green (ed.), *Pontnewydd Cave — A Lower Palaeolithic Hominid Site in Wales* (Cardiff, 1984). It should be borne in mind that radio-carbon dates (cited as 'bc.') may differ considerably from approximate 'calendar' dates (cited as BC) and that scientists have not so far agreed on a standard system for correcting the former.

[8] J.A. Taylor, 'Environmental Changes in Wales during the Holocene Period' and R.M. Jacobi, 'The

Early Holocene Settlements of Wales', in Taylor, *Culture and Environment*, 101–30 and 131–206 respectively.

[9] C.F. Fox, op. cit.

[10] H.N. Savory, 'The Neolithic in Wales' in Taylor, *Culture and Environment*, 207–32, updated by C. Smith and F. Lynch, *Trefignath and Hen Dryfol*, and W. Britnell and H.N. Savory, *Gwernvale and Penywyrlod* (of which only the latter has so far appeared, *Cambrian Archaeological Monographs* No. 2 (1984)).

[11] P. Dixon, 'Crickley Hill', *Current Archaeology*, No. 76 (1981), 145f.

[12] P.D. Moore, 'The Influence of Prehistoric Cultures upon the Initiation and Spread of Blanket Bog in Upland Wales', *Nature*, 241, No. 5388, 350–3.

[13] C. Burgess, *The Age of Stonehenge* (London, 1980); A. Burl, *The Stone Circles of the British Isles*, (1976); I.F. Smith, 'The Neolithic' in C. Renfrew (ed.), *British Prehistory* (1974), 100–36.

[14] C. Burgess, 'The Bronze Age in Wales', in Taylor, *Culture and Environment*, 243–78.

[15] C. Burgess, *Age of Stonehenge*, 52–61, 165–8 and 235–7; H.N. Savory, *Guide Catalogue of the Bronze Age Collections* (Cardiff, 1980), 15–23.

[16] *Archaeology in Wales* (C.B.A. Group II), 22 (1982), No. 3.

[17] J.P. Northover, 'The Analysis of Welsh Bronze Age Metalwork' in H.N. Savory, *Guide Catalogue of the Bronze Age Collections*, 229–36; and C. Burgess and J.P. Northover, *Bronze Age Metallurgy in Wales* (to be published).

[18] J.G. Evans, *Environment of Early Man.*, 147–9; and Taylor, *Culture and Environment*, 125–7.

[19] *Ordnance Survey Map of Southern Britain in the Early Iron Age* (Chessington, 1962).

[20] *Antiquity* (1947), 122, and Willoughby Gardner and H.N. Savory, *Dinorben, a Hill-fort Occupied in Early Iron Age and Roman Times* (Cardiff, 1964), 222–5.

[21] H.N. Savory, 'Welsh Hillforts: a Reappraisal of Recent Research', in D.W. Harding (ed.), *Hillforts* (1976), 238–93.

[22] S.C. Stanford, *Croft Ambrey* (Hereford, 1974).

[23] C.R. Musson, 'Excavations at the Breiddin, 1969–73', in Harding, *Hillforts*, 293–302.

[24] G.C. Guilbert, 'Moel y Gaer (Rhosesmor), 1972–3: an Area Excavation in the Interior', in Harding, *Hillforts*, 303–17, and 'Planned Hillfort Interiors', *Proc. Pre. Soc.*, (1975), 203–21.

[25] Savory, *Welsh Hillforts*, 250f. and Burgess, 'The Bronze Age' in Taylor, *Culture and Environment*, 270–3.

[26] G. Guilbert, 'Llanstephan Castle, 1973 Interim Report', *Carms. Antiq.*, 10 (1974), 37–48.

[27] *Arch. in Wales*, 19 (1979), No. 95; 20 (1980), No. 37; 21 (1981), Nos. 46–8; 22 (1982), No. 26.

[28] B. Cunliffe, 'Danebury, Hampshire: Second Interim Report on the Excavations 1971–5', *Antiquaries Journal*, (1976), 198–216; 'Third Interim Report', (1981), 238–54'.

[29] Savory, *Welsh Hillforts*, 276f., Figure 13; *Arch. in Wales*, 22 (1982).

[30] H.N. Savory, 'Some Late Bronze Age Hoards — Old and New', *Archaeologia Atlantica*, I (ii) (1975), iii-25; ibid, 'The Late Bronze Age in Wales: Some new discoveries and new interpretations', *A.C.*, CVII (1958), 3–63.

[31] C.F.C. Hawkes, 'Cumulative Celticity in Pre-Roman Britain', *Études Celtiques*, 13, (2), 590–611.

[32] H.N. Savory, *Welsh Hillforts*, 279–82.

[33] M.G. Jarrett (ed.), *The Roman Frontier in Wales* (Cardiff, 1969), with summaries of subsequent work annually to date in *Archaeology in Wales*.

[34] For Caerwent see J. Wacher, *The Towns of Roman Britain* (1974); for Carmarthen, see J. Wacher, ibid., 389–93, and *Arch. in Wales*, (1980); No. 41; (1981), No. 51; and (1982), No. 30; for Cowbridge, see Glamorgan-Gwent Archaeological Trust *Annual Report* (1977–8), 17–21, (1980–1), 15–26, (1981–2), 7–21, (1982–3), 14–30, and (1983–4), 59–65.

[35] H. James and G. Williams, 'Roman Settlements in Roman Dyfed', in D. Miles (ed.), *The Romano-British Countryside: Studies in Rural Settlements and Economy*, B.A.R., British Series, 103 (ii), (1982), 289–312; H.C. Mytum, 'Rural Settlement of the Roman Period in North and East Wales, ibid., 313–35.

[36] See n.34 for reference to recent work on Caerwent and Carmarthen.

[37] V.E. Nash-Williams, *Early Christian Monuments of Wales* (Cardiff, 1950), Nos. 103 and 126.

[38] Savory, *Welsh Hillforts*, 282–90.

[39] For the social ranking of Roman villas, see P. Salway, *Roman Britain* (Oxford, 1981), 601–6; J.T. Smith 'Villas as a Key Social Structure', in E.M. Todd (ed.), *Studies in the Romano-British Villa* (Leicester, 1978), 149–85.

[40] E.g. Skomer (Pembs.), *A.C.*, CI (1950), 1–20.

[41] Gardner and Savory, *Dinorben*, 66–72, 103–7.

[42] A. Fox, 'Early Christian Period', in Cambrian Archaeological Association, *A Hundred Years of Welsh Archaeology* (Gloucester, 1946), 105–28; L. Alcock, *Arthur's Britain* (Harmondsworth, 1971).

[43] L. Alcock, *By South Cadbury is that Camelot* (London, 1972); P.J. Fowler et al. *Cadbury Congresbury, Somerset, 1968* (Bristol, 1970); I. Burrow, *Hillfort and Hill-top Settlement in Somerset in the First to Eighth Centuries A.D.*, B.A.R., British Series, 91, (1981).

[44] Wacher, *The Towns of Roman Britain*, 389.

[45] J.L. Davies, D.B. Hague and A.H.A. Hogg, 'The Hut-settlement on Gateholm, Pembrokeshire', *A.C.*, CXX (1971), 102–10.

[46] W. Davies, 'Roman Settlements and Post-Roman Estates in south-east Wales', in P.J. Casey (ed.), *The End of Roman Britain*, B.A.R. 71, (1979), 153–73.

[47] Alcock, *Arthur's Britain*.

[48] H.N. Savory (ed.), *Glamorgan County History* II (Cardiff, 1984).

[49] Jacoby, 'Upper Palaeolithic' in Taylor, *Culture and Environment*, 50.

[50] Savory, *G.C.H.*; Jacoby, 'Early Holocene' in Taylor, *Culture and Environment*.

[51] P. Evans, 'The Intimate Relationship: an Hypothesis concerning pre-Neolithic Land Use', in J.G. Evans, S. Limbrey and H. Cleere, (eds.) *The Effect of Man on the Landscape in the Highland Zone*, CBA Research Report II (1975), 43–8.

[52] Savory, 'The Neolithic in Wales', in Taylor, *Culture and Environment*, and D.P. Webley, 'How the West was Won: Prehistoric Land Use in the southern Marches', in G.C. Boon and J.M. Lewis (eds.), *Welsh Antiquity* (Cardiff, 1976), 19–35.

[53] Savory in Taylor, *Culture and Environment*; F. Lynch, 'The Megalithic Tombs of North Wales', in T.G.E. Powell (ed.), *Megalithic Enquiries in the West of Britain* (Liverpool, 1969); R.C.A.H.M, *An Inventory of the Ancient Monuments in Caernarvonshire*, [Caern. Inv.] 3 vols., (1956–64); R.C.A.H.M., *An Inventory of the Ancient Monuments in Glamorgan*, [Glam. Inv.] I, Pt. 1, (1976).

[54] W.A. Cummins, 'Stone Axes as a Guide to Neolithic Communications' in *Proc. Pre. Soc.*, 46 (1980), 45–60.

[55] C.H. Houlder, 'Stone Axes and Henge-Monuments', in G. Boon and J.M. Lewis *Welsh Antiquity*, 55–62. For an air photograph see J.K.S. St. Joseph, 'Aerial Reconnaissance in Wales' *Antiquity*, (1961), 263–75, Plate xxxv. H.N. Savory, *Guide Catalogue of the Bronze Age Collections*, no. 103.

[56] H.N. Savory, *Guide Catalogue of the Bronze Age Collections*, no. 103.

[57] R.B. White, 'Rhosgoch to Stanlow Shell Oil Pipeline: Archaeological Work carried out on behalf of the Department of the Environment on the Anglesey Section of the Pipeline in the summers of 1973 and 1974', *B.B.C.S.*, XXVII (iii), (1977), 470–6.

[58] C.H. Houlder, *Welsh Antiquity*, 59.

[59] W.E. Griffiths, 'Excavation of Stone Circles near Penmaen-mawr, North Wales', *Proc. Pre. Soc.*, (1960), 305–39.

[60] *Glam. Inv.* I, Pt. 2, Nos. 711–15; *Caern Inv.* III, xcii–v.

[61] H.N. Savory, 'The Excavation of a Bronze Age Cairn at Saint-y-nyll, St Brides super-Ely (Glam.)', in *T. Cardiff Nat. Soc.*, (1959–60), 9–30, and 'Copper Age Cists and Cist Cairns in Wales: with special reference to Newton, Swansea and other 'Multiple-cist' cairns in F. Lynch and C. Burgess (eds.), *Prehistoric Man in Wales and the West* (Bath, 1972), 117–39.

[62] C.F. Fox, 'Two Bronze Age Cairns in South Wales: Simondston and Pond Cairns, Coity Higher Parish, Bridgend', *Archaeologia*, LXXXVII (1938), 129–80.

[63] W.F. Grimes, 'A Barrow on Breach Farm, Glamorgan', *Proc. Pre. Soc.*, (1938), 107–21.

[64] Savory, *Guide Catalogue of the Bronze Age Collections*, Nos. 505–6, fig. 72.

[65] Glamorgan-Gwent Archaeological Trust, *Annual Report* (1979–80), 12–15; *Arch. in Wales*, (1980), No. 19.

[66] J.P. Northover and C.B. Burgess, *Bronze Age Metallurgy* (to be published); Savory, *Guide Catalogue of the Bronze Age Collections*, 49.

[67] Savory, *Welsh Hillforts*, 271–82.

[68] C.B. Burgess, 'The Bronze Age in Wales', in Taylor, *Culture and Environment*, 272, fig. 7.2.

[69] *Caern. Inv.* III, lxx–xxx1; and Savory, *Welsh Hillforts*, 267–71.

[70] H.N. Savory, 'An Early Iron Age Metalworker's Hoard from Worm's Head, *A.C.*, CXXIII (1974), 170–4.

[71] G.C. Boon, 'A Graeco-Roman Anchor-stock from North Wales', *Archaeologia Atlantica*, 1(2) (1975), 195–9.

[72] Savory, 'Welsh Hillforts: a Reappraisal of Recent Research' in D.W. Harding (ed.), *Hillforts* (London, 1976), 279–82.

[73] H.N. Savory, *Guide to the Early Iron Age Collections* (Cardiff, 1976), Nos. 17–22, Figs. 13–30.

[74] Glamorgan-Gwent Archaeological Trust, *Annual Report* (1977–8), 17–21; (1980–1), 15–21; (1981–2), 7–21; and (1982–3), 14–30.

[75] H.N. Savory, 'The Excavation of an Early Iron Age Fortified Settlement on Mynydd Bychan, Llysworney (Glam.)', *A.C.*, CIII (1954), 84–108; and CIV (1955), 14–51.

[76] P.V. Webster, 'The Roman Period', in *G.C.H.* II (1984). For Caer Ddynnaf, Llanfleiddan see *Glam. Inv.* I, (Pt. 2), No. 670 and frontispiece (air photograph). For Dinas Powys see *Arch. in Wales*, (1978), No. 64.

[77] Tacitus, *Agricola*, 18, 'Caesaque prope universa gente'.

[78] *Caern. Inv.*, III, lxxxi–vi.

[79] The 'VCP' pottery used by C.A. Smith (see n. 80 below) to suggest that the enclosed hut group at Pant-y-saer, Anglesey is of pre-Roman origin, is not securely stratified.

[80] *Caern. Inv.*, xcvii–cvii; C.A. Smith, 'A Morphological Analysis of Late Prehistoric and Romano-British Settlements in North-west Wales', *Proc. Pre. Soc.* (1974), 157–69; idem, 'Late Prehistoric and Romano-British Homesteads in North-west Wales', *A.C.*, CXXVI (1977), 38–52; and N.D. Johnson, 'The location of Rural Settlement in Pre-Medieval Caernarvonshire', *B.B.C.S.*, XXIX (1981), 381–417; and H.C. Mytum, *Romano-British Countryside*.

[81] P.V. Webster in *G.C.H.* II (1984).

[82] R.G. Collingwood and J.N.L. Myres, *Roman Britain and the English Settlements* (1937), 284–6.

[83] G.C. Boon, *Caernarvon-Segontium* (Cardiff, 1974).

[84] *Glam. Inv.*, No. 758.

[85] L. Alcock, *Dinas Powys: An Iron Age, Dark Age and Early Medieval Settlement in Glamorgan* (Cardiff, 1963). For a review of the present state of knowledge of Dark Age Glamorgan see J.K. Knight in *G.C.H.* II (1984), chs. VIII and IX.

[86] H.N. Savory, 'Excavations at Dinas Emrys, Beddgelert (Caern.), 1954–6', *A.C.*, CIX (1960), 13–77; L. Alcock, 'Excavations at Degannwy Castle, Caernarvonshire, 1961–6', *Arch. Journ.*, (1967), 190–201.

[87] D.M. Robinson, 'Medieval Vernacular Buildings below the Ground: a Review and Corpus for South-east Wales' in Glamorgan-Gwent Archaeological Trust, *Annual Report* (1981–2), 94–123.

[88] *Caern. Inv.* III, (Pt. 2), clxxviii–ix.

[89] *Glam. Inv.* III, (Pt. 2), 307.

[90] M. Davies, 'Field Patterns in the Vale of Glamorgan', *T. Cardiff Nat. Soc.*, (1954–5), 5–14.

[91] *Glam. Inv.*, III, (Pt. 2), 17–42.

[92] Ibid., 219–43.

The Dark Ages

GLANVILLE R. J. JONES

THE task of re-creating a picture of settlement and society in Dark Age Wales is fraught with difficulty for the strictly contemporary sources are so few and fragmentary. The fullest testimony for early social organization and the various kinds of associated early settlements is that presented, albeit in indirect form, in medieval redactions of customary law.[1] Of these, even the oldest extant text of Welsh law can be dated no earlier than the thirteenth century and is therefore much later than the reign of Hywel Dda (*ob. c.*950) to whom is attributed the assembling and clarification of then existing customary practice. Some part of this practice must have had an ancient application but the problem is to determine which part of the older strata of Welsh law can be ascribed to an earlier period. Fortunately this can be determined to some extent from the contents of the lawbooks themselves. Moreover, although they are few in number, there are some strictly contemporary sources which provide confirmation that the highly stratified society and the stable territorial organization portrayed in the lawbooks were old established.

Among these strictly contemporary sources are some five charters written into the margins of *Llyfr Teilo* (The Book of Teilo) during the ninth or tenth centuries.[2] To these can be added the 149 charters contained in the twelfth-century *Liber Landavensis* (The Book of Llandaff), but which refer to land grants made to the Church from the early seventh century onwards,[3] and also the fourteen charters which although appended to the *Vita Cadoci* (The Life of Cadog) in a manuscript of *c.*1200 appear to relate to the seventh and eighth centuries.[4] The survival in many cases of the place-names in these charters permits the location of the land to which they refer. At the close of the Dark Ages, Domesday Book provides a survey of fiefs and of fiscal obligations, but only for parts of the borders of Wales is information given in detail.[5] Some slight, but nevertheless significant, further written testimony is provided in the *De Excidio Britanniae* (The Ruin of Britain), largely a work of moral exhortation written by Gildas in the sixth century,[6] and in the *Historia Brittonum* (The History of the Britons),[7] a compilation put together in 829.[7] This can be supplemented by information derived from the *Annales Cambriae* (The Welsh Annals) compiled from the late eighth century onwards and the royal genealogies, whose originals were probably put together in the tenth century.[8] Early poetry also provides a tenuous strand of information which can be used as evidence from the ninth century onwards.[9] To this testimony can be added the evidence of material remains as provided by archaeological excavation, and by the classification of the so-called early Christian monuments.[10] Yet, even when assembled, the record of all these strictly contemporary written and material sources is so fragmentary that it is best viewed in terms of the models of territorial organization presented in the medieval lawbooks.

According to the very schematic and obviously idealized model of territorial organization presented in the texts of *Llyfr Iorwerth* (The Book of Iorwerth), which relate to Gwynedd, there were fifty vills (*trefi*) in every commote or half-hundred.[11] These vills or townships were small rural districts, the real units for working the land. Pride of place was accorded to the two vills reserved for the use of the king: one was the *maerdref* or vill of the reeve, which contained the mensal land cultivated in the main by the bondmen of the reeve's vill for the sustenance of the royal court (*llys*); the other was the king's distant summer pasture land (*hafod-tir*). The remaining forty-eight vills were ascribed to twelve *maenolydd* each containing four vills. Each *maenol* therefore contained a multiplicity of settlements and formed a small multiple-estate. One *maenol* of four vills was held by the greater reeve in return for his services to the king and a second *maenol* was held by the king's bailiff. Six *maenolydd* were held by free notables in return for military service and an annual food-rent (*gwestfa*). The remaining four *maenolydd* were held by the king's bondmen who, in return, owed more onerous services such as construction of the various buildings of the royal court, assistance with the cultivation of the royal demesnes, and the donation of a food-gift (*dawnbwyd*) twice every year.

In this well-articulated organization the food-rent obtained from the free *maenol* had consisted originally of the produce of both arable and pastoral farming, loaves, flour, mead, bragget or ale, and oat sheaves as well as the carcass of an ox or a cow, a pig, a salted flitch and butter. Likewise the food-gifts of the bondmen were made up of the produce of mixed farming.[12]

In the free *maenol* the vill (*tref*) was envisaged as comprising four holdings each with a homestead site (*tyddyn*) of four *erwau* (small acres), and arable land amounting to sixty *erwau* lying in four sharelands. These very notional dispositions applied to hereditary land in which equal shares in the patrimony (*tref tad*) were inherited by brothers on their father's death.[13] Thus each heir acquired rights in arable land to which further rights over pasture were appurtenant. The rules governing these inheritance customs presuppose a long antecedent occupancy of land. Thus provision was made under certain conditions for the re-partition of rights in land among all the surviving male descendants of a common great-grandfather or in other words a four-generation inheritance group of close relatives. At an earlier date therefore such hereditary land had been shared by the members of a four-generation inheritance group.[14] As Gerald of Wales reported, such sharing had been displaced long before 1188 by equal division among brothers,[15] with the result that the kindred was no longer split, as hitherto, with the passage of each generation. Instead the kindred increased in size with each new generation and typically had grown into a large lineage, or expanding descent group. The term *gwely*, originally used of a bed, came to mean a marriage bed, and hence probably ancestors; but it came to be used of a lineage, or segment of a lineage, and ultimately of the joint holding of the expanding descent group, in the sense of its permanent stake in the soil. Nevertheless, the notion that each heir had originally held at least a standard holding (*gafael*) is implied by the schematized disposition of holdings in the *tref* (vill). That the size of such standard holdings, however notional, was necessarily changed with growth in population over time is indicated by the statement in the Book of Iorwerth that Bleddyn ap Cynfyn (*ob.* 1075) changed the allocation of *erwau* to the *tyddyn* (homestead).[16]

In addition there was nucleal land (*tir corddlan*), apparently a variant of hereditary land which, according to the Book of Iorwerth, was 'not to be shared as homesteads, but as gardens'.[17] These gardens appear to have been small strips or quillets of land arranged in radial fashion, like the petals of a flower, around some kind of nucleus. Although such nucleal land typically appears to have formed part of the possessions of the members of a free kindred, it was usually occupied by their undertenants. Such possessions had earlier included what were described as the three ornaments of a kindred (*tri thlws cenedl*), namely a mill, a weir and an orchard.[18] As ornaments these were not to be divided but instead their produce was to be shared between those with a right to it. Later, after equal division among brothers was adopted, such ornaments of a kindred came to be in common among brothers. Even a church could be a possession in common among brothers and thus some nucleal lands consisted of *erw* (acre) strips disposed radially around churchyards.[19]

A third kind of land, which appears to have been characteristic of the vills of the bond *maenol* as recorded in the Book of Iorwerth, was reckoned land (*tir cyfrif*). This land, held by bondmen, was to be shared equally among all the adult males of the vill, irrespective of lineage, with the shares being allocated by the greater reeve and the king's bailiff. In return the bondmen owed to the king joint obligations and communal renders which did not vary whether the bond tenants were few or many.[20] Similarly the bond tenants of the *maerdref* (reeve's vill) held equal shares of reckoned land in return for joint obligations and communal renders, but their shares were allocated to them by the lesser reeve.

The models of territorial organization presented in the lawbooks which relate to south Wales were much less elaborate. According to *Llyfr Cyfnerth* (The Book of Cyfnerth), which perhaps contains some of the most original expressions of the laws co-ordinated by Hywel Dda, there were two kinds of estates.[21] On the one hand there was a *maenol* of seven vills and, on the other, a *maenor*, seemingly occupied by notables, which embraced thirteen vills. *Llyfr Blegywryd* (The Book of Blegywryd), attributed to *c*.1300, records that there were seven vills in the lowland estate (*maenor fro*) and thirteen vills in the upland estate (*maenor wrthtir*), but the same lawbook also refers to a group of vills known as *maerdrefi y llys* (the reeve's vills of the court).[22]

Within both the larger and the smaller *maenor* of the south-Welsh lawbooks, lesser territorial subdivisions were envisaged. Thus, according to the Book of Cyfnerth there were four sharelands (*rhandiroedd*) within each free *tref* (vill) and three sharelands within each bond *tref*. Each shareland (*rhandir*) contained 312 acres (*erwau*), 'between clear and brake, and wood and field, and wet and dry'.[23] To judge from the stipulated width of the boundary between two sharelands the foot on which the eighteen-foot rod of Hywel Dda was based contained only nine inches.[24] Thus the acre of the Book of Cyfnerth, measuring eighteen such rods in length by two rods in breadth, contained only 729 statute square yards, so that the shareland of 312 acres would have contained slightly less than 47 statute acres. According to the Book of Blegywryd, in the lawful shareland (*rhandir*) of 312 acres the owner could have 'arable, pasture and fire-wood' in the 300 acres and 'space for buildings' on the 12 acres.[25] Since the acre of the Book of Blegywryd appears to have contained only 512 statute square yards the 300 acres devoted to arable, pasture and fire-wood would have covered slightly less than 32 statute acres, and the 12 acres for buildings

$1\frac{1}{4}$ statute acres. Thus on the area reserved for building in this shareland, or standard holding, there was room enough to accommodate not only the dwelling of the proprietor but also the houses of his undertenants. With the larger acre recorded in Latin Redaction B, a law-text of the mid thirteenth century, the space for buildings would have embraced nearly $2\frac{1}{2}$ statute acres and the 300 acres, for arable, pasture and fire-wood, precisely 60 statute acres.[26]

According to the Book of Cyfnerth, of the four sharelands in the free *tref* (vill), three were for occupancy and the fourth was pasture for the three. From such a *tref* the king was to receive a food-rent (*gwestfa*) similar to that recorded as being due from the free *maenol* of the Book of Iorwerth, but including a vat of honey instead of butter and omitting the pig as well as the salted flitch.[27] In the three sharelands of the bond *tref* there were said to be three bondmen in each of two sharelands and the third was pasturage for the two. From these bondmen the king received two food-gifts, one in winter consisting largely of arable produce, and one in summer consisting almost entirely of pastoral produce.[28]

Different arrangements were recorded in Latin Redaction A, another text of the mid thirteenth century, so that the full *maenor* was said to contain seven 'portions (*particulae*) that is *rantyr*' but each portion appears to have been the equivalent of a free *tref* (vill), for from each portion the food-rent consisted of loaves, cheeses, a vessel (*ryschen*) of butter, and a cask of beer containing four *modii*. The land of a *modius*, however, was said to contain 312 acres in which the possessor had 300 acres for arable, pasture and fire-wood, and 12 acres for buildings.[29] In other words, the land of a *modius* matched exactly the shareland (*rhandir*) of the Book of Blegywryd and other south-Welsh lawbooks. The acres involved, however, were slightly larger than those recorded elsewhere so that the 300 acres embraced $67\frac{1}{4}$ statute acres.[30]

The kinds of territorial organization envisaged in the models presented in the medieval lawbooks appear to have been old established. Yet the model presented in the south-Welsh lawbooks appears to relate to an earlier phase than that envisaged for north Wales in the Book of Iorwerth, hence the smaller size of the *maenol* in north Wales with only four vills as compared with the *maenorydd* of seven or thirteen vills in south Wales. Not surprisingly therefore there was some uncertainty about the make-up of the *maenor* on the part of the redactor of Latin Redaction D, a law-text of *c*.1300. Thus immediately after stating that there 'are seven sharelands in a *maenor*' the redactor adds 'Others say that a full *maenor* contains 13 vills, that is in the uplands (*yn gwrthir*)'.[31]

Long before the oldest extant texts of Welsh medieval law were committed to writing such groups of vills were already in being. Thus, according to Domesday Book, in Gwent where Welshmen were recorded as 'living under Welsh law' there were in 1086 four distinct groups of vills under the control of four different Welsh reeves.[32] Appropriately enough two of these groups comprised thirteen vills, but the other two comprised fourteen vills. A remaining group, which earlier had apparently comprised fourteen vills, was by 1086 subdivided so that, for example, three vills were held by Berddig the poet, two vills were held by the Archdeacon of Gwent, single vills were held by individuals and one vill, said to be in the alms of the king, rendered to the church '2 pigs, 100 loaves and beer'. Moreover, another group of seven demesne vills recorded for Gwent in Domesday Book is known to have existed in 1075.[33]

Again, in Ystrad Alun near the north-eastern border of Wales, the estate of Bistre in 1086 embraced thirteen vills. This extended from the floor of Moldsdale on to the flanking hills. Yet, the Domesday Survey records that within the thirteen constituent vills there was land for only seven ploughs. According to Domesday Book in this 'same manor' King Gruffudd ap Llywelyn of Gwynedd (*ob.* 1063) 'had 1 plough in demesne and his men 6 ploughs'; and 'when the said king came thither every plough rendered him 200 *hesthas* [*sic*], and a vat (*cuvam*) full of beer and a vessel (*ruscam*) of butter',[34] a food-rent which compares with that obtained from each of the seven portions of a full *maenor* as recorded in Latin Redaction A.

Much earlier, in the ninth century, a marginal entry in the Book of Teilo records the existence of one *maenor*, that of Meddyfnych in Dyfed,[35] but the Book of Llandaff records the existence of no less than twelve *maenorau* in various parts of south Wales from the western bank of the Wye to western Dyfed, and for dates extending from the early seventh to the late eleventh century.[36] It is especially significant that the charters incorporated into the Book of Llandaff should reveal that the dimensions of the vills granted to the Church were closely in accord with those described in the south-Welsh lawbooks. For ninety-two land grants recorded in the Llandaff charters measurements were given, either in *modii* of land or in larger units called *unciae* said to contain twelve *modii*. Of the sixty-nine grants recorded in *modii* of land at least 57 per cent were for three *modii* and a further 14 per cent were for multiples of three *modii*. On the other hand, only 14 per cent of these land grants were for four *modii*, and there were no multiples of four *modii*. As we have seen, according to Latin Redaction A, the land of a *modius* contained 312 acres, that is the exact equivalent of a shareland as recorded in the south-Welsh lawbooks; and there were said to be three such sharelands in a bond vill. A majority of the measured land grants recorded in the Book of Llandaff were therefore bond vills of precisely the dimensions recorded in the south-Welsh lawbooks. Among them was the grant, made to the Church *c.*765, by a notable, of three *modii* of land at *Dinbirrion* in Gwent; and appropriately enough a charter appended to The Life of Cadog reveals that the donor, who gave himself to the Church with this same land at *Lisdin Borrion*, was to receive from it annually 'six *modii* of beer with bread and flesh and honey'.[37] Evidently, since the land grants measured in *modii* of land in the Llandaff charters appear to have been made as early as the seventh century, the kinds of territorial arrangements portrayed in the medieval lawbooks had long been in being.

Even more old established were the royal courts which figure in the jurists' models. Already in the mid sixth century, as Gildas indicates, Maelgwn had a royal court in his kingdom of Gwynedd. According to the Welsh Annals, it was at *Llys Rhos* that Maelgwn died of the plague in 547.[38] This court was probably located at the vill of Dinorben Fawr in Rhos Isdulas, at a site near Fardre (*maerdref*), some half-a-mile south-west of Dinorben hill-fort.[39]

The lawbooks, besides portraying the general features of territorial organization, yield evidence about the nature of settlement forms and patterns. As might be expected the fullest information was provided for the king's court (*llys*), albeit in an over-schematized fashion. This king's court in each commote comprised a group of separate buildings within the enclosing wall of the court. They included the king's hall, his chamber, the chapel, the refectory, the queen's chamber, the stable, a gatehouse which doubled as a prison, and some other lesser structures.[40] There was, however, ambiguity in the lawbooks about the name and thus the function of one of these structures; this was known variously in different texts as the *cyfordy*, the *cynordy*, or the *cynhordy*, referring respectively to the brew-house, the kennel, or the porch-house.[41] In itself this ambiguity implies that the complex of buildings in the court had long been established by the time the lawbooks were written.

The archaic material in the section of the lawbooks dealing with 'the laws of the court' also refers to the lodgings of the king's officers and servants when on circuit. Thus in the settlement which contained the *llys* the presence of other dwellings is recorded. The steward (*distain*) was to share the lodgings, allocating 'to himself the nearest to the court and all the officers with him'. The head of the household troop 'lodged in the largest and most central house (*tŷ*) in the *tref*' for, apart from those of the troop he chose to be with him, the remainder were to stay around his lodging. With the head of the household dwelt the bard of the troop and also the physician; but the priest of the troop, with the king's clerks and the queen's priest lodged in the house of the chaplain.[42]

Outside the court too were the king's barn and his kiln. These, according to one variant of The Book of Iorwerth, were to be erected 'on the *maerdref*' by the bondmen who apparently lived in the hamlet called the *maerdref* which adjoined the king's court.[43] Close at hand was the king's barn in which, when on circuit, the head falconer lodged 'in case his birds should catch the smoke'. In the house (*tŷ*) nearest this barn lodged the head-groom and with him the groom of the queen. On the other hand, in order to counter hazards from fire the king's kiln was at some little distance from the hamlet, yet it was here that the head-houndsman lodged, presumably in the kiln-house.[44] Clearly therefore the *tref* in every commote which contained the king's court was a composite and fairly substantial settlement, probably a village.

The emphasis placed on fire hazards in even the earliest lawbooks indicates that there were other old-established nucleations of settlement. Thus no compensation was paid for fire damage caused by the smithy of a hamlet (*trefgordd*) if the smithy were nine paces, or more, distant from the settlement and roofed with broom or turves. The same applied to damage caused by the fire used for heating in the hamlet bath-house or washing-place.[45] A typical nucleation, recorded in a later law-text, was the hamlet of nine houses, whose complement was one plough, one kiln, one churn, one cat, one cock, one bull, and one herdsman. This indicates a strictly communal agrarian organization appropriate for reckoned-land (*tir cyfrif*) whether in a bond vill (*tref gyfrif*), or, as one law-text indicates, in a shareland (*rhandir*).[46]

On nucleal land (*tir corddlan*) there were other, probably smaller, clusters of dwellings occupied by the undertenants of more substantial proprietors. Some of these substantial proprietors no doubt dwelt in the small nuclei but more frequently they appear to have occupied outlying homesteads. According to the lawbooks the permanent residence of the typical free notable was a substantial cruck-built hall with an attached chamber. Associated with this dwelling were a number of outhouses, among them a barn, a kiln, a cow-house, a pigsty and a sheep-cote. In addition the notable might have two temporary and much less substantial, dwellings, a summer-house (*hafty*) and an autumn-house (*cynhafty*).[47] The summer-house was located on summer pasture and the autumn-house probably in woodland, but the hall with its outhouses was sited near arable land. The hall might well be placed towards the corner of a homestead site (*tyddyn*), thereby affording opportunities for the accommodation of heirs who wished to establish their dwellings near the parental homestead in the old settlement (*hendref*). Many heirs would have wished to live there not solely for reasons of sentiment but also because the *hendref* was sited near the very best land for cultivation within the vill. Hence the emergence characteristically of a loose patrilocal cluster of dwellings and outhouses at the *hendref*. With shared inheritance in the four-generation group such clusters are particularly likely to have developed, but even at that stage the physical limits to settlement expansion would soon have been attained and subsidiary clusters would have been established at a distance from the *hendref*. When equal division among brothers was adopted most heirs, save the youngest in any family, appear to have established their dwellings away from the *hendref*. They sited these dwellings on the peripheries of arable sharelands so as to economize on increasingly scarce resources of crop land; hence the development of what may be described as girdle patterns of homesteads with each girdle of homesteads flexibly adapted, as it were, to the contour.[48] It was for these reasons that a later law-text states that 'every habitation ought to have two footpaths: one to its church and one to its watering place'; and likewise 'every habitation ought to have a by-road to the common waste of the vill', the width of the by-road being seven feet.[49]

When bondmen became proprietors of hereditary land similar settlements developed. Among them were aliens who could become proprietors in the fourth generation after they had been settled on the waste belonging to the king or to notables. Such aliens, after they had become proprietors, were to have 'their homesteads (*tyddynnod*) on the land, and land to them also; and their land, excepting such, to be land of plough-share and coulter between them'.[50] These rules indicate that, over time, others could gain the same rights to arable land as freemen; and they also suggest that the bond undertenant could acquire his homestead (*tyddyn*), the site of his hall and outhouses only in the fourth generation. By so doing they provide a pointer to the process whereby a girdle pattern of homesteads could be established in place of a smaller nucleal settlement.

ABERFFRAW

Of all the kinds of settlements portrayed in the lawbooks by far the most significant were those associated with royal courts. Paramount among these was Aberffraw in Anglesey, the traditional principal seat of Gwynedd and, as early verse suggests, already a royal court by the early seventh century, if not much earlier.[51] It is fortunate therefore that at Aberffraw there remain to this day clear vestiges of the kinds of settlements associated with the king's court, the *maerdref* and the *gwelyau* of court officers (Fig. 42).[52] Occupying gently rising ground by the tidal estuary of the Ffraw, at the lowest point for fording this river, yet not easily visible from the sea, the site of Aberffraw was favoured for early settlement; for here too, close at hand, were extensive areas of readily cultivable land, among them, in the area extending to Pen y Maes (The Head of the Open-Field), the former arable open-field of Maes y Maerdref (The Open-Field of the Reeve's Vill). The court (*llys*) of Aberffraw

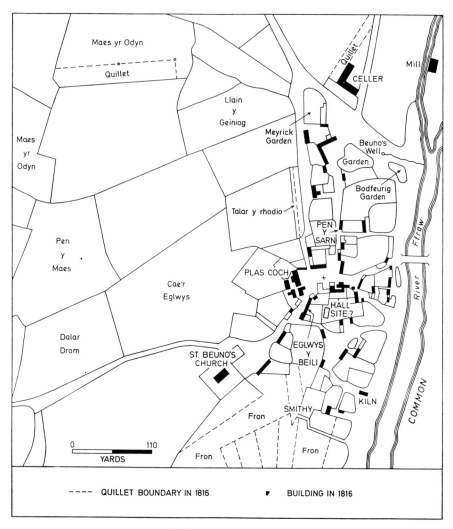

Fig. 42   The form of settlement in Aberffraw.

appears to have been sited on the flank of this former open-field, to the south-east of
the stone rampart uncovered near Plas Coch. This rampart, which formed part of
the defences of a multi-phased enclosure, is tentatively ascribed to the reign of
Maelgwn Gwynedd.[53] The curious shape of the central open space in the village to
the east of Plas Coch was probably a consequence of its inclusion within the
enclosing wall of the court complex; hence the perceptible narrowing of the
roadways leading from this central open space, as, for example, at Pen-y-Sarn (The
Head of the Causeway). Within the formerly enclosed area of the court complex
was the site of the court chapel at Eglwys y Beili (The Church of the Enclosure) and
immediately to the east what was probably the site of the king's hall. To the south,
loosely clustered around the triangular open space, were the dwellings in the bond

hamlet of Maerdref, with the kiln and the smithy at some distance in the interests of fire prevention.[54] To the north and east in the area between Pen-y-Sarn and the river crossing were the homesteads of the freemen of Gwely y Porthorion (The Gwely of the Porters) who were responsible for making and repairing a length of wall on either side of the gateway into the court. Within the vill of Aberffraw there was also a second bond hamlet called Garddau (Gardens), which was occupied by lesser bond tenants each with an acre of land. These were probably located at the northern end of the village in the vicinity of Beuno's Well. Here also appear to have been located other gardens, some disposed radially around Beuno's Well. Among them was Bodfeurig Garden, probably the garden of an undertenant of Gwely Bodfeurig, the free *gwely* centred at the outlying settlement of Bodfeurig, a mile to the west.[55] Aberffraw proper with, besides the royal court, its four free *gwelyau*, one free holding of a carpenter, and two bond hamlets was not only an ancient settlement but also a composite one whose morphological complexity matched the very diverse social composition of its inhabitants.

In the same neighbourhood of Malltraeth commote were other early settlements closely associated with Aberffraw. Among them was the vill of Eglwys Ail to the north-east beyond the common pasture of Tywyn Aberffraw. Eglwys Ail was recorded in the fourteenth century as being 'free and held of St Cadwaladr the King'.[56] As the name of this tenure implies, and fourteenth-century accounts confirm, the two *gwelyau* in the vill were held as sanctuary lands, exempt from renders and services save that certain rights were reserved to the king.[57] These *gwely* lands consisted, in part, of nucleal gardens radiating outwards from the churchyard of Eglwys Ail at Llangadwaladr, and also of outlying arable sharelands adjoined by homesteads.[58] Yet King Cadwaladr, whose name was preserved alike in that of the tenure and in that of the church, was sixth in descent from Maelgwn Gwynedd and ruled that kingdom during the seventh century. Clearly therefore the settlements in the vill of Eglwys Ail were already in being during the seventh century. Moreover the presence in the church itself of an early seventh-century tombstone commemorating King Cadfan, the grandfather of King Cadwaladr,[59] indicates that already in the seventh century Eglwys Ail was the principal church associated with the seat of the dynasty at Aberffraw.

Elsewhere in Malltraeth commote there were vills, named after officers listed in the laws of the court, and likely therefore to have been old established. Such was Trefwastrodion (The Vill of the Grooms) which contained six free *gwelyau* including, significantly, Gwely Gwalchyddion (The Gwely of the Falconers), and one bond *gwely*. Among the obligations of the heirs of these free *gwelyau* was the duty of making part of the king's chamber at Aberffraw, but the obligations of the heirs of the bond *gwely* were far heavier and included, besides the circuits of the falconers and the king's warhorse, the duty of making part of each house of the court of Aberffraw.[60]

LLANYNYS

Although religious establishments do not figure very prominently in the lawbooks, the more important of these establishments, like the royal courts, gave rise to significant early settlements. Such was Llanynys in the fertile vale of Clwyd for, already by the ninth century, its church was perhaps the one named in Welsh verse as the 'Lanfawr (Great Church) beyond Bannawg, where the Clwyd joins the Clywedog'.[61] In any event, by the thirteenth century and probably long before, it had become a *clas*, or community of canons under an abbot, all sharing the revenues of the Church.[62] As a hereditary property-holding religious community its possessions included not only hereditary land but also nucleal land. Clear traces of both kinds of possessions have survived at Llanynys, thus making very evident their relationship to early settlement. Llanynys, placed perhaps significantly near a prehistoric enclosure, occupied an island-like spread of well-drained Dyfnog soils elevated above the floor of the vale (Fig. 43). The church and graveyard lay within the northern part of what appears to have been a larger, roughly circular enclosure, which was perhaps the original *llan* (enclosure) within which the dwellings or courts of the canons of this community were located. Outside this enclosure lay nucleal land (*tir corddlan*) held apparently by undertenants of the *clas*. These resided in chambers located immediately outside the *llan*. Beyond lay their gardens, strips or quillets, disposed in radial fashion, like the surviving croft (*crofft*) of glebe land in the field known as Gerddi duon (Black gardens) or Cae'r llan. To the north-west in Bryn castell (Castle hill) were yet other radial gardens, but beyond them in turn were the hereditary lands held by the portionaries of the *clas*.[63] As in Maes isa (Lower open-field) and Maes ucha (Upper open-field), where quillets of former hereditary land survived to a late date, the arable lands of any heir consisted of strips lying intermingled in unenclosed sharelands (*rhandiroedd*).[64] The rights of the portionaries in arable lands were exercised over the well-drained Denbigh soils and, in the northernmost Trefechan (little *tref*), over lighter Dyfnog soils.[65] Attached to these arable holdings were appurtenant rights over meadow and common pasture. The meadows, as indicated by surviving field-names in Dôl and Gweirglodd, were on the fringes of the arable sharelands, but the common pastures extended over the ill-drained lands designated as Gwern (Alder Marsh), Cors (Bog) and Mawndir (Peat-land). It was, however, proximity to their largest shares of arable land that determined the locations of the outlying homesteads of the portionaries of Llanynys and they were therefore sited on the outer edges of arable sharelands, as near the north-western limits of Maes isa and Maes ucha, or near Tŷ-coch on the margins of the former sharelands of the northernmost Trefechan.

MAENOR MEDDYFNYCH

Incontrovertible testimony of the stability of territorial organization in Dark Age Dyfed is provided by a memorandum inscribed on the margins of the Book of Teilo in the early ninth century. This gives the perambulation of *Mainaur Med Diminih* (Maenor Meddyfnych) by means of a series of named features which can be identified.[66] Starting and finishing at Aber Huer, but proceeding in a clockwise direction, these include, among others, Byrfaen in Pen y Coed, Cymer, the source of Nant y Carw, Aber Istill and Llygad (Fig. 44). The area thus defined was nearly conterminous with the parish of Llandybïe save for two exceptions: one, the upland area to the south-west of Nant y Carw and Coed Bannau, and the other, the

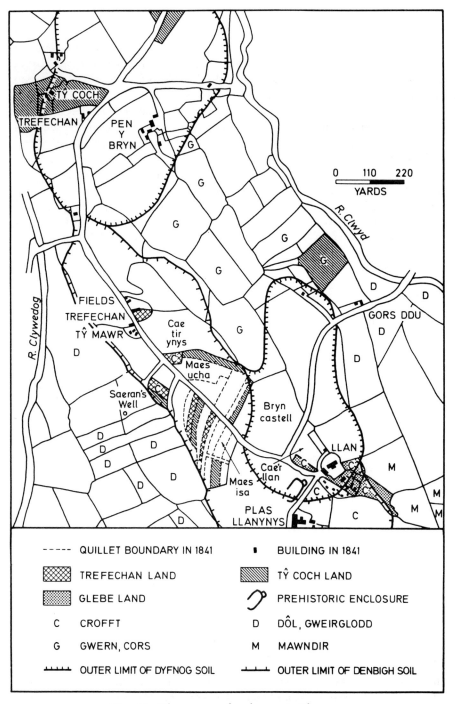

Fig. 43 The pattern of settlement in Llanynys.

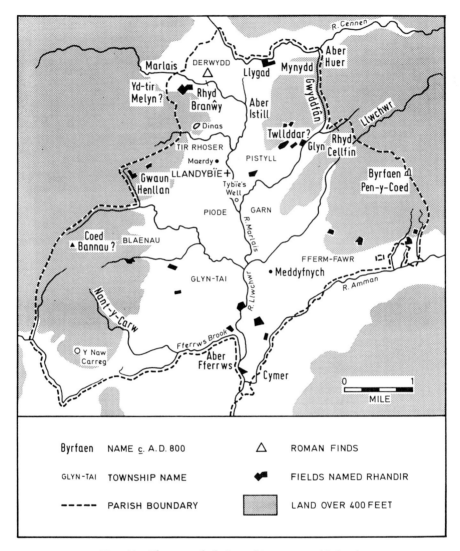

Fig. 44   The perambulation of Maenor Meddyfnych.

lowland township of Derwydd in the north where Roman remains indicate the presence of a substantial Romano-British homestead. Nevertheless the estate of Meddyfnych was huge, covering some 9000 acres, an area which embraced precisely seven townships.[67] As the names in the perambulation indicate there was woodland on the flanks of the hills near Pen y Coed (Top of the Wood) and at Coed Bannau (Wood of the Summits). Yet in more favoured settings even at this date cultivation was practised near the estate boundary; hence, the Yd-tir Melyn (Yellow Cornland), in an area near the north-western boundary where the field-name *rhandir* (shareland) has frequently survived. The frequent survival elsewhere of the name *rhandir*, sometimes applied to land where quillets of arable or meadow lay intermingled, or of the name *maes* (open-field), suggests that settled agriculture was old established in many parts of the estate (Fig. 44).[68] Among them in the township of Fferm Fawr (Large Farm) was Meddyfnych, after which the *maenor* was named. The principal settlement, however, was at Llandybïe, nearly two miles away from Meddyfnych. Llandybïe was already old established, for the perambulation refers to a Gwaun Henllan (Meadow of the Old Church). A productive upland meadow, this lay at an altitude of about 500 feet a mile or so to the west.[69] That a distant upland meadow should thus be ascribed to the Old Church in itself indicates that Llandybïe, with its church and holy well dedicated to St Tybïe, was then several centuries old. The disposition of the glebe land here suggests that Llandybïe was a small nucleation characterized by radial gardens. Yet attached to this old nucleation were outlying homesteads, such as Maerdy (Reeve's house), well placed between Llandybïe and the elevated strong point (*din*) of Dinas. That there were other outlying homesteads distant from the main settlements after which the townships were named is revealed by the dispositions of names in *hendref* (old settlement) near the boundaries of Glyn Tai and Tir Rhoser.[70] Evidently therefore as early as the ninth century, Maenor Meddyfnych in the interior of Dyfed was a multiple estate containing far more than one significant settlement.

MAINAURE IN ERGYNG

In the area of the early kingdom of Ergyng similar territorial arrangements can be discerned. Already by the mid ninth century the northernmost part of Ergyng had been lost to the English and by 1066 the whole of Ergyng, now known as Archenfield, had been annexed to Herefordshire. Accordingly it was surveyed in Domesday Book, yet even in 1086 the Welsh foundations of the pattern of territorial organization were evident. Thus Domesday Book records the existence of a *Mainaure* in 'the border (*in fine*) of Archenfield'.[71] A twelfth-century transcript of the Domesday survey for Herefordshire reveals that this *Mainaure* consisted in 1086 of the Birches, that is the two vills of Much Birch and Little Birch[72] (Fig. 45). Then in part occupied by a Welshman, this *Mainaure* was cultivated by four ploughs and rendered to Roger de Lacy, besides cash, a characteristic Welsh render of sesters of honey. Comprising only two vills, it was by 1086 a late surviving vestige of a once wider *maenor* fissioned by the alienation of its other former components; for Domesday Book records, under the rubric Wormelow Hundred, the manor of Westwood which was held by the Monastery of St Peter of Gloucester. The *caput* of Westwood, which had been held by King Edward in 1066, was apparently to the west of Much Birch in the parish of Much Dewchurch, and probably at the settlement named Much Dewchurch. At Westwood there were six hides, one of which was said in Domesday Book to have 'Welsh custom and the others English'.[73] An early twelfth-century list of tenants indicates that only two of these hides were held by the Church of St Peter. These were in the *Villa Asmacun*, equated with Westwood in the twelfth-century transcript, and thus referring to the vill literally below Aconbury hill-fort, in other words Much Dewchurch, later a manor of St Peter. The same sources reveal that two of the six hides were in the part of the manor of Westwood held in 1086 by Roger de Lacy at Wormeton Tirel; and that the

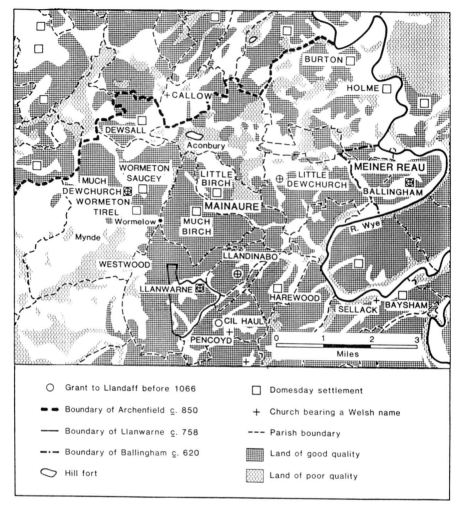

Fig. 45   Early territorial organization in northern Ergyng.

remaining two, in the part held by Ralph de Saucey, were in Wormeton Saucey. It was this latter part of the manor of Westwood which contained the Welsh hide, located, as later sources reveal, in The Mynde (*la Montayne*).[74] In other words the Welsh hide held in 1086 by a Welshman, the subtenant of Ralph de Saucey, and cultivated by half a plough-team was in the uplands to the south of Much Dewchurch, whereas the five English hides, on which no less than ten plough-teams were at work in 1086, were on lowlands of much better quality to the north. Still further north, at Dewsall, was yet another component of the manor, and recorded as a part of Westwood. Within the limits of Westwood apparently, but belonging to Holme, a manor of the canons of Hereford in Dinedor Hundred by 1086, was the church of Llanwarne in Archenfield. To the south of Holme but within Archenfield was a manor, not named in Domesday Book, where four freemen with four plough-teams rendered four sesters of honey and 16d. as customary due. This was identified in the twelfth-century transcript as Ballingham and also as *Meiner Reau*. The latter, it may be tentatively suggested, was a late corrupt form of Maenor Fro, meaning Lowland Maenor, a suggestion reinforced by the typically Welsh dues owed at Ballingham. A late medieval entry in the twelfth-century transcript indicates that there was a Manor of Wormelow, named after the Domesday hundredal moot at Wormelow Tump, probably as a result of the alienation of the six hides of Westwood. This Manor of Wormelow embraced a wide area of Archenfield, including *Meiner Reau, Mainaure* and Westwood.[75] It may be suggested, therefore, that earlier there had been one wider *maenor* in northern Ergyng including both a *maenor wrthtir* and a *maenor fro*. The *maenor wrthtir*, or upland estate, embraced Aconbury hill-fort but the former *llys* (court) was probably at Much Dewchurch (*Villa Asmacun*), the royal *caput* of Westwood in 1066; and the *llan* was at Llanwarne, hence the tithes it later received from the Minster Farm at Much Birch. The *maenor fro*, adjoining the Wye, was a lowland estate whose *caput* was in Holme parish, at Burton, 'the settlement belonging to the fort', until that district was lost to the English (Fig. 45). The former *llys* of *maenor fro* was probably at Burton, for its wood remained in royal demesne in 1086, whereas the former *llan* was at Holme.

  That this wider *maenor* was a very deeply-rooted estate is indicated by the grants of churches, and of the means for their support, recorded in the Llandaff charters. Among them was a grant of a religious settlement (*podum*) at *Lann Iunabui* (Llandinabo), with an *uncia* of land, which was made to St Dyfrig by King Peibio.[76] Dyfrig was a sixth-century leader, in the tradition of a Roman territorial bishop, and the grant was presumably made to his church rather than his person, probably in the early seventh century.[77] To judge from its later perambulation this grant was carved out of a wider territorial entity (Fig. 45), and, significantly, the *Iunabui* (Inabwy) after whom it was named was a cousin to King Peibio. Later in the seventh century King Gwrgan gave the religious settlement (*podum*) of *Lann Budgualan* (Ballingham) with two-and-a-half *unciae* of land around it (*incircuitu podi*) to Bishop Inabwy.[78] Within the bounds specified in a later perambulation this donation covered an area of some 1285 statute acres, so that each *uncia* contained about 515 statute acres.[79] Again in the eighth century, after the Saxon devastation, King Ithel returned to the Church a number of churches which, like *Lann Budgualan* (Ballingham), had previously belonged to the church of Dyfrig, among them *Lann Iunabui* (Llandinabo) and *Lann Deui* (Much Dewchurch). All these grants were made by kings as was that of *Cil Hal* (Cil Haul) donated in the seventh century and said specifically to be part of King Erb's inheritance.[80] Later grants, however, were made by non-royal laity. Among them was the grant of land made *c.*758 by *Catuuth* son of *Coffro* to *Hennlennic*, literally the old subsidiary church, that is *Lannguern* (Llanwarne), on the bank of the Gamber in Ergyng. This grant was for an *ager* (land) of three *modii* which was defined in this particular charter as a quarter of an *uncia*.[81] The perambulation indicates that this land (*ager*) lay between the River Gamber, the old ditch, and the hyacinthine way, which latter can be none other than the Roman road which led to Wormelow Tump. The area thus delimited amounted to some 530 statute acres, or about one *uncia*, so that the three *modii* granted, as is implied by the reference to a quarter of an *uncia*, was not a specific area marked out by bounds but rather a fractional share of a larger expanse lying, probably unenclosed, to the south of the long pre-existing church hamlet of *Hennlennic* (Llanwarne). In the case of these three *modii* moreover a direct link with Domesday plough-teams can be suggested; for at Llanwarne in 1086 there were precisely three plough-teams but, presumably because of its earlier donation to *Hennlennic*, the land of this church of Llanwarne was said in 1086 to be free from the payment of geld.[82] Accordingly the *modius* was the equivalent not only of the shareland of the Welsh lawbooks, but also of the land cultivated by one plough-team; and the latter was probably the equivalent of the Welsh hide which, at least in and near Archenfield, appears to have contained an area of some 60 statute acres, or sometimes less.

LANN HELICON IN MORGANNWG

A rare insight into the detailed pattern of settlement associated with hereditary land in the Dark Ages is provided by the charter in the Book of Llandaff which records the grant of *Lann Helicon* to the Church. With King Brochfael's guarantee *Elivid, Conone, Guoidcen* and *Erdtibiu*, sons of *Euguen*, gave an '*ecclesia cum castello agri circa eam* (a church with a *castell* of land about it)' free of all lay services.[83] The church was named in the title of the grant but neither *Lann Helicon* nor the land about it have hitherto been identified.[84] Nevertheless the church can be equated with the Llan which is located near Castellau Uchaf in Morgannwg (Fig. 46). Although a mere farmhouse by the nineteenth century this was then still known as *The Lan*.[85] The site is a commanding one at an altitude of nearly 700 feet, on a spread of well-drained cultivable soils islanded amidst less well-drained soils.[86] Towards the south-western edge of this same spread of well-drained soils is the farmhouse of Castellau Uchaf but, appropriately enough, the farmhouse of Pentre (Edge of the *Tref*) is on the very edge of this same spread. Near the centre, however, was the *llan* granted with a *castell* (castle) of land about it, for the term *castell* besides being used of a fortification or stronghold could also be used of a measure of land.[87]

    The grant has been ascribed to *c*.780, and as the description of the estate appears to have been integral to the charter, rather than a later addition, the description probably portrays the conditions of settlement obtaining in the early eighth century. The church and the *castell* of land, until granted, had formed part of the hereditary possessions of the four brothers. Since the brothers did not give themselves to the church they presumably retained their other hereditary possessions. These probably lay in the vill or township of Castellau which extended from Nant Mychydd to Nant Castellau and as far north as the uplands beyond Waun Castellau (Castellau Moor). Within these limits there were in the nineteenth century four farmsteads named Castellau, and likewise in 1570 there were four separate holdings named Castellau.[88] Like Castellau Uchaf these were located on the edges of patches of well-drained soils suitable for cultivation. Similarly in the early eighth century there were probably four homesteads named Castellau, one for each brother, with the *hendref* (old settlement), the abode of the youngest brother and earlier the father, probably at the southernmost Castellau, later the site of a sixteenth-century mansion. The other homesteads were likewise dispersed in accordance with the lie of the land, near

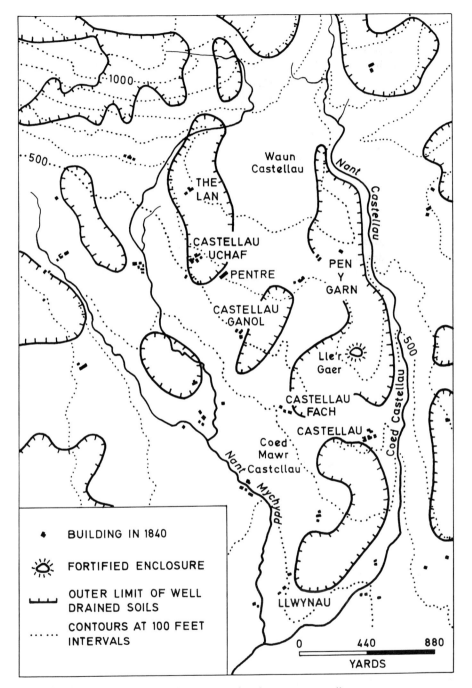

Fig. 46 The pattern of settlement in Castellau.

four spreads of arable land which even in the eighth century were possibly divided into sharelands. On the other hand the *castell* about *Lann Helicon* was probably nucleal land, as was the Bryn *castell* at Llanynys; for certainly, before it was donated to the church, *Lann Helicon* appears to have been a treasure common among brothers. The homesteads of Castellau *c.*708 were dispersed but linked as they had been to *Lann Helicon* they were not isolated; and, as their disposition in relation to the fortified enclosure of the Iron Age at Lle'r Gaer suggests,[89] this organic dispersal was already old established long before the eighth century.

All the evidence available for Wales in the Dark Ages points to the existence of a society, entirely rural, in which the occupancy and possession of land was of paramount importance alike as a source of status and of wealth. This resulted in the existence of an old-established pattern of permanent settlement, notably in the lowlands where conditions of soil and climate were suitable for cultivation.[90] Such settlement was rarely close but over the course of the Dark Ages it is likely to have increased in density, so that already by the eighth century ecologically favoured areas were fairly well settled. Thus Bede could report *c.*730, on the basis of estimates probably made a century earlier, that in Anglesey there was land for 960 families by the English reckoning of the hide; and since this implies for Anglesey an average of some 180 statute acres of land, wood and waste per hide the typical holding is likely to have required labour from outside the nuclear family.[91] Nor was Anglesey entirely exceptional, for on the richer lands of Ergyng the replacement of the *uncia* of some 528 statute acres, by the *modius* of about 44 statute acres, a change largely effected before the close of the eighth century, is likely to reflect a reduction in the size of the average holding.[92] Elsewhere average holdings were no doubt larger and the density of settlement correspondingly lower. So too forms of settlement varied, ranging usually from dispersed homesteads to hamlets, but with larger agglomerations only at royal courts or ecclesiastical centres. Yet even the dispersed homesteads were rarely isolated for, as the associations between homesteads and the treasures of the kindred suggest, there were developed linkages between settlements. The presence of these linkages betokens an already well-established territorial organization.

NOTES

[1] D. Jenkins (ed.), *Damweiniau Colan* (Aberystwyth, 1973); H.D. Emanuel (ed.), *The Latin Texts of the Welsh Laws* (Cardiff, 1963); S.J. Williams and J.E. Powell (eds.), *Llyfr Blegywryd* (Cardiff, 1961); M. Richards (ed.), *The Laws of Hywel Dda* (Liverpool, 1954); A.W. Wade-Evans (ed.), *Welsh Medieval Law* (Oxford, 1909); A. Owen (ed.), *Ancient Laws and Institutes of Wales*, 2 vols. (1841).

[2] J. Gwenogvryn Evans and J. Rhys (eds.), *The Text of the Book of Llan Dav (Llyuyr Teilo vel Liber Landauensis)* (Oxford, 1893), xlii–xlvii.

[3] Ibid., 72–8, 121–9, 140–280; Wendy Davies, *The Llandaff Charters* (Aberystwyth, 1979).

[4] A.W. Wade-Evans (ed.), *Vita Sancti Cadoci*, in *Vitae Sanctorum Britanniae et Genealogiae* (Cardiff, 1944).

[5] A. Farley (ed.), *Domesday Book*, 2 vols. (1783).

[6] M. Winterbottom (ed.), *Gildas, The Ruin of Britain and other works* (Chichester, 1978).

[7] J. Morris (ed.), *Nennius, British History and The Welsh Annals* (Chichester, 1980).

[8] J. Williams 'ab Ithel' (ed.), Rolls Series 20, (*Annales Cambriae* 1860); E. Phillimore, 'The *Annales Cambriae* and Old Welsh Genealogies from Harleian MS. 3859', *Y Cymmrodor*, 9 (1888), 141–83.

[9] Ifor Williams (ed.), *Canu Llywarch Hen* (Cardiff, 1955); R. Geraint Gruffydd, 'Canu Cadwallon ap Cadfan' in Rachel Bromwich and R. Brinley Jones (eds.), *Astudiaethau ar yr Hengerdd* (Cardiff, 1978), 25–43.

[10] V.E. Nash-Williams, *The Early Christian Monuments of Wales* (Cardiff, 1960).

[11] *Llyfr Iorwerth*, 59–60.

[12] Ibid., 56.

[13] Ibid., 53–4, 60.

[14] *Welsh Medieval Law*, 53: T.M. Charles-Edwards, *A Comparison of Old Irish with Medieval Welsh Land Law* (University of Oxford D.Phil. thesis, 1971), 188–9; idem, 'Kinship, Status and the Origins of the Hide', *Past and Present*, 56 (1972), 8–21; D. Jenkins and Morfydd E. Owen (eds.), *The Welsh Law of Women* (Cardiff, 1980), 199–202.

[15] J.F. Dimock (ed.), *Giraldi Cambrensis Opera*, Rolls Series 21, 6, (1868), 211–12.

[16] *Llyfr Iorwerth*, 53, 60.

[17] Ibid., 58; *Llyfr Colan*, 38, 155–6.

[18] *Llyfr Iorwerth*, 58.

[19] *Damweiniau Colan*, 10; *The Latin Texts of the Welsh Laws*, 231, 289; *Ancient Laws and Institutes of Wales 2*, 888–9; G.R.J. Jones, 'Post-Roman Wales' in H.R.P. Finberg (ed.), *The Agrarian History of England and Wales*, I (ii) (Cambridge, 1972), 340–9; idem, 'Early Customary Tenures in Wales and Open-Field Agriculture' in T. Rowley (ed.), *The Origins of Open-Field Agriculture* (1981), 210–15.

[20] *Llyfr Iorwerth*, 54; *Llyfr Colan*, 36; D. Jenkins, 'A Lawyer looks at Welsh Land Law', *T.C.S.* (1967), 235–6.

[21] *Welsh Medieval Law*, 55, 205, 344.

[22] *Llyfr Blegywryd*, 27, 71.

[23] *Welsh Medieval Law*, 54, 204.

[24] Ibid., 54–5, 204, 206; *Ancient Laws and Institutes of Wales, 2*, 268–9.

[25] *Llyfr Blegywryd*, 71; *The Laws of Hywel Dda*, 75.

[26] *The Latin Texts of the Welsh Laws*, 226.

[27] *Welsh Medieval Law*, 54–6, 204–7.

[28] Ibid., 55–7.

[29] *The Latin Texts of the Welsh Laws*, 135–7.

[30] Ibid.

[31] Ibid., 383.

[32] *Domesday Book*, 1, f.162a.

[33] Ibid., 1, f.185b.

[34] Ibid., 1, f.269a.

[35] *The Text of the Book of Llan Dav*, xlvii.

[36] Ibid., 62, 72, 124–5, 165–6, 180, 254–5.

[37] Ibid., 210; *Vita Sancti Cadoci*, 135.

[38] *Gildas*, 32–3, 102: *Nennius*, 85.

[39] G.R.J. Jones, 'Field Systems of North Wales' in A.R.H. Baker and R.A. Butlin (eds.), *Studies of Field Systems in the British Isles* (Cambridge, 1973), 465–7; R. Geraint Gruffydd, 'A New Look at Cunedda Wledig', *Studia Celtica*, (to be published).

[40] *Llyfr Iorwerth*, 62; *Llyfr Colan*, 40.

[41] Ibid., 172; *The Latin Texts of the Welsh Laws*, 204–5; *Llyfr Blegywryd*, 188.

[42] *Llyfr Iorwerth*, 5–16, 20.

[43] *Llyfr Colan*, 40.

[44] *Llyfr Iorwerth*, 11–12.

[45] *The Latin Texts of the Welsh Laws*, 123, 201, 336, 451; *Llyfr Blegywryd*, 114; *Welsh Medieval Law*, 130, 274; *Llyfr Iorwerth*, 81.

[46] *Ancient Laws and Institutes of Wales*, 672–93; *Llyfr Iorwerth*, 54; *Llyfr Colan*, 36; *Damweiniau Colan*, 18, 24, 32; *The Latin Texts of the Welsh Laws*, 382.

[47] *Llyfr Blegywryd*, 95–6; *Welsh Medieval Law*, 102–3; *Llyfr Iorwerth*, 91–2.

[48] G.R.J. Jones, 'The Distribution of Medieval Settlements in Anglesey', *T.A.A.S.*, (1955), 33.

[49] *Ancient Laws and Institutes of Wales, 2*, 270–1.

[50] *Llyfr Iorwerth*, 58–9; *Ancient Laws and Institutes of Wales, 2*, 76–7.

[51] R. Geraint Gruffydd, in *Astudiaethau ar yr Hengerdd*, 42–3; R. White, 'New Light on the Origins of the Kingdom of Gwynedd', in ibid., 350–5.

[52] G.R.J. Jones, 'Rural Settlement in Anglesey', in S.R. Eyre and G.R.J. Jones (eds.), *Geography as Human Ecology* (1966), 211–15; A.D. Carr, *Medieval Anglesey* (Llangefni, 1982), 123, 152; H. Ellis (ed.), *The Record of Caernarvon*, Record Commission, (1838), 45–9.

[53] R.B. White, 'Sculptured Stones from Aberffraw, Anglesey', *A.C.*, CXXVI (1977), 140–5; idem, 'Excavations at Aberffraw, Anglesey, 1973 and 1974', *B.B.C.S.*, XXVIII (1978–80), 319–41.

[54] University College of North Wales, Bangor, Bodorgan MS., Llysdulas 53.

[55] *The Record of Caernarvon*, 48–50; G.R.J. Jones in *Studies in Field Systems*, 461–5.

[56] *The Record of Caernarvon*, 46–7.

[57] Public Record Office (hereafter P.R.O.), Special Collections 6, 1170/5.

[58] G.R.J. Jones, *Origins of Open-Field Agriculture*, 213–15.

[59] V.E. Nash-Williams, *Early Christian Monuments*, 55–7.

[60] *The Record of Caernarvon*, 45–6.

[61] *Canu Llywarch Hen*, 22, 153–8.

[62] G.R.J. Jones, *Ag. Hist.* I(ii), 343–9.

[63] P.R.O., Wales 15/8.

[64] P.R.O., Special Collections 2/224/4.

[65] D.F. Ball, *The District around Rhyl and Denbigh*, Memoirs of the Soil Survey of Great Britain (1960), 39–45.

[66] *The Text of the Book of Llan Dav*, xlvii; G.R.J. Jones, *Ag. Hist.* I(ii), 309–11.

[67] M. Richards, *Welsh Administrative and Territorial Units* (Cardiff, 1969), 109.

[68] National Library of Wales (hereafter N.L.W.,), Dynevor MSS: 603, 682, 694, 741: Tithe Apportionment and Map, Llandybïe, 1839.

[69] N.L.W., Dynevor MSS: 601, 605, 606.

[70] N.L.W., Tithe Apportionment and Map, Llandybïe, 1839.

[71] *Domesday Book*, I, f.181a.

[72] V.H. Galbraith and J. Tait (eds.), *Herefordshire Domesday c.1160–1170*, Publications of the Pipe Roll Society, 63 (1950), 20.

[73] *Domesday Book*, I, f.181.

[74] *Herefordshire Domesday*, 78, 127; W.H. Hart (ed.), *Monasterii Sancti Petri Gloucestriae*, Rolls Series, 33, 2, (1865), 224; N.L.W. Mynde Park Deeds and Documents, 207, 346, 994.

[75] *Domesday Book*, I, f.181; *Herefordshire Domesday*, 19–21, 25, 87; P.R.O. Calendar of Inquisitions Post Mortem, 13 (1954), 196.

[76] *The Text of the Book of Llan Dav*, 73.

[77] E.G. Bowen, *The Settlements of the Celtic Saints in Wales* (Cardiff, 1954), 38, 44; K. Hughes, 'The Celtic Church. Is This a Valid Concept?', *Cambridge Medieval Celtic Studies*, (1981), 1–20.

[78] *The Text of the Book of Llan Dav*, 164–5.

[79] Compare Wendy Davies, '*Unciae*: Land Measurement in the *Liber Landavensis*', *Ag. Hist. Rev.*, 21 (1973), 111–21; idem, *An Early Welsh Microcosm. Studies in the Llandaff Charters*, Royal Historical Society Studies in History Series, 9, (1978), 32–4; F. Noble, in M. Gelling (ed.), *Offa's Dyke Reviewed*, B.A.R., British Series, 114 (Oxford, 1983), 16.

[80] *The Text of the Book of Llan Dav*, 75, 171, 192; Wendy Davies, *An Early Welsh Microcosm*, 50–4.

[81] *The Text of the Book of Llan Dav*, 200; Wendy Davies, *The Llandaff Charters*, 119.

[82] *Domesday Book*, I, f.181b.

[83] *The Text of the Book of Llan Dav*, 205–6.

[84] Wendy Davies, *The Llandaff Charters*, 205.

[85] N.L.W., Tithe Apportionment and Map, Llantrisant, 1840.

[86] C.B. Crampton and D.P. Webley, 'The Correlation of Prehistoric Settlement and Soils: Gower and the South Wales Coalfield', *B.B.C.S.*, XX (1963–4), 326–39.

[87] *Geiriadur Prifysgol Cymru*, I (Cardiff, 1950–67), 438; G.P. Jones (ed.), *The Extent of Chirkland (1391–1393)* (Liverpool 1933), 8.

[88] N.L.W., Tithe Apportionment and Map, Llantrisant, 1840; Bute MS. 32,

[89] R.C.A.H.M.W., *An Inventory of the Ancient Monuments in Glamorgan* I, Pt. 2 (Cardiff, 1976), 30.

[90] G.R.J. Jones, 'The Distribution of Bond Settlements in North-West Wales', *W.H.R.*, 2 (1964), 19–36.

[91] B. Colgrave and R.A.B. Mynors (eds.), *Bede's Ecclesiastical History of the English People* (Oxford, 1969), 162–3.

[92] Wendy Davies, art. cit., *Ag. Hist Rev.*, 21 (1973), 111–21.

The Middle Ages[1]

D. HUW OWEN

SETTLEMENT patterns in medieval Wales were inevitably influenced by the major political and military events of the period. Successive phases of military conquest were achieved by Norman forces in the late eleventh and early twelfth centuries and by Edward I's armies in the late thirteenth century. The native princes of Gwynedd embarked upon state-building enterprises in the thirteenth century, and Owain Glyndŵr proclaimed his independent Welsh state in the early fifteenth century. The rulers of medieval Wales, whether they were Welsh princes, Norman lords or English kings, encountered opposition, based on well-established local allegiances, from their subjects. Political life was characterized by turbulence and disorder. Border communities were devastated as a result of the destructive raids mounted by Gruffudd ap Llywelyn in the mid eleventh century. Four centuries later the dynastic struggles which repeatedly imperilled the English throne split the loyalties of the articulate Welsh bards and their patrons amongst the emergent gentry families.[2]

All Welsh localities, irrespective of fluctuating political fortunes and masters, were critically affected in terms of settlement forms and agrarian practices by topographical conditions. A wide range of documents, including modern geological and soil surveys, emphasize the influence of aspect, altitude, coastal location and especially soil quality on the nature and distribution of settlement on the island of Anglesey. More advanced economic and social trends may be observed in those lowland areas of north and west Wales which were not conquered until the late thirteenth century. An examination of the extent of commutation into cash payments of the traditional renders of freemen in Gwynedd in the period leading up to the Edwardian Conquest has revealed striking regional variations: the incidence of commutation was nearly complete in Anglesey and the adjacent mainland but was of negligible proportions in the mountainous areas of Snowdonia.[3]

The lordships established by Norman barons in south Wales and along the English border, comprising the Welsh March, were divided into two zones, the Englishry and Welshry, and the boundary was normally located along the 600' contour line. The upland Welshry was characterized by a widespread survival of traditional customs whilst the Englishry, occupying coastal or valley areas, experienced a far greater extent of disruption and change as a direct consequence of the imposition of Norman rule.[4] An awareness of the three clearly-defined topographical regions of Glamorgan — the upland and lowland areas known as *Blaenau Morgannwg* and *Bro Morgannwg*, and the intermediate zone, 'The Border Vale' — contributes to an understanding of the pattern of Norman conquest and settlement.[5] The lordship of Glamorgan was frequently associated with the earldom of Gloucester, and ecclesiastical property in Glamorgan was conferred on the abbeys of Gloucester and Tewkesbury.[6] Personal and tenurial connections may be traced between the coastal belt of south Wales and south-western England with both lords and tenants bound by links which extended across the Bristol Channel.[7] In the lordship of Pembroke — the lowlands north of Milford Haven — the *cantrefi* of Rhos and Daugleddau experienced an extensive Flemish settlement in the reign of Henry I (*c*.1107–11). This plantation of Flemings, supervised and controlled by royal officials, had a profound impact on this area: in 1188 Gerald of Wales commented on the distinctive characteristics of local inhabitants.[8]

The castle was the proof and symbol of Norman domination and the course of the Norman Conquest may be reconstructed from an appraisal of the distribution of numerous motte and bailey castles, with some, including those at Cardiff and Loughor, built on the sites of Roman forts. Several of these early castles were later rebuilt or strengthened in stone but the castle of Chepstow was originally built in stone with its keep, constructed in the period 1067–72, one of the earliest buildings of this type in Britain. Further innovations and improvements in military architecture led to the impressive fortresses built in the thirteenth century by marcher lords at Caerffili and Cydweli, Rhuthun and Denbigh, and by Edward I in the conquered lands of north, mid and west Wales. The military strongholds from the outset fulfilled administrative functions and from the late eleventh century Pembroke castle was the administrative centre for the lordship and later earldom of Pembroke.[9]

The spiritual and commercial requirements of the conquerors were satisfied by the building of churches and monasteries and the foundation of towns. Surviving remains again illustrate these processes and of particular value in this context are the early monastic church at Ewenni and the town walls of Conwy and Denbigh.[10] The history of the priory and town of Carmarthen in the twelfth and thirteenth centuries displays those elements of continuity and change which may be observed, in varying degrees, in several localities subject to Norman control.[11] After the abandonment of the first Norman castle built at Rhyd-y-gors, which was probably about one mile south-west of the town of Carmarthen, a second castle was built towards the end of the first decade of the twelfth century.[12] This castle was rebuilt in stone and in the late thirteenth century royal possessions in south-west Wales were administered by officials based at this massive fortress. The castle was sited in the outer defences of an old Roman fort near to a crossing point of the River Tywi and was to the west of the Roman town whose continued existence into the Norman period is implied by the use of the term 'Old Carmarthen' to describe the settlement centred on the church of St Teulyddog. This church was granted in the early twelfth century to Battle Abbey but soon afterwards was re-formed as an Augustinian abbey which came to control Old Carmarthen. The more important Norman town, known as New Carmarthen, was established in the shadow of the castle and a market was held outside the main gate of the castle. The market and two annual fairs dominated commercial activities in the fertile lower Tywi Valley. The building of shops, increase in population and extra-mural expansion all contributed to the urban growth of Carmarthen in the thirteenth century. It was the only Welsh town, apart from the episcopal centres, which appeared on Matthew Paris's map of Britain drawn towards the middle of the century.[13] The main medieval features are also clearly depicted in John Speed's early seventeenth-century town plan.[14]

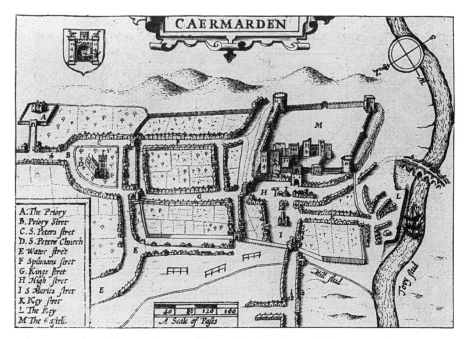

Plate XI   Plan of Carmarthen in John Speed, *The Theatre of The Empire of Great Britain* . . . (1611).

Plate XII   Artist's impression of the town of Cydweli (Alan Sorrel, *Early Wales Re-Created* (Cardiff, 1980)).

The burgesses of Carmarthen were granted a variety of administrative, commercial and judicial privileges in a charter granted by the Lord Edward, probably in 1256–7. This charter resembled those granted to numerous early Welsh boroughs in that it was based on the Hereford charter which in turn was modelled on that of Breteuil in Normandy. William Fitz Osbern, Earl of Hereford and grantor of the borough charter, was clearly influenced by the customs enjoyed by the residents of his town of Breteuil. The burgesses of Carmarthen were therefore allowed to bequeath land freely, use local woods, fields and rivers, and try offences committed inside the borough. The tradition of conforming to the Hereford model was also followed in the royal and seigneurial charters which accompanied the creation of a second generation of boroughs in the late thirteenth century.[15]

The prerogatives and privileges associated with burghal tenure contrasted with the regulations imposed on the manors. The organization and exploitation of demesne lands cultivated by a dependent bond population for the maintenance of the lord and his followers may be observed in the Normanized lowlands. Lowland villages, with their bond tenants, were adapted to conform to the requirements of a manorial system. Entries in Domesday Book relating to border areas suggest that conditions frequently favoured the acceleration of manorial enterprises.[16]

Robert Fitzhamon, the first Norman lord of Glamorgan, held the manors of Roath and Leckwith, both of which were situated near to his stronghold and administrative centre at Cardiff Castle. Roath, a mile to the east, originally seems to have been a dairy manor whilst Leckwith, two miles south-west of the castle, predominantly comprised customary tenants whose labour services, as described in the early fourteenth century, were discharged throughout the shire-fee, that is, the coastal plain conquered at the end of the eleventh century during the initial phase of the Norman Conquest. Robert Fitzhamon also held the manor of Llantwit, fifteen miles west of Cardiff in the Vale of Glamorgan. This manor included the township of Llysworny: the original form of the place-name, Llyswrinydd, suggests that here was located the *llys* (court) of the *cantref* of Gwrinydd which was one of the administrative units which comprised the pre-conquest kingdom of Morgannwg.[17] Similarly, the castle built by Henry, Earl of Warwick, at Swansea on the right bank of the River Tawe and which became the *caput* of the lordship of Gower established early in the twelfth century, was probably sited near to the court of the native ruler of the pre-Norman commote of Gŵyr. The lord of Gower held the manor of Trewyddfa which lay to the north of the castle and which may well have formed the demesne-property and administrative centre for the pre-conquest Welsh rulers.[18] In both the lordships of Glamorgan and Gower, which in the sixteenth century formed the main components of the shire of Glamorgan, the territory in the coastal lowlands, to the west of the *caput*, which was not retained by the lord was parcelled out as fiefs to Norman knights who had participated in the original conquest and who henceforth owed military service at the central castle: Cardiff or Swansea. In these lowland areas, numerous castles, manors and boroughs constituted characteristic features of the Englishries of the two lordships, but elusive evidence suggests that a greater measure of continuity and survival of pre-conquest elements seems to have prevailed than was once envisaged.

Information derived from those western and northern areas subject to a later phase of military conquest also implies the presence of a quasi-manorial system which had prevailed over a long period of time. Bond communities held land by means of *tref gyfrif* tenure which involved the recurrent partition and allocation of equal shares of arable land. The agrarian activities of the bondmen were carefully regulated by the *maer biswail* or land mayor and his main settlement, the *maerdref* (reeve's township) was situated near to the *llys*, the local court, and to the *tir bwrdd* (demesne land) on which the bondmen performed their traditional labour services. The bondmen also held small arable plots dispersed in the open fields. A multiple estate, comprising a number of distinct settlements, has been identified at Aberffraw (Anglesey), the traditional capital of Gwynedd. Bondmen occupying several hamlets, including 'Maerdref', were responsible for labour services at the court and for the cultivation of the demesne.[19]

In contrast to the nucleated villages and hamlets associated with the manor and *maerdref* a dispersed settlement pattern characterized the *tir gwelyawg* holdings (hereditary land) which were usually occupied by groups of free clansmen. The movement which involved the creation of the *gwely* began in the early twelfth century in the north-east borderlands on territory recovered by Welshmen from English and Norman occupants, spread westwards to reach Anglesey in the second half of the century and then advanced southwards. The *gwely* was occupied by members of the *gwelygordd* (free agnatic kindred). The *priodor* (free clansman) exercised proprietary rights in the *tir priod* (appropriated land) consisting of a *tyddyn* (homestead) and *tir gwasgar* (scattered arable plots), and also in the pasture, wood and wasteland. The homesteads surrounded the *rhandir* (shareland) which consisted of open arable fields. Restrictions were placed upon the *priodor's* ability to dispose of his property and also upon the redistribution of appropriated land. Proprietary rights were inherited according to the principle of *cyfran* (partible succession) with the original homestead of the *gwely*-founder bequeathed to his youngest son. The establishment of secondary settlements by the co-operative efforts of groups of kinsmen, together with the operation of *cyfran*, resulted in an irregular pattern of holdings in the *rhandir* with plots belonging to several *gwelyau* intermingled in the open fields. Detailed regulations governing three possible successive phases of partition appear in sections of the law books which are concerned with *tir gwelyog* holdings.[20]

Assessments of lands conquered in the late thirteenth century provided evaluations of actual and potential sources of revenue. The inclusion of information on some resources which had become obsolescent by the time of the Edwardian Conquest enhances the value of these documents as sources containing unique and invaluable evidence for an understanding of settlement-patterns and the social framework of several localities both before and after the military conquest. The Survey of the Lordship of Denbigh, compiled in 1334, presented a detailed examination of eighty-one lay townships or *trefi* in the lordship of Denbigh which, formed in 1282, comprised an extensive area lying to the east of the River Conwy. The main components of the lordship were the commotes of Is Dulas and Uwch Dulas in the *cantref* of Rhos and the commotes of Is Aled, Uwch Aled and Ceinmeirch in the *cantref* of Rhufoniog. The evidence suggests that its social organization had formerly been of a bond character but that, by 1344, most of the

Welsh tenants listed in the Survey were freemen with a large number belonging to the predominant clans. The property of the clan of Hedd Molwynog was concentrated in one locality along the River Aled. A solid block of territory was therefore held in the commote of Uwch Aled by the progenies of Rand Fychan ab Asser. This was an exception to the trend whereby clan groupings were dispersed over a wide area and numerous secondary foundations, often located at a considerable distance from the original settlement, were established by the Braint Hir, Marchweithian (Fig. 47) and Edrud ap Marchudd clans.[21]

Marchudd ap Cynan, whose name is associated with the latter clan, seems to have lived in the late eleventh or early twelfth century.[22] This date, together with that of *c.*1170 suggested for the existence of Carwed and Griffri, who appropriated old-established bondlands attached to the *llys* (court) at Llysddulas, Anglesey, supports the argument advanced with regard to the chronological spread of the *gwely* movement. Following the deaths of Carwed and Griffri, who were probably brothers, their lands were divided between their seven sons who are regarded as the founders of the agnatic kindred-groups whose occupation of *gwelyau* in Llysddulas is recorded in a 1294 rental, 1352 extent and 1549 Crown rental.[23] In Eifionydd many free *gwelyau* were probably established by the descendants of Collwyn ap Tangno, the main landowner in the twelfth century: two large *gwelyau* mentioned in the *Record of Caernarvon* (1352) bear the names of Collwyn's grandson Gwgan and his great-grandson, Gwyn ab Ednowain, who lived *c.* 1200.[24]

In some localities, including Merioneth, and Arllechwedd Isaf and Nanconwy, in Caernarfonshire, and also the lordships of Chirk, Oswestry and Bromfield and Yale, clan-land was described not as a *gwely* but as a *gafael* (holding), a related but distinct agrarian and tenurial institution. In the lowlands of Arllechwedd Isaf the *gafael* represented a dispersed form of land tenure with scattered holdings intermingled with those belonging to other *gafaelion*. The *gafael* was therefore regarded as the product of the partition of an established and older *gwely*.[25] Fragmented *gafaelion* may be identified in upland localities of Merioneth.[26] Entries relating to these areas in the 1415–20 survey have suggested that the *gafael* may have been a specific and compact territorial unit and a similar argument has been advanced for the Ogwen Valley in Caernarfonshire.[27]

Occasional references to the *gwely* appear in the Black Book of St David's which, compiled in 1326, records a survey of episcopal lands. These estates were scattered throughout south-west Wales and the *gwely* system had evidently been adopted in several localities, including Llangyfelach in the Welshry of the lordship of Gower. The *gwely* seems to have been introduced into Ceredigion during the thirteenth century. This area had experienced political upheaval in the twelfth century and the restoration of order by Rhys ap Gruffudd, the Lord Rhys, had resulted in the imposition of a territorial resettlement. This is implied by the uniform distribution of *gwestfa* districts and the artificial nature of *gwestfa* renders assessed on the *gwely* units: the term *gwestfa*, representing the food renders paid to the Welsh ruler and his household, reminds us of a much earlier and more primitive period of the history of Wales.[28]

The later Middle Ages witnessed the collapse of the agrarian and tenurial institutions associated both with manors and with kindred groupings. The manors

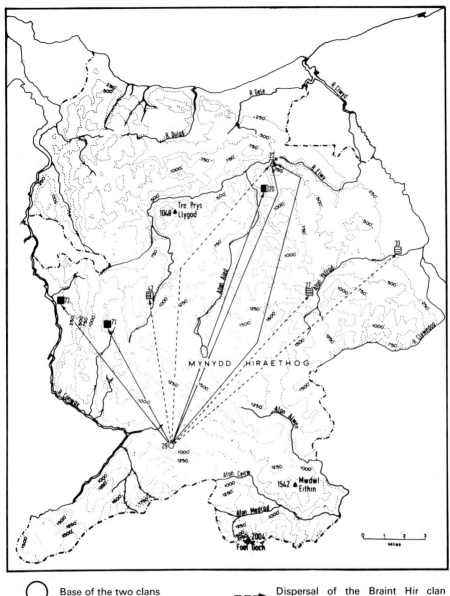

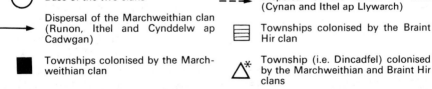

Fig. 47 The expansion of the Marchweithian and Braint Hir clans in the twelfth and thirteenth centuries. The numbers on the map relate to the list of townships which appeared in the *Welsh History Review*, VI (1972), 137. The key townships in the expansion of these two clans are: 20 — Carwedfynydd, 22 — Dincadfel, 27 — Nantglyn Cynon, 29 — Prys, 33 — Ystrad Cynon (in the commote of Is Aled); 42 — Gwytherin (in the commote of Uwch Aled); and 71 — Garthgyfannedd; and 72 — Llanrwst (in the commote of Uwch Dulas).

of the marcher lordships were certainly not immune from the demographic, financial and military pressures which curtailed and terminated demesne-land cultivation throughout the whole of western Europe. In the thirteenth century, emphasis had been placed in several lordships on the production and marketing of cereals and this was the most valuable source of revenue in the financial accounts compiled in 1256–7 for the lordships of Monmouth and Abergavenny. Profit margins, however, were frequently small and this was increasingly the trend in the fourteenth century when low yields and high labour costs contributed to the abandonment of direct cultivation in numerous lordships and the adoption of a system involving the leasing of the demesne. Demesne lands in Senghennydd, in the lordship of Glamorgan, had been leased before 1307 and in the lordship of Chirk by 1324.[29]

The *gwely* system contained within itself elements which would ultimately account for its disintegration. Physical limitations were inevitably placed on those processes of territorial expansion which were an innate feature of the *gwely* movement. At an early stage efforts were made to obviate the combined effects of the pressure exerted by an expanding population on limited territorial resources and also of *cyfran* (the Welsh law of partible succession) but assarting and encroachments on to waste land were confined and eventually terminated by the non-availability of land.[30] Rural communities were also critically affected by the policies adopted by the thirteenth-century rulers of Gwynedd and these, designed to establish the framework of a feudal state, lessened the authority of kindred groupings over the ownership and occupation of land.[31]

Entries in the Survey of Denbigh 1334 illustrate the tenurial consequences of political action in Gwynedd Is Conwy, the area lying to the east of the River Conwy. The descendants of Ednyfed Fychan, seneschal to Llywelyn ab Iorwerth, prince of Gwynedd (1202–40) occupied their lands by means of a privileged arrangement and the only obligation imposed on them was that of rendering military service to the ruler. References are also found in the Survey to *tir cynnyf*, land purchased or acquired by means other than hereditary right, and to *prid*, a perpetual mortgage or vifgage which constituted the most common form of clan-land alienation in the later Middle Ages.[32] The *prid* was a lease for a term of years with the *priodor* (clansman) allowed to transfer his property for a consideration. Licences were purchased to secure a *prid* transaction and the princes of Gwynedd seem to have been aware of the benefits accruing from a carefully-regulated land market.[33] Traditional labour services and cash renders had been commuted into cash payments and in many localities the process had been completed by 1334. An urban centre also seems to have been established at Llanrwst and this represented another aspect of the attempt to establish a money economy in the thirteenth century.[34]

Surveys compiled by Edwardian officials for localities in north-west Wales illustrate the impetus given by the native rulers to the growth of urban centres in thirteenth-century Gwynedd. An extent compiled in 1284 refers to the establishment by the princes of a small Welsh town at Caernarfon with a port and a 'borough court'. The largest of the pre-conquest towns of north-west Wales was situated in Anglesey at Llan-faes which had evolved from a *maerdref* and a similar origin may be traced for the small towns of Pwllheli and Nefyn which were identified as urban centres by the royal officials who surveyed Llywelyn ap Gruffudd's estates in the Llŷn Peninsula in 1284. These towns continued to function throughout the later Middle Ages without the displacement of population experienced at Llan-faes and at Caernarfon.[35]

The Welsh town of Caernarfon had been succeeded by an Edwardian borough occupied by settlers brought in from outside Wales. The foundation of boroughs was an integral element of the Edwardian settlement of Wales. They were invariably closely associated with the castles which were built at this time and which had the primary aim of defending the new order in Wales. The charters, again based on the Hereford model, conferred on the burgesses various privileges. The allocation of administrative functions gave a further impetus to the newly-established towns, and Caernarfon and Carmarthen became the administrative centres for the north-west and south-west respectively.[36]

The surviving returns of the Lay Subsidy imposed in 1292–3 throw light on the social character of the newly-established boroughs. Attention has been drawn to the limited impact of the 'urban explosion' in the shire of Merioneth. The number of taxpayers at the chartered boroughs of Bere and Harlech was only sixteen and twelve respectively. In Flintshire, on the other hand, there were seventy-six taxpayers in Flint and seventy-five in Rhuddlan. These towns contained a considerable number of English settlers but one-third of the taxpayers of Bere and Harlech had Welsh names. Subsidy assessments for Cilgerran in the south-west suggest that there was a predominantly Welsh population in this town. The borough of Rhuthun, established in 1282, had a mixed Anglo-Welsh population and the 1324 rental records that forty of the seventy burgesses were Welshmen.[37]

Welshmen were excluded, however, from the borough of Denbigh, founded in 1285 and re-established c.1300 after the collapse of the initial attempt to launch the urban enterprise. The borough was located in close proximity to the castle which was the administrative centre for the lordship of Denbigh. Territory had been acquired partly by means of the operation of escheat with tenants who had committed an offence, or had been unable to render their dues, or had been involved in rebellion, deprived of their lands. Other local inhabitants were granted lands in other townships in exchange for their original holdings. Extensive areas of land were acquired by these two methods and immigrant English families, including the Hultons, Pigots, Salusburys and Swynemores, encouraged to settle here. Surrounding the five centres of English settlement in the lordship of Denbigh were parallel centres of Welsh influence formed as a result of the concentration of displaced tenants: the creation of distinctive zones of influence resembled the pattern which prevailed in the older marcher lordships, which were divided into Englishries and Welshries.[38]

Urban expansion and the movement of peoples, through encouragement and compulsion, together with the colonization of wasteland contributed to the substantial population figures which have been tentatively estimated for the late thirteenth century. A comparative survey of the available statistics for Merioneth has prompted the suggestion that the population of the shire, based on the evidence of the 1292–3 subsidy returns, was well in excess of 10,000 persons and that this was higher than the population implied by the subsidy returns of 1543.[39]

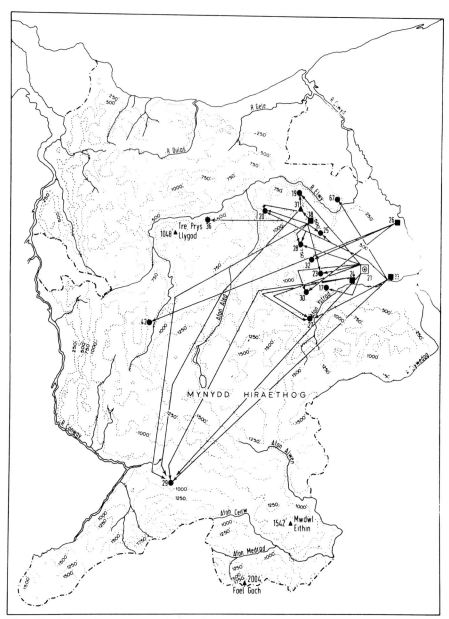

Fig. 48 The colonization and resettlement processes in the lordship of Denbigh (1282–1334): (a) the dispersal of the Welsh population at the time of the Edwardian Conquest; (b) the five centres of English settlement in the lordship of Denbigh.

◙ The manor and borough of Denbigh. ■ Township from which the original Welsh population was despatched. ▲ A township from which Welshmen were despatched and which also served as a reception centre. ●'Reception' centre

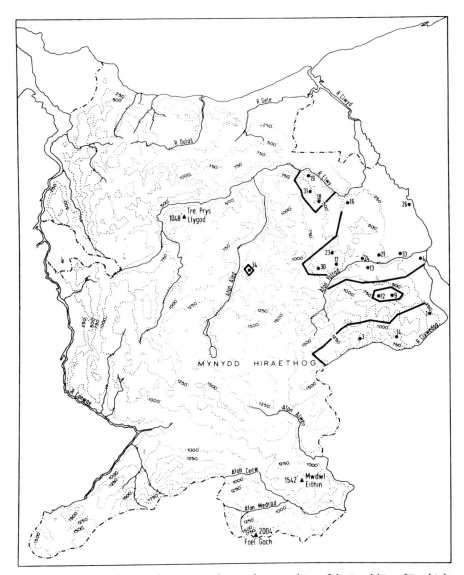

Fig. 48b   The numbers on these maps relate to the townships of the Lordship of Denbigh listed in 'Tenurial and Economic Developments in North Wales in the Twelfth and Thirteenth Centuries', *W.H.R.*, VI (1972), 137. The townships include Archwedlog (34), Berain (18), Dinbych/Denbigh (21), Gwenynog Cynon (24), Lleweni (26), Nantglyn Cynon (27), Prŷs (29), Segrwyd (13), Sgeibion (14), Wigfair (67), and Ystrad Cynon (33).

The demographic decline of the later Middle Ages was critically affected by periodic outbreaks of pestilence. The chronicler Geoffrey le Baker referred to the spread of the plague to Wales in 1349, and entries in the financial accounts and legal records of numerous localities emphasize the ravages of the visitations of 1349–50, 1361 and 1369. Among the areas which suffered severely from the outbreak of 1349–50 were the marcher lordships of south-east and north-east Wales: the court records of Rhuthun provide illuminating evidence of the extent to which the lordship was afflicted by the disease in the summer of 1349. Similarly ministers' accounts for the principalities of north and south Wales record the deaths of all twelve tenants-at-will who occupied the demesne-land on the manor of Llan-llwch, near Carmarthen in 1349, and also the numerous vacant holdings, in Anglesey and Caernarfonshire in 1351, caused by the poverty or death of their former occupants. References to the plague (*y Farwolaeth Fawr*) appear in contemporary poetry and Ieuan Gethin of Baglan vividly described the horrifying symptoms of the Plague which had resulted in the deaths of five of his children.[40]

It is evident that the successive outbreaks of pestilence had a considerable effect on local communities but, despite the inclusion of specific references in contemporary sources, problems are involved in the evaluation of its full impact. The undeniably terrifying character of the Plague possibly induced contemporary observers — chroniclers, officials and poets and also later historians — to overemphasize its importance in relation to the various economic difficulties of the period. The consequences of pestilence at times may well have been blamed by local officials who were unable for various reasons to collect revenue (this failure admittedly was often an indirect consequence of the plague with bondmen able to leave their traditional holdings and evade their communal obligations).[41] Moreover, the effects of plague may be placed in perspective when one considers the problems experienced in the early fourteenth century, *before* the first major outbreak of pestilence, with the manorial and kindred organizations already subject to strain and tension.

The fabric of Welsh society was subject to further change as a result of the extensive damage caused by Welsh forces and royal armies in many areas of Wales during the course of the Glyndŵr rebellion in the first decade of the fifteenth century. Owain Glyndŵr was described by Adam of Usk as 'a second Assyrian, the rod of God's anger' and the chronicler also commented on his 'deeds of unheard of cruelty with fire and sword' in the diocese of Llandaff.[42] The first attack of the rebellion was significantly launched on the borough of Rhuthun in September 1400 and throughout the revolt the privileged boroughs, together with the manors located in the Englishries of lordships, represented prime targets for the Welsh forces. The financial accounts again are illuminating sources for the devastation and dislocation caused to various localities and communities. An account of 1411 described the manorial borough of Pwllheli, regarded as an alien institution despite the fact that it was occupied by Welshmen, as 'destroyed and laid waste' and the tenants had apparently fled from the area.[43] Another account, compiled in 1410, records that tenements on the manor of Llantrisant, in the lordship of Usk, had been burned and devastated.[44] Moreover, ministers' accounts for the lordship of Newport record that mills destroyed during the rebellion had not yet been repaired.[45] Memories of the violence associated with the rebellion survived for many generations. Sir John Wynn, writing at the end of the Tudor period, provided a vivid description of the desolation caused at Llanrwst, that 'greene grasse grewe one the market place' and he also commented that 'it was Owen Glyndoores policie tobringe all thinges to wast, that the Englishe should find not strength nor restinge place in the Countrey'.[46]

The outbreaks of pestilence and the damage caused during the Glyndŵr rebellion had a shattering impact on communities comprising kindred groupings and also on manorial centres. The bond inhabitants were particularly vulnerable to the effects of plague, and their occupation of nucleated settlements may well explain the reduction in the bond population which may be observed in this period. *Tref gyfrif* tenure involved the imposition of rents on a communal basis, and therefore excessive pressure was exerted on those bondmen who survived the plague. The financial accounts of the Principality of North Wales record the suspension in some localities of payments of *staurum*, a render traditionally levied on bondmen, and the restoration of these payments by 1362 denotes a measure of recovery.[47] However, further opportunities were presented during the Glyndŵr rebellion for bondmen to escape from their financial obligations and entries in fifteenth-century accounts, derived from all parts of Wales, confirm the decay of bond settlements. Some bondmen secured their enfranchisement and in several localities there was a blurring of the traditional differences between bond and free tenures.[48] Bond settlements were frequently located on favourable soils and the disintegration of bond communities attracted the attention of the more enterprising and acquisitive freemen. In the early years of the reign of Henry VII Maredudd ab Ieuan decided to leave his hereditary lands in Eifionydd and move to Nanconwy so that 'he shoulde finde Elbowe roome in that wast countrey amonge the bondmen': an action which was probably the key factor in the growth of the landed estate of the Wynn family of Gwydir.[49]

Ambitious burgesses also exploited the opportunities presented by the pressure on bond communities and the boundaries of the boroughs of Conwy and Beaumaris were extended, in 1355 and 1366 respectively, as a result of the addition of lands formerly held by bondmen.[50] The residents of the plantation boroughs of north Wales also gained possession of small clan-holdings located in the adjacent rural hinterlands. The finest example of this trend was the acquisition of hundreds of small properties in the commote of Arllechwedd Isaf by Bartholomew Bolde, a burgess of Conwy, in the period 1420–53. The extreme morcellation of holdings in this commote was a feature of the mid fifteenth-century rental prepared for Bolde.[51] His daughter and heiress had married William Bulkeley of Beaumaris and the lands acquired by Bartholomew Bolde formed a substantial portion of the Caernarfonshire section of the Bulkeley estate.

The foundation of the Bulkeley estate illustrates the successful policies adopted by a settler family in north Wales to further its territorial, social and political ambitions. William Bulkeley the elder came from Cheshire to Beaumaris where he held various offices in the borough and castle and purchased properties in the town, building a residence, Henblas, near to the church in the last quarter of the fifteenth century.[52] Native gentry families (*uchelwyr*) were at this time in a dominant position in many areas of Wales. Penrhyn in north-west Wales and Raglan in the south-east were renowned as centres of bardic patronage and a succession of poets sang in praise of the Gruffudd and Herbert families. Poetic compositions frequently contain valuable information on the buildings and life-style of gentry families, in addition to the personal qualities of the patrons who were extolled in return for their hospitality. Rhys Goch Eryri, in a poem composed after 1405, contrasted Penrhyn, a white-washed timber building which was not yet the main residence of the Gruffudd family, with the heavily fortified Eagle tower at Caernarfon castle.[53] Dafydd Llwyd of Mathafarn, in the second half of the fifteenth century, provided both a lengthy description of a feast at Penrhyn and also of the various means whereby the residents of Raglan amused themselves: the leisure activities and amenities included dancing, carousel, card-playing, dog-handling, parks and wine-gardens. The size of the mansion had clearly impressed the poet and the number of chambers, towers, parlours, gates, chimneys, bonfires and lofts in each case was given as a hundred. Dafydd Llwyd also referred to a vast great new hall, a 'cellar which is the width of the building', a 'high lead (roof)', and 'the dance held above the dungeon'.[54]

In the late fourteenth century Iolo Goch had described in detail Owain Glyndŵr's residence at Sycharth: a timbered house with four lofts 'on four marvellous pillars, tiled roofs and chimneys that cannot nurse smoke'. Associated with the mansion were an orchard, mill, vineyard, deer-park, dovecot and fishpond and the house occupied what was probably the only example of a moated site in the locality:

> Mewn eurgylch dwfr mewn argae.
> Pand da'r llys, pont ar y llyn,
>
> (Moated with water's gold round
> Fine manor, bridge on the moat)[55]

A poem composed by Guto'r Glyn in the mid fifteenth century provides valuable information on another moated site: the parsonage sited beside the church at Llandrinio (Montgomeryshire).

> Dŵr yn gaer i'w droi'n ei gylch
> Llyn perffaith fal llun pwrffil
>
> (By water girt a moated fort provide;
> A lake surrounds the whole in shapely guise)

The new long hall is roofed with tiles and contains nine rooms which include a parlour for the host who shares the wine: 'Parlwr i'r gŵr a rôi'r gwin'.[56]

A total of 130 probable and possible moated sites have been identified in Wales with a concentration in the lowland areas of the eastern borderlands and the southern coastal belt. Most had seigneurial functions and served as manorial centres: it is probable that the majority represented an alternative for the lesser lords, and also for the paramount lords on their less important lands, to the provision of a stone castle to protect the manor.[57] It has been argued, however, that a group of moated farmsteads in Maelor, the detached portion of Flintshire, had been established as centres for the colonization of the waste and the clearing of woodland.[58] One of the few excavated sites is the one at Highlight (north of Barry). A sub-manor of the lordship of Dinas Powys, it formed an administrative centre for the de Sumeri family from the late twelfth century to the early fourteenth century. Occupied in the late twelfth century and certainly moated by the thirteenth century, it was abandoned in the fifteenth century as a result of the building nearby of a larger manor house which became the home of a cadet branch of the St John family of Fonmon.[59]

Defensive buildings, such as St Donat's castle, the residence of the Stradling family, were the homes of most of the predominant magnates in the later Middle Ages, but a significant trend may be observed towards the end of the period with the occupation of undefended houses. Some of these, such as New Place (Swansea), Castleton (near St Athan's), and Castle Farm (St George's), were manor houses which incorporated adaptations of earlier fortifications. Several of the surviving medieval domestic buildings in Glamorgan were the residences of clergymen, and these include Glebe Farm, Cheriton (Gower) and three parsonages at St Donat's, Llantwit Major and St Andrew's. A distribution map of these houses again emphasizes the greater degree of survival in the lowlands of Glamorgan and the same was true of the monastic granges, with the cluster of Neath Abbey granges in the Dulais and upper Neath Valleys constituting an exception to this trend. The surviving remains of these monastic farms, which include the Great Barn at Monknash and the Dovecot, Gatehouse and lower portions of the walls of the tithe barn at the Grange of Abbot's Llantwit, provide valuable information on agrarian practices and domestic conditions in the later Middle Ages.[60]

The fluctuating fortunes of monastic farms mirrored contemporary economic developments. The expansion of Cistercian estates had occasionally involved the displacement of tenants and the acquisitive methods employed by the monks of Neath and Margam were condemned respectively by Walter Map and Gerald of Wales. In his *Speculum Ecclesiae* Gerald narrated how the consolidation by Margam Abbey of the grange of Llangewydd, near Laleston, had involved the dismantling at night of the existing castle and church and the expulsion of parishioners from their homes. The encroachments of sea and sand led to the depopulation of settlements along the southern coast. Those granges located in the coastal lowlands near to Margam Abbey were affected by the encroachment of sand dunes in Margam Burrows and Kenfig Burrows and the grange at Kenfig had been abandoned for this reason by the middle of the fourteenth century. Extensive damage was caused on the south-west coast of Anglesey in 1331 and 186 acres of the lands of Newborough were covered by sand and tide and rendered unfit for further cultivation.[61]

The creation of monastic granges and the consequences of sand-drift, plague and rebellion all contributed to the desertion of hamlets and villages in this period. Archaeological evidence suggests that in Glamorgan the villages of Gwmcidy, Highlight, Barry, Sully and Radyr, which were examples of linear-type settlements with houses following trails or streets, experienced shrinkage during the late fourteenth century (of the eighteen sites in Glamorgan which survive either as earthworks or as excavated remains Wrinstone seems to be the only example of a nucleated village clustered around a green).[62] A combination of pressures intensified by the effects of plague and rebellion led to the decline of nucleated settlements in the lordship of Laugharne.[63] Physical damage caused during the Glyndŵr rebellion was responsible for the desertion of the hamlets of Sutton and Northdown in the lordship of Ogmore. However, entries in surveys prepared in 1429 and 1502 and relating to six manors in the same lordship denote substantial increases in the number of tenants and in the extent of cultivated land.[64] Ministers' accounts compiled for Wrinstone (in 1416–17) and Michaelston(in 1428–9) indicate that a demographic recovery had taken place on these manors situated in the south-eastern Vale of Glamorgan.[65] The availability of land in the early fifteenth century stimulated both a mobility of tenants and an active land-market. Recolonization of desolate land was accompanied by encroachments on to waste and wooded lands. This process seems to have been well advanced by the end of the fifteenth century as was the conversion of *hafodydd*, originally summer-dwellings in the mountain-moorlands, into separate and later independent farms.[66]

Another important development which was in progress at this time was the enclosure of open fields. This was the period when Rice Merrick's informants considered that 'great part of the inclosures [in the Vale of Glamorgan] was made in those days'.[67] Another sixteenth-century commentator, George Owen of Henllys, referred to the widespread survival of open fields in north Pembrokeshire.[68] Estate records and manorial and tithe surveys contain entries which reflect the division of arable fields into strips. Remains of open-field farming, in strips, have survived to the present day in parts of Gower and the Vale of Glamorgan. At Rhosili arable strips in a surviving manorial open field, known as 'The Vile', are still separated by uncultivated balks, termed 'landshares', but in some places there are permanent boundaries in the form of dry-stone walls or earth banks.[69]

Reference has already been made to the cultivation of open fields by freemen and bondmen in settlements occupied respectively by *gwely* and *tref gyfrif* tenure.[70] Climatic, soil and topographical conditions had a critical influence on the extent and distribution of open-field cultivation and also on the adoption of crop-rotation systems. Only a limited number of specific references signify the existence of a three-field system.[71] Ministers' accounts record the arrangement of fields into three groups on the manor of Llantrisant in the lower Usk Valley in the period 1323–6. The predominant crops were wheat and oats, and the latter, widely cultivated in medieval Wales, provided a staple diet and also constituted a source of winter fodder for animals.[72] Local conditions restricted corn production to the fertile coastal lowlands and river valleys and Gerald of Wales commented on the exceptional fertility of Anglesey which justified his use of the phrase 'Môn Mam Cymru' (Anglesey, the Mother of Wales): 'When crops have failed in all other regions this island, from the richness of its soil and its abundant produce, has been able to supply all Wales.'[73] In the sixteenth century John Leland remarked on 'very good plenty of corne and grasse' between Nefyn and Aberdaron in the Llŷn Peninsula.[74]

The unsuitability of some portions of the demesne lands for the cultivation of wheat explains irregularities in the systematic application of a three-course rotation. An unequal balance characterized the open fields at Llantrisant: those on which wheat and oats were cultivated comprised between fifty and sixty acres, whilst the fields used for the growing of the less important crops of barley, peas and beans were under ten acres in extent.[75] A contrast may be observed between the south and north of the former shire of Pembroke in that the absence of two or three-field systems in the north is suggested by George Owen's comment that winter corn was not sown. The information contained in Owen's writings concerning the adoption of infield/outfield agrarian arrangements in both the southern and northern areas is clearly relevant for the late-medieval period, and lands used for temporary forms of cultivation in other regions of Wales, described as *terra montana* or *tir y mynydd*, corresponded to the outfield.[76]

The character of ploughing arrangements is revealed by the evidence contained in legal texts and contemporary poetry. Financial penalties and valuations emphasize the qualities of the ideal plough-ox, and the practice of co-tillage was outlined in the regulations which governed the cultivation of twelve 'acres' with one acre each belonging to the ploughman, ox-driver, owners of the plough-frame and plough-irons, and the owners of the eight oxen forming the plough-team, respectively. The language, imagery and content of contemporary poetry vividly illustrates agrarian practices involved in crop cultivation. Detailed descriptions of ploughs were presented by the poets Iolo Goch and Lewys Glyn Cothi, and the manuscript of a legal text compiled in Ceredigion contains an illustration of a plough. *Cywyddau* composed by Ieuan Deulwyn towards the end of the fifteenth century refer to a late-surviving example of the long-yoke, with eight oxen arranged four abreast of each other, and also to a long-team, a more popular arrangement by this time, whereby the oxen were grouped in pairs with one pair following the other.[77]

Vivid descriptions are also provided on the various breeds and colours of the cattle of late-medieval Wales.[78] The importance of cattle-rearing had been appreciated by the native rulers of Gwynedd whose strategically-placed vaccaries, including four cattle-farms near to the royal residence at Aber, formed a crucial element of their military policies.[79] An examination of the Edwardian extents reveals that although sheep were more numerous than cattle, they were found on less than 60 per cent of farms in north-west Wales, in contrast to the 90 per cent of farms whose livestock included cattle.[80] In the second half of the fourteenth century, vaccaries in Fforest Fawr and Fforest Fach in the lordship of Brecon were supervised by stock-keepers and provided for the requirements of the castles and manors of the lordship, and also for other estates held by the lord.[81]

The limited extent of sheep-farming in some localities was caused by the unsuitability of the terrain, the prevalence of disease, marketing difficulties, and the lack of protective facilities. Sheep-rearing enterprises were particularly associated with the estates of Cistercian abbeys and marcher lords. The statistics contained in the 1291 *Taxatio* and the poll tax return of 1379 should be handled with care, but they clearly illustrate the maintenance of large sheep-flocks on the estates of Margam, Neath, Strata Florida and Tintern.[82] Sheep-rearing activities on the lands of Strata Florida in mid and west Wales were based on an integrated system of dispersed granges with the sheep driven from the uplands used for summer grazing to the lowlands for the winter months.[83] The Bohun lands in the Marches contained important sheep-rearing centres and approximately 3,000 sheep were kept in 1372 by the Earl of Hereford in the lordship of Brecon. Permanent sheep-folds had been built at Bronllys, the main sheep farm, and at Bryndu. Over 18,000 fleeces were produced on the Bohun estates in the period 1367 to 1372 and a substantial number were sent in 1371 for sale in London.[84] The wool produced in Wales and the border shires was of an extremely good quality and the flocks of Abbey Dore, Margam and Tintern were renowned for their high-grade wool. Critical comments, however, were made on the standard of wool exported from Carmarthen, and in 1341 Welsh wool was described as 'being coarse and of little value.'[85] The increasing importance of wool production was reflected by the designation in 1326 of Carmarthen and Cardiff as staple towns.[86] Declining soil fertility and climatic deterioration, together with the depopulation and devastation caused by pestilence and rebellion, contributed to the conversion of arable land to pasture, and the scarcity of tenants — even more than the price of wool — was an incentive for an expansion in sheep-rearing farming activities.[87]

Fifteenth-century Customs' Accounts record not only a reduction in the amount of wool exported from Welsh ports but also an increased emphasis on cloth production.[88] In contrast to the expanding English cloth industry which was not primarily dependent upon local supplies of high quality wool, large flocks of sheep produced the raw material for the fulling-mills of the Welsh Marches. The distribution of the 202 fulling-mills identified in Wales and the Marches before 1547 signifies the existence of cloth-producing centres in many localities, but with a concentration in the marcher lordships. Earlier developments were in the southern march but there was an increasing investment in northern areas in the later Middle Ages. The important local centres in the south included Brynmill along the coast to the west of Swansea. This formed in the fifteenth century a self-contained industrial area which comprised four *pandai* and at least two grain mills. To the west, a concentration of mills in the lordship of Cydweli centred on the urban centres of Cydweli and Llanelli whilst another industrial area developed beneath the priory in Carmarthen: the priory's involvement was an exception to the trend of a largely secular industry. In the north an industrial complex was formed on the River Ceiriog near Chirk whilst the borough of Rhuthun was one of the main centres of the cloth trade in north Wales.[89] Cloth produced in Wales was not only sold locally but was also taken to markets in border towns or sent to the annual St Bartholomew Fair in London. Large quantities of friezes were also exported to overseas markets either directly from Welsh ports, including Beaumaris, Carmarthen and Rhuddlan or from Bristol which, as a major manufacturing centre, featured prominently in the Welsh export trade.[90]

Information relating to the exploitation of mineral resources in the Middle Ages signify the existence of other groups of small industrial settlements. Domesday Book refers to an iron-mine in north-east Wales, probably at Bodfari and to a mint established by the Norman lord, Robert of Rhuddlan.[91] Gerald of Wales, in the late twelfth century, also commented on silver-mining operations in this area as he travelled from St Asaph to Basingwerk and he also drew attention to the Forest of Dean as a significant iron-working area.[92] The adjoining lordship of Monmouth was also important in this respect and iron-producing communities have also been identified in numerous areas of Wales, including the lordships of Abergavenny, Brecon, Builth and Llandovery. Lead was mined in north Cardiganshire, and at Llanddewibrefi a small supply of lead was obtained in 1326 from a mine owned by the Bishop of St David's.[93] The lead-miners of Minera in the lordship of Bromfield and Yale formed an autonomous community which enjoyed legal and administrative privileges in the fourteenth century.[94] Metal-smelting enterprises were fuelled by charcoal supplies, and considerable amounts of charcoal were made and sold in Flintshire and in Gwent.[95] There was only a limited demand for coal at this time, even for domestic purposes, but there is evidence of coal-mining enterprises in Flintshire and in Bromfield and Yale.[96] The outcropping of coal measures to the surface explains the location of coal-mines on the periphery of the south Wales coalfield, in the coastal areas of the lordships of Pembroke, Cydweli, Gower and Kilvey. Here, at Llansamlet to the east of the River Tawe, net profits by the end of the fourteenth century were estimated at £90 per annum.[97]

On the whole, mining operations were on a confined scale and economic activity was largely based on agriculture. In addition to the woollen and cloth industries leather was produced for footwear and harness, and numerous cobblers appear in analyses of the names of persons living in Merioneth and Anglesey. The production of millstones was an important industry in Anglesey, with local stones being used in the fourteenth century for rebuilding royal mills on the island and also exported for royal mills at Chester and Dublin. Brewing may also be considered as an agriculture-based industry. Relevant information is provided in court rolls which record fines for licences to brew and amercements for unlicensed brewing: the alehouse seems to have been a social centre for communities in medieval Wales.[98]

Churches were other, and more revered, social centres in an 'Age of Faith'. Aspects of their development have already been considered and this reflects the extent to which they were affected by the main trends of the period. The siting of churches is an indication of the existence and vitality of communities and their isolated location today in some areas suggests the abandonment of a bond settlement which had previously clustered around the church.[99] The small and more concentrated parishes of lowland Glamorgan, in contrast to those of Blaenau Morgannwg, probably resulted from the capacity of the more fertile lowlands to support a larger population. Parish boundaries corresponded to those of secular administrative units and they occasionally seem to have been based on the boundaries of estates which existed before the Norman Conquest.[100] The effects of successive phases of conquest, pestilence and rebellion were experienced on ecclesiastical and monastic estates but renewed church-building activity in the fifteenth century confirms the evidence for a more general economic recovery. The enlargement of the village of Tythegston, in Glamorgan, as a result of a population movement from Candleston, Newton Burrows and Merthyr Mawr Warren explains the rebuilding of the church in the fifteenth century.[101] An expanding urban population also accounted for the construction in the late fifteenth century of the church of St John's in the centre of Cardiff. The impressive tower of this church has been attributed to the patronage of Isabel Nevill, duchess of Clarence (d. 1476), and Jasper Tudor, Henry VII's uncle, is associated with the building of the spire of St Mary's church, Tenby and also the north-west tower of Llandaff Cathedral, known as 'Jasper's Tower'.[102] In north-east Wales elegant towers characterized the group of 'Stanley' churches built at Gresford, Mold and Northop.[103]

Evidence of decay and growth also illustrates the varying experiences of urban communities in this period. Several towns had succumbed to contemporary economic pressures, and this was particularly true of those urban communities whose existence depended almost entirely on their location near to a castle. Towns in this category which were either in a depressed state or had disappeared completely included Bere, Dolforwyn, Dinefwr, Dryslwyn and Caerffili. Substantial sand encroachments were responsible for the abandonment of Kenfig but the artificial nature of town plantation accounted for the decay of many urban settlements. The outstanding example of this process is probably the gradual decline of Tre-lech, which today is a modest village in Gwent but was one of the largest towns in late-thirteenth-century Wales with 378 burgages recorded in 1288. In 1298, 102 burgages were described as vacant following an attack launched during the rebellion which had erupted in 1294–5. It is also known that this area suffered heavily from the outbreak of pestilence in 1369.[104]

Some towns, however, recovered from the debilitating effects of plague and rebellion. Rhuthun and Cydweli, which were both attacked by Owain Glyndŵr's forces, were the centres of a prosperous cloth industry in the late fifteenth century. At Cydweli, urban development had significantly occurred not in the 'old Toun', described in the sixteenth century by John Leland as 'near desolate' but in the area situated on the other side of the River Gwendraeth.[105] Urban expansion into areas removed from the castle and into suburban localities emphasizes that commercial factors, rather than strategic considerations, were becoming increasingly important. This was true of the four towns identified as being at the head of an 'urban hierarchy' in the sixteenth century and also probably in a pre-eminent position from the information available for the late fifteenth century.[106] Damage had been inflicted on Caernarfon and Denbigh during the rebellion of 1294–5, and on Denbigh again during the dynastic wars of the fifteenth century. Moreover, Brecon, Caernarfon and Carmarthen had been besieged by Glyndŵr's forces. All four towns, however, had recovered from the attacks launched on them and were in a reasonably prosperous condition by the late fifteenth century.[107]

In these four towns, as in numerous others, Welshmen struggled, with varying degrees of success, to be allowed to hold offices and property. Resistance was encountered from members of settler families especially in the plantation boroughs of north Wales. However, racial distinctions were often ignored as Welshmen were accepted as full and equal members of the urban community. Relations between urban and rural inhabitants consequently improved. The diminution of other social distinctions, including those between freemen and bondmen, suggests the formation of a new society, with accompanying novel settlement patterns.

NOTES

[1] The work which have proved to be of exceptional value in relation to this chapter include F.G. Cowley, *The Monastic Order in South Wales, 1066–1349* (Cardiff, 1977); R.R. Davies, *Lordship and Society in the March of Wales, 1282–1400* (Oxford, 1978); R.A. Griffiths (ed.), *Boroughs of Mediaeval Wales* (Cardiff, 1978); A.O.H. Jarman and G.R. Hughes (eds.), *A Guide to Welsh Literature* 2, (Swansea, 1979); T. Jones Pierce, *Medieval Welsh Society*, ed. J. Beverley Smith, (Cardiff, 1972) [M.W.S.]; G.R.J. Jones, 'The Tribal System in Wales; a Re-assessment in the Light of Settlement Studies', *W.H.R.*, I (1961–2), 111–32; E.A Lewis, *The Medieval Boroughs of Snowdonia* (1912); T.B. Pugh (ed.), *Glamorgan*

County History, III, The Middle Ages (Cardiff, 1971); W. Rees, South Wales and the March (Oxford, 1924); Glyn Roberts, Aspects of Welsh History (Cardiff, 1969); Glanmor Williams, The Welsh Church from Conquest to Reformation (Cardiff, 1962); K. Williams-Jones (ed.), The Merioneth Lay Subsidy Roll 1292–3 (Cardiff, 1976). A number of important legal studies have been published in recent years and an evaluation of the evidence contained in legal texts appears in G.R.J. Jones, 'Field Systems of North Wales' in A.R.H. Baker and R.A. Butlin (eds.), Studies of Field Systems in the British Isles (Cambridge, 1973), 430–9.

[2] J.E. Lloyd, A History of Wales from the Earliest Times to the Edwardian Conquest, II, (1911); D. Walker, The Norman Conquerors (Cardiff, 1977); Glanmor Williams, Owen Glendower (Oxford, 1966); H.T. Evans, Wales and the Wars of the Roses (Cambridge, 1915).

[3] G.R.J. Jones 'Rural Settlement in Anglesey' in S.R. Eyre and G.R.J. Jones (eds.), Geography as Human Ecology (1966), 199–230; T. Jones Pierce, 'The Growth of Commutation in Gwynedd during the Thirteenth Century' in M.W.S., 119–20. R.H. Hilton, in A Medieval Society, The West Midlands at the End of the Thirteenth Century (1966) identifies two major distinctive settlement forms in this region: areas of early settlement with large nucleated villages, open-field agrarian systems and emphasis on arable farming; and areas of later development with dispersed settlements, enclosed fields and extensive pastoral districts.

[4] W. Rees, South Wales and the March, 28-31; Davies, Lordship and Society, 302–18.

[5] J. Beverley Smith, 'The Kingdom of Morgannwg and the Norman Conquest of Glamorgan' in G.C.H. III, 11–12.

[6] Ibid., 9–10, 15, 17, 27–8; F.G. Cowley, 'The Church in Glamorgan from the Norman Conquest to the Beginning of the Fourteenth Century', ibid., 95–6.

[7] R.A. Griffiths, 'Medieval Severnside: The Welsh Connection' in R.R. Davies, R.A. Griffiths, Ieuan Gwynedd Jones, and Kenneth O. Morgan (eds.), Welsh Society and Nationhood, Historical Essays presented to Glanmor Williams (Cardiff, 1984), 74–89.

[8] I.W. Rowlands, 'The Making of the March: aspects of the Norman settlement in Dyfed' in R. Allen Brown (ed.), Proceedings of the Battle Conference on Anglo-Norman Studies, III (1980), 146–8; Gerald of Wales, The Journey through Wales and The Description of Wales, trans. with introd. by Lewis Thorpe (1978), 141–2, 145–7.

[9] Douglas B. Hague, 'The Castles of Glamorgan and Gower', G.C.H. III, 426–7, 443; C.J. Spurgeon and H.J. Thomas, 'Glamorgan Castles (General), Early Castles in Glamorgan', Archaeology in Wales, Group 2, 20 (1980), 64–9; D.F. Renn, 'The Anglo-Norman Keep, 1066–1138', Jnl. Brit. Arch. Assoc., 3rd Ser. XXIII, (1960), 1–23; W. Rees, Caerphilly Castle (Cardiff, 1937); R.A. Brown and H.M. Colvin;' The Royal Castles 1066–1485' in H.M. Colvin (ed.), The History of the King's Works, 11, The Middle Ages (1963), 685–7; A.J. Taylor, The King's Works in Wales 1277–1330 (1974), 293–408; D.J. Cathcart King, 'Pembroke Castle', A.C., CXXVII (1978), 75–121.

[10] C.A. Ralegh Radford, Ewenny Priory (Ministry of Works Guide, 1952); Conway Castle and Town Walls (Ministry of Works Guide, 1956); L.A.S. Butler, Denbigh Castle, Town Walls and Friary (1976), 26–33.

[11] See the editor's chapter in Griffiths, Boroughs of Mediaeval Wales, 130–63; T. James, Carmarthen: An Archaeological and Topographical Survey (Carmarthen, 1980), 23–46.

[12] Thomas Jones (ed.), Brut y Tywysogyon, Peniarth MS 20 (Cardiff, 1941), 26–7; idem (ed.), Brut y Tywysogyon or The Chronicle of the Princes, Peniarth MS 20 Version (Cardiff, 1952), 19–20.

[13] F.J. North, 'The Map of Wales', A.C., XV (1935), 30–4, reproduction in C. Platt, The English Medieval Town (1976), plate 1.

[14] See Plate XI for reproduction of plan of Carmarthen included in John Speed, The Theatre of the Empire of Great Britain . . . (1611), and Plate XII for copy of artist's impression of the neighbouring town of Cydweli in the mid fifteenth century (Alan Sorrel, Early Wales Re-Created (Cardiff, 1980), 55).

[15] J.R. Daniel-Tyssen, Royal Charters and historical documents relating to the town and county of Carmarthen . . . ed. A.C. Evans (Carmarthen, 1876), 7; M. Bateson, 'The Laws of Breteuil', E.H.R., XV (1900), 302–18, 495–523, 754–7, and XVI (1901), 92–110, 332–45; D. Walker, 'Hereford and the laws of

Breteuil', *Trans. Woolhope Naturalists' Field Club*, XL(1) (1970), 55–65; Lewis, *Medieval Boroughs*, 17, 40.

[16] M. Davies, 'Field Systems of South Wales' in Baker and Butlin (eds.), *Studies of Field Systems*, 482–4; Davies, *Lordship and Society*, 109; J.S. Moore (ed.), *Gloucestershire, Domesday Book*, gen. ed. J. Morris (Chichester, 1982) 162–3.

[17] J.B. Smith, *G.C.H.* III, 15–16, 19.

[18] Idem and T.B. Pugh, 'The Lordship of Gower and Kilvey in the Middle Ages', ibid., 209, 214.

[19] G.R.J. Jones, *W.H.R.*, 1 (1961–2), 119–21; idem, *Geography as Human Ecology*, 211–14; idem, in *Studies of Field Systems*, 434, 460–71; T. Jones Pierce, 'Pastoral and Agricultural Settlements in Early Wales' in *M.W.S.*, 342–7.

[20] Ibid., 340–2; idem., 'Agrarian Aspects of the Tribal System in Medieval Wales' in *M.W.S.*, 332–6; idem, 'Landlords in Wales, The Nobility and Gentry' in J. Thirsk (ed.), *The Agrarian History of England and Wales*, [*Ag. Hist.*] IV, 1500–1640 (Cambridge, 1967); Jones in *Studies of Field Systems*, 432–3;D. Jenkins (ed.), *Llyfr Colan* (Cardiff, 1963); idem, 'A Lawyer looks at Welsh Land Law', *T.C.S.* (1967), 220–47.

[21] P. Vinogradoff and F. Morgan (eds.), *Survey of the Honour of Denbigh, 1334* (Oxford, 1914); D.H. Owen, 'Tenurial and Economic Developments in North Wales in the Twelfth and Thirteenth Centuries', *W.H.R.*, VI (1972), 117–42 for discussion on information contained in the Survey on bond and free units and distribution-maps of property held by the four predominant clans. Figure 47 displays the expansion of the Marchweithian and Braint Hir clans in the twelfth and thirteenth centuries.

[22] G.P. Jones, 'Rhos and Rhufoniog Pedigrees', *A.C.*, V (1925), 300.

[23] T. Jones Pierce, 'An Anglesey Crown Rental of the Sixteenth Century', in *M.W.S.*, 87–101; idem. 'Medieval Settlement in Anglesey', ibid., 253–8.

[24] C.A. Gresham, *Eifionydd, A Study in Landownership from the Medieval Period to the Present Day* (Cardiff, 1973), 146–7.

[25] T. Jones Pierce, 'The Gafael in Bangor Manuscript 1939', in *M.W.S.*, 220–4.

[26] G.R.J. Jones, 'The Distribution of Bond Settlements in North-West Wales', *W.H.R.*, II (1964), 28; idem, in *Studies of Field Systems* 457–8.

[27] C. Thomas, 'Social Organisation and Rural Settlement in Medieval North Wales', *Jnl. Mer. H.R.S.*, VI (1970), 128–30; J.R. Jones, 'The Development of the Penrhyn Estate up to 1431', (Univ. Wales MA Thesis 1955), 174.

[28] J.W. Willis-Bund, (ed.), *The Black Book of St. David's*, Cymmrodorion Record Series, 5, (1902), 284–9; T. Jones Pierce, 'Medieval Cardiganshire, a Study in Social Origins' in *M.W.S.*, 317–24.

[29] G. Duby, *Rural Economy and CountryLife in the Medieval West* (1968), 312–31; A.J. Roderick and W. Rees (ed.), 'The Lordship of Monmouth', *S.W.M.R.S.*, 4 (1957), 5–29; Davies, *Lordship and Society*, 113–15; J. Beverley Smith, 'The Lordship of Senghennydd' in *G.C.H.* III, 315–16; Llinos O.W. Smith, 'The Lordships of Chirk and Oswestry: 1282–1415', (Univ. London Ph.D thesis 1970), 139–40.

[30] Jones Pierce, *Ag. Hist.* iv, 360–1; G.R.J. Jones, 'Some Medieval Rural Settlements in North Wales', *T. Inst. Brit. Geog.*, (1953), 60.

[31] Jones Pierce, *M.W.S.*, 119–24.

[32] Owen, *W.H.R.*, VI (1972) 123–34; Vinogradoff and Morgan, *Survey of the Honour of Denbigh*, ff. 49, 196, 269.

[33] Llinos Beverley Smith, 'The Gage and the Land Market in Late-Medieval Wales', *Ec.H.R.*, XXXIX (1976), 537–50; idem, 'Tir Prid: Deeds of Gage of Land in Late-Medieval Wales', *B.B.C.S.*, XXVII (1977), 263–77.

[34] Owen, op. cit., 134–5; Vinogradoff and Morgan, op. cit., ff.254–5.

[35] Williams-Jones, 'Caernarvon' in Griffiths, *Boroughs of Mediaeval Wales*, 75. T. Jones Pierce, 'A Caernarvonshire Manorial Borough: Studies in the Medieval History of Pwllheli', *M.W.S.*, 132–51; ibid., 121–3, 279–81; F. Seebohm, *The Tribal System in Wales* (1895), Appendix A, 3–25.

[36] Griffiths, *Boroughs of Mediaeval Wales*, 72–101, 130–63.

[37] Williams-Jones, *Merioneth Lay Subsidy Roll 1292–3*, lx–lxiv, 51–2, 65–6; P.G. Sudbury, 'The Medieval Boroughs of Pembrokeshire' (Univ. Wales MA thesis 1947), 111; R. Ian Jack, 'Records of Denbighshire Lordships, 11: The Lordship of Dyffryn Clwyd in 1324', *T.D.H.S.*, XVII (1968), 13–18.

[38] D.H. Owen, 'Denbigh' in Griffiths, *Boroughs of Mediaeval Wales*, 165; idem, 'The Englishry of Denbigh: An English Colony in Medieval Wales', *T.C.S.* (1974 and 1975), 57–76. Figures 48a and b illustrates the colonization and resettlement processes in the area featured in Figure 47.

[39] Williams-Jones, *Merioneth Lay Subsidy Roll 1292–3*, xxxv–liv.

[40] W. Rees, 'The Black Death in Wales., *T.R.H.S.* 4th Ser. III, (1920), 120–3; Jones Pierce, 'Some Tendencies in the Agrarian History of Caernarvonshire during the Later Middle Ages', in *M.W.S.*, 43–4, G.J. Williams, *Traddodiad Llenyddol Morgannwg* (Cardiff, 1948), 28–9; C.W. Lewis, 'The Literary Tradition of Morgannwg down to the middle of the Sixteenth Century', in *G.C.H.* III, 498–9.

[41] D.L. Evans, 'Some Notes on the History of the Principality of Wales in the Time of the Black Prince, (1343–1376)', *T.C.S.* (1925–6), 80.

[42] E. Maunde-Thompson, (ed.), *Chronicon Ade de Usk* (1904), 247.

[43] Jones Pierce, *M.W.S.*, 156; P.R.O. S.C. 6/1175/9.

[44] Rees, *South Wales and the March*, 278; P.R.O. S.C. 6/928/20.

[45] T.B. Pugh, *The Marcher Lordships of South Wales, 1415–1536* (Cardiff, 1963), 167–9.

[46] Sir John Wynn, *The History of the Gwydir Family*, (ed.) J. Ballinger, (Cardiff, 1927), 52–3.

[47] E.A. Lewis, 'The Decay of Tribalism in North Wales.', *T.C.S.*, (1902–3), 44; Jones Pierce, *M.W.S.*, 43–4.

[48] C. Thomas, 'The Social and Economic Geography of Rural Merioneth from the Dark Ages to the Act of Union', typescript of chapter for forthcoming Merioneth County History, 11, 23. I am grateful to Dr Thomas for allowing me to read a manuscript copy of this chapter prior to its publication.

[49] Wynn, *History of the Gwydir Family*, 54; Gresham, *Eifionydd*, 87–9; J. Gwynfor Jones, 'The Wynn Estate of Gwydir: Aspects of its Growth and Development *c.* 1500–1587', *N.L.W. Jnl.*, XXII (2) (1981), 141–2.

[50] Lewis, *The Medieval Boroughs of Snowdonia*, 46, 50.

[51] Jones Pierce, *M.W.S.*, 195–217; C.A. Gresham, 'The Bolde Rental (Bangor MS. 1939)', *T.C.H.S.*, 26 (1965), 31–49.

[52] D.C. Jones, 'The Bulkeleys of Beaumaris 1440–1547', *T.A.A.S.*, (1961), 1–4; A.D. Carr, *Medieval Anglesey* (Llangefni, 1982), 217–21.

[53] G. Roberts, 'Wyrion Eden, The Anglesey Descendants of Ednyfed Fychan in the Fourteenth Century' in *Aspects of Welsh History*, 210, 213; H. Lewis, T. Roberts, Ifor Williams (eds.), *Cywyddau Iolo Goch ac eraill* (Cardiff, 1972), 310–13.

[54] E. Rowlands, 'The Continuing Tradition' in Jarman and Hughes, *A Guide to Welsh Literature 2*, 312–13.

[55] Lewis, Roberts, Williams, *Cywyddau Iolo Goch*, 36; J.P. Clancy, *Medieval Welsh Lyrics* (Cardiff, 1965), 136.

[56] D.R. Thomas, 'Llandrinio in the 15th century. Two Poems by Gutto'r Glyn *c.* 1430–70', *Mont. Coll.*, XXXIII (1904), 143–54, Ifor Williams (ed.) *Gwaith Guto'r Glyn* (Cardiff, 1961), 275–6.

[57] Royal Commission on Ancient and Historical Monuments in Wales, *An Inventory of the Ancient Monuments in Glamorgan* [Glam. Inv.], III, Pt. 2 (Cardiff, 1982), 69–118.

[58] D. Pratt, 'Moated Settlements in Maelor', *Jnl. Flints. H.S.*, XXI, (1964), 110–20.

[59] *Glam Inv.* III (ii), 107–10.

[60] R.A. Griffiths, 'The Rise of the Stradlings of St. Donat's', *Morgannwg*, VII (1963), 15–47; *Glam. Inv.* III, Pt. 2, (124–8, 148–55, 159–63, 179, 182–6, 188, 194–5, 247, 262–6, 299–303.

[61] Walter Map, *De Nugis Curialum*, trans. M.R. James, ed. E.S. Hartland, Cymmrodorion Record Series, IX, (1923), 56; *Giraldi Cambrensis Opera*, (1861–91), 129–43; *Glam. Inv.* III, (Pt. 2), 249, 278; L.S. Higgins, 'An Investigation into the Problem of the Sand Dune Areas on the South Wales Coast', *A.C.*, LXXXVIII (1933), 26–67; Jones, *Geography as Human Ecology*, 225–6; A.H.W. Robinson, 'The Sandy Coast of South-West Anglesey', *T.A.A.S.* (1980), 54–5; *Calendar of Inquisitions Miscellaneous, 1307–1349*, no. 1275, 312.

[62] *Glam. Inv.* III (Pt. 2), 215–17, 224–8, 231–6, 238–40.

[63] W.S.G. Thomas, 'Lost Villages in south-west Carmarthenshire', *T. Inst. Brit. Geog.*, 47 (1969), 191–200.

[64] R.R. Davies, 'The Lordship of Ogmore' in *G.C.H.* III, 300–4; Glanmor Williams, 'The Economic Life of Glamorgan 1536–1542' in *G.C.H.* IV, 22.

[65] M. Griffiths, 'The Manor in Medieval Glamorgan: The Estates of the De Ralegh Family in the 14th and 15th Centuries', *B.B.C.S.*, XXXII (1985).

[66] Jones Pierce, *Ag. Hist.*, iv. 379; Elwyn Davies, 'Hendre and hafod in Merioneth', *Jnl. Mer. H.R.S.*, VII, 13–27; idem, 'Hendre and hafod in Denbighshire', *T.D.H.S.*, 26 (1977), 49–72.

[67] Rice Merrick, *Morganiae Archaiographia, A Book of the Antiquities of Glamorganshire*, ed. B. Ll. James, South Wales Record Society, 1, (1983), 14.

[68] George Owen, *The Description of Penbrockshire*, in H. Owen (ed.), Cymmrodorion Record Series, 1, (1902), 61.

[69] Davies in *Studies of Field Systems*, 480–529; *Glam. Inv.* III, (Pt. 2), 307–12.

[70] See above, 202–3.

[71] Examples are provided in Rees, *South Wales and the March*, 140, B.E. Howells, 'Open Fields and Farmsteads in Pembrokeshire', *Pembs Hist.*, 3 (1971), 11.

[72] Rees, *South Wales and the March*, 190–3; P.R.O., S.C.6/923/29,30; S.C.6/924/1,2,3.

[73] Gerald of Wales, *Description of Wales*, 187.

[74] John Leland, *The Itinerary in Wales in or about the years 1536–9*, ed. L. Toulmin Smith (1906), 87.

[75] See above, n. 72.

[76] B.E. Howells, 'Pembrokeshire Farming circa 1580–1620', *N.L.W. Jnl.*, IX (1955–6), 324–6; Owen, *The Description of Penbrockshire*, 1, 61; Jones, in *Studies of Field Systems*, 422–4.

[77] Aneurin Owen, (ed.), *Ancient Laws and Institutes of Wales* 1, (1841), 274, 314, 316, 318, 320, 332; F.G. Payne, *Yr Aradr Gymreig* (Cardiff, 1954), 73–7; idem, 'The Welsh Plough Team to 1600' in J. Geraint Jenkins (ed.), *Studies in Folk Life, Essays in Honour of Iorwerth C. Peate* (Cardiff, 1969), 236–47; idem. *Cwysau, Casgliad o Erthyglau ac Ysgrifau* (Llandysul, 1980), 7–29; Lewis, Roberts, Williams, *Cywyddau Iolo Goch*, 80; T. Lewis (ed.), *The Laws of Howel Dda* (Cardiff, 1912), frontispiece; N.L.W. Llanstephan MS. 116; Ifor Williams (ed.), *Gwaith Ieuan Deulwyn* (Cardiff, 1909), 42, 44.

[78] Payne in *Studies in Folk Life*, 237–8, 247–50.

[79] G.R.J. Jones, 'The Defences of Gwynedd in the Thirteenth Centuries', *T.C.H.S.*, 30 (1969), 38–9.

[80] C. Thomas, 'Peasant Agriculture in Medieval Gwynedd', *Folk Life*, 13 (1975), 30–1.

[81] W. Rees, *The Great Forest of Brecknock* (Brecon, 1966), 10; Davies, *Lordship and Society*, 116; P.R.O. D.L. 29/671/10810; S.C.6. 1156/18; S.C.6/1157/2.

[82] Cowley, *The Monastic Order in South Wales* 86–9; Williams, *The Welsh Church from Conquest to Reformation*, 174.

[83] E.G. Bowen, 'The Monastic Economy of the Cistercians at Strata Florida', *Ceredigion*, 1 (1950–1), 34–7.

[84] Rees, *South Wales and the March*, 256–7; P.R.O., S.C.6/1156/13, 15, 18.

[85] D.H. Williams, *The Welsh Cistercians, Aspects of their Economic History* (Cardiff, 1969), 68; E. Power, *The Wool Trade in English Medieval History* (1941), 22–3.

[86] T.H. Lloyd, *The English Wool Trade in the Middle Ages* (Cambridge, 1977), 115; *Calendar of Patent Rolls*, 1324–7, 269, 274.

[87] Davies, *Lordship and Society*, 116–19; Duby, *Rural Economy*, 350–1; Jones in *Studies of Field Systems*, 451; Lewis, *T.C.S.*, (1902–3), 47; T.H. Lloyd, 'The Movement of Wool Prices in Medieval England', *Ec. H. R. Supplement*, 6 (1973), 28–30.

[88] E.A. Lewis, 'The Development of Industry and Commerce in Wales during the Middle Ages', *T.R.H.S.*, XVII (1903), 51–61.

[89] Thirsk, 'Industries in the Countryside' in F.J. Fisher (ed.), *Essays in the Economic and Social History of Tudor and Stuart England in Honour of R.H. Tawney* (Cambridge, 1961) 72–4; R.I. Jack, 'The Cloth Industry in Medieval Wales., *W.H.R.*, X (1981), 443–60; idem, 'Fulling-mills in Wales and the March before 1547' *A.C.*, CXXX (1981), 70–130.

[90] Lewis, *T.R.H.S.*, (1903), 159–61; Lloyd, *The English Wool Trade in the Middle Ages* (1977), 54–5, 132; E.M. Carus-Wilson, 'The Overseas Trade of Bristol' in E. Power and M.M. Postan (eds.), *Studies in English Trade in the Fifteenth Century* (1933), 185–8; Griffiths in *Welsh Society and Nationhood*, 86–9.

[91] W. Rees, *Industry before the Industrial Revolution* 1, (Cardiff, 1968), 30; P. Morgan (ed.), *Cheshire, Domesday Book*, gen. ed. J. Morris (Chichester, 1978), 269.

[92] Gerald of Wales, *Description of Wales*, 114, 196, 225–6.

[93] Rees, *Industry before the Industrial Revolution*, 29–30, 36–42; *Black Book of St David's* 198–9.

[94] D. Pratt, 'The Leadmining Community at Minera in the Fourteenth Century', *T.D.H.S.*, 12 (1962), 28–36; idem. 'Minera, Township of the Mines'; ibid., 25 (1976), 114–54.

[95] W. Linnard, *Welsh Woods and Forests, History and Utilization* (Cardiff, 1982), 39–40.

[96] Rees, *Industry before the Industrial Revolution*, 35; K. Ll. Gruffydd, 'Coal-Mining in Flintshire during the Later Middle Ages', *Jnl. Flints. H.S.*, 30 (1981–2), 107–24.

[97] Rees, *Industry before the Industrial Revolution*, 34–5, 79–80, 94; Smith and Pugh, *G.C.H.* III, 250 and n. 236.

[98] Williams-Jones, *Merioneth Lay Subsidy Roll, 1292–3*, cii–iii; Carr, *Medieval Anglesey*, 106–10.

[99] Jones, *W.H.R.*, I, (1961–2), 127–8.

[100] Cowley, *G.C.H.* III, 117.

[101] L.A.S. Butler, 'Medieval Ecclesiastical Architecture in Glamorgan and Gower' in *G.C.H.* III, 403.

[102] Ibid., 401, 406; W.G. Thomas, 'The Architectural History of St Mary's Church, Tenby', *A.C.*, CXV (1986), 158–60.

[103] Williams, *The Welsh Church from Conquest to Reformation*, 433.

[104] I. Soulsby, *The Towns of Medieval Wales* (Chichester, 1983), 24–7, 256–9; idem, 'Trelech, a Decayed Borough of Medieval Gwent', *The Monmouthshire Antiquary*, IV (1981–2), 1, 41–4.

[105] Leland, *The Itinerary in Wales*, 59.

[106] Carter, *The Towns of Wales: a study in urban geography* (Cardiff, 1965), 32–9.

[107] R.R. Davies, 'Brecon', K. Williams-Jones, 'Caernarvon', Griffiths, 'Carmarthen', Owen, 'Denbigh', in Griffiths, *Boroughs of Mediaeval Wales*, 67–70, 89–101, 155–63, 165, 184–7.

The Emergence of the Modern Settlement Pattern, 1450–1700[1]

MATTHEW GRIFFITHS

B Y the middle of the fifteenth century the social and agrarian reorganization that was the child of epidemic and war throughout Wales was well in train. To borrow a phrase, 'a new society was emerging from the cracking shell of the old'.[2] It was the social and economic needs of this new society that in the succeeding two hundred years or so would reshape the Welsh landscape, bringing into existence the pattern of field and farm, hamlet and village with which we are familiar today. The sixteenth and seventeenth centuries saw the working out of processes already underway in the later Middle Ages, but now against a background of renewed demographic growth and economic expansion.

So much may be confidently asserted. However, a systematic explanation of changing patterns of settlement and agrarian organization during this period is by no means easy, since we lack a detailed understanding of the causes, timing, and local incidence of the economic and demographic trends that underlie them. When, for example, we consider the desertion or shrinkage of villages and hamlets in the southern March in the fourteenth and fifteenth centuries, or examine field-name evidence for the extension of the frontiers of colonization under the Tudors, it is impossible to avoid the fact no one has yet tackled an overall study of late-medieval and early-modern social and economic developments in Wales. In fact, research on landscape history and settlement patterns seems to have run ahead of a more general attack on Welsh social change between the Glyndŵr revolt and the industrial revolution. Even so, coverage of the Principality as a whole has been patchy. No work on south Wales can match the sophistication of analyses of the decay of the *gwely* system and the disappearance of the bond vills in Gwynedd. The best that can be attempted here is to bring together the results of research to date, cast some fresh light on themes which have been misunderstood, and indicate some of the directions in which work of this kind could be advanced.

DEMOGRAPHIC AND ECONOMIC DEVELOPMENTS

The Black Death and subsequent epidemics dramatically reduced the Welsh population in the mid to late fourteenth century. In so doing, plague accelerated changes already at work in the medieval economy and society. The Glyndŵr revolt has been viewed as an even greater catalyst, leading to economic distress and administrative breakdown throughout Wales between 1400 and 1410.[3] Perhaps the specific effects of plague and war have been overdramatized, but it remains true that the decline in population after 1350 (if not before) and its subsequent recovery were among the chief determinants of the new social formation of Tudor and Stuart

Wales. Escheats, the commutation of dues and services, the leasing of the demesne, and an active land market, were all contributory factors to the breakdown of the old pattern of life in medieval Wales before 1350, but declining population and the effects of the revolt enormously accelerated the pace of change. In consequence, the greater part of the fifteenth century — with food plentiful and cheap, land freely available for those with a little cash, bond or servile status and tenures fast disappearing — was a time of economic and social opportunity. In fifteenth-century documents, the lineaments of early modern society are readily apparent. In the period before 1500 the dissolution of ancient patterns of landscape and settlement gathered strength throughout Wales; the century and a half which followed saw the processes at work in the later Middle Ages taken to their conclusions as increasing population again altered the balance between people and land.

To appreciate fully the nature of changing patterns of settlement and agricultural organization we need to look a little more closely at the demographic and economic context. There are few reliable statistics for the Welsh population, locally or nationally, before 1801; none the less we can form a general impression of the size of the population of the individual counties and the Principality and of the pattern of change in our period. What we cannot at present do, in the absence of reliable parish register data before the early eighteenth century, is more than to guess at the rate of change at different periods and at the respective roles of fertility, nuptuality and mortality in this process.

Leonard Owen suggested that the population of Wales in the middle of the sixteenth century amounted to some 225,800 people and calculated that by 1670 this figure had increased by roughly 52 per cent to about 342,000. These estimates were based on the Lay Subsidy assessments of the 1540s, the 'Bishop's Census' of Elizabeth's reign, and the Hearth Tax returns of the 1660s and 1670s.[4] Some useful conclusions can be drawn from Owen's figures, which are calculated for boroughs, hundreds and counties, but they must none the less be treated with great caution. Two recent local studies have revealed that Owen did not always count accurately and that he misunderstood his original data in ways that make his estimates untrustworthy, though useful as a basis of comparison.[5] His evidence does show very clearly that, as we might expect, it was the southern counties of Monmouth, Glamorgan, Carmarthen, Pembroke and Cardigan that were most densely settled in the early to mid sixteenth century, especially the parts where farmers laid stress on crops as well as the pasturing of cattle and sheep. By comparison, the pastoral upland counties of mid and north Wales were sparsely peopled. Owen's figures give some idea also of the extent and location of population growth in the early modern period. As Frank Emery has pointed out, north Wales witnessed a remarkable expansion of its population, indicating that more intensive use of land enabled such counties as Caernarfon (where the increase was c.76 per cent), Merioneth (85 per cent) and Anglesey (66 per cent) to support far more people.[6] The increase of numbers in the uplands was not general, however, for the populations of Breconshire and Radnorshire grew relatively little.

Recent work on Glamorgan suggests that further investigation of the Lay Subsidy assessments and Hearth Tax returns from the point of view of population might be worthwhile. Examination of the documents at parish level shows that both in the 1540s and 1670s there were significant variations in the density of population even between neighbouring communities, whether in the uplands or in the lowlands of Gower and the Vale of Glamorgan. Moreover, in the mixed-farming lowlands it would appear that a substantial recovery of population had occurred by the later years of Henry VIII's reign, however severe had been the decline in the fourteenth and fifteenth centuries. Some parishes in Gower and the Vale were as thickly peopled as parts of Leicestershire and East Anglia. These communities experienced little if any growth in the later sixteenth and in the seventeenth centuries; the greatest increases occurred in the uplands where population levels were lowest in the 1540s.[7] Despite these generalizations, what is most impressive is the diversity of local experience.

As for the pace of population growth in the Principality as a whole we must, for the time being, assume that the Welsh experience paralleled that of England. Recovery, as the Glamorgan experience suggests, may have been widespread by Henry VIII's reign. Subsequently, we may envisage a steep rise in numbers until around 1600, probably reflected, as we shall see, by the intensive colonization of marginal land, after which the increase may have continued less dramatically until the middle of the seventeenth century. After 1650 the growth of the English population was much slower (it may even have contracted), and we must assume that, save perhaps where industry was developing, this was also true in Wales.[8]

Increasing population underlies many aspects of social and economic change in sixteenth- and seventeenth-century Wales. It stimulated increased activity in the land market and the expansion of inland and maritime trade. Its impact on prices created opportunities for some individuals and families, those well placed by virtue of their ownership of land or possession of a substantial farm; for others, small farmers, cottagers and labourers, the chances were less good. Just as the wealth of some classes in the countryside is reflected in improved standards of housing in the later sixteenth and seventeenth centuries, so the increased number of poor and the problems they generated is indicative of the lot of the victims of the consequences of population growth and its concomitant inflation. From the particular point of view of this survey, the increase in numbers meant the physical expansion of settlement and the colonization of previously waste or marginal land; likewise the need to increase productivity, to grow more food and graze more animals, brought about significant structural changes in the organization of farming and the use of land. In the new conjuncture of economic forces that prevailed from the early sixteenth century until the Civil Wars the reshaping of the landscape and pattern of settlement that had begun in the later Middle Ages was brought to fruition.

THE TOWNS

Tudor and Stuart Welsh towns have been little studied. In so far as the boom in urban history has affected Wales it has enlarged our knowledge of towns in medieval and modern Wales while passing over the sixteenth, seventeenth and eighteenth centuries. The development of urban archaeology may help to remedy this situation — indeed, it has yielded two useful monographs on Carmarthen and

Cowbridge which deal in detail with our period — but much basic groundwork will have to be done before we can confidently generalize about the nature of urban life and the fortunes of towns in early modern Wales.[9]

Harold Carter has produced the only synthetic study of Welsh urban development. He regards the sixteenth and seventeenth centuries as a time of 'sorting out' or readjustment of the roles of particular towns in the local and regional economies of the Principality, and views the early modern period as an age of fluctuating fortunes in which many settlements, already on the decline in the later Middle Ages, continued to decay. The growth of towns was restricted by the thinly distributed population of the Principality and the problems posed to marketing by poor communications. Towns remained largely isolated centres of activity, dependent on the prosperity, or lack of it, of their hinterlands. By the early eighteenth century, however, an interim stability had been achieved and a balanced pattern of 'service centres' had emerged. This pattern was no sooner established than it was disrupted by the growth of industry.[10] Ian Soulsby's study of medieval Welsh towns likewise views the sixteenth and seventeenth centuries as typified by urban decay and adjustment. In this case the decline of urban life is thought to have continued into the nineteenth century, and it is true that eighteenth- and early nineteenth-century travellers left unflattering accounts of settlements that pretended to urban status.[11] In this context a reappraisal of Welsh towns in the early modern period would be a useful stimulus to further research. Here we can only examine a few of the themes relevant to such a task.

There is considerable evidence, despite the sparsity of the documentary sources, for the decline of many Welsh towns in the fourteenth and fifteenth centuries. In many cases this decline is hardly surprising, for it has been demonstrated that thirteenth-century Wales had acquired far more towns than could be justified by economic needs. Urban life in Wales was in its origins largely an artificial creation; the majority of the medieval boroughs were planted rather than organic settlements (a reversal of the situation that obtained in England) and had been established for political and military reasons.[12] Once the strategic value of such towns had been undermined, those which had not acquired or could not develop an economic rationale to their existence were liable to dwindle into villages. Some towns disappeared altogether.

The turbulent conditions of the fourteenth and early fifteenth centuries provided the initial period of trial for those towns that had not already proved, like Bere (Merioneth) or Caerffili (Glamorgan) abortive foundations. Epidemic and the Glyndŵr rebellion are the villains of the piece, although signs of contraction were already apparent in the early fourteenth century. When we look at the towns in the early sixteenth century, whether through the eyes of Leland, or with the aid of rentals and tax assessments, it is hard not to be impressed by signs of decline, even in the case of the larger boroughs. Leland notes fifty-eight Welsh towns in his Itinerary (1536–43) and in thirty of these his descriptions suggest urban stagnation or decline.[13] Aberystwyth, which at its peak in 1300–1 had 120 occupied burgages, could only muster 68 adult males between the ages of sixteen and sixty in 1539.[14] In the case of Tenby, which seems to have made a rapid recovery from pestilence in the later fourteenth century, evidence from the end of the fifteenth century points to falling revenues from tolls and customs and to a large number of vacant burgages. Although Leland found the town and its port 'very wealthy by merchandise', early sixteenth-century Tenby was a pale reflection of its former self.[15] Comparable evidence for real or apparent decline is legion and has been fully rehearsed by Soulsby, whose study is particularly useful for its catalogue of failed medieval plantations.

We should not, however, regard the later Middle Ages as entirely bleak. Some towns held their own, or even enjoyed modest growth. Brecon's burgesses increased in number in the fifteenth century, and the town benefited from its position on the main route from west Wales to England and from its role as the *caput* of a major marcher lordship.[16] Carmarthen's population had probably fallen by the early fifteenth century, but there is evidence that, after the vicissitudes of the Glyndŵr revolt, the town regained its confidence rapidly, rebuilding its walls and many of its houses, with its success sustained by its role as the administrative and economic capital of the southern Principality and by the overseas links of its port.[17] There are signs too of a healthy commercial life in Rhuthun, where a weavers' and fullers' guild was founded in 1447 and, by 1496, a guild for the corvisers of the borough.[18] For Welsh towns, the later Middle Ages were a time of winnowing, and it is likely that for many the period of trial extended well into the sixteenth century.

To get a perspective on the development of the urban network in the early modern period we may glance at estimates of town populations. Owen gives figures for a number of the larger boroughs which, though they need to be treated cautiously, help to establish a basis of comparison. In about 1550 Carmarthen seems to have been the only Welsh town to have had more than 2,000 inhabitants. With some 2,150 people it was some way ahead of Brecon (1,750), Wrecsam (1,515) and Haverfordwest (1,496). Next in size ranked Cydweli (1,120), Cardiff (1,008) — the largest town in Wales at the close of the thirteenth century, Swansea (960), Tenby (950) and Denbigh (898). Caernarfon had some 800 inhabitants and Pembroke about 630; while places such as Conwy, Bangor, Welshpool and Knighton could number no more than 400–500 folk. Owen also gives figures for Cardigan (260), Montgomery (308) and Radnor (360) but, as Emery had pointed out, he omitted some thirty or so centres which, like Cowbridge or Newtown, may have had populations of between 200 and 400 people.

Inevitably we are struck by the small scale of even the more populous of these towns. Small they were to remain even in the later seventeenth century. By then Wrecsam, again using Owen's figures, was the largest town in terms of population, with some 3,200 people. Carmarthen, Brecon and Haverfordwest each had about 2,000 inhabitants; Caernarfon, Cardiff and Swansea hovered around the 1,700 mark, while Pembroke had about 1,200 people. The remaining towns for which Owen produced estimates had late seventeenth-century populations of between 500 and 1,000. We can at present only speculate about the size of the smaller market towns.[19]

The majority of the early modern Welsh towns thus tended to be smaller than most of the local market centres that ranked at the bottom of the English urban hierarchy. In Tudor times such English market towns generally had populations of between 600 and 1,000 — often around the 900 mark — with a very few numbering about 2,000 folk. No Welsh town matched the 'regional capitals' of early modern England — places such as Bristol, Norwich and Newcastle which had figures of 7,000+ c.1500, 11,000+ c.1700. Nor did any but the three or four largest Welsh boroughs compare in terms of size with the 'regional centres' and county towns of the English shires, whose populations in the early sixteenth century typically lay in the 1,500–5,000 range.[20]

On the other hand we can detect strong similarities between the Welsh and English urban networks when we consider *function* rather than size alone. This may be the particular value of Carter's carefully-elaborated urban hierarchy. The towns which this author places at the top of the ladder in the mid sixteenth century — Brecon, Carmarthen, Denbigh and Caernarfon — functioned economically and administratively as regional capitals. Not only were they major market centres serving large regions (Carmarthen, for example, was effectively the economic capital of south-west Wales and carried on a thriving import-export trade with the west of England, Ireland and France) but because of their physical accessibility the Acts of Union had endowed them with chanceries, exchequers and assizes. The second tier of towns in Carter's scheme all had functions which elevated them above the status of 'mere market towns', even if they lacked the administrative importance of Carmarthen or Caernarfon. Places such as Cardiff, Haverfordwest, Swansea, Abergavenny and Rhuthun, in their various ways, might be considered analogous in their roles to the 'regional centres' in Clark and Slack's model of the English urban structure. The coastal location of the majority of these centres should be noted. The fortunes of the towns which Carter places in this second rank were diverse. Some clearly declined in the course of the sixteenth century, Cardigan and Newport (Monmouthshire), for example; others had their growth restricted by the proximity of better-placed centres — thus Monmouth, despite the development of its capping industry, ultimately suffered from competition with Abergavenny. Towns such as Cowbridge, Dolgellau and Machynlleth served limited or poor hinterlands but discovered a political and social significance out of proportion to their size. Finally, at the bottom of the Welsh hierarchy, as of its English counterpart, were those towns which existed simply as local marketing centres.[21]

Carter's model is useful, but it must remain provisional until we have learnt more about the history of particular places and have acquired a clearer understanding of the roles of towns and markets in the economy of Tudor and Stuart Wales. One would question whether decayed New Radnor should be placed above Conwy, Builth or Welshpool. We have a long way to go before we may generalize about patterns of urban success and decay, though here again analogies with the situation in England seem useful. We know that both the larger English country towns and the 'regional capitals' experienced mixed fortunes in the fifteenth, sixteenth and seventeenth centuries, although controversy still attaches to the models that seek to chart periods of decline and recovery. By contrast, as internal trade quickened and the economy grew in the sixteenth and early seventeenth centuries it seems that the English *market towns* thrived as a class, though often to be confronted with problems of adjustment after the Restoration as improved communications enabled many local markets to be bypassed. We may be justified in seeing a parallel situation in Wales and indeed Everitt has suggested that from about the 1570s onwards the Welsh market towns tended to prosper.[22]

Population figures alone indicate that the larger Welsh boroughs did not develop evenly in the sixteenth and seventeenth centuries, with growth rates varying considerably. Caernarfon increased in numbers by some 120 per cent between 1550 and 1660, Wrecsam by 112 per cent. Brecon's population grew by about a quarter in the same period, as did that of smaller towns such as Beaumaris and Knighton; while Carmarthen, for all its success, added only 2 per cent on Owen's calculations. Population growth is not always an indicator of economic prosperity, however, for an increase in numbers could pose serious social problems; nevertheless where urban numbers declined in this period then surely we are seeing signs of contraction. Significant declines in population were experienced by Cydweli (by 42 per cent, from 1,120 to 600) and Tenby (by 13 per cent, from 950 to 826), while Denbigh's lack of growth owing to the development of Wrecsam is demonstrated by its stability in population between the mid sixteenth and the later seventeenth centuries.

A number of recently published case studies enable us to trace specific examples of contraction or success in the sixteenth and seventeenth centuries. These deal chiefly with the more important medieval boroughs. Brecon and Carmarthen, for example, amongst the towns that were given the attributes of administrative centres for the four quadrants of the Principality in 1542, built on their late medieval prosperity and flourished commercially and socially. By contrast Denbigh, its growth hindered from the start by difficulties of site, was rapidly outstripped in the fifteenth and early sixteenth century by neighbouring Wrecsam, which was more advantageously placed as a commercial centre. Thus, although Denbigh became the county town, 'county days' were held in the two towns alternately and the assizes met in both towns.[23] In the case of smaller centres, such as Pembroke and Tenby, we can trace the fortunes of places that became less significant in our period than they had formerly been. Haverfordwest came to dominate the economy and society of Pembrokeshire and ranked second in importance in west Wales to Carmarthen.[24] Tenby, in serious decline at the end of the fifteenth century, continued in a depressed state until the reign of Elizabeth, but was eventually able to reshape its trading links, surrendering its foreign connections to Carmarthen and Haverfordwest and refounding its economy on coastal and cross-channel shipping. Pembroke, however, failed to discover a niche in this restructured regional economy; Speed's account records that the borough had 'more houses without inhabitants than I saw in any one city in my journey'.[25]

More local studies, not just of the larger towns, but of more humble market centres are very much needed. Of the smaller towns, only Cowbridge[26] has been studied in depth, but it is studies of this kind that may help us test the hypothesis that, while the experience of larger boroughs may have been variable, the majority of local markets prospered.[27]

Work of this kind needs to be undertaken not just from the social, economic and administrative point of view but should have a strong topographical content. This may seem a hard request, since plans of the early modern town in Wales are so few. Our point of departure here has to be the tithe maps and early Ordnance Survey maps of the nineteenth century, together with eighteenth-century estate surveys. These can serve as the basis for a retrogressive analysis linked to the study of documents such as deeds and rentals. At present we are very hazy as to the physical changes undergone by the majority of towns in the sixteenth, seventeenth and eighteenth centuries. Soulsby's plans are helpful, but not always accurate. We know little about the development of the suburbs of the walled towns, nor how space was used within mural areas. Were the increased populations of expanding towns accommodated within or without the boundaries of the walls? In the case of the towns for which Speed provides visual evidence there seems to have been plenty of space available for building within the walls, and in Cardiff it was on this kind of land that new houses were erected, the medieval suburb of Crockherbtown undergoing little expansion. Gardens, pastures, orchards and waste plots gave many sixteenth- and seventeenth-century Welsh towns a rural appearance.

The character of urban building is also largely unknown. The interest in rural vernacular architecture in Wales has not been accompanied by a parallel interest in town houses. Certainly, in places such as Cardiff and Swansea nineteenth-century and later building has all but obliterated earlier evidence. Elsewhere, in Monmouth or Brecon, we have examples of seventeenth- and eighteenth-century buildings of quality that give us an idea of the standards that urban dwellers and corporations could achieve in favourable circumstances. This subject requires a much more systematic appraisal that may prove to be as much the task of the archaeologist as the architectural historian.

THE COUNTRYSIDE

Outside the Anglicized lowlands of the south and south-west, the modern Welsh countryside exhibits a pattern of scattered farms in which nucleations of any size are few and far between. We understand best how this settlement pattern emerged in the context of north and north-west Wales, on which recent research has been concentrated. It has been argued that a dispersed pattern of settlement evolved here in the later Middle Ages and in the century or so after 1500, when the hamlets and 'girdle settlements' that characterized the thirteenth- and fourteenth-century landscape decayed to be succeeded by consolidated farmsteads whose inhabitants tilled and grazed enclosed fields. Hand in hand with this process of consolidation and engrossing, especially as the sixteenth century progressed, went an attack on former waste and common land fuelled by population pressure and the developing land market. Grazing which formerly had been open became subject to encroachment and enclosure; transhumance agriculture decayed as many *hafodau* were converted into permanent steadings.

T. Jones Pierce, Glanville Jones, and Colin Thomas have been chiefly responsible for the elaboration of this model, and have identified a number of factors at work in this reshaping of agrarian organization and landholding.[28] Some were inherent in the nature of medieval Welsh society; even before 1350 escheat was contributing to the break up of the clanlands; likewise, the commutation of rents and services reflected the development of a cash economy in which land was increasingly treated as an alienable commodity; and the seeds or the dissolution of the *gwelyau* were inherent in the practice of *cyfran* — partible inheritance or gavelkind. As land became divided amongst successive generations of co-heirs, a point would ultimately be reached where, with territorial expansion impeded by natural limitations to settlement, holdings would become too small to support a family. Such excessively fragmented holdings were a natural prey to more substantial men. The *prid* mortgage was under Welsh land law a vehicle which could facilitate the alienation of clanland and the acquisition of estates. *Prid* enabled the bans imposed on the buying and selling of land by the Crown and by private landlords to be circumvented; its use helped to finance the purchase of property and contributed to the formation of a wealthy sector in Welsh society, in Carmarthenshire as in north Wales.[29]

The latter pressures were internal. External agents of change were represented by plague and war. Depopulation contributed to the dissolution of the ancient settlement pattern in north Wales, for the decline in numbers ensured the rapid disappearance of the bond hamlets in the fourteenth and fifteenth centuries. As fiscal obligations devolved on the few surviving bond tenants of depopulated townships those who remained were driven to quit these settlements. Vacant land thus escheated in vast quantities to the Crown and became available for leasing to speculators. Other decayed bond vills became subject to encroachment by neighbouring freeholders. W. Ogwen Williams has drawn attention to the social transformation that took place as a result of these circumstances in Caernarfonshire between the middle of the fifteenth century and the 1530s, a revolution that underlay the demands for enfranchisement that the Crown met in the Principality in 1507. Part and parcel of the redistribution of land that took place in late fifteenth- and early sixteenth-century Caernarfon — accompanied by a concomitant restructuring of the rural landscape — was the emergence of that class of native gentry that was a willing recipient of the benefits of the Union legislation.[30]

Various classes were active in the late-medieval land market in north-west Wales, making use of *prid* to acquire clanland and leasing escheat land from the Crown. Eager buyers were burgesses from the north Walian boroughs, such as the Bulkeleys of Conwy and Beaumaris and the Salusburies of Denbigh. So too were men of the native officialdom to whom administration in the Principality had almost wholly devolved by the later fifteenth century, men who were ready to invest the profits and perquisites of office in the building up of estates. Also well developed by the reign of Henry VII was a class of minor native gentry and lesser freeholders whose estates originated in the *gwelyau* and provided a basis for the amalgamation and enclosure of strips in the sharelands and the hedging of land that had previously been common grazing. Such men competed for the tenements of those reduced to poverty by the remorseless operation of partible inheritance and for the possession of former bond land. It was as a result of these transactions that the highly morcellated sharelands were acquired by estate consolidators and the landscape itself reshaped. Open field was taken into severalty and girdle settlements and bond hamlets shrank to be replaced by dispersed *tyddynnod* standing in their own fields.

Considerable advances had been made in this direction in north Wales by the beginning of the sixteenth century, a period when land was comparatively cheap and the total population much smaller than it had been in the early fourteenth century. However, the process was by this date far from complete. T. Jones Pierce has estimated that small peasant proprietors whose rights in land derived from clan status were still predominant in north Wales before the Acts of Union. The *gwely* remained the framework within which much land was held; still, for a time, an administrative reality. The subdivision of holdings in the *gwelyau* was continuing apace, many tenements by this time consisting of no more than one or two acres whereas 150 years before a farmstead of ten acres might have been more typical.[31] However great had been the changes of the fifteenth century, the alienation and consolidation of *gwely* land and the enclosure of open fields and appurtenant common grazing accelerated thereafter.

Several factors gave a new dimension to these activities after 1500. Firstly, there was the impact of the recovery of population that took place in Tudor and early Stuart Wales, perhaps especially rapidly between *c.*1540 and 1600. Also of importance were the legal and social changes initiated by the Tudor state: the abolition of *cyfran* (formally, if not practically) in 1542 — after which date partibility of land became a matter of choice rather than obligation — and the release of large tracts of land on to the market as a consequence of the dissolution of the monasteries. The harmonization of Welsh and English land law undoubtedly gave a new impetus to estate-building, for primogeniture made it easier to maintain intact the lands that a family had carefully acquired. Also of significance are more purely economic factors, especially the growth of the cattle trade. By the middle of the sixteenth century this was in full sway, with animals being driven annually to the markets and fairs of the Midlands and beyond. These pressures combined to accelerate the alienation and concentration of *gwely* land in north Wales; moreover, as land hunger increased, the margins of colonization were extended beyond their medieval frontiers, common and waste taken into severalty, and many *hafodau* transformed into farms that were occupied all the year round.

Glanville Jones has used the example of Llysdulas township in Anglesey to illustrate how some of these processes might function in practice. A detailed rental of the township was drawn up in 1549 and this illustrates the extent to which land had been redistributed and landownership consolidated. Gavelkind had created a class of vulnerable and impoverished smallholders and better-off families had made use of the *prid* mortgage to acquire small parcels of clanland. Shares in the open fields had been laid together and hedged, and common pasture and meadow had also become vulnerable to enclosure. In 1549 thirty-one landholders controlled 125 parcels of *gwely* land; however, ninety-four of these holdings were in the possession of just six men. The advent of primogeniture made these estates less likely to be partitioned and the consolidation of holdings in the township continued in the second half of the sixteenth century to the extent that by 1600 farms of fifty to one hundred acres were typical of the locality.[32]

We could do with more local analyses of this kind. Much of the research on this theme has been carried out by historians charting the decay of medieval society rather than the creation of a new social formation, and it would be especially useful to have studies of changes in particular communities covering the period down to, say, 1650, and charting the final disappearance of the sharelands in the later sixteenth and early seventeenth centuries. Meanwhile, Llysdulas may serve as a model for their evolution in the lower-lying settlements of north Wales.

On higher ground, where the sharelands had historically been less extensive, it seems that few traces of the medieval settlement pattern outlived the sixteenth century. Here, a more prominent development in the early modern period was the acquisition by landowners and tenants of parcels of waste and common land, and the amalgamation of such land with territory already appropriated and associated with dispersed farmsteads. A prominent feature of this process of encroachment and enclosure was the erosion of the old summer grazing settlements.

Some measure of the attack on waste and common land that developed in the sixteenth century has been provided by Colin Thomas's studies of agrarian change in Merioneth. A late sixteenth-century rental of Crown lands lists over 400 encroachments comprising more than 100,000 acres in the commotes of Ardudwy, Penllyn, Talybont and Ystumanner. It was 'the embryonic gentry . . . aided by their tenants and their less famous neighbours' who undertook the enclosure of the upland grazings. Two kinds of terrain were in fact under assault. New colonization was mainly concentrated on the upland pastures or *ffriddoedd*, formerly the grazing lands of medieval townships or monastic granges, but one should not ignore the parallel interest in lowland meadow, pasture and marshland. This process was fuelled by the need to provide pasture and hayland for the great cattle herds which were the mainstay of the economy of the hill country.[33]

Some attempt has been made to trace this process in more detail and to refine its chronology by the analysis of place- and field-names derived from eighteenth-century estate maps and the tithe maps of the mid nineteenth century. This seems practical because, in the context of the dispersed settlement pattern that typifies the Welsh countryside outside the extreme south and parts of the borders, the names of fields and farmsteads have had a remarkable longevity. Certain elements recorded in eighteenth- and nineteenth-century documents are assumed to indicate the location of former open field: for example, *erw*, *maes*, *llain*, *cyfer*, *dryll*, *talar*. Where a sixteenth-century document records *tŷ*, *tir*, or *tyddyn*, it has been argued that we may be able to identify sites occupied in the Middle Ages, especially if these elements are found in association with field-names implying the former existence of shareland. It has likewise been claimed that the less specific term *cae* may represent land that was subject to 'early' appropriation and enclosure. Such elements, when plotted in relation to relief, tend to occur at a lower level than the upland pasture that was being enclosed in the second half of the sixteenth century. Thomas has therefore suggested that the relative chronology of the expansion of colonization can be deduced from the presence of field-names indicating the enclosure of damp pasture, woodland and marsh. In particular, it was the *ffriddoedd* that were subject to colonization in Elizabethan and early Stuart times, generally higher in altitude than the limits of medieval settlement but lower than the vast areas that were to be enclosed by Act of Parliament in the later eighteenth and nineteenth centuries. Analysis on these lines has been attempted largely in the context of north Wales, and not every scholar would accept the proposed dating Thomas derives from the plotting of his toponyms, but this clearly represents a fertile area for further research which should be attempted elsewhere.[34]

We have little evidence from mid and south Wales to set alongside the meticulous studies of the landscape of the north and north-west. It would seem generally reasonable to suppose that analogous developments occurred elsewhere in Wales; in particular that the same type of land was subject to consolidation and encroachment.

Doubt, however, attaches to the assumption that a network of bond and free townships, girdle settlements and nucleated hamlets, shareland and *cytir* evolved in other parts of non-Anglicized Wales as it did in the north. Sylvester, for example, doubts whether co-aration and nucleation were marked features of the medieval landscape of much of Breconshire, Radnorshire and the borders, save where there had been contact with manorialism, or where there had been a *maerdref*.[35] It would seem, too, that the medieval settlement pattern of much of west and south Wales evolved differently to that of Gwynedd. In Cardiganshire the *gwely* was a late development, perhaps only a couple or so generations old *c.*1300, and the result of appropriation of land within the uniform pattern of *gwestfau* and *rhandiroedd* into which both Cardiganshire and parts of Carmarthenshire had been divided by resurgent native rulers in the later twelfth century following the disruption of the ancient web of *llys*, *maerdref* and *tref gyfrif* by Anglo-Norman and north Walian incursions. Jones Pierce has suggested that as a result the transition in this area from medieval to modern social conditions was more prolonged than in other parts of Wales; this is an assumption that requires further exploration.[36]

In the Welshries of Pembrokeshire, the *gwely* made only a peripheral appearance in the Middle Ages, although Welsh law and custom were otherwise strongly rooted. Just as it spread into Cardiganshire from north Wales at a relatively late date so Howells has suggested that 'the English conquest of most of Welsh Pembrokeshire early in the twelfth century prevented the introduction of the *gwely* and preserved the social sub-stratum upon which it was imposed in other areas'. Welsh settlement here was based on the hamlet, occupied by free (? formerly servile) clansmen, cultivating arable land in strips or *lleiniau*, probably organized into some form of infield and outfield. Alongside these hamlets isolated farmsteads standing amidst their own fields had also developed by the later sixteenth century and it would seem that, aided by the abolition of gavelkind, enclosure and the consolidation of quillets were very much features of the late sixteenth- and the seventeenth-century landscape of northern Pembrokeshire.[37] George Owen attributed the intermingling of holdings in the 'Welsh country' to gavelkind:

> so that in process of time the whole country was brought into small pieces of ground and intermingled up and down one with another, so as in every five or six acres you shall have ten or twelve owners.

Since its abolition, however,

> in many parts the ground is brought together by purchase and exchanges and hedging and enclosures much increased, and now they fall to tilling of this winter corn in greater abundance than before.[38]

Estate maps indicate none the less that in many communities open field persisted into the later eighteenth and nineteenth centuries. Likewise, in the manorialized parts of the county the process of enclosure seems to have been much slower than it was, for example, in the Vale of Glamorgan.

Given our assumptions about agrarian organization in early medieval Wales, and taking into account the social implications of *cyfran*, it is surprising how little evidence there is for the medieval settlement pattern in the Welshries of south

Wales. The Book of Cynferth indicates that a version of the multiple estate—the *maenor* — was to be found in pre-Norman south Wales. Arguably, traces of such pre-Norman multiple estates can be discovered in late medieval documents, but by the time these manuscripts were drawn up the agrarian system had been so heavily modified by Norman and English influence and attenuated by the changes generally underway in the later Middle Ages, that one must be very careful not to read too many assumptions into the evidence we have. Place-names indicate that in the twelfth and thirteenth centuries there were a few nucleated settlements associated with the cultivation of arable demesnes by Welsh customary tenants in Gower *Wallicana*. Further eastwards in the lordships of Neath, Glynrhondda, Meisgyn and Senghennydd, inquisitions *post mortem* — notably that of Joan de Clare (1307) — indicate the existence of small arable demesnes (already subject to partial leasing) both on the fringes of the *blaenau* and further north, in Gelli-gaer and Merthyr Tudful, where, on favourable terrain, there were hamlets inhabited by Welsh bond tenants. The place-name element *maerdref* is to be found in several locations within the old lordship of Glamorgan. By the fifteenth century these demesnes had been wholly leased out and some had been transmuted into consolidated farms.[39]

It is possible that throughout much of the south Wales hill country the bond population had historically been of negligible importance and that settlement had taken a form that might be comparable to that in the *gafaelion* of north Wales, largely dispersed and free from servile obligations. By 1450, the bond population in the Glamorgan *blaenau* was certainly of little account; later medieval documents reveal a population of freemen working small estates handed down by *cyfran*.[40] Unfortunately we have very little evidence of the form these freemen's settlements may have taken. The numerous platform houses, generally lying between 500 and 1,000 feet in altitude, were clearly peasant habitations, and these often occur in small groupings. However, there is considerable doubt as to how far these hut-groups may represent all-year-round steadings. Some at least may have been summer shelters for transhumance graziers. Only excavation will help to determine the true nature of these enigmatic sites.[41]

These uncertainties apart, however, other features of the changing landscape of upland Glamorgan in our period, as far as can be judged from the limited research carried out to date, mirrored developments elsewhere in Wales and may be assumed to have had common economic and social roots. Evidence from the Glyncorrwg area indicates that the period from about 1450 onwards witnessed a great consolidation of landholding into single units, effectively complete by 1600. Accompanying this consolidation of holdings ran a general assault on the waste; in the Afan Valley virtually every farm snatched small parcels from the mountain during the sixteenth century and it was probably in the early seventeenth century that there ensued a more systematic enclosure of that waste that had not so far been subjected to colonization. As elsewhere in Wales, this period saw the building up of estates by the ambitious gentry, whose fortunes had been swelled by the dispersal of monastic land. Roger Brown thinks that the economic perils of the late sixteenth and early seventeenth centuries forced many small farmers to mortgage their freeholds and ultimately sell out to the cormorant rich, such as Lewis Thomas of Betws, whose lands subsequently became the core of the great Dunraven estate. In this area, too, he argues, a concomitant of the extensions of the margins of colonization was the erosion of the summer pastures and the conversion of former *hafodau* into permanent farmsteads.[42] No systematic study has, however, been made of this subject in the context of south Wales.

We must turn again to the experience of the north for a detailed idea of what was entailed by the decline of transhumance grazing. A series of papers by Elwyn Davies has made the major contribution to this subject through the detailed exploitation of estate and tithe maps. Farmsteads whose names include the elements *hafod*, *hafoty*, *lluest* and *llety* appear on such maps surrounded by enclosed fields, usually at a higher altitude than *tyddynnod* of more ancient foundation. Their association with field names such as *ffridd* indicate that such fields have often been taken in from formerly open grazing.[43] Allen's excavations at Hafod y Nant Criafolen in the Brenig Valley have yielded a vivid picture of the kind of settlement once represented by the former *hafodau*. At Hafod y Nant Criafolen, there was a group of seven structures with associated enclosures suitable for use as cattle pens, or the safeguarding of sheep and goats. Each domestic building was a crude structure having a rectangular plan with an entrance in one of the lateral walls. Hearths were rudimentary, generally formed of two or more slabs laid on the floor. These huts appear to have been without windows, their low rubble walls surmounted by turf roofs through which escaped the smoke from the fire. The pottery assemblage from this site suggests occupation from some point in the fifteenth century until the reign of Queen Elizabeth.[44]

Settlements such as that excavated by Allen could be natural growth points for permanent dwellings. From the mid sixteenth century onwards, the hunger for land supplied an excellent motive to convert summer pasture into enclosed grazing managed in severalty. None the less, the decline of transhumance was a long drawn out process of which the timing can only be sketchily charted. Perhaps the increased interest in sheep farming in the uplands that developed in the second half of the seventeenth century did much to complete the job that population pressure and the active land market of the previous century had begun. Sheep farming was a less labour-intensive occupation than the management of dairy cattle and did not require the continual presence of the farmer and his family. The new sheep flocks and the herds of dry cattle that accompanied them could be visited less often. Thus, while the *hafodau* persisted into the nineteenth century in some parts of the country, it is clear that they had entered their final decline by the middle years of the eighteenth century, when they excited the curiosity of writers such as Thomas Pennant.[45]

The history of landscape and settlement in the Anglicized, manorialized lowlands of the south and the borders has been studied in less depth than the changes which took place in *pura Wallia*. Accounts of the early modern landscape in the coastlands of Pembrokeshire, Carmarthenshire, Glamorgan and Monmouthshire, or the river valleys of Breconshire, Radnorshire and Montgomeryshire, have tended to be more descriptive than analytical, despite Dorothy Sylvester's pioneering work on the English and Welsh March.[46] Little real attempt has been made to show how, for example, the medieval open arable fields of this zone were replaced by the familiar modern quilt of lane and hedge. Still less has there been any attempt to examine the historical evolution of the relationship between nucleated villages and hamlets, and single farms, in this milieu. In part this may be due to the fact that the countryside of the Vale of Glamorgan, for example, has a deceptively 'English' feel; in part there is a problem of documentation. This is an undertaking which will require the collaboration of historian and archaeologist, but that the effort will be worthwhile is demonstrated by the Welsh Royal Commission's recent survey of non-defensive secular medieval monuments in Glamorgan and by the fortuitous concentration of much recent rescue archaeology in south Wales on deserted and shrunken medieval villages.[47]

The decay of the open fields is one of the more obvious and more dramatic features of agrarian change in the manorialized lowlands. The development of field systems is an intrinsically interesting study, but one that is central also to the understanding of more general aspects of lowland settlement; in particular, the relationship between nucleation and dispersal in the modern rural landscape. Since the 1950s a mass of evidence has been arrayed to demonstrate that open arable fields, and in some places common meadows, were the basis of medieval agriculture in the manorialized zone. We realize that these were seldom open fields on the generous scale of the English midlands, but as a rule smaller and less regular in structure, as seems to have been the case in Devon. This lack of regularity can be seen partly as a function of the uneven landscape of much of the south; probably it has much to do also with the early medieval pattern of land use inherited by the Anglo-Norman conquistadors and their followers in the late eleventh and twelfth centuries. As yet there is little evidence for communal regulation of cropping and grazing, though this may be due to the lack of the kind of documentation — such as medieval court rolls — in which we might discover such rules and by-laws. Margaret Davies and Dorothy Sylvester have shown that the final extinction of open field and common meadow was not accomplished in some parts of south Wales and the March until the second half of the nineteenth century. In consequence several tithe maps — from the Caldicot levels of Monmouthshire, for example — record surviving open field systems. Elsewhere, eighteenth, nineteenth and twentieth-century maps reveal strong residual traces of former open field strips. Wales even has its own Laxtons, where relict open fields can be seen today; at Laugharne, for instance, or at Llan-non in Cardiganshire.[48]

We have therefore been taught to recognize the legacy of former open field systems in both documentary sources, such as estate and tithe maps, and also in the modern countryside. Unfortunately little progress has been made in analysing the origins and morphology of open field systems, or in charting their decay. We have not progressed beyond the observation that enclosure occurred at a very early stage in some places and remarkably late elsewhere, for there has been little attempt to investigate in detail the enclosure history of particular settlements or to explain why the experiences even of neighbouring communities should have differed so considerably. Accordingly, the published evidence for the distribution and survival of open field will not be rehearsed again here; an attempt will be made instead to highlight those factors which may underlie the disappearance of the open fields. We shall concentrate on Glamorgan and southern Monmouthshire, for it is these areas that have been studied in most detail.

The origins of the modern landscape must inevitably be sought in the changes that took place in the later Middle Ages. This was a period of crisis and transition in the manorial Englishries just as much as in *pura Wallia*. Depopulation and the effects of rebellion had their impact on this society, too, although many of the economic, social and tenurial changes of the period after 1350 were already foreshadowed at the beginning of the fourteenth century. We have recently become aware of the extent to which the villages and hamlets of the Englishries experienced desertion, or more often, shrinkage, in the fourteenth and fifteenth centuries. The Glamorgan list published by the Royal Commission in 1983 has been extended by more recent fieldwork, yielding a total of over thirty deserted or shrunken sites, chiefly of medieval date, in the Vale and in Gower. A few examples are also known from Gwent, but further fieldwork and excavation is needed in the case of the latter county to establish an accurate total and a chronology of desertion.[49] These desertions are suggestive evidence of the extent of depopulation in the later Middle Ages; in the case of the limited number of excavated sites, the curtailment of occupation seems to have occurred during the second half of the fourteenth century, so that plague has tended to be selected as the likely villain of the piece. R. R. Davies has drawn attention also to the physical impact of the Glyndŵr rebellion in the lordship of Ogmore, enabling men with cash to invest to engross the tenements of peasant families who had fled or been killed. Extensive depopulation created the circumstances in which wealthier peasants could accumulate vacant holdings; where land was being redistributed, then enclosure was a likely concomitant of the rationalization of landholding, and we should perhaps expect that it was in these conditions that a more familiar landscape begins to emerge. On the other hand, there is a certain amount of evidence that, for other Vale of Glamorgan villages, recovery from plague was rapid and the impact of Glyndŵr less traumatic. This seems to have been the case in the manors of Wrinstone and Michaelston, where the population recovered quite quickly, but where in the fifteenth century we can similarly trace a growing disparity in the size of holdings and evidence of early enclosure in the period 1400–1550.[50]

Despite this caveat, the general economic circumstances of the later fourteenth and fifteenth centuries in southern Glamorgan and Gwent are well known. Depopulation did occur, and on the grand scale; land became relatively cheap, tenants scarcer and wage-labour more costly for manorial lords. Demesnes were leased either *en bloc*, or in parcels, at economic rents; villeinage mutated into various forms of customaryhold. That we should look to the fifteenth century for the first signs of a widespread retreat from the common fields is suggested both by these circumstances, and by the testimony of the Glamorgan chorographer, Rice Merrick, writing in Queen Elizabeth's reign, that

> This part of the country . . . was a champion and open country, without great store of inclosures; for in my time old men reported that they remembered in their youth that cattle in some time, for want of shade, to have from the Portway run to Barry, which is 4 miles distant, whose forefathers told them that great part of the inclosures was made in their days.[51]

As yet, as R. R. Davies has pointed out, this process can be traced only tentatively; the relevant documents are few and far between, and in any case were not drawn up to meet the needs of the historian. It might be thought that at this early date enclosure would be most prominent on the demesnes, and in the case of meadow and pasture. Indeed, early fourteenth-century extents of the de Ralegh manors in the Vale of Glamorgan suggest that a certain amount of enclosure had affected demesne parcels of arable, meadow and pasture by 1307.[52] Medieval enclosure would no doubt also be represented by assarts on the periphery of the open fields, giving rise to the distinctive and irregular enclosures associated with some isolated farmsteads on tithe and estate maps.

Developments in the late medieval economy and society can only have encouraged enclosure; none the less, its pace varied considerably from place to place. Open arable was very extensive, for example, in Gower and Pembrokeshire in the later sixteenth century; in many parishes in the latter county the balance of enclosure took place in the eighteenth century.[53] The historian's task is to explain why this should have been the case; why should one, for instance, have found working open field systems on the Caldicot levels in the early nineteenth century, whereas over most of the Vale of Glamorgan unfenced strips had become a rarity a hundred years earlier? We should be searching not only for factors that would encourage enclosure but for those which would retard it. There is a further aspect of this question that we need also to explore: the physical enclosure of groups of strips by hedges was only a part of the process that we have to chart. Enclosure might or might not be accompanied by the related phenomena of engrossment and consolidation. In many parishes, enclosure left farmers with a legacy of small, narrow fields that preserved the outlines of former open-field strips and were often intermingled with fields belonging to their neighbours.

A comparison of the experiences of three parishes in the Vale of Glamorgan — Barry, Merthyr Dyfan and Cadoxton — exemplifies the different paths that could be followed by neighbouring communities. An exceptionally early map shows that the small parish of Barry was wholly enclosed by 1622.[54] Analysis of sixteenth-century court rolls in conjunction with this map and its accompanying terrier suggests that the bulk of enclosure in Barry had in fact been achieved no later than 1570. Farms in the parish in the seventeenth century ranged from about twenty to about eighty acres, and while the field pattern bore traces of its champion past, it underwent little change until much of the parish was urbanized in the 1880s and 1890s. While farms varied in size, and were to be reorganized and amalgamated in the later eighteenth and early nineteenth centuries by improving landlords, the early modern Barry farmer rarely had to cross a neighbour's field to gain access to his land; enclosure had been accompanied by the rationalization of farm layouts. The situation in Cadoxton and Merthyr Dyfan was very different. Former demesne land may have succumbed at an early date, but the enclosure of tenement land took place at a much slower rate than in Barry. In 1545 Cadoxton's 'West' Field appears still to have been quite extensive; thereafter enclosure proceeded with no obvious dispute throughout the later sixteenth and the seventeenth centuries. As late as the 1760s there was a substantial residue of unfenced strips in Cadoxton, and here and in Merthyr Dyfan the legacy of such slow, piecemeal activity was a landscape which was marked by many small, fossilized open-field strips, and in which farmland remained inconveniently intermingled into the nineteenth century.

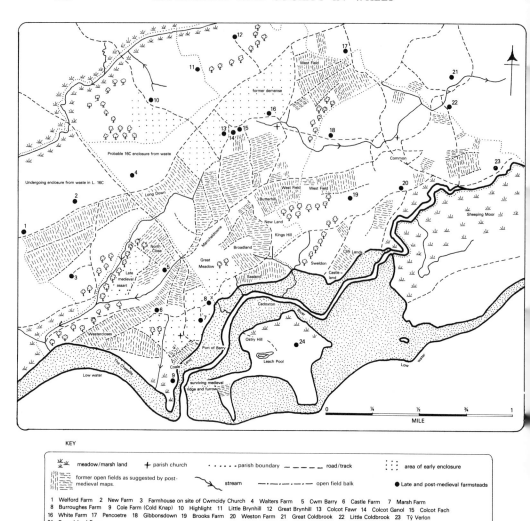

Fig. 49 Late and post-medieval farmsteads in the parishes of Barry, Cadoxton and Merthyr Dyfan.

A partial explanation, at least, for the varying development of these three parishes may be sought in the structure of landownership in the district. In Barry, manor and parish were practically coterminous, freehold minimal, and landownership otherwise undivided. In Merthyr Dyfan and Cadoxton, ownership was divided amongst several manors and sub-manors whose lands were inextricably intermixed. The presence of extensive freeholds may have complicated matters further. It may be thought that this situation prevented landlords or tenants from co-operating in the effective rationalization of farming. At Wrinstone, also in the south-east Vale, the survival of small freeholds has likewise been seen as a factor retarding enclosure

until the Jones, and then the Jenner, estates achieved a consolidation of ownership in
the township in the late eighteenth century. A further factor that may enter into the
situation is lack of capitalization. Cadoxton and Merthyr Dyfan farms were
typically smaller than those in Barry, where the relative wealth of local copyholders
is attested by the extensive 'rebuilding' that took place in the late sixteenth and early
seventeenth centuries. In Cadoxton and Merthyr Dyfan such rebuilding seems
largely to have been a late eighteenth- and early nineteenth-century phenomenon. If
lack of capital is a relevant factor, then this may be one explanation for the similarly
slow process of enclosure in much of the Gower peninsula, where farms were on
average smaller and the local agriculture less rewarding than in many Vale parishes.
We should in certain cases be looking, too, at the role of other elements in a
communal agriculture. Common arable was sometimes only one element in a larger
system. In the case of parishes such as Magor, Undy and Caldicot on the coastal
levels of Monmouthshire, where extensive open field arable persisted until enclosure
took place by statute in the 1850s, the strong communal organization that was
necessary for the regulation of the common meadows and pastures may have acted
as a bulwark for the open fields.[55]

In the case of Barry, Merthyr Dyfan and Cadoxton we understand developments
a little more deeply because a detailed archaeological and documentary study has
been made of these communities in the Middle Ages and the early modern period.
Landscape history is an area of study where the microscopic investigation of events
at the level of the manor and parish is of particular value if we want to try and
understand what was taking place more widely. However, some temporary
assumptions may be made about matters in the manorialized lowlands as a whole.
The first is that enclosure from open field was, as a rule, not a contentious process,
although there is some evidence from late sixteenth-century Pembrokeshire that it
could occasionally cause dissension.[56] In this, south Wales differs from parts of
England, where enclosure, conversion to pasture, and depopulation were linked in
contemporaries' minds as a social evil until the middle of the seventeenth century.
The difference probably lies in the fact that enclosure in the Englishries of south
Wales was not normally linked to a reduction in tillage, but was intended to increase
the productivity of arable as much as to make pasturing animals easier. The region
generally was not short of grazing. The piecemeal nature of enclosure similarly
meant that the process was seldom controversial. It was a matter in which farmers
and landlords co-operated; not until the period after 1750 do we see signs of
gentlemen taking the initiative to improve their estates and reorganize communities
wholesale. Unlike the contemporary attack on waste and common land, enclosure
of the arable did not provoke contemporaries to extensive litigation.

If we look again at Barry, Merthyr Dyfan and Cadoxton, we can see how
enclosure was accompanied by other, connected, changes in the pattern of
settlement. Figure 49 on page 242 reconstructs the former extent of open field arable
in these three parishes. It also seeks to show the location of new farmsteads of late-
and post-medieval origin in these communities. The period after c.1450 witnessed a
strengthening of the element of dispersal in the landscape. New farmhouses were
planted on former demesne land, on land that had once been common, and on land
that had been waste and wood in the Middle Ages. The recovery and subsequent

expansion of population in the district in the sixteenth and seventeenth centuries were accompanied by the physical expansion of settlement beyond its medieval bounds. This took place, very often, away from the hamlets and villages that had formed the nuclei of these communities in 1300. Cadoxton also accommodated increased numbers by the encroachment of small cottages on the margins of its common. Similar developments must have taken place throughout south Wales, but this aspect of early modern settlement has attracted little attention.

It is landscape history pursued at the level of the local community which is likely to be most helpful in charting the progress of enclosure and the creation of new farms and smallholdings. We should not, however, lose sight of more general underlying factors. In its earlier phase, enclosure was probably encouraged by the opportunities for the engrossment of holdings that existed in the later Middle Ages and was the work of larger peasant farmers and demesne lessees. In the sixteenth and early seventeenth centuries, rising population and prices placed new and different pressures on farmers, and in this conjuncture, the most obvious response was the intensification of production to which enclosure could make a contribution. It may be that after 1650, when arable prices slumped and population growth slowed, the pressures for change were reduced and the rate of enclosure slowed, leaving loose ends to be tidied up in the course of the following century, when landed gentlemen became interested in improving their estates. It must be emphasized, however, that local circumstances, perhaps especially the structure of landownership and the size and profitability of farms, would govern the pace of progress in individual communities.

Detailed local investigation would also enable a more systematic appraisal of pressure on common, waste and wood land. Parts of the countryside, such as the Vale of Glamorgan, had relatively little common land; elsewhere, in Gower, for example, and in Gwent, common, wood and waste land was much more extensive in the early sixteenth century. Courtney has argued that the sixteenth and seventeenth centuries saw much of the waste in Monmouthshire put to agricultural use; deer parks, likewise, were converted to farmland, and richer tenants made every effort to extend their holdings. This was part of a process of erosion of common rights that lasted into the nineteenth century. In the Vale of Glamorgan, too, there was considerable pressure on what common there was, reflected, for example, in the late sixteenth century, in disputes between the tenants of Wick and those of St Brides Major and Southerndown over grazing rights, and in the resistance that was mounted in Queen Elizabeth's reign to enclosure of the King's Wood and Flemingsdown Wood in Ogmore lordship. All classes, it seems, participated none the less in encroachment on the waste; gentleman, tenants, and poor squatters.[57]

It is the activities of squatters that from the point of view of the development of settlement could, in particular, do with greater examination at the level of the local community. In southern Glamorgan it appears that it was those parishes with extensive commons which grew most in population in the later sixteenth and the seventeenth centuries and where, in the 1670s, large proportions of the poor were concentrated. Where landlord control was for one reason or another minimal, poor families who could not establish themselves elsewhere could find a refuge on the common-edge. Very often the fines that were levied on such squatters were in practice *de facto* rents. In Caerau (Glamorgan), in 1666, thirty cottages were said to have been established on common land; earlier, Duchy of Lancaster surveys of the manors of White Castle and Skenfrith in Monmouthshire (1609–13) contain long lists of encroachments and cottages built without licence on roadside and common. It would be well worth looking in more detail at the social structure and settlement geography of such communities.[58]

CONCLUSIONS

By 1700 the modern landscape of rural Wales had come, in its essentials, into existence. This is not to say that the following 250 years have not seen great changes. The later eighteenth and the nineteenth centuries were to see further massive attacks on upland wastes and commons, reflected in the regular patterns of parliamentary enclosure; the expansion and contraction of population in rural areas led to further extension of the margins of colonization and a subsequent retreat from farmsteads established on difficult land. The essential characteristics of the rural settlement pattern of modern Wales had none the less already been established: a pronounced dispersal of settlement in the uplands and in the lowlands of *pura Wallia*, accompanied by the disappearance of the hamlets and girdle-settlements of the high Middle Ages; in the manorial Englishries, the development of an enclosed landscape of field and hedgerow that replaced the champion countryside of earlier centuries. These processes we can trace with some confidence in their outlines; what is now required is a more rigorous attempt to reconstruct changes in the landscape at the local level in the context of changes in social structure, economic activity and demographic growth. In the early modern period, too, we need to develop a more detailed understanding of the relationship between countryside and town as it was before the development of industry and improved communications disrupted the urban network of the sixteenth and seventeenth centuries. In this respect settlement studies can make a major contribution to the construction of a fuller history of Welsh society in the pre-industrial era.

NOTES

[1] The following works provide a general outline of the topics discussed in this chapter: H. Carter, *The Towns of Wales: a study in urban geography* (Cardiff, 1965); Margaret Davies 'Field Systems of South Wales' and G.R.J. Jones 'Field Systems of North Wales' in A.R.H. Baker and R.A. Butlin (eds.), *Studies of Field Systems in the British Isles* (Cambridge, 1973); F.V. Emery, 'West Glamorgan Farming circa 1580–1620' in *N.L.W. Jnl.*, IX (1955–6); idem, 'The Farming Regions of Wales' and T. Jones Pierce, 'Landlords in Wales: the nobility and gentry' in Joan Thirsk (ed.), *The Agrarian History of England and Wales*, [*Ag. Hist.*] IV (Cambridge 1967); P. Flatrès, *Géographie rurale de quatre contrées Celtiques* (Rennes, 1957); B.E. Howells, 'Pembrokeshire Farming, 1580–1620', *N.L.W. Jnl.*, IX (1955–6); Leonard Owen, 'The Population of Wales in the Sixteenth and Seventeenth Centuries', *T.C.S.* (1959); Dorothy Sylvester, *The Rural Landscape of the Welsh Borderland* (1969); C. Thomas, 'Place-name Studies and Agrarian Colonisation in North Wales', *W.H.R.*, X (1980–1); M.I. Williams, *The Making of the South Wales Landscape* (1975).

[2] Gwyn A. Williams, 'Owain Glyn Dŵr', in A.J. Roderick (ed.), *Wales through the Ages*, I (Llandybie, 1959), 177.

[3] For an assessment of the disruptive effects of the Glyndŵr revolt see, for example, R.R. Davies, *Lordship and Society in the March of Wales, 1282–1400* (Oxford, 1978), 425 *et seq.*

[4] Leonard Owen, 'The Population of Wales in the Sixteenth and Seventeenth Centuries', *T.C.S.* (1959), 99–113.

[5] Royston Stephens, 'Gwynedd, 1528–1547: economy and society in Tudor Wales' (University of California, Los Angeles, Ph.D. dissertation, 1975), 115, 160 (n.3); M. Griffiths, 'The Vale of Glamorgan in the 1543 Lay Subsidy returns', *B.B.C.S.* XXIX (1980–2), 718–19.

[6] F.V. Emery, 'The Farming Regions of Wales' in *Ag. Hist.* IV, 142–5.

[7] Comments based on work in progress for an edition of the Glamorgan 1543–5 Lay Subsidy returns; cf. also M. Griffiths, *B.B.C.S.,* XXIX (1980–2), 722–5.

[8] E.A. Wrigley and R.S. Schofield, *The Population History of England, 1541–1871* (1981), publishes the results of the work of the Cambridge Group for the History of Population and Social Structure on trends in the English population; chapter 5 of Peter Laslett's *The World we have lost: Further Explained* (1983) takes account of Wrigley and Schofield and is considerably more entertaining.

[9] D.M. Robinson, *Cowbridge: the archaeology and topography of a small market town in the Vale of Glamorgan* (Swansea, 1980); T. James, *Carmarthen: an archaeological and topographical Survey* (Carmarthen, 1980).

[10] H. Carter, *The Towns of Wales*, 29–68. Cf. idem, 'The Growth and Decline of Welsh Towns', in D. Moore (ed.), *Wales in the Eighteenth Century* (Swansea, 1976), 47–62.

[11] I. Soulsby, *Towns of Wales* (Chichester, 1983), 27–8.

[12] M. Beresford, *New Towns of the Middle Ages* (1967), 339–47; 527–32; H. Carter, *Towns of Wales*, 14–28; M.W. Barley (ed.), *The Plans and Topography of Medieval Towns in England and Wales*, C.B.A. research report no. 14 (1976).

[13] John Leland, *The Itinerary in Wales in or about the years 1536–9*, ed. L. Toulmin Smith (1906). Contemporary descriptions of Welsh towns may also be found in William Camden's *Britannia* (1586) and in George Owen's *The Description of Penbrockshire* (1603), ed. H. Owen, I, Cymmrodorion Record Series, 1, (1902). Rice Merrick's account of Cardiff *c.* 1578 is in Rice Merrick, *Morganiae Archaiographia, A Book of the Antiquities of Glamorganshire*, ed. B.Ll. James, South Wales Record Society, 1, (Barry, 1983), 86–92.

[14] See the editor's chapter on 'Aberystwyth' in R.A. Griffiths (ed.), *The Boroughs of Mediaeval Wales* (Cardiff, 1978), 44.

[15] R.F. Walker, 'Tenby', in ibid., 311–19.

[16] R.R. Davies, 'Brecon', in ibid., 66–70.

[17] James, *Carmarthen: an archaeological and topographical survey*, 30–2; R.A. Griffiths, 'Carmarthen' in *Boroughs of Mediaeval Wales*, 154–6.

[18] B. Ian Jack, 'Ruthin', in ibid., 255–7, 259.

[19] Owen, *T.C.S.* (1959), 107–13.

[20] For English towns see P. Clark and P. Slack, *English Towns in Transition 1500–1700* (Oxford, 1976), 7–11, and passim, and P. Clark (ed.), *The Early Modern Town: a reader* (Oxford, 1976).

[21] Carter, *Towns of Wales*, 32–46; Emery, *Ag. Hist.* IV, passim; relevant articles in *Boroughs of Medieval Wales*.

[22] A. Everitt, 'The Marketing of Agricultural Produce', in *Ag. Hist.* IV, 475–8; cf. ibid., 589 *et seq.*

[23] A.H. Dodd, *A History of Wrexham* (Wrexham, 1957), 34.

[24] B.G. Charles (ed.), *Calendar of the Borough Records of Haverfordwest, 1539–1660* (Cardiff, 1967), 1–2.

[25] Walker, 'Tenby' in *Boroughs of Mediaeval Wales*, 314–18; John Speed, *Theatre of the Empire of Great Britaine* (1611), part 2 (1676 ed.), 101.

[26] Robinson, *Cowbridge*; cf. Brian Ll. James and D.J. Francis, *Cowbridge and Llanblethian: past and present* (Cowbridge, 1979) for an accurate, readable account of the social history of the borough.

[27] A. Everitt, *Ag. Hist.* IV.

[28] See in particular, apart from the works cited above, the essays by T. Jones Pierce reprinted in *Medieval Welsh Society*, [M.W.S.] ed. J. Beverley Smith (Cardiff, 1972); T. Jones Pierce, 'Landlords in Wales: the nobility and gentry' in *Ag. Hist.* IV, 357–81; Jones in *Studies of Field Systems*, 430–79; C. Thomas, 'Patterns and Processes of Estate Expansion in the Fifteenth and Sixteenth Centuries' *Jnl. Mer. H.R.S.*, VI (1972).

[29] For *prid*, see Llinos Beverley Smith, 'The Gage and the Land Market in Late Medieval Wales', *E.C.H.R.* 2nd series, XXIX (1976), 537–50.

[30] W. Ogwen Williams, *Tudor Gwynedd* (Caernarfon, 1958), 17, 37–53, and passim.

[31] G.R.J. Jones in *Studies of Field Systems*, 460–71; T. Jones Pierce, *Ag. Hist.* IV 360–1.

[32] Jones, in *Studies of Field Systems*, 451–7.

[33] Thomas, *Jnl. Mer. H.R.S.*, VI (1972), 338–41; idem, 'Enclosure and the Rural Landscape of Merioneth in the Sixteenth Century', *T. Inst. Brit. Geog.*, XLII (1967), 153–62; R. Elfyn Hughes, 'Environment and Human Settlement in the Commote of Arllechwedd Isaf', *T.C.H.S.*, II (1940), 1–25; Elwyn Evans, 'Arwystli and Cyfeiliog in the Sixteenth Century', *Mont. Coll.*, LI (1949–50), 23–37.

[34] C. Thomas, 'Place-name Analysis in the Geographical Study of the Rural Landscape of Wales', *Studia Celtica*, VIII (1973), 299–318; idem, 'Colonisation, Enclosure and the Rural Landscape', *N.L.W. Jnl.*, XIX (1975–6), 132–46; Place-name Studies and Agrarian Colonisation in north Wales', *W.H.R.*, X (1980–1), 155–71.

[35] Sylvester, *Rural Landscape*, 224.

[36] T. Jones Pierce, 'Medieval Cardiganshire: a study in social origins', in *M.W.S.*, 309–24; idem, 'Pastoral and Agricultural Settlements in Early Wales', ibid. 344–51.

[37] Howells, *N.L.W. Jnl.*, IX (1955–6), 314–15, 322–6.

[38] Owen, *Description of Penbrockshire*, I, 61.

[39] Cf. J. Beverley Smith and T.B. Pugh, 'The Lordship of Gower and Kilvey in the Middle Ages', in T.B. Pugh (ed.), *Glamorgan County History*, [G.C.H.] III (Cardiff, 1971), 214–15; J. Beverley Smith, 'The Lordship of Senghennydd', in ibid., 314–15.

[40] Ibid., 323–6.

[41] Royal Commission on Ancient and Historical Monuments in Wales, *An Inventory of the Ancient Monuments in Glamorgan*, [Glam. Inv.] III (ii), (Cardiff, 1982), 17–41.

[42] Roger Lee Brown, 'Afan Argoed', *Afan Uchaf*, II (1979), 1–27.

[43] Elwyn Davies, '*Hendre* and *Hafod* in Caernarfonshire', *T.C.H.S.*, XL (1979), 17–46; idem, '*Hendre* and *Hafod* in Denbighshire', *T.D.H.S.*, XXVI (1977), 49–72; '*Hendre* and *Hafod* in Merioneth', *Jnl. Mer. H.R.S.*, VII (1973), 13–77; Melville Richards, '*Hafod, Cynaefdy* and *Hendre* in Welsh Place-names', *Mont. Coll.*, LVI (i) (1958), 177–87; idem, '*Hafod* and *Hafoty* in Welsh Place-names', ibid., LVI (ii) (1959), 13–20.

[44] D. Allen, 'Excavations at Hafod y Nant Criafolen, Brenig Valley, Clwyd, 1973–4', *Post-medieval Archaeology*, XIII (1979), 49 *et seq.*

[45] Thomas Pennant, *Tours in Wales*, ed. John Rhys (1883), II, 325–6.

[46] See especially Sylvester, *Rural Landscape*; and Davies in *Studies of Field Systems*, 480–529.

[47] *Glam. Inv.* III (ii), 215–43.

[48] Davies in *Studies of Field Systems*, passim; idem, 'Rhossili Open Field and Related South Wales Field Systems', *Ag. Hist. Rev.*, IV (1956), 80–96; Dorothy Sylvester, 'The Common Fields of the Coastlands of Gwent', *Ag. Hist. Rev.*, VI (1958), 9–26.

[49] A useful listing of deserted and shrunken village sites in south-east Wales is given in 'Deserted Medieval Villages in Glamorgan and Gwent', in H.N. Savory and G. Dowdell (eds.), *Glamorgan-Gwent Archaeological Trust Annual Report 1979–80* (Swansea, 1980), 39–45.

[50] R.R. Davies, 'The Lordship of Ogmore', in *G.C.H.* III, 298–304; M. Griffiths, 'The Manor in

Medieval Glamorgan: the estates of the de Ralegh family in the 14th and 15th centuries', *B.B.C.S.*, XXXII (1985).

[51] R. Merrick, *Morganiae Archaiographie*, 14.

[52] Davies, *Lordship and Society* 432, *et seq.*; Somerset Record Office, D/D WO 47/1.

[53] Howells, *N.L.W. Jnl.*, IX (1955–6), 314 *et seq.*; F. Emery in ibid., 399.

[54] Glamorgan Record Office, manorial map of Barry manor surveyed by Evans Mouse (1622); M. Griffiths, 'Manor Court Records and the Historian: Penmark, Fonmon and Barry, 1570–1622', *Morgannwg*, XXV (1981), 54–9. The following material on the Barry area is based on the latter article and on my two chapters in Donald Moore (ed.), *Barry — the Centenary Book* (Barry, 1984).

[55] P. Courtney, 'The Rural Landscape of Eastern and Lower Gwent, *c.* A.D. 1070–1750' (Univ. Wales Ph.D. thesis, 1983), 280 *et seq.*; for Wrinstone, see B.E. Vyner and S. Wrathmell, 'The Deserted Village of Wrinstone, South Glamorgan', *Trans. Cardiff Naturalists' Society*, XCVIII (1978), 21–3.

[56] Howells, *N.L.W. Jnl.*, IX (1955–6), 327–9.

[57] Courtney, (thesis, 1983), 310–46; M.E. Thomas, 'Glamorgan 1540–1640. Aspects of social and economic history' (Univ. Wales M.A. thesis, 1973), 101–2.

[58] Joanna Martin, 'The Landed Estate in Glamorgan *circa* 1660 to 1760' (Univ. Cambridge Ph.D. thesis, 1978), 83; W. Rees (ed.), *A Survey of the Duchy of Lancaster Lordships in Wales 1609–1613* (Cardiff, 1953), 95, 115–17.

Rural Settlements in the Modern Period

COLIN THOMAS

IF a contemporary traveller through rural Wales could be transported backwards to the early eighteenth century, he would find much that would be quite unfamiliar to him. Not only would there be coarser landscape textures to meet the eye and a very different pace and quality of material life, but equally strange would be the experience of social and cultural attitudes and economic practices that survive, if at all, today in only their most attenuated forms. Throughout the generations under consideration those profound transformations of rural landscapes, economies and societies reflected reappraisals of natural resources, technological innovations both within and beyond the Principality, population changes and fluctuations in the relative power of socio-economic groups. The period, partly because of its length, exhibited conflicting and contrasting trends, a turbulence that was further complicated by regional variation.

POPULATION AND DEMOGRAPHIC TRENDS

The fourfold growth of the population from 0·587 millions in 1801 to 2·421 millions in 1911 was significant in itself and also as evidence of the country's increasing capacity to support greater numbers of people with its own varied resources, more of which were being exploited by concentrated capital investment and improved technology. Published results of the first ten censuses[1] chart aggregate changes in density and distribution, yet more crucial in the long term were the internal shifts that occurred both regionally and structurally in economic life.

By 1891 so widespread had been the impact that more than half of the total population was to be found in Glamorgan and Monmouthshire, counties which in 1801 had sustained only one-fifth of Wales's inhabitants. During the upheaval, then, not only were major absolute gains recorded in most counties, but equally indicative were changes occurring in the rank order and share of the total population held by specific counties as a consequence of broad regional revaluations of community and personal opportunities. For example, in 1801 Montgomeryshire housed 8·2 per cent of the Welsh total and was the fifth most populous county: by 1891 it had slipped to ninth place and its share had been reduced to 3·3 per cent. Glamorgan remained first but its share more than trebled to 38·8 per cent: Monmouthshire climbed from sixth to second rank and its share almost doubled. Whereas at the beginning of the century Radnor had been the only county with less than 5·0 per cent of the total population, at the close of the century it had been joined in that depressing distinction by Anglesey, Brecon, Cardigan, Flint, Merioneth, Montgomery and Pembroke. On this scale of analysis, already in the 1840s Merioneth, Montgomery and Radnor had also begun to register absolute intercensal decreases and the rural south-west — Cardigan, Carmarthen and Pembroke — showed signs of stagnation or incipient decline, features that were to become more extensive in succeeding decades.

Census data alone offer no comprehensive explanations of processes responsible for these trends, though footnotes relating to particular parishes may provide brief insights into short-term local events or characteristics, such as an inflow of men seeking employment in expanding coalfield settlements or the temporary influx of labourers for a construction project. For details of demographic mechanisms one must turn to alternative sources and adopt a different perspective. Two such mechanisms need to be examined and two documentary sources contain the primary evidence.

The first process is that of the demographic transition, whereby initially high oscillating birth- and death-rates were stabilized over several generations at greatly reduced levels and the excess of births over deaths was itself diminished. Throughout Europe the net result was that the high rates of natural increase, especially among rural populations, which had contributed substantially to the pronounced regional contrasts, were gradually eliminated in many countries. Underlying influences on this trend are still incompletely understood, although it is clear that important roles were played by improvements in housing, sanitation, hygiene and diet, together with the application of preventative measures to curb the worst effects of cholera,[2] smallpox and typhoid epidemics, themselves chronicled in local newspapers and mid-nineteenth-century reports from public health commissioners. Synchronized changes in social attitudes and material well-being were also involved.

As yet a definitive account of the historical demography of Wales has still to be undertaken; all that can be sketched here is an outline of trends and suggested courses for further research. Prior to the Civil Registration Act of 1837 quantitative evidence for long-term national or regional variations in fertility and mortality can only be deduced from analyses of information on baptisms and burials contained in parish registers, kept with varying degrees of accuracy and completeness by clergy of the Established Church since the Reformation. Despite the attention paid to these sources elsewhere in Britain, research of this nature has rarely been attempted in Wales even on a small scale.[3] In its absence we will be obliged for some time to come to rely upon aggregate summaries collated by John Rickman and published with the 1831 census.[4]

The potential pitfalls of using parish register data, particularly in areas like Wales where Nonconformity was so prevalent, are well known,[5] and the intricate and time-consuming effort required to extract statistically valid samples from either the original baptismal, marriage and burial registers or from the Bishops' Transcripts held at the National Library in Aberystwyth may deter the most ardent amateur scholar. Even so the rewards of tabulating monthly, seasonal or annual demographic events over a lengthy time-span, or the establishing of possible relationships between occupations and age at marriage, family size, birth intervals, life expectancy and age at death are enormous to the local historian and geographer. Comparative studies may be conducted between different periods and different small communities, measured against evidence available from more extensive research in progress in rural England and possibly blended with similar material derived from contemporary Nonconformist and Roman Catholic registers.

As background to such projects, tabulations in the Parish Register Abstracts for 1801–40 enable some tendencies to be discerned for the 13 counties and 83 hundred divisions of Wales[6]. During the first three decades of the nineteenth century, almost universally high fertility resulted in a surplus of births over deaths at county level, although local adverse trends were beginning to emerge. Between 1811 and 1821 only border districts of Flintshire and Radnorshire, and to a lesser extent Merioneth, deviated from the large natural gains promoted by high post-Napoleonic birth-rates, while death-rates peaked some years later. The southern counties and Caernarfonshire continued to record steady unspectacular population increases, but in mid and north Wales generally future decreases were already being foreshadowed. Subject to the reservations which must be held concerning parish register evidence, mathematical and logical regularities appear to distil from analysis of data from 72 hundreds for which it has been possible to derive calculations for 1821–31. Whereas crude birth-rates in Carmarthenshire, Glamorgan and Pembrokeshire ranged between 16 and 23 per thousand inhabitants in 1821, mid Wales districts conformed more closely to the national range of 17 to 28 per thousand and those were exceeded in the north. Precise figures, when viewed in the context of later nineteenth-century statistics for England and Wales, seem relatively low and may need to be adjusted upwards by as much as 25 per cent to allow for registration error, total omission or lack of evidence from some parishes, and unrecorded illegitimate births. However, the same sources reveal that by 1831 the broad north–south differential remained, albeit on a lower scale. The other really significant feature was the apparent sharp reduction of both birth- and death-rates over the decade, to such an extent that several areas even exhibited excesses of deaths over births in the latter year. Such examples of natural population decrease occurred along the northern flanks of the Brecon Beacons, Mynydd Eppynt and the Black Mountains, in the hundreds of Caerffili and Miskin on the coalfield and the whole tract from St David's Head eastwards through Preseli into the south Cardiganshire and north Carmarthenshire hills. Similar in the north was the area extending from the Dyfi Valley through Mawddwy and Penllyn to southern Snowdonia. In contrast high rates of natural increase remained characteristic of the lowlands of north-east Wales and the middle borderland.

The more reliable evidence of civil registration statistics examined by Lawton for the 1851–1911 period confirms that there followed a phase of slower rural natural increase almost everywhere in Wales, usually of the order of 6–10 per cent per decade.[7] Higher rates were experienced only in the industrial south-east, where the former influx of young people was now having a marked demographic impact in raising the birth-rate.

The second process superimposed on fertility–mortality relationships is that of migration. The conflicting stimuli of post-Napoleonic agrarian depression and early industrialism at selected locations enabled even prosperous rural districts to attract short-distance migrants in considerable numbers, though seldom was that magnetism attributable to purely agricultural resource exploitation. Already in the

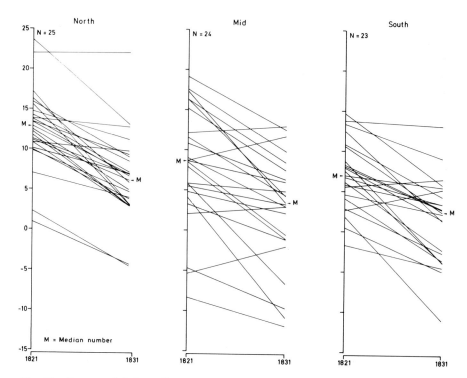

Fig. 50   Excess and deficit of baptisms over burials for Welsh hundred divisions, 1821–31.

eighteenth century, far-sighted entrepreneurs, including several estate owners, had been encouraged to prospect for minerals in the Ordovician and Silurian rocks which yielded ores of silver, copper, lead and zinc. From Carboniferous series, coal and iron were being mined in increasing quantities, and in Snowdonia, Preseli and the Berwyns from the 1760s slate and other building stone were widely quarried.[8]

Industrial intrusions into the countryside undoubtedly deterred some potential migrants from leaving rural under-employment and submitting to the material enticements of new coalfield towns or the even more distant lights of Liverpool, the English Midlands or London.[9] However, those same developments did magnetize not only Welshmen, but also English and Irish entrepreneurs, engineers, craftsmen and labourers. For example, published birthplace data by counties in the censuses of 1851, 1871 and 1891 quantify the population mobility which operated on a substantial scale to modify the trends of natural increase described above. In gross numbers, migration initially widened the size differential between rural and urban settlements, and between agrarian and industrial counties by shifting the balance of labour from areas of surplus to those of deficit. Consequently in 1871 more than 30 per cent of the inhabitants of the counties of Brecon, Glamorgan and Monmouth had not been born there. Conversely, Anglesey, Caernarfon, Cardigan, Carmarthen, Montgomery and Pembroke each represented the birthplace for 80–90 per cent of their respective residents.[10] That feature does not indicate that such counties and their people were in any sense introspective: on the contrary, thousands of men and women then living in the industrial south-east had originally belonged to farming families in the north and west, as may be demonstrated from calculation of net lifetime migration balances between counties and mapping the resultant flows. Similar techniques and sources help to explain Lawton's conclusion that, for the period 1851 to 1911, virtually all central and south-west Wales experienced a net loss of population because out-migration exceeded natural gain, whereas northern districts, which were more isolated from the sources of change, achieved small net gains despite migration losses.

A further element in the equation was cross-border interaction with England, which accelerated in both directions towards the end of the century. As the filter's mesh opened up, most of the influx was directed towards Glamorgan and Monmouthshire where in 1891 some 200,000 residents were not Welsh by birth. The majority could trace their origins to adjacent parts of Gloucester, Somerset, the West Midlands, Cheshire and Lancashire.[11] A reverse movement had taken even larger numbers of Welsh-born people to similar, though more urban, destinations in England. Demographically, one effect of migration within, to and from Wales was to increase the ratio of males to females in industrial localities and to decrease it in rural districts, thereby creating an imbalance which was to have far-reaching repercussions on all aspects of rural life for succeeding generations. For a time urban birth-rates and death-rates were deflated by the flood of young immigrants, but the natural increase soon revived as new families established themselves. In the countryside, cumulative loss of future parents was to become the hallmark of Welsh communities from the 1840s to the present day.

For more vivid appreciations of the nature of local society there is need to change both the perspective and scale of investigation by making use of information on households and individuals contained in the unpublished census schedules for enumeration districts. Released sequentially from the Public Record Office under the hundred-year rule governing confidentiality, these documents are especially valuable for 1851 onwards when accuracy improved and classifications became more sophisticated.[12] Regrettably few studies of this source have been conducted with the methodological rigour that would come from standardized analysis of themes, particularly from data-processing by means of microcomputer programs. Nevertheless, several published and many more unpublished works[13] have demonstrated how the schedules enable composite pictures to be compiled by building up from details of a single residence to a village or parish, with further potential to regional or county levels. Evidence of personal names, age, occupation, place of birth and relationship to the head of household all contribute to a more profound understanding of static views derived from published statistics. In the immediate context, birthplace data, when related to age, sex and occupation, allow one to trace not only the history of families at specific addresses, but also the character of whole communities. For various locations in Cardiganshire, for instance, Lewis[14] and Thomas[15] have shown how immigration was age- and sex-selective and how the initially narrow spheres of population mobility in relatively remote areas gradually broadened to embrace individuals and families of widely different social, economic and cultural backgrounds, extending the range of local experience and skill while simultaneously giving rise to other tensions in traditional society.

It was from such communities under stress that people came to participate in a third process, which was in many respects a variant of the second, namely overseas migration since the 1840s. Total numbers of emigrants are imprecisely known,[16] and their story largely lies beyond the scope of this discussion, except in so far as their loss from rural Wales exacerbated still further that caused by quantitatively greater internal migration within the British Isles. From a few well-documented cases the forces which engendered those movements become sharply distinguishable, whether the traffic began in the countryside or in urban contexts under the guidance of professional men. Some followed Michael D. Jones to Ohio or the Pennsylvania coalfield;[17] others stumbled half-intentionally to the Chubut Valley of Patagonia;[18] yet others travelled more bewildered still with John Hughes to help initiate the Russian industrial revolution in the basin of the Ukrainian River Don.[19] All laid the foundations of a trans-oceanic Wales that would be built upon by other generations seeking expanded social or economic horizons, and in all cases their gradual acculturation by host communities was a clear image of what occurred in Wales itself.

SETTLEMENT LIMITS, FORMS AND LANDSCAPES

For those who remained at home their form of habitat was equally diverse and fluid in the eighteenth and nineteenth centuries. To recapture some flavour of the age one may scan the landscapes depicted by classical or romantic painters and poets,[20] and the often less romantic impressions recorded by English visitors during the course of tours through the Principality.[21] However entertaining or intrinsically interesting they may be, description is distorted by perception in these travellers' tales, though to retrace the routes of Thomas Pennant, George Kay, Walter Davies, George Borrow, Charles Hassall or Benjamin Heath Malkin can be a delight. Samuel Lewis's *Topographical Dictionary*,[22] too, is a supplementary source for selected places in the early nineteenth century, providing contemporary detail that may be interwoven with the increasingly comprehensive documentation to emerge at a national level.

Intensified population growth inevitably brought about a steady remodelling of the landscape to meet changing needs. The censuses themselves indicate the relative potency of two conflicting trends, the abandonment of some houses and the building of others, while any alert observer today may detect further material proof of the variety of housing distribution, size and style that accrued to the early modern pattern. In the uplands that pattern consisted primarily of dispersed homesteads, often of medieval origin as place-names testify. Farms generally lay in the midst of their own irregularly-shaped fields and were linked to each other by a web of footpaths, narrow cart tracks and minor roads. Where favourable conditions of soil, slope and aspect permitted, settlement was not uncommon at 300 metres above sea-level, with appurtenant rights on the exposed treeless moorlands beyond. Quite a different sight was presented by the island of Anglesey, the northern and southern coastal lowlands and the broader valleys leading westwards from the English border. There historic factors of manorial colonization, the nature of a farming system based more upon tillage than pastoralism, and the requirements of trade had offered opportunities for the development of nucleated villages, often nestling around ruined castle and solid parish church.[23] Those agglomerations not only provided homes for farmers who journeyed daily into their outlying fields, some of which still bore morphological traces of intermixed medieval cultivation strips, but also harboured a variety of service provision for their hinterlands. Set within that gentler scenery were ancient market towns that articulated all the needs of the common people and provided a social and economic focus for a modestly present middle class and gentry.

For all the antiquity of both landscape types, documentary and cartographic evidence reveals that they had undergone slow transformation since the Elizabethan era.[24] Anyone wishing to reconstruct any of those past realities should turn first to successive editions of the Ordnance Survey maps,[25] though without excessive expectations since the earliest six-inch to one-mile maps for Wales date only from the mid 1860s. Somewhat earlier patterns of settlement distribution, roads and field boundaries are preserved in the tithe maps and schedules, compiled on a parish basis in the 1830s and 1840s by teams of land surveyors[26] who may themselves have been responsible for drafting enclosure maps and awards, or even estate surveys which pre-date them.

The very existence of such documents is symptomatic of several processes active throughout the modern period — the gradual extinction of ancient customary rights to common land, the creation of new fields and farmsteads, the territorial extension of the margins of agrarian occupancy, the remolding of existing structures, the consolidation of land ownership in fewer hands, and the socio-economic realignments that arose from all these causes. Moreover all historical sources identified thus far portray, and themselves reflect, the progressive specialization and differentiation occurring in rural society, partly in response to technological innovation. After all, surveyors like John Matthews of Mold,[27] Richard Owen of Llanynghenedl and Robert Williams of Llandygái may have been smallholders in their own right, yet their expanding profession could not have flourished without the demands made upon it by their more wealthy employers, and indeed would not have been possible without that spirit of invention and application of science which epitomized their age. Their services were acknow-ledged directly in fees, but for future generations they were beyond price because arduous years of careful measurement and artistry have bequeathed to us a vast store of cartography and statistics on land quality, ownership, occupancy and exploit-ation, which may involve as much pleasure and creativity in its rediscovery as its original compilation. Using modern Ordnance Survey maps as a base, eighteenth or nineteenth-century landscape textures may be standardized for scale, transposed and reconstituted. Land-use elements can be identified as they are changed, as can property boundaries.[28] When analysed alongside farm deeds, rentals and account books, the intricate but sturdy framework of an older agrarian way of life re-emerges from obscurity.

A considerable part was played in that transformation by the enclosure movement.[29] Physically it spread novel geometric field systems over hills and moorlands that had hitherto seen few tangible limitations of individual or joint proprietorship.[30] Land hunger, stimulated by population growth, dotted those fields

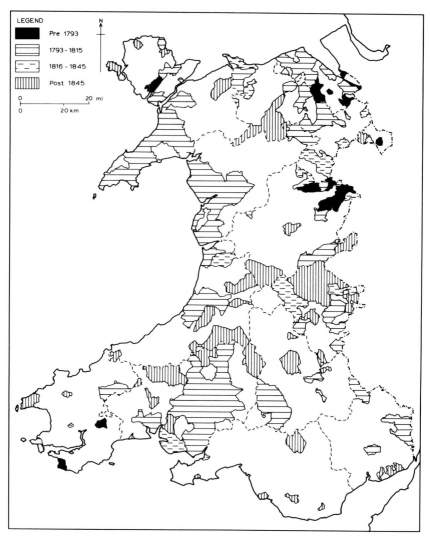

Fig. 51   Parishes subject to Parliamentary Enclosure Awards.

with farmhouses, from which rough grazings were converted to improved pastures or even cultivated plots. Yet neither development should be divorced from its antecedents, for Parliamentary enclosure, proceeding slowly from peripheral lowlands into more inhospitable regions of Wales especially between 1790 and 1815, merely continued a trend which had been initiated during the later Middle Ages. Since the sixteenth century the *cytir* had been subjected to widespread illegal encroachment by squatters, whose resort to the *tŷ un nos* tradition was even encouraged by some landowners who were not averse to the practice themselves. In the fifteen years before the Act was passed to enclose uplands in Llanddwywe, Merioneth (1810), the Mostyn estate of Corsygedol had constructed 8,000 yards of new field walls on the commons[31] and in due course obtained 97 per cent of its

3,185-acre allotments. Formal contrasts between a tortuously distended field wall, hedge or ditch and a large rectilinear enclosure should not blind us to their similarities of purpose, namely to bring common land into exclusive private possession. Likewise, the solid cottages appearing on commons allotments and dignified with Welsh names in reality differed from the squatters' hovels, whether 'Liberty Hall' or 'Clod Hall', only in style, not in function. Its occupant has been poignantly likened to 'an outcast, an Ishmael in society, living on the verge of destitution and predisposed towards criminal acts'.[32] As settlement margins were pressed beyond normal ecological limits, outlying buildings, once islands in an ocean of rough pasture and peat bog, took upon themselves the form and appearance of permanently-occupied independent farmsteads, but retaining their tell-tale names — Hafod, Lluest or Beudy.[33] In such locations all the natural disadvantages of altitude, exposure, isolation and sheer distance meant that temporary agricultural gains along the ragged moorland edge were short-lived. Within a generation of the Napoleonic period's economic high water mark, they were once again stranded, their tiny arable fields having reverted to heath or scrub and the houses fallen into disrepair and eventual dereliction.[34] Surprisingly, some huts with earth walls and roofed with thatch, turf or slate survived for a century or more, for example at Rhoshirwaun on the Vaenol estate in Caernarfonshire,[35] standing in stark contrast to neat stone cottages rebuilt and modernized by landed proprietors elsewhere in Snowdonia, or indeed to the rows of quarrymen's houses planted and appropriately named at Tan-y-bwlch, Llandygái.

Optimistic colonizations which reinforced primary dispersion of settlement in Napoleonic Wales were rueful memories by the middle of the nineteenth century. As agricultural margins retreated downslope, homesteads were abandoned and their lands amalgamated, leaving in the present scenery only tumbledown fieldwalls and derelict shells of isolated houses. Rural society had begun a withdrawal to the comparative security of compact clusters which alone could sustain amenities and service provisions that were every family's expectation and right. Yet not all was loss. For each example where a 'landscape by design' progressed no further than a surveyor's idealistic plan, other real gains may be cited. In the Vale of Ffestiniog, or Morfa Harlech and the lower Dysynni Valley rich meadows emerged from laboriously reclaimed tidal marshes,[36] while at Traeth Mawr in the Glaslyn estuary W. A. Madocks accomplished the most spectacular turning of the tide by employing proven expertise from the Lincolnshire Fens.[37]

LAND TENURE AND THE RURAL ECONOMY

Since land was wealth, either directly or indirectly, its acquisition in greater quantities by fewer families between the Tudor period and the Victorian age accomplished a distinctive shift of power and status from a freeholding peasantry to a landed oligarchy.[38] By its very legal mechanisms, enclosure contributed to a process that was already dynamic. Estate deeds, and comparison of estate surveys of the eighteenth century with the same localities on tithe maps, reveal the territorial extent of property consolidation and how it was achieved. Preliminary charting of an estate's growth also provides a framework for studies of all manner of economic change, landlord–tenant relations, social and cultural transition, into which may be woven evidence drawn from several sources.[39]

Statistics on landownership compiled by Bateman[40] in the 1870s require far more critical appraisal than they have received hitherto, if only because of the exclusion of woodlands, an equivocal attitude to rough grazings, and serious methodological faults in the presentation of data by counties. Published evidence in the 1851 census may be similarly flawed, certainly if the contents of individual enumerators' schedules are any guide. An ideal procedure would be to tabulate information for sample years on specific estates with a view to accumulating a composite picture. Generally it would seem that many larger estates (over 10,000 acres) were found in north Wales, perhaps because of historic tenurial pressures and the impact of enclosure, whereas southern gentry counterparts were often less massive. That disposition is apparently reversed when farm size is examined, although in broad terms Wales was characteristically a land of smallholdings of less than 50–100 acres.[41] Regional variation is evidently a key feature and indeed analysis of different farm-size patterns between estates suggests that there may have been contrasting policies operated by individual proprietors.

Management of freeholds and tenant farms also varied widely according to temporal, national, local and personal factors. Land-use changes may be traced at either parish or farm scale from estate papers, the 1801 crop returns,[42] tithe schedules, or the post-1867 June returns. Cartographic and statistical analyses show how the balances between arable, meadow, pasture and woodland, or between particular crops, fluctuated over time and contrasted in space in harmony with changing demographic, economic, technological and ecological constraints. After the stimuli of war and blockade in the early 1800s, the dominant trend thereafter was towards pastoralism at the expense of tillage, a shift which had repercussions on labour as well as landscape.[43]

When manpower in farming ceased to be cheap, when its surplus was creamed off by industry or replaced by mechanization, profound social changes swept the countryside. Census schedules for 1851 and 1861, for example in south Cardiganshire, confirm that traditional family farm units survived with little need for paid labour, other than a few resident servants or workers, usually in their teens or early twenties. Between 1851 and 1871 in Wales, the census records an abrupt decline in total labour inputs, including losses of over 11,000 male agricultural labourers, almost 10,000 female farm servants and 33,000 farm family members, 88 per cent of them females.[44] Simultaneously, significant increases were registered in the average age of heads of farming households. Socially- and economically-motivated migration has already been noted as one cause, but parallel to it were structural shifts taking place in the rural society as evidenced by its occupation composition, even at the scale of the 48 census registration districts.

Functional diversity, which could always be detected in the past by detailed analysis, now became widespread, and regional employment emphases easily discerned with simple quantitative techniques to measure degrees of locational concentration. However deeply rooted in direct exploitation of the soil, Welsh rural communities had always been heterogeneous in geographical origins, employment structure, social class, cultural and political attitudes, and the complexity of inter-

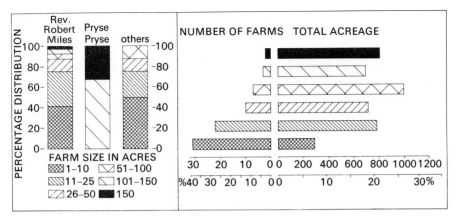

Fig. 52 Farm size distribution in the parish of St Mary's, Cardiganshire, 1839.

personal relationships. The generalized occupation classifications of earlier censuses and labour books of estate home farms portray the range of jobs available and the seasonal nature of some activities.[45] Every village had its craftsmen in stone, wood, metal, leather or textiles, its carters, tradesmen and even professional elements. Innumerable coastal hamlets from Llŷn to Gower sheltered their fishermen and sailors, while larger harbours along the shores of the Bristol Channel and Irish Sea offered work for shipwrights, merchant seamen and master mariners in trade that linked together crafts and ports from all over Britain, though the places themselves may have been quite isolated by poor overland communications.[46] Nevertheless long before Telford's enterprises, networks of carters, mail coaches and drovers[47] travelled well-worn routes over the mountains to integrate distant populations and their material produce with more commercially-oriented English industrial society. Along those tracks, later multiplied and rivalled by turnpike roads and railways, Welsh butter, cheese, beef, mutton and lamb probed wider markets through intermediary towns that had served local hinterlands for centuries.

The structure and role of such market centres may be reconstructed not only from the censuses but also from surviving visible relics and the descriptions provided by early topographies and trade directories.[48] All sources perform the triple service of firstly offering details of physical appearance at a specific date and place, secondly enabling systematic comparisons to be made which locate individual towns in a wider hierarchical arrangement, and thirdly assessing temporal re-sorting within that ranking.[49] Some reorientation resulted from the scale of population growth as larger nucleations in the countryside expanded to the detriment of villages nearby, but synchronized with and underpinning that shift was usually a boost given to a town's economic status by improved communications and augmented industry. In extreme cases, narrowly-based slate-quarrying settlements like Bethesda, Blaenau Ffestiniog, Nantlle, Dinorwic and Llanberis could never have existed without their related tramways and railways, which in turn stimulated the trade of Porthmadoc, Caernarfon and Bangor.[50] Amlwch and Aberystwyth flourished on the strength of short-lived exports of copper and lead-zinc ores respectively.[51] Brecon's prosperity was greatly enhanced on completion of the canal links with the Monmouthshire coalfield which acted as a supplier of its fuel needs and a market for its agricultural products.[52]

While extractive industries scarred remote pastoral slopes and attracted immigrants from similar specialist regions like Cornwall, Shropshire or the Derbyshire Dales as well as from the adjacent Welsh counties, more traditional crafts were transformed into factory manufacture along the Teifi and Severn, where woollen mills used agricultural raw materials and the softer power of water.[53] Employment concentrations of miners, quarrymen, millworkers, weavers emerge from parish registers[54] and census schedules,[55] where early references to retail and professional services run alongside more emphatic listings in trade directories published primarily for advertising purposes. Company records, diaries, news-papers, and private correspondence all bring to life cold facts drawn from official sources. In the non-productive sphere, omens of a new rural function begin to surface at Llandrindod,[56] Builth and Llanwrtyd where the fashion of visiting spas brought brief grandeur when railways promoted greater personal mobility and the concept of tourism and recreation on a larger scale than ever before.

If change was everywhere to be seen it should not wholly mask those facets of continuity that were equally potent in the countryside, the cross-currents of stability and impermanence representing rewarding research themes. While enclosure and amalgamation enlarged some farms, many remained untouched. On the Rhiwlas estate near Bala few holdings varied in acreage or even their assemblages of fields from Richard Owen's 1797 survey until after the tithe apportionment fifty years later. Land utilization patterns were reshuffled, yet field-names diagnostic of soil or vegetation types endured.[57] Among tenants and labourers, too, studies of succession and turnover can be enlightening. Numerous workers' names recur decade after decade in account books of the Bodrhyddan and other estates in north Wales,[58] though absolute continuity of employment throughout the year was less secure for women and children outside the harvest seasons, and declined generally by the 1870s. At off-peak times, home farm labourers on the Mostyn estates could expect to find themselves transferred to unfamiliar work in their employer's Flintshire coalpits[59] or temporarily laid off completely during exceptionally inclement weather.

Under such circumstances occupancy of the smallest plot of land was a cushion against adversity that not all could obtain or afford. While pioneer quarrymen and miners in Wales were among Europe's first 'peasant-workers', competition for better quality agricultural land and the gradual replacement of long leases by yearly tenancies eroded former patterns of security, deterred innovatory initiative or even adequate maintenance of properties, encouraged increased rents and fostered other grievances. The 'land question' culminated in March 1893 in the establishment of a Royal Commission, the proceedings of which, like many another, are more useful for their presentation of vast bodies of evidence than for their conclusions. Foremost among the findings of the Commission was the impossibility of disentangling political and cultural issues from superficially economic and social considerations, and once again the contrasting experience emanating from regional peculiarities. Political evictions, or at least the failure of landlords to renew tenancies where ideological conflict intervened, were demonstrated on Wynnstay, Peniarth, Rhiwlas and Glanllyn estates in Merioneth after the General Election of 1859,[60] yet other proprietors had recourse to no such strictures against their tenants. Equanimity in itself did not mean that peasant dynasties operated as an unbroken subculture over long periods. Nevertheless, by comparing the names of occupiers of 259 farms and smallholdings sampled from the 1837–39 tithe schedules for six South Cardigan-shire parishes[61] with those in the 1851 and 1861 censuses, a consistent continuity rate of 64 per cent was calculated for the 1837–51 and 1851–61 periods when either the same individual or a relative remained in residence for over a decade. The census confirms that the rate would have been higher had it not been for lack of male heirs, the death of an aged original occupier, or if it had been possible to trace transfers to other holdings in the vicinity.

CULTURE AND SOCIETY

However subtle the interpretation of themes and sources outlined above, they alone will not define adequately all the identities contained in rural Wales. A deeper understanding should involve probing further into the realms of non-material culture, attempting to evaluate how its changes have been dependent on, or independent of, those factors already discussed.

Having drawn attention to overall patterns when discussing rural settlement form and distribution, two elements in those patterns may now be brought into focus as buildings symbolic of the cultural traits they enshrine, namely the school and the church or chapel. The often proposed primary indicators of culture, religion and language, are singularly apt when applied to Wales where they have been for generations, if not centuries, inextricably bound up with education and political belief, themselves intertwined with economy and demography.

The more ancient establishment, the church, was held by E. G. Bowen to be a key feature in crystallizing settlement during the early medieval period, allied as it often was to the veneration of a regional or local Celtic saint and providing sanctuary in very turbulent times.[62] For the most part ecclesiastical records date from the Reformation and G. J. Lewis has succinctly described a model of increasing religious complexity arising from the progressive rejection of Roman Catholicism and Anglicanism.[63] After Dissenting meeting places were licensed by the 1689 Toleration Act, Wales adhered massively to Nonconformist creeds. Arguing that their initial spread was retarded by physical isolation, population immobility and a language barrier, Lewis emphasized how Methodism radiated throughout the Principality from Trefeca and Llangeitho by means of its itinerant Welsh-speaking preachers and the spawning of circulating schools to promote literacy and religious knowledge.

Distinct regional variations in denominational adoption rates were revealed by data compiled in the 1851 census concerning the numbers of places where services were conducted, their seating capacity, and figures for morning and evening attendances on 30 March of that year.[64] Supporting evidence is available from each denomination's annual reports and the membership lists of individual churches, many of which also kept registers similar to those of the Established Church prior to the introduction of civil registration of births, marriages and deaths.

Olive Anderson has noted that nearly half of the population did not appear to attend any place of worship in 1851 and that high incidences of civil marriage in nineteenth-century Wales may be attributable to forces other than purely religious ones, though the ceremony could be conducted in either Welsh or English.[65] When increasing numbers of chapels were registered for the solemnization of marriages after the mid 1850s, more Nonconformist institutions imitated the Anglican ceremonial with the result that all places of worship acquired an additional cohesive function in their respective communities. Building on their ethical and educational roles they became increasingly social nuclei and formal guardians of those cultural and behavioural norms that were especially potent in rural localities.

Despite the general atmosphere of strict Sabbatarianism, temperance, codes of private morality and public obedience to the law of the land, acute poverty and social tensions would periodically strain the capacity of religious organizations to cope with the everyday needs of their members. Indeed, against a strong background of rural unrest,[66] perhaps the most remarkable thing is the lack of correlation between statistics on crime and pauperism.[67] Moreover, on a local scale, sectarianism could act as an agency of fragmentation, cutting across those networks of relationships based on economic or kinship ties that ran so deeply in Welsh communities. Alwyn D. Rees cites an example, that can not be unique, of problems that arose in Llanfihangel-yng-Ngwynfa over the acquisition of land from the Anglican squire as a site for a Nonconformist chapel which many of his tenants would have attended.[68] Only a generation ago within the confines of Tregaron's Presbyterian chapel, Emrys Jones detected a cameo of rural society as a whole in the subtle reflections of class and status which found expression in tacit seating arrangements around the pulpit.[69] On a more expansive canvas, regional predispositions towards various denominations were clearly alive at the time of the 1851 enquiry and numerous patterns have been interpreted in terms of wholly non-theological factors.[70]

Formal education is a more recent phenomenon than institutionalized religion, though paradoxically many of the earliest charity schools had rural locations.[71] Similarly, Sunday Schools formed an integral part of the process whereby much of rural Wales was converted to Calvinistic Methodism in the eighteenth and nineteenth centuries. Wider geographical significance may be attached to those established by the National School Society and the British and Foreign School Society, supplemented by a small number of philanthropic industrialists who set up voluntary schools for children of their employees.[72] The effectiveness of these schools in reaching the mass of the population may be gauged by their distribution in relation to population densities, the volume of capital investment prior to the Elementary Education Act (1870), and the numbers of school teachers and scholars identified in the census schedules for 1851–81. On all criteria, education in Wales was a fragile phenomenon in mid Victorian times. Of £50,000 received by the British Society between 1833 and 1843, less than £2,000 was spent in the Principality and Idwal Jones has concluded that 'the places influenced were all coastal with comparatively big populations: the rural areas, which were poorest but most truly Welsh, were not influenced in the slightest degree'.[73] A major contributory factor was that whereas the National Schools were offshoots of the Established Church, committed to instruction through the medium of English and therefore unacceptable on two counts to the majority of the people, the non-denominational or Nonconformist leanings and tolerance of Welsh in British schools could not be matched by that Society's capacity to provide adequate buildings or qualified teachers. Particularly interesting might be detailed investigations of enrolments at various types of institution, including their seasonal oscillations in harmony with local agricultural activities, and the family background of scholars recorded in the 1851, 1861 and 1871 censuses.[74]

References to social, spatial and temporal variations in the use of the Welsh language have already intruded into consideration of several themes in this chapter, but it should not be overlooked as a central cultural trait in its own right. Ebbs and flows of the language have been researched as independent topics[75] and in association with other facets of regional particularism and change.[76] Several writers have shown that as the population drifted from the rural west and north to urban industrial Wales and across the border, the language divide retreated in the opposite direction. According to census returns, between 1901 and 1981 the proportion of persons over the age of three and living in Wales who were able to speak the language has declined from one-half to one-fifth. Alternative sources of information for the period before 1891, when it was first sought officially, suggest that in the mid nineteenth century Welsh was widely understood everywhere except in southern Pembrokeshire, Gower, parts of the Vale of Glamorgan and the eastern borderland from Gwent to Montgomeryshire, and the detached portion of Flint. At parish or community scale its steady loss of dominance can be retraced in religious services, schools, social organizations and newspaper circulation. Sociologically, its function may be viewed, like that of denominationalism, as a force simultaneously serving unity and exclusion, cohesion and division, and throughout the past two centuries that dual attribute has been inseparable from other economic and political struggles and issues impinging upon the daily life of country people. Contentious matters such as education provision, payment of tithes, land ownership and occupancy, and electoral behaviour and political allegiance were all tainted with religious and linguistic overtones in some district or another. Even industrial urbanism in its first generations cannot be held uniquely responsible for shifts in the fortunes of the Welsh language: after all, its position in the iron and coal towns was initially buttressed by the influx of migrants from the Welsh-speaking regions, as were pioneer minority colonies set up overseas.

Ultimately, a profound understanding of the continuous adjustments being made in rural life, whether initiated internally or externally, can only be achieved by systematic analyses of individual behaviour and community organization over protracted timespans. Such research should base its conclusions about society at large upon a knowledge of families and households, their relationships with each other at home, school, work, worship and leisure, and by placing the minutiae of local circumstance firmly in the context of wider horizons and more universal processes. By their very nature those processes are expressed in different quantities and types of data sources, the character of which has altered over a lengthy time-span. The main feature has been the emergence of standardized quantifiable evidence and cartographic illustration which permit specific local analyses to be dovetailed into methodologically comparable national frameworks. The picture revealed is far from uniform or stereotyped at the lowest level, and it is a great virtue of all the sources referred to above that at any scale they may be made to contribute to our knowledge of the whole.

NOTES

[1] *Census of Great Britain, Population Tables*, various years 1801–1911.

[2] G.P. Jones, 'Cholera in Wales', *N.L.W. Jnl.*, X (1957–58), 281–300.

[3] R.T. Jenkins and W. Rees (eds.), *Bibliography of the History of Wales* (Cardiff, 1962), 66–9; C.J. Williams and J. Watts-Williams (compilers), *Cofrestri Plwyf Cymru: Parish Registers of Wales* (Aberystwyth, 1986).

[4] *Census of Great Britain 1831, Parish Register Abstracts* (1833), 416–85.

[5] E.A. Wrigley (ed.), *An Introduction to English Historical Demography* (1966), 44–95.

[6] G. Melville Richards, *Welsh Administrative and Territorial Units* (Cardiff, 1969).

[7] R. Lawton, 'Population Changes in England and Wales in the Later Nineteenth Century: An Analysis by Registration Districts', *T. Inst. Brit. Geog.*, 44 (1973), 55–74.

[8] A.H. Dodd, *The Industrial Revolution in North Wales* (Cardiff, 1951).

[9] C.G. Pooley, 'Welsh Migration to England in the Mid-Nineteenth Century', *Journal of Historical Geography*, 9 (1983), 287–306.

[10] *Census of Great Britain 1871, Population Abstracts*, III (1873), 608–11.

[11] *Royal Commission on Land in Wales and Monmouthshire* (1896), Appendix E, 289–91.

[12] *H.M.S.O. Guides to Official Sources, No. 2; The Census of Great Britain, 1801–1951* (1952).

[13] For example, G.J. Lewis, *A Study of Socio-Geographic Changes in the Central Welsh Borderland, 1850–1960* (Univ. Leicester PhD thesis, 1960); K.M. O'Kelly, *A Demographic Study of Central Snowdonia and its Coastlands in the Nineteenth Century*, (Univ. Manchester, MA thesis, 1961); W.T.R. Pryce, *The Social and Economic Structure of Northeast Wales, 1750–1891*, (CNAA PhD thesis, 1971).

[14] G.J. Lewis, 'Mobility, Locality and Demographic Change: the case of North Cardiganshire, 1851–71', *W.H.R.*, 9 (1979), 347–61.

[15] C. Thomas, 'Rural Society in Nineteenth-Century Wales: South Cardiganshire in 1851', *Ceredigion*, 6 (1971), 388–414.

[16] D. Williams, 'Some figures relating to emigration from Wales', *B.B.C.S.* 7 (1935), 396–415.

[17] A.H. Dodd, *The Character of Early Welsh Emigration to the United States* (Cardiff, 1953).

[18] G. Williams, *The Desert and the Dream: A Study of Welsh Colonization in Chubut, 1865–1915* (Cardiff, 1975); E.G. Bowen, 'The Welsh Colony in Patagonia 1865–1885', *Geogr. Jnl.*, 132 (1966), 16–31.

[19] Idem, *John Hughes (Yuzovka) 1814–1889* (Cardiff, 1978).

[20] D. Moore (ed.), *Wales in the Eighteenth Century* (Swansea, 1976), 127–51; J. Zaring, 'The Romantic Face of Wales', *Annals of the Association of American Geographers*, 67 (1977), 397–418.

[21] R.L. Gant, 'The Topography as a Resource for Welsh Urban Studies', *N.L.W. Jnl.*, XIX (1976), 217–26.

[22] S. Lewis, *A Topographical Dictionary of Wales*, 2 vols., (1833).

[23] C. Thomas 'Rural Settlement' in H. Carter (ed.), *National Atlas of Wales* (Cardiff, 1982–4).

[24] D. Sylvester, *The Rural Landscape of the Welsh Borderland* (1969).

[25] D.A. Bassett, *A Source-Book of Geological, Geomorphological and Soil Maps for Wales and the Welsh*

Borders (1800–1966) (Cardiff, 1967); J.B. Harley, *Maps for the Local Historian: A Guide to British Sources* (1972).

[26] P. Eden and Avril Thomas (eds.), *Dictionary of Land Surveyors and Local Cartographers of Great Britain and Ireland, 1550–1850*, 3 vols. (Folkestone, 1975–9).

[27] C. Thomas, 'Land Surveyors in Wales, 1750–1850: the Matthews family', *B.B.C.S.*, XXXII (1985), 216–32.

[28] Idem, 'Estate Surveys as Sources in Historical Geography, *N.L.W. Jnl.*, XIV (1966), 451–68.

[29] I. Bowen, *The Great Enclosures of Common Lands in Wales* (1914); C. Thomas, 'Colonization, Enclosure and the Rural Landscape', *N.L.W. Jnl.*, XIX (1975), 133–46.

[30] The pre-enclosure importance of access to common grazings may be judged by its inclusion in sale particulars of farms, for example in the Dolgellau area in 1766; U.C.N.W. Mostyn Ms. 6037.

[31] U.C.N.W. Mostyn Ms. 6774.

[32] D. Williams, *The Rebecca Riots: A Study in Agrarian Discontent* (Cardiff, 1955).

[33] E. Davies, 'Hafod, Hafoty and Lluest: their distribution, features and purpose', *Ceredigion*, 9 (1980), 1–41.

[34] C. Morgan, *The Effect of Parliamentary Enclosure on the Landscape of Caernarvonshire and Merioneth*, (Univ. Wales MSc. thesis, 1959); G.I. Lewis, *An Investigation of Changes in Population Density and Distribution, together with Changes in Agricultural Practice, in Pembrokeshire during the period 1831–1931*, (Univ. Birmingham MA thesis, 1937).

[35] E. William, 'Peasant Architecture in Caernarvonshire', *T.C.H.S.*, 43 (1982), 83–107; R.O. Roberts, *Farming in Caernarvonshire around 1800* (Denbigh, 1973); P. Smith, *Houses of the Welsh Countryside* (1975); I.C. Peate, *The Welsh House* (Liverpool, 1944).

[36] C. Thomas, 'Merioneth Estates 1790–1850: a study in agrarian geography', *Jnl. Mer. H.R.S.*, 5 (1967), 221–38.

[37] E. Beazley, *Madocks and the Wonder of Wales* (London, 1967).

[38] P.R. Roberts, *The Landed Gentry in Merioneth circa 1660–1832, with special reference to the estates of Hengwrt, Nannau, Rug and Ynysymaengwyn*, (Univ. Wales MA thesis, 1963).

[39] D.W. Howell, 'The Economy of the Landed Estates of Pembrokeshire, c. 1680–1830', *W.H.R.*, 3 (1967), 265–86; C. Thomas, 'Estates and the Rural Economy of North Wales, 1770–1850', *B.B.C.S.*, 28 (1979), 289–304.

[40] J. Bateman, *The Great Landowners of Great Britain and Ireland* (1886 edition reprinted Leicester, 1971); B.L. James, 'The Great Landowners of Wales', *N.L.W. Jnl.*, 14 (1966), 301–20.

[41] *Census of Great Britain 1851*, Population Tables II, Vol. II (1854), 884–5. In total 49 per cent of farms were less than 50 acres in size and 73 per cent were below 100 acres.

[42] D. Thomas, *Agriculture in Wales during the Napoleonic Wars* (Cardiff, 1963); T.R.B. Dicks, *The South-Western Peninsulas of England and Wales: Studies in Agricultural Geography, 1550–1900* (Univ. Wales PhD thesis, 1964).

[43] D.W. Howell, *Land and People in Nineteenth-Century Wales* (London, 1977); A.W. Ashby and I.L. Evans, *The Agriculture of Wales* (Cardiff, 1944).

[44] Census, 1851 and 1871; Occupations; *Royal Commission on Land*, Appendix XI–XII, 276–82.

[45] C. Thomas, 'Seasonality in Agricultural Activity Patterns; examples from estates in the Vale of Clwyd, 1815–1871', *Jnl. Flints. H.S.*, 26 (1976), 96–113.

[46] M.E. Hughes, *The Historical Geography of the Sea-faring Industry of the Coast of Cardigan Bay during the Eighteenth and Nineteenth Century* (Univ. Wales MA thesis, 1962); C. Thomas, 'The Shipping Trade of the River Conway in the Early Nineteenth Century', *T.C.H.S.*, 32 (1972), 233–45; J.G. Jenkins, *Maritime Heritage. The Ships and Seamen of Southern Ceredigion* (Llandysul, 1982); L.W. Lloyd, 'Sails on the Mawddach; the account books of David Evans, boatman', *Maritime Merioneth*, 7 (1981).

[47] R.J. Colyer, *The Welsh Cattle Drovers: Agriculture and the Welsh Cattle Trade before and during the Nineteenth Century* (Cardiff, 1976).

[48] D.R. Lewis, 'Early Victorian Usk', *Park Place Papers*, 10 (Univ. Coll. Cardiff, Department of Extra-Mural Studies), (1982).

[49] C.R. Lewis, 'Trade Directories — A Data Source in Urban Analysis', *N.L.W. Jnl.*, 19 (1975), 181–93; idem, 'The Analysis of Changes in Urban Status: a case study in Mid-Wales and the middle Welsh Borderland', *T. Inst. Brit. Geog.*, 64 (1975), 49–65.

[50] J.G. Jones, 'The Ffestiniog State Industry: the industrial pattern, 1831–1913', *Jnl. Mer. H.R.S.*, 6 (1970), 191–213, D.D. Pritchard, *The State Industry of North Wales: a study of changes in economic organisation from 1780 to the present day* (Univ. Wales MA thesis, 1935).

[51] W.J. Lewis, *Lead Mining in Wales* (Cardiff, 1967); J.R. Harris, *The Copper King* (Liverpool, 1964).

[52] R.L. Gant, 'The Townscape and Economy of Brecon, 1800–1860', *Brycheiniog*, 16 (1972), 103–24.

[53] J.G. Jenkins, *The Welsh Woollen Industry* (Cardiff, 1969).

[54] J.M. Powell, *An Economic Geography of Montgomeryshire in The Nineteenth Century*, (MA thesis, Univ. Liverpool, 1962); idem, 'Parish Registers and Industrial Structure', *N.L.W. Jnl.*, 15 (1968), 325–34.

[55] G. Davies, 'Community and Social Structure in Bethesda, 1840–1870', *T.C.H.S.*, 41 (1980), 107–27.

[56] I.E. Jones, 'Growth and Change in Llandrindod Wells since 1868', *Trans. Radnorshire Soc.*, 45 (1975), 9–21.

[57] C. Thomas, 'Place-name Analysis in the Geographical Study of the Rural Landscape of Wales', *Studia Celtica*, 8–9 (1973–4), 299–318.

[58] Idem, 'Agricultural Employment in Nineteenth Century Wales: A New Approach', *W.H.R.*, 6 (1972), 143–60.

[59] U.C.N.W. Mostyn 6517.

[60] *Royal Commission on Land*, I (1895), 160 et seq.

[61] *N.L.W. Tithe schedules*; Aberporth, Blaenporth, Llandygwydd, Mwnt, Tremain and Verwig: *1851 Census Enumerators' Schedules*; PRO H.O. 107/2481: 1861 *Census Enumerators' Schedules*; PRO RG9/4175, 4178.

[62] E.G. Bowen, *Saints, Seaways and Settlements in the Celtic Lands* (Cardiff, 1969); idem, *The Settlements of the Celtic Saints in Wales* (Cardiff, 1954).

[63] G.J. Lewis, 'The Geography of Religion on the Middle Borderlands of Wales in 1851', *T.C.S.*, (1980), 123–42.

[64] *Census of Great Britain 1851, Religious Worship in England and Wales* (1853), 120–9; I.G. Jones, *The Religious Census of 1851, a calendar of the returns relating to Wales*, 2 vols. (Cardiff, 1977 and 1980); W.T.R. Pryce, 'The 1851 Census of Religious Worship: an introduction to the unpublished schedules for Denbighshire', *T.D.H.S.*, 23 (1974), 147–92.

[65] O. Anderson, 'The Incidence of Civil Marriage in Victorian England and Wales', *Past and Present*, 69 (1975), 50–87.

[66] D.J.V. Jones, *Before Rebecca; Popular Protests in Wales, 1793–1835* (London, 1973).

[67] *Royal Commission on Land*, Appendices E. (Crimes) 300, and J (Poorlaw), 410–19; A.E. Davies, 'The New Poor Law in a Rural Area, 1834–1850', *Ceredigion*, 8 (1978), 245–90; D. Jones, 'Pauperism in the Aberystwyth Poor Law Union', *Ceredigion*, 10, (1980), 78–101.

[68] A.D. Rees, *Life in a Welsh Countryside* (Cardiff, 1950).

[69] E. Jones, *Welsh Rural Communities*, edited by E. Davies and A.D. Rees (Cardiff, 1962).

[70] G.J. Lewis, *T.C.S.*, (1980), noted how English-derived cells of Baptists and Wesleyans were to be found in Breconshire, Radnorshire and Montgomeryshire villages which had long economic connections with the denominations' nuclei in Hereford and Shropshire, and W.J. Lewis, *Lead Mining in Wales* (1967), suggested that Wesleyan Methodism took root in some north Cardiganshire lead-mining settlements such as Ystumtuen and Goginan where families from the Stannaries had made their homes in 'Cornishman's Row'.

[71] W. Rees, *An Historical Atlas of Wales* (London, 1972), plates 61–3.

[72] L.W. Evans, 'Ironworks Schools in Wales, 1784–1860', *Sociological Review*, 43 (1951), 203–28.

[73] I. Jones, 'The Voluntary System at Work. A chapter in Welsh Education, based on unpublished material', *T.C.S.*, (1931–32), 72–146.

[74] B.I. Coleman, 'The Incidence of Education in Mid-Century', in E.A. Wrigley (ed.), *Nineteenth Century Society: Essays in the Use of Quantitative Methods for the Study of Social Data* (Cambridge, 1972), 397–410.

[75] W.T.R. Pryce, 'Welsh and English in Wales, 1750–1971, a spatial analysis based on the linguistic affiliation of parochial communities', *B.B.C.S.*, 28 (1978), 1–36.

[76] B.S. John, 'The Linguistic Significance of the Pembrokeshire Landsker', *Pembs. Hist.*, 4 (1972), 7–29; G.J. Lewis, 'The Geography of Cultural Transition: the Welsh Borderland, 1750–1850', *N.L.W. Jnl.*, 21 (1979), 131–44.

Urban and Industrial Settlement in the Modern Period, 1750–1914

HAROLD CARTER

INTRODUCTION:
THE GROWTH OF URBAN POPULATION 1750–1914

THE most effective way to interpret the general map of the distribution of towns in Wales is through visualizing it as composed of a series of successive and superimposed networks, each related to a phase of urban genesis modified by its subsequent development.[1] The conforming of each succeeding net to its predecessor was at best partial. Each one of the Roman, Norman and Renaissance/Baroque networks made its contribution, although the first was greatly attenuated by the time of the Norman foundations and the impact of the last in Wales, in terms of town founding, was minimal. The industrial genesis of towns can be considered as setting up a further net, but again one only in part conformable to what had developed from the Norman genesis.

If Leonard Owen's translation of the 1670 Health Tax returns[2] into population totals be accepted, then in the late seventeenth century the largest Welsh towns in rank order were Wrecsam (3,225), Brecon (2,210), Carmarthen (2,195), Haverford-west (2,137), Cardiff (1,771), and Caernarfon (1,755). This hierarchy still preserved the situation which had devolved from the Act of Union of 1536 when Caernarfon, Denbigh, Carmarthen and Brecon had been nominated as the locations of Chanceries and Exchequers, that is to be the respective 'capitals' of the four quadrants of Wales. Wrecsam, largely due to its superior nodal location, had replaced Denbigh but the others remained, joined by supplementary centres at Haverfordwest, a one time county in its own right, in the south-west and Cardiff in the south-east. This is a fair representation of the situation some eighty years later in 1750 at the beginning of the period under review, but even by the first census of 1801 that ordering had been considerably amended. The older centres still showed through with Carmarthen still fourth in rank, Wrecsam fifth, Haverfordwest sixth and Caernarfon seventh, but the first three positions were now occupied by Merthyr Tudful, Swansea and Holywell, presaging the much more revolutionary changes which were to characterize the nineteenth century as the new industrial network of towns was established. The description 'revolutionary' is seen to be justified if the rank ordering of the first ten towns in 1801 and 1901 is compared (Table 1).

These changes brought about by industry can be considered in four phases which although they succeeded each other in chronological order quite clearly also overlapped. The first and earliest of these can be regarded as 'pre-industrial'. In 1584 the Mines Royal Society began the smelting of copper at Neath, whilst lead and silver were also being produced. In 1717 this type of activity appeared at Swansea (Landore) and, due to the greater ease of traffic on the Tawe, that town soon

Table 1. Rank order of the ten largest Welsh towns in 1801 and their ranks in 1901

Town	Rank in 1801	Rank in 1901
Merthyr Tudful	1	4
Swansea	2	3
Holywell	3	73
Carmarthen	4	28
Wrecsam	5	19
Haverfordwest	6	49
Caernarfon	7	30
Monmouth	8	55
Dolgellau	9	76
Brecon	10	50

outstripped Neath. Similar activities were extended west to Pen–clawdd (pre 1797) and Llanelli (1805), and east to Aberafan (Tai–bach 1727). It was the metal industries which carried Swansea to its second ranking in 1801, when Neath was twelfth. Likewise in north Wales early development at Bersham reinforced the role of Wrecsam, whilst by the latter half of the eighteenth century the smelting of copper and lead, together with zinc as a basis of brass production, and the beginnings of textile manufacture, all underpinned the growth of Holywell. Finally, this pre-industrial period was also characterized by the early woollen industry, especially the production of webs at Dolgellau (which was as high as rank 9 in 1801), and of flannel along the Severn Valley at Llanidloes, Newtown and Welshpool.

The second phase began the industrial period proper and was initiated in the south with the beginning of the iron industry at Dowlais, near Merthyr Tudful, in 1759. This was quickly followed by the establishment of other ironworks in Merthyr itself and along the northern outcrop of the south Wales coalfield, creating towns such as Aberdare, Rhymney, Ebbw Vale, Tredegar and, in the extreme east, Pontypool. The bases of this new iron industry were the blast furnace and the coking of coal, and the locational controls which operated are sufficiently well known to need no discussion. In the north the iron industry at Bersham and Brymbo sustained the growth of Wrecsam, whilst Holywell remained the centre for lower Deeside. This period also saw the beginning and growth of slate-quarrying on a major scale in north Wales and the creation of dependent settlements.

The third phase was initiated some one hundred years later when the mining and export of coal became the predominant activity. In south Wales this brought about the major development phase in the Rhondda Valley and of those parts now referred to as 'the hearts of the valleys'. This is the period when it is difficult to distinguish between mining villages and functioning towns. After local government reorganization in 1894 the small mining settlements were grouped into urban districts so that

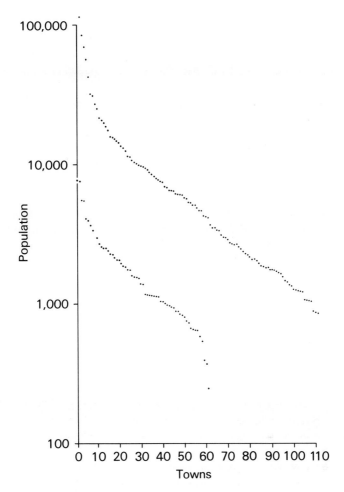

Fig. 53   Rank-size graphs of the towns of Wales in 1801 and 1901.

few had independent administrative status, and omnibus titles, such as the Rhondda, came into being referring to no specific settlement. The demand for roofing slate led to a major revival of slate quarrying in the north.

The fourth phase demonstrates most clearly the degree of overlap. The settlements created in phases two and three demanded service and administrative centres, and hence towns emerged with those primary functions. Pontypridd, which at mid century was merely the name of a bridge crossing the River Taff, is the best example. Export also demanded ports and Cardiff, which to that role also added those of service and administration, grew rapidly to become the largest Welsh town in 1881. Other ports also became resorts to meet the new demand for holidays. Such were Barry and Porthcawl in the south, whilst in the north Llandudno, Rhyl and Prestatyn grew more specifically as seaside towns meeting the demand from north-west England.

Against this background some generalizations about the period can be adduced. It must first be noted, however, that the very small settlements in 1801 are a relic of the medieval inheritance still administratively extant. In addition, it is evident that the Welsh towns did not constitute an independent system but even if the towns of the borderland are included the basic shapes of both the graphs in Figure 53 are not changed.

The first and most obvious point is the increase in the number of towns. Using census definitions which refer to administrative areas and not physically distinct settlements, the urban total had increased from some 61 in 1801 to 111 in 1901. If a more realistic definition were used the increase would be revealed as much greater. Along with this went another immediately apparent feature, a marked growth in the size of towns. In 1801 the largest was Merthyr Tudful with a population of 7,705; by 1901 Cardiff had reached 164,333. When, however, rank-size arrays on a log-normal basis for the two dates are compared (Figure 53) no great differences in the shape of the resultant curves appear in spite of the evidently revolutionary period of change. In short, some form of allometric process was in operation by which growth in the number of towns along one axis was compensated by increase in the sizes of towns measured along the other. To observe an allometric process is one thing, to offer an explanation another. There is an implied relationship between increasing numbers and larger sizes of towns and this indicates that a relationship via population numbers, and the services which were demanded by them, echoed through the whole system from bottom to top.

A further point follows in this review of urban growth. The increase in functional range, and especially the creation of industrial, mining and quarrying settlements which bore no relation to demand from a hinterland or to role as service or market centre, meant that any simple, stepped hierarchical ordering of towns was disrupted. Already by 1801 it is difficult to discern any such systematized structure but by the end of the period it is clear that a continuum characterized the array of Welsh towns. It is hardly permissible to call this a 'maturing' of the system but the implication is that with growth and greater functional variety during the period 1750–1914 a simpler, hierarchical structure derived from purely market functions became transformed into a continuum reflective of modernity.[3]

THE DETERMINANTS OF URBAN STRUCTURE

Against the background of the growth in urban populations which has been presented it is possible to consider the major determinants of the new physical structuring of Welsh towns. This can be carried out under three headings: the *processes* which were operative, the *elements* which were contributory, and *organization* of patterns on the ground.

Processes

Fig. 54 attempts to summarize the dominant processes which were effective during the nineteenth century.[4] The four most dominant processes are described as economic, social, political and environmental. These are then subdivided so that some fourteen 'processes' are identified. It is not feasible to undertake a seriatim

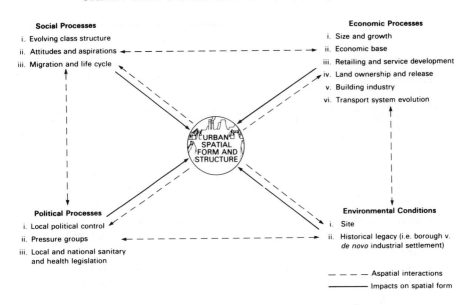

Social Processes

i. Evolving class structure

ii. Attitudes and aspirations

iii. Migration and life cycle

Economic Processes

i. Size and growth

ii. Economic base

iii. Retailing and service development

iv. Land ownership and release

v. Building industry

vi. Transport system evolution

URBAN SPATIAL FORM AND STRUCTURE

Political Processes

i. Local political control

ii. Pressure groups

iii. Local and national sanitary and health legislation

Environmental Conditions

i. Site

ii. Historical legacy (i.e. borough v. *de novo* industrial settlement)

— — — — Aspatial interactions

——————— Impacts on spatial form

Fig. 54   Urban spatial form and structure: a summary of processes.

review of each of these, although they all had a clear impact. Three of the most important can be selected for illustrative discussion.

(i) Landownership. Amongst the most significant of controls of urban development was that of ownership of land and the willingness to release it for building, together with the related restrictions or covenants placed on lessees and builders. The ownership itself divided into two, that constituting the common lands of pre-existing boroughs and that in private hands. As soon as pressure for extension began to be exerted one clear way of relief was to enclose, subdivide and sell or lease common land which no longer served its initial purposes. The form of towns was in this way considerably influenced by the date at and the circumstances under which common land was developed. At Aberystwyth (Fig. 55) the growth of its function as a resort at the end of the eighteenth and during the early nineteenth century led to an increase in the demand for building land. Some leases of common land had been granted from the late 1750s, but in 1813 the Court Leet recorded 'we the jury direct that part of the waste land called Morfa Swnd be mapped and divided into convenient spots for building'.[5] The division was a near grid with some adjustment for site and this added a distinctive area to the town, one which is still readily discernible on present-day maps.

In contrast to this we find attempts by private landowners to develop complete towns on their estates. This can be seen in the early part of the nineteenth century at Aberaeron, Milford Haven and Tremadoc, but perhaps the most successful was the somewhat later venture to create a seaside resort on the Mostyn estate at Llandudno. It was undertaken by the second Baron Mostyn after the necessary land had been accumulated, in this case by an enclosure award which gave some 859 out of 950 acres fronting Llandudno Bay to Edward Mostyn as Lord of the Manor. A modified

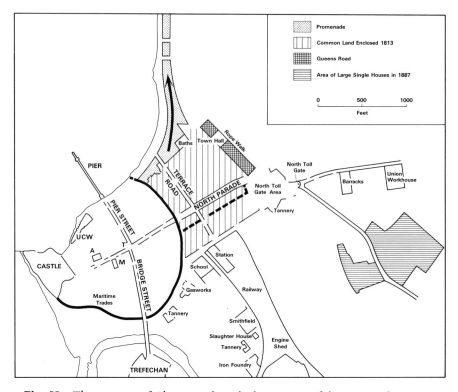

Fig. 55   The structure of Aberystwyth in the last quarter of the nineteenth century.

grid plan was drawn up, the modification being related to the curve of the bay and the form of the small existing settlement. The sale of land took place in 1849 but a series of building regulations, subsequently reinforced by the Llandudno Improvement Act of 1854 which created town commissioners to oversee its provisions, controlled the nature of development. Indeed, *The Tourists Guide* of 1849 noted that 'Great care has been taken to provide salutory restrictions, without making them exceedingly irksome, and to classify the whole locality, one neighbourhood for large houses and another for a smaller description . . . with a view to provide for the health and comfort of all who may visit or settle in this district the . . . code of building regulations has been prepared and designed to ensure proper ventilation, sewerage and uniformity of frontage and elevation which bestow value upon property to the injury of none.'[6]

The regulations themselves were unexceptional, but it is worth noting that duplicate plans of proposed buildings had to be deposited with the town commissioners and 'that the person so lodging the plans and specifications shall not consider them approved of until signed by the vendor or his agent . . . If such building be begun of, or made without such written consent, the vendor may cause such buildings . . . to be demolished.'[7] In this way not only the plan of Llandudno but the nature of its buildings were carefully controlled by the landowner.

Restrictive covenants were fairly common in attempts to ensure high quality development and this is a good Welsh example.

The most ubiquitous influence of landowners was, however, in the control of the way in which established towns developed. Two examples can been considered, the one from north Wales, the other from the south. At the beginning of the period, Bangor was but a tiny settlement gathered about the cathedral. By the beginning of the nineteenth century, however, the population was increasing largely in consequence of the slate export trade. The ownership of lands is shown in Fig. 56a and to meet the demand for building land the Dean of Bangor began after 1809 to lease plots of land in '. . . that field or parcel of land with the barn and garden thereunto belonging, commonly called Cae Scybor . . . containing by admeasurement 8 acres 3 roods and 6 perches'.[8] As P. E. Jones notes, 'This field which sloped gently down from High Street to the banks of the River Adda lay midway between the cathedral and the sea. The settlement was laid in a rectangular form around a central thoroughfare Dean Street, which was named after the administrator of the land.'[9] The Dean and Chapter were equally willing to lease land near the Adda mouth. There are numerous references in the Carter Vincent collection of manuscripts to the Dean of Bangor's leasing plots of land '. . . in a field adjoining the

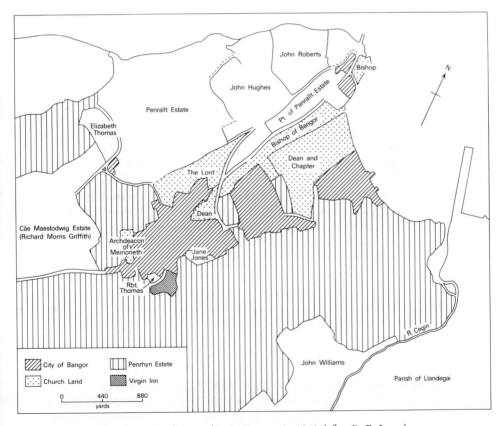

Fig. 56a   Landownership in Bangor in 1840 (after P. E. Jones).

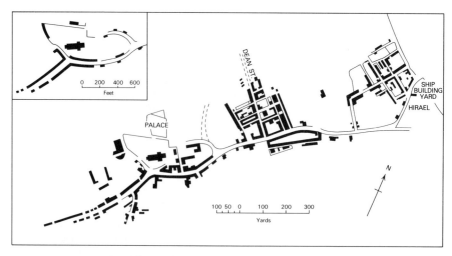

Fig. 56b   Bangor in 1834 (inset, the city in 1610).

coast, Cae Glanymor, alias Weaver's Field'.[10] The subsettlement of Hirael grew in this port location so that by the mid 1830s Bangor showed a clear threefold structure — the city, the Dean Street area and Hirael (Fig. 56b). This was largely the result of the willingness of the Dean to lease land for development.

Daunton's detailed work on the city of Cardiff again presents excellent illustrations.[11] Thus he notes that by the later nineteenth century many of the smaller land holdings had been developed and the Bute estate had become the major provider of urban land. However, because the early development of Butetown, itself a carefully planned urban extension, had declined disastrously in social cachet, the Bute estate determined to set higher standards for future development. Daunton records that the plainest working-class housing was avoided. 'Where possible, development was for the well-to-do middle class with a high standard of planning; for lower-middle class or artisan housing, the standard on the Bute estate was always somewhat higher than usual. In south Roath, where the Tredegar estate laid out a grid of working-class streets, the Bute estate laid out a square surrounded by higher-class houses ... The Bute–Windsor boundary in Grangetown is immediately apparent, the Bute area marked by street gardens, houses with bay windows and front gardens; exactly the same point applies to the southern part of Canton.'[12] All this landowner action meant that townscape was intimately determined by the details of ownership.

Cardiff also displays a larger scale and most impressive example. The Bute estate had acquired by careful purchase most of the land about Cardiff castle; the details are traced in John Davies's *Cardiff and the Marquesses of Bute*.[13] As Davies points out, control of so much land gave a major opportunity for planning of city centre growth but the estate displayed no interest in this. 'The chief glory of central Cardiff today is the result of negative rather than positive action by the Bute estate. By refusing to lease Cathay's Park, Cooper Fields and much of the farms of Maendy, Mynachdy, Pontcanna, Plasturton and Blackweir for building purposes, the

Marquesses preserved a vast tract of open land in the heart of Cardiff long enough to ensure that its value would be recognised and that it would be preserved in perpetuity.'[14] Thus the great wedge of open land which extends northwards from the castle not only gives a distinctive feature to the city's layout but it also provided the opportunity for the subsequent monumental building which characterizes central Cardiff and gives it an administrative core proper to the national capital. This was the direct consequence, negative though it may have been initially, of the control exercised by the prime landowner.

(ii) Class Structure. High amongst the determinants of the internal character of towns between 1750 and 1914 was the evolving class structure, a greatly complex issue which properly demands discussion in its own right. That discussion is made all the more complex when the critical point relative to settlement patterns becomes the extent to which class, or socio-economic status, was spatially expressed — or indeed, since it needs to be considered, the extent to which the physical separation of social classes affected their development and relations. But the towns of 1914 are so near to the classic segregated settlements of the inter-war period that to fail to consider this most central of processes would make any attempt at the discussion of urban evolution unreal. There is no need, however, in a reductionist way to seek the socio-economic bases of the class system, for it is the reality of differential economic reward which primarily affects the town, although perceptions of status were of obvious significance.

Industrialism in all its ramifications demanded wide ranges of skills, and the varying financial rewards for those skills laid the basis for that elemental division into the skilled, semi-skilled and the unskilled which is still used in the census. Status, especially that of the artisan élite, was vigorously defended against dilution and was one of the bases of trade unionism. Commercial operations produced not only a new managerial sector but also an immense increase in clerical occupations which were characteristic of the bulk of the lower middle class. There was an equal burgeoning of the professions which, together with the managers of business, produced a superior middle-class layer. All these groups as they became self-consciously aware of status sought to distance themselves from what they considered to be their social inferiors, and that word 'distance' carries explicit spatial implications. The process which dominated the period, therefore, was a progressive sorting of populations by status through internal migration so that towns moved towards residential areas segregated according to class, and ultimately towards exclusive single-class residential areas. Whereas the process is clear, whether segregation was characteristic of Welsh towns by 1914, let alone single-class areas, remains open to question, for the final stages were reached with the more extensive suburban estates and commuter villages of the inter-war period. The Welsh towns between 1750 and 1914 are best considered, therefore, as undergoing a period of transformation, rather than seeing that transformation completed.

The process of transformation can be illustrated by two examples of towns of contrasting sizes and functions. At Merthyr Tudful[15] until the middle of the nineteenth century those highest in the social scale, the isolated houses of the ironmasters and their managers apart, lived in the centre of the town, mainly along

High Street. There was segregation, but it existed only at a front street–back street level. The census enumeration districts containing the bulk of those in the upper socio-economic groups also show as many in the lowest groups. But by 1871 there was an incipient movement of those of high status out of the central location to the somewhat higher rising ground to the east at Thomastown, which showed at that date a predominance of those in professional occupations. But there was inevitably a limit to development on the sloping valley side and though streets of later date and increasing social status characterize the steeply rising area, a later and different growth of higher social status took place to the north-east in the area between the parkland surrounding the residences of two of the ironmasters, Cyfarthfa Castle and Penydarren House. The consequences by the end of the period was a clear sectoral extension of relatively higher social class residence north-eastward from the town, very much in the way suggested by Hoyt where open ground, proximity to parkland, higher ground and the residences of the leaders of society were the attracters of growth.

A similar process can be traced at Aberystwyth, a much smaller and older borough town and one growing as a seaside resort.[16] In 1851 Bridge Street, one of the intramural medieval axes, was still the fashionable place to live. As late as the 1820s the Pryses of Gogerddan, one of the landowning families of the hinterland, had built an imposing town house there. But the extension of the town by enclosing and leasing part of its common land after 1813, a feature already discussed under landownership, gave the opportunity for some newer and large houses to be built either on the sea front or the major street of the new area, North Parade. This carried social cachet away from the old town and by 1871 the most fashionable housing was at the boundary between the common land and the surrounding privately owned land. Well before 1914 large single houses in their own grounds had been built still further out on Llanbadarn Road (Fig. 55).

What can be identified, therefore, both in Merthyr and Aberystwyth are staged shifts of the high status residential areas from an initial emplacement in the town centre towards the periphery, in a sectoral form. Social-class divisions were being translated into residential locations which were locally identified and recognized. But in both cases it would be premature to propose that separation and segregation had been accomplished by the First World War.

(iii) Migration. It has already been stressed that population growth was the fundamental element in the substantial changes in towns after 1750. That growth was mainly brought about by immigration and the varied sources from which the migrants were derived played a considerable part in the internal structuring of the larger towns, although it is not easy to distinguish this process of differentiation by population origin from that by class division already discussed, since there were always strong associations between them. The fastest growing town wholly dependent on immigration until the latter part of the nineteenth century was Merthyr Tudful and the pattern of birthplaces of household heads provides a basis for analysis.[17]

A clustering procedure was undertaken in which nine variables were used, these being birthplaces classed as (i) local (Merthyr and adjacent parishes); (ii) adjacent

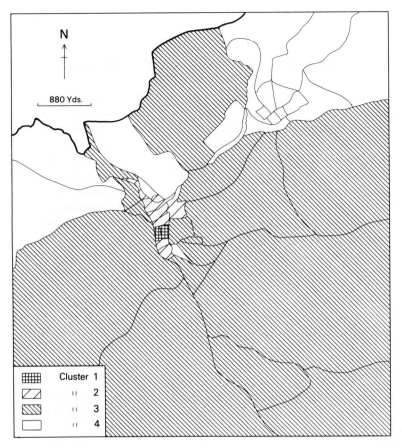

Fig. 57 Merthyr Tudful in 1851: birthplace clusters by enumeration districts, the four-cluster stage.

counties, that is Glamorgan, Breconshire and Monmouthshire; (iii) south-west Wales, that is, Carmarthenshire and Pembrokeshire; (iv) mid Wales, that is, Cardiganshire, Montgomeryshire and Radnorshire; (v) north Wales; (vi) south-west England; (vii) the remainder of England and Scotland; (viii) Ireland; (ix) foreign. The four-cluster stage is shown in Fig. 57. Cluster 1 is dominated by those born in England and Scotland; cluster 2 is characterized by those born outside England and Wales, mainly the Irish together with the foreign; cluster 3 is a local and adjacent county grouping; cluster 4 is made up of those from rural, west and mid Wales. One reservation has to be entered. The data are those of birthplace and Merthyr's industrial growth had started some 100 years before 1851, the year to which they relate. Inevitably some of those classed as locally born were part of early migratory flows, but there is no way of avoiding this difficulty.

Those locally born (cluster 3) can be regarded as making up a background group dominating the rural surrounds together with sporadic coal-mining nodes of settlement within it. They were also predominant in the most southern of the ironworking areas, that at or south of Pentre-bach. The migration streams that can be identified from the remaining clusters were targeted towards different sections of the town. The English born (cluster 1) moved mainly to the centre of the town where they constituted a significant part of the professional and commercial occupations which were found there. The Irish (cluster 2) were markedly concentrated in two areas, respectively north (China) and south (Caedraw) of the town centre in the area which today would be called the 'inner city'. It was an area of quite appalling physical and social degradation which attracted those lacking in urban skills and seeking the cheapest accommodation. At a time before mechanization these populations met the great demand for unskilled labour. Cluster 4 was characterized by immigrants from rural Wales who, often continuing family links via migration chains, provided the skilled and semi-skilled labour required in the iron industry. In origin, of course, they were no more skilled than the Irish but the associations of over a hundred years gave them access to that training from which the Irish were quite overtly debarred. It must be stressed that these are not exclusive clusters, and migrants from all sources can be found in each of the areas, town centre, inner city, and industrial suburb. Even so, it is possible to suggest a caricature of the situation described above with each immigrant group related to specific areas. The centre was dominated by the English, Anglican in religion (they built a new church in the centre where the language was to be English) and high on the social scale. The ironworking 'suburbs', such as Dowlais, were made up of the Welsh born, Nonconformist in religion and in skilled or semi-skilled labouring occupations. The 'inner city' was characterized by the Irish, Roman Catholic in religion and found in the lowest social status group. The locally born constituted the matrix into which these distinct elements were set, though represented in all of them. In the way these caricatures have been presented the overlap with social class is clearly apparent.

If that was the situation in 1851 it was greatly modified in the years before 1914. The main trend was the blurring of this association of origin and area as migration flows became less significant and as subsequent generations were assimilated. A process of internal migration was the mechanism of mixing. That mechanism is extremely difficult to establish. It can only be done by using anecdotal information such as family diaries or by tracing families through the available censuses and that is only feasible between 1841 and 1881. Moreover, it is a difficult and immensely time-consuming task given the similarities of Welsh surnames. To date there are no Welsh studies to provide empirical evidence and hence internal movements have to be presumed.

By 1914 the well-attested 'ethnic' areas which had been produced in the larger towns by the immigration process had been largely dispersed, but there was one which was the creation of the later part of the period under review and was to remain as perhaps the only immigrant area in Wales, losing the notion of immigrant and becoming one of Welsh-born ethnic character. This was Cardiff's Butetown which had been intended as a high quality suburb but, due to its dockland location, had rapidly deteriorated into the Tiger Bay of Welsh urban mythology. By the outbreak of the First World War it was the only major urban 'region' in Wales of distinct ethnic make-up as a result of immigration.

(iv) Land-use Segregation. So far the processes operative in structuring Welsh towns between 1750 and 1914, the sale or lease of land, the developing class system and the migration of population, have been discussed in the context of the emerging residential areas of the town. However, these constituted but one use amongst many to which urban land was put. In 1750 the very small Welsh towns exhibited few distinctive arrangements and different kinds of land-use were scattered through the settlements in inchoate form.[18] Shops and craft industries were generally central, although noxious crafts were confined to the margins and trade was largely dominated by the temporary stall erected for the weekly market. This situation was radically and completely transformed by 1914.

This was the period of industrial revolution and so the lead can be ascribed to industrial technology. The new industries were factory based and required extensive areas of land. The town centres, where towns existed, were inadequate and so new urban regions came into being dominated by massive associations of plant, transportation facilities and spoil heaps. The old craft trades were slowly eliminated as mass-produced factory goods were delivered by the new railway system. Manufacturing was concentrated into large and distinctive sections of the town.

Along with an industrial revolution went one in retailing. The weekly market gave way to the market hall and then to the permanent shopping centre when shops were open for six days of the week. The key was the vastly increased demand from the assembled populations and their increased spending power. The history of Marks and Spencer, as narrated by Goronwy Rees,[19] epitomizes the changes taking place. Marks started in Leeds as a pedlar or packman, a type of figure well known in the towns of industrial south Wales and which can be linked with the most primitive of retail systems. By 1884 he had a stall in the open market at Leeds which operated on two days of the week. From there he moved to the covered market, which had been started in 1857, and which was open on every weekday. The next stage was to open stalls in other markets. By 1890 he had five, and in 1895 he opened a penny bazaar in Cardiff market, one year after the start of his partnership with Spencer. By these processes the old mixed-use cores of the towns, or part of them, were converted to specialized retail use. Along with all the changes taking place arose a great demand for professional services. Attorneys and surgeons were the most obvious but a variety of others grew offering services to businesses and dealing in finance and insurance. These, too, sought central locations and became part of what by 1914 can be called a Central Business District (CBD). In the largest towns these non-retail demands for CBD land developed sufficiently to need extensive areas which themselves became separated and specialized. Such were warehousing, wholesale and financial regions. Welsh towns were too small for distinctive segregation at such a level of detail to emerge, but Cardiff's Butetown, especially the area about the Coal Exchange and Mountstuart Square, can be considered as a distinctive financial and commercial region of the city during the latter part of the period.

These processes can be illustrated in simple form by Neath which grew from a town of 2,512 in 1801 to 13,720 in 1901, and where the impact of that growth upon its internal structure was fundamental. The prime stimulus was the growth of a well-defined industrial region (Fig. 58). The controls of location were the transport

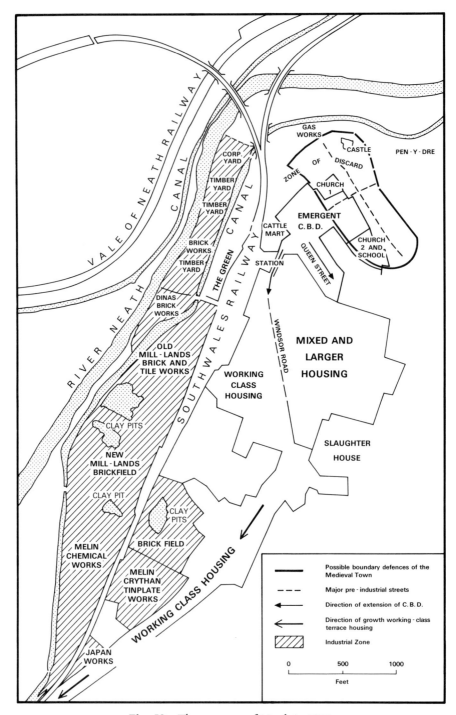

Fig. 58   The structure of Neath in 1875.

lines formed by the River Neath, the Neath Canal (1791) and the South Wales Railway (1850). The components were predominantly brickworks, and steel, tinplate and chemical works which built up an elongated region extending south from the medieval core to the 'outport' at Briton Ferry. With the growth of the town and its hinterland, retail and trading functions also increased and a clear central business district was created. As this occurred the central business district also shifted south and developed away from the old core so that the medieval High Street with its market hall became no more than a decadent part of the shopping area, a relic of the old system of weekly markets and a true zone of discard. Even its name was symbolically changed from High Street to Old Market Street. The causes of this shift were probably simply a demand for space which was more easily available because of site conditions to the south, but it also echoed the southward growth of the town before the land of the Gnoll estate was released for building. Fig. 58 indicates these two regions and also relates them to the growth of residential areas which has been, in part, already considered.

One further use of city-centre land, namely local government and administration, became gradually more significant, especially after the reorganization of the 1880s. As local government responsibilities and functions multiplied so more space was demanded. Initially, *ad hoc* arrangements led to locations in adapted and scattered buildings, not infrequently the large houses of those high in the social scale, which had been abandoned in the move to the suburbs. But ultimately these were brought together in administrative areas. The one in Wales with the greatest distinction was again that in the largest city, Cathays Park at Cardiff. Cardiff had made several attempts to buy the land from the Bute estate and as an historian of the civic centre writes, 'in the early 1890s the question of acquiring the Park came up in another form (i.e. as against a memorial park to Queen Victoria). Cardiff had now developed into a large town and was still growing rapidly. Its existing administrative, educational and judicial institutions were becoming inadequate to meet its growing needs. Sites were being sought for a new Town Hall and Law Courts, Museum, Intermediate and Technical Schools, as well as for the proposed new University College. The old Town Hall in St. Mary Street was too small to accommodate the fast-increasing Corporation staff, and the judges were severely criticising the lack of adequate provision for the administration of justice. The question of new accommodation was becoming urgent . . .'[20] The quotation epitomizes all the reasons for the emergence of what have been called so far administrative regions, but which became popularly referred to as civic centres. Cathays Park was purchased in 1898, a plan was drawn up in 1899 and development began in 1903, a development which was to give not only Cardiff and Wales but the United Kingdom one of its most distinctive urban regions devoted to administration and education.

Elements

The preceding section has examined some of those processes which were primarily instrumental in determining the internal structure of the towns. The actual townscapes were, however, the consequences of the way in which the pattern of areas was reflected in actual buildings, that is by the elements which composed the visual scene. Again, it is not easy within a limited compass adequately to represent the wide array of buildings, many of them fine examples of their period, such as the Coal Exchange at Cardiff (1886), the City Hall and Law Courts (1904) in the same city, or the Old College at Aberystwyth (1864). But some selected examples of the predominant elements can be presented and since residential uses made up the greatest physical extent it is appropriate to begin with housing. But the period also marked the ascendancy of Nonconformity and the chapel became a ubiquitous and characteristic urban building during the period. Finally by the turn of the present century the chain store and department store began increasingly to dominate the town centres.

(i) Housing. Urban housing studies[21] have been dominated by working–class housing, although the total stock was much more varied. The whole period between 1750 and 1914 saw a progressive standardization of house types to which the successive Public Health Acts, and the by-laws derived from them, contributed considerably. The Act of 1875 was the one under which many local authorities drew up their by-laws, adopting the model issued by the Local Government Board in 1877 so that the national (UK) uniformity of the three-bedroomed terrace house became apparent. It was in the earliest industrial times, therefore, especially in the iron-working towns, that local and unique forms were generated, although few have survived to the present. The most well-known single example, probably because its destruction became a prominent conservation issue, was The Triangle at Pentre-bach, near Merthyr Tudful. A restored example is Stack Square and Engine Row at Blaenafon. J. B. Lowe identifies this as 'part of one of the earliest industrial settlements to be seen in Wales. The two parallel rows of houses are joined by a third range of buildings which, in the early nineteenth century, contained the company shop and perhaps the offices of the proprietor. The whole group was built between 1789 and 1792, at the same time as the first two Blaenavon furnaces.'[22]

The need for entrepreneurs to provide housing was a consequence of the development of new settlements about the ironworks: hence Stack Square, and The Triangle which was built for Anthony Hill of the Plymouth Works. But as the towns grew housing on a more extensive scale was needed, and this demand was met by the creation of what were almost company towns, as at Dowlais and Georgetown in Merthyr. In this provision, characteristic types were developed. Lowe has identified a group of 'catslide roofed outshot' houses which were built between 1795 and 1830 and strongly localized in the Taff Valley and nearby areas (Fig. 59). 'A simple correlation of this distribution (using the actual numbers identified), with the areas that were exploited for the several iron-works, shows that the catslide outshot house is associated not only with the Merthyr Tudful area, but more particularly with the Crawshay family, proprietors of the Cyfarthfa works.'[23] The Crawshays, as indeed many of the ironmasters, were relatively enlightened employers and the houses they built were adequate for the times. They deteriorated with age, however, and were overtaken by higher standards, but even so remained into recent times making up significant parts of Welsh towns.

It was often due to the operations of small–scale builders that the worst conditions

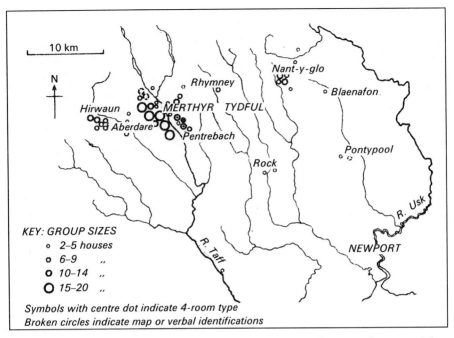

Fig. 59   The distribution of catslide outshot houses in south-east Wales, 1973 (after J. B. Lowe).

ensued. The poorest parts of Merthyr in socio-economic terms have already been noted as areas of extreme physical degradation. Henry de la Beche's description of the district called China in his 'Report on the Sanitary Condition of Merthyr Tydfil', published in 1845, has been often quoted. 'The most wretched part of the town would appear to be that known as the cellars, near Pont Storehouse, and supposed to contain about 1,500 persons. Though so named, they are not cellars, but a collection of small houses of two stores, situated in a depression between a line of road and cinder heap, a line of slag from the furnaces, the lower portion of this collection abutting upon the river Taffe. The space between these houses is generally very limited; and an open stinking and nearly stagnant gutter, into which household refuse is, as usual, flung, moves slowly before the doors. It is a labyrinth of miserable tenements and filth.'[24] Another description reads, 'The houses are mere units of stone — low, confined, ill-lighted, and unventilated; they are built without pretensions to regularity and form a maze of courts and tortuous lanes, hardly passable in many places, for house refuse, rubbish and filth. In some places they are considerably below the level of the road, and descent is by ladders.'[25]

It was to remedy these conditions that the successive Public Health Acts of the nineteenth century were passed enabling local authorities to introduce by-laws to regulate housebuilding. Much of industrial south Wales was developed late in the century, especially the mining valleys, so that extensive areas of terraced housing of uniform character are the product by the by-laws. Similar features can be identified in the slate-quarrying settlements of north Wales. Thus Lowe has contrasted the earlier central parts of Bethesda, developed in the 1820s and made up of an 'irregular layout of houses of different types, the unfenced plots of land, the meandering unpaved footpaths, the many awkward junctions of buildings and ground level which all bring to mind Methyr Tudful at the beginning of the nineteenth century'.[26] In contrast are the planned developments of later years, such as Gerlan which was laid out in 1864. 'The layout and all the buildings were approved by the commissioners appointed under the Bethesda Improvement Act of 1854, and their influence is visible today. The houses are ranged in straight rows, with roads of statutory width (21 feet) and regulation size access courts at the back of the houses.'[27]

In a paper called 'Housing Areas in the Industrial Town: a case study of Newport, Gwent, 1850–1880', C. R. Lewis used housing quality and character to establish meaningful units for social area analysis.[28] His basic data source was rateable values. In 1880, based on valuation lists, he establishes three clusters or groupings of values. The first two correspond to the types already identified. These were the early cottages, often arranged in courts and alleys, some of which had already been cleared during the period 1850–80 by the Newport Local Board of Health, and the more substantial streets of terraced houses, partly a consequence of the operation of the Local Board. The third group, however, was very different and more recent, 'semi detached and detached villas . . . high value houses which were built in the period 1854 to 1880. Particularly striking are the concentrations in Gold Tops and Clytha Park, and in Summerhill and Maindy'.[29] This group, to the north-west and east of the town and built at higher elevations, represents the beginnings of that suburban extension which, by the end of the period covered by this chapter, was becoming the predominant process. Indeed, to a considerable degree, 1914 does mark a turning-point. The successive housing acts from The Lodging Houses Act (Shaftsbury's Act) of 1851 to the Housing of the Working Classes Acts of 1885, 1890, 1900 and 1903 leading to the Housing and Town Planning Act of 1909 had moved the country towards a position where it was possible for local authorities to provide houses. The major step forward, however, where it became incumbent on local authorities to make provision, came with the Housing and Town Planning Act (Addison's Act) of 1919. The eventual product was the municipal housing estate. In the private sector, the Garden City movement produced no town in Wales but sparked off the garden suburb. Even before 1914 Rhubina Fields at Rhiwbeina, Cardiff, had been started (1913) to a plan designed by Raymond Unwin, one of the great protagonists of the Garden City Movement.[30] Another example is Barry Garden Suburb designed by T. Alwyn Lloyd and developed between 1915 and 1925. These developments were the forerunners of the private suburban housing estate. But in 1914 the impact of these two crucial forms of urban extension lay in the future.

(ii) Chapels. Welsh towns before 1750 were small and insignificant; after that date they were the creations of industry so that the country, with but few exceptions, lacks an urban architecture of any distinction. Even the magnificent Victorian gothic town halls of England have no equivalents in Wales. But one predominant and characteristic building there was, the Nonconformist chapel. There are two general sources of evidence, the Census of Religion of 1851[31] and the 1911 Royal

Commission on the Church of England and Various Religious Bodies in Wales and Monmouthshire. But though much has been written about Nonconformity there is surprisingly little on the buildings. Hilling, however, includes an excellent chapter in his book *Cardiff and the Valleys*, and he writes, 'the fecundity of Nonconformism resulted in a proliferation of chapels across southern Wales to such an extent that in the Valleys they dominated the street scene . . . In a society more concerned with rhetoric and revivals than with the visual arts, the chapel was often the most important building and the only evidence of anything approaching deliberately conceived architecture . . . Although concentrated almost entirely on the front facade the designs display a virile imagination, part folk-art and part an adaptation of historic styles introduced from across the border, that ranges from masculine simplicity and urbane sophistication to exotic mannerism.'[32] There is, in general, an evolution in style from a primitive early phase, to one where larger buildings in classical style predominated, to a later variation and elaboration, in some cases a Gothic element leading to a similarity with churches. This evolution can, in part, be related to the evolution of settlement. The large classical chapels are often town-centre buildings, the primitive, the plainer and the smaller are characteristic of the working-class suburbs and of the breakaways or offshoots of the larger central chapels. Gothic elaboration is part of the beginning of middle-class suburbia. In this way the whole settlement from centre to periphery was characterized by these buildings.

So significant was the chapel that settlements were named after them and although these were mainly villages some achieved urban status. An example is the settlement which grew in the parish of Llanllechid as a result of the development of the Penrhyn quarry and which in 1820 took the name of one of its chapels, Bethesda. There were also Carneddi (Calvinistic Methodist) and Jerusalem, also C.M. and the largest. The chapels 'were all sited within stone's throw of each other. The areas they occupied were prime building sites in the High Street.'[33] Indeed between 1801 and 1851 the number of chapels in the parish increased from 1 to 13,[34] so that the town centre along High Street, and all the subsidiary nuclei, were dominated by the chapels.

It is also worth noting briefly that the Church of England also responded to the changing settlement pattern of the industrial period. 'Church building and repair were of the essence of the revival of the Anglican Church in the nineteenth century.'[35] The new central areas of Neath and Merthyr were dominated by new churches dedicated to St David, whilst a new St Michaels was built at Aberystwyth. The old parish system was slowly adapted to the new settlement and population distribution so that between 1831 and 1906 some 827 additional churches were built in Wales.[36]

(iii) Shops. Geraint Davies in his study of community and social structure in Bethesda notes that the quarrymen who lived initially in High Street were gradually displaced by those in trades and professions as the settlement grew. It was a process analogous to that in Merthyr Tudful where the higher social status of the High Street in the middle of the nineteenth century has already been noted. By 1881 Davies observes there were in High Street, Bethesda, 'an additional accountant's

office, three banks, even more public houses (and these despite temperance opposition), hotels, four "carriage owners", insurance agents, a solicitor and land estate agents, and a string of specialized traders in linen and woollen goods, china ware, grocery and ironmongery.'[37]

This process of transformation of the centre has been considered in the section on the segregation of land-uses. It was characteristic of all Welsh towns as the inchoate nuclei of earlier times became the shopping centres which were commonplace by 1914. Again it has already been noted that the intermediate stage was often the building of a market hall to replace the weekly street market or the limited provision of town or guild hall. These latter were the product of circumscribed demand where low population density, limited mobility and relative poverty could not provide the bases for the permanent shop. These restricting conditions were removed during the period of growth, and the market hall was part of the change where overhead costs were still limited. Many towns built market halls in the first part of the century and Lewis's *Topographical Dictionary* is full of references to such constructions — 'A new market-house and shambles were built in 1831, at the expense of the corporation'[38] (Caernarfon); 'A very commodious market-house has lately been erected; it is a spacious quadrilateral building, containing covered shambles for eighty butchers, with ample accommodation for the sale of poultry, butter, vegetables, and hardware'[39] (Haverfordwest). Aberystwyth's market hall was opened in 1822, while the Merthyr Market Act was passed in 1835. The *Morning Chronicle* correspondent recorded, 'The shops of Merthyr are numerous, well furnished, and show all the bustle and activity of a thriving trade. The market-house, which is very capacious, may be termed a "bazaar of shops". The scene from six to ten o'clock on Saturday evenings is one of the most extraordinary I have ever witnessed. In this interval what one might suppose the entire labouring population of Merthyr passes through its crowded halls . . . outside the market-house are booths and shows, with their yellow flaming lamps, flaunting pictures and obstreperous music.'[40]

The 'numerous shops' of Merthyr indicate that there was a growing central business district. By the end of the century the chain stores of grocers, chemists and shoe shops were to bring another element whilst the main department stores in Cardiff had also been established by 1914; James Howell had set up business in 1865, David Morgan in 1879.[41]

The three elements which have been considered, housing, chapels and shops, were only three out of a much larger number, but it was they which contributed very greatly to the townscapes which had materialized by 1914.

Structures

The processes which were in operation and the elements which were involved gave rise to certain recurrent structures which characterized the Welsh settlement pattern. Two of these can be considered here: (i) the multinucleated structures of the coal-mining valleys and the slate-quarrying areas, the latter of which is sometimes ignored; and (ii) the fringe belt and infill structuring of established towns.

(i) Multi-nuclear settlements. The most illuminating study of these forms is that by P. N. Jones of colliery settlements in the south Wales coalfield between 1850 and

1926.[42] Jones identified three major growth phases. The first, from 1850 to 1878, he called a pioneer phase since it covered the period of initial development, where there was an intimate and symbiotic relationship between mine and settlement. Housing provision was largely made by colliery companies and coal-owners, often in the form of isolated terraces. The second phase from 1878 to 1898 marked an intermediate period when expansion was mainly in the centre and east. It was during this phase that the housing by-laws came into operation. The third division after 1898 was generally one of high activity in house construction related to a peak in mining activity. In these later phases the early simplicity of the mining settlement disappeared as more complex relations developed. There were, in particular, large compact and regularly laid out additions, which Jones calls 'adjunctive' as opposed to the 'accretionary' infill and ribbon extensions. The agencies of provision also changed, with speculative builders and building clubs becoming dominant and even the Welsh Garden cities company contributing, whilst the colliery companies were much less important.

Fig. 60 shows the Garw Valley in the second phase. Development in phase one had been slight and had only begun with the construction of the railway in 1876. The two pits were still in process of development and settlement was confined to rows of houses at Braichycymmer on the western valley side and lower down the valley at Llest and Pontyrhyl. Jones notes that in 1877 a director of the Ffaldau Steam Colliery Company had asked the Dunraven estate to grant land for workmen's cottages, but on that being refused the company built its first houses on a small field belonging to Braichycymmer farm (K on Fig. 60) whilst many poor quality rows were built on the main part of the farm on the west of the river.[43]

In the second phase larger collieries, together with the housing by-laws, produced bigger pit-head settlements of which Blaengarw, built as a colliery-company enterprise in the 1890s, is a good example. Infilling and ribbon development took place, as in the ribbon extension between Blaengarw and Pontycymer. But the main feature of growth was adjunctive units, which in the case of Pontycymer involved a shift from the original western valley side location to one on the east and the establishment of a regular grid layout. Second phase development was concentrated on the lands of Nantyrychen farm (H on Fig. 60), but in the third phase the Dunraven estate took an interest. Jones notes an entry in the Register of Deposited Plans of Ogmore and Garw U.D. for 1903 — 'plan of proposed new streets at Pontycymer (Tŷ Meinwr) for the Dunraven estate'. Tŷ Meinwr farm (G on Fig. 60) became the main development area with speculative builders and other agencies submitting plans for street blocks also. Thus most growth was channelled into adjunctive extension of Pontycymer although there were isolated developments at Pontyrhyl, and at Pwllcarn near the International Colliery.

This brief example demonstrates the manner in which the characteristic valley settlements of south Wales came into being. At first these were straggling and closely related to the locations of pits, but with increasing flexibility nuclei developed which by addition became the nodes in the lines of ribbon growth.

Such a process was also apparent in the north Wales slate-quarrying areas. Blaenau Ffestiniog is the best example. The site of the settlement is a narrow horseshoe-shaped break of slope at the head of Cwmbowydd, at between 600 and

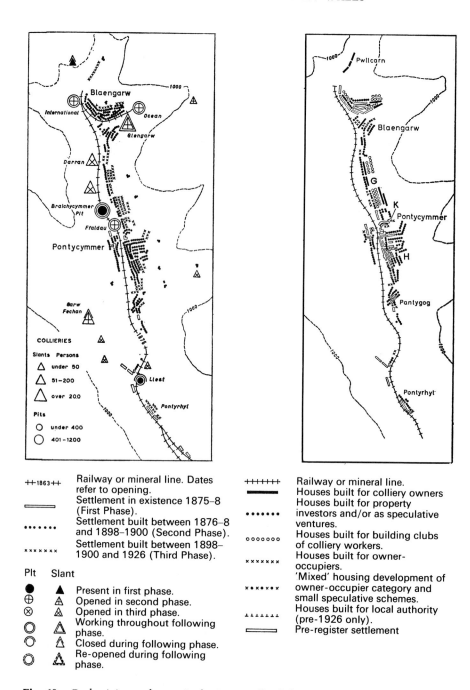

++1863++		Railway or mineral line. Dates refer to opening.
▭		Settlement in existence 1875–8 (First Phase).
• • • • • •		Settlement built between 1876–8 and 1898–1900 (Second Phase).
x x x x x x x		Settlement built between 1898–1900 and 1926 (Third Phase).

Plt	Slant	
●	▲	Present in first phase.
⊕	⊿	Opened in second phase.
⊗	⊿	Opened in third phase.
○	⊿	Working throughout following phase.
○	⊿	Closed during following phase.
○	⊿	Re-opened during following phase.

++++++	Railway or mineral line.
▬▬▬	Houses built for colliery owners
• • • • • •	Houses built for property investors and/or as speculative ventures.
o o o o o o o	Houses built for building clubs of colliery workers.
x x x x x x x	Houses built for owner-occupiers.
x•x•x•x	'Mixed' housing development of owner-occupier category and small speculative schemes.
⊥⊥⊥⊥⊥⊥⊥	Houses built for local authority (pre-1926 only).
▭	Pre-register settlement

Fig. 60 Coal-mining settlement in the Garw Valley (after P. N. Jones): (a) The growth of colliery settlement; (b) Agencies of housing provision.

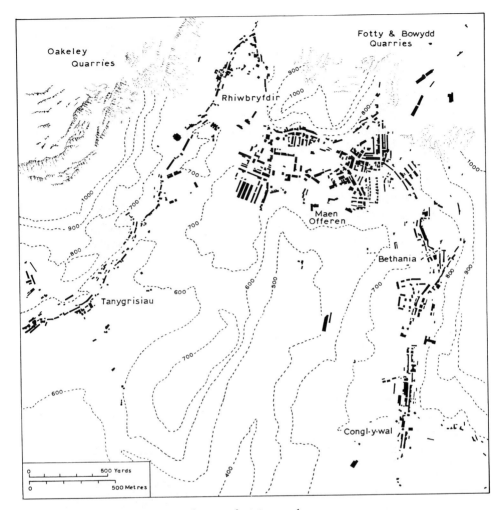

Fig. 61   Blaenau Ffestiniog: settlement structure.

750 feet (Fig. 61). Above that break the valley sides rise precipitously. At the beginning of the eighteenth century there was only a series of scattered farms located on this bench but as quarrying developed they became the nuclei about which settlement collected, often in the first instance with barracks for the quarrymen. These partly separated nuclei were Congl-y-Wal, Bethania and Tabernacl, both named after chapels, a characteristic already discussed, Rhiwbryfdir and Tanygrisiau. Development was most rapid between 1820 and 1830 and the most favoured location was about the farmsteads of Maenofferen and Blaenbowydd where the shelf was at its widest. To the north was the entrance to the Fotty and Bowydd quarries and this crossed the main road from Congl-y-Wal and Bethania. On this street, Lord Street, the first market was established in 1832 and Four Crosses became the predominant nucleus of the straggling settlement. Finally, the period 1880–1914 saw a renewed phase of rapid growth when construction was concentrated at that

nucleus and the town of Blaenau Ffestiniog was consolidated. The parallels with the south Wales pattern are evident both in the evolutionary process and the final multinucleated structure of settlement.

(ii) Fringe Belts and Infill. As towns grew in physical extent the consequent structure was not a simple additive one like the successive growth rings of a tree. Growth itself was uneven with periods of 'still-stand' alternating with periods of rapid growth. This has given rise to the notions of fixation lines, boundaries which mark the edges of settlement during periods of little growth and which can remain stable over lengthy periods, and fringe belts where extensive users of land became located during such stable periods when they could more effectively compete, and by which subsequent growth was conditioned.[44] At the same time, growth was achieved not only by extension into the fringe belt but by infilling open spaces within the already built-up area. These features can be illustrated by Aberystwyth, whose physical structure during the nineteenth century can be related to the existence of two fixation lines and two fringe belts (Fig. 62).

The inner and first fixation line was that of the medieval town walls, together with the physical limits of the small, extra-mural bridgehead settlement of Trefechan (literally 'little town'). Apart from Trefechan, no houses were built outside the walls until late in the 1790s, although minor encroachments had taken place during the eighteenth century. The medieval, inner or first fixation line lasted, therefore, for some 500 years. To a large degree it remained inviolate because the town itself was but a skeleton of streets, and a good deal of open land remained within the walls, even in the second half of the nineteenth century. Beyond this fixation line lay the Inner Fringe Belt. This was composed of the extra-mural common lands of the borough, which were made up of three tracts of marshland surrounding the small hill on which the town had been established in 1277. These were Morfa Swnd (Sandmarsh), Morfa Mawr (Great Marsh) and Morfa Bach (Little Marsh). Since there was ample intra-mural space, little specifically urban use was made of these lands, other than the location of the cattle market, the pound and the town gallows! Fringe uses, therefore, did not characterize them in any distinctive way, other than by the manner in which they contributed to those agricultural activities in which the burgesses themselves were involved. For small, remote towns in a period before effective transport, the provision of food can be regarded as a distinctive fringe use, although the conventional view of such uses is one which is dominated by the growth of nineteenth-century urban institutions. It was not until 1813 that these lands of the Inner Fringe Belt were formally divided and leased.[45] The trigger for this decision was the demand for land brought about by the first growth phase identified above. Morfa Swnd was enclosed, divided and leased, as was Morfa Mawr, but the latter remained in agricultural use.

With the extension of the town in this manner, a new and second fixation line was created. This was at the limit of borough common land, which had previously been classed as marshland, and which was clearly marked by the steep slopes of the Rheidol Valley both to north and south. Beyond this line, land was in private hands, mainly those of two prestigious local families, the Pryses of Gogerddan and the Powells of Nanteos. It is also interesting to observe that at two points a use, derived

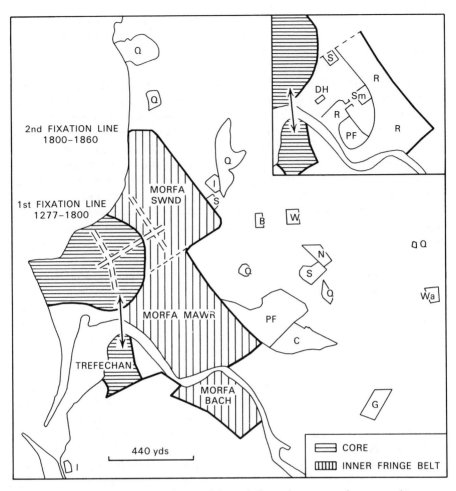

Fig. 62   Aberystwyth: fixation lines and fringe belts in the nineteenth century. (Compare with Fig. 55.) Inset Morfa Mawr, fringe belt uses in 1900. The streets of the shopping area in 1900 are indicated. I Infirmary; S School; W Union Workhouse; Wa Waterworks; G Gasworks; C Cemetery; PF Playing Fields; Q Quarries; R Railways; Sm Smithfield; DH Drill Hall.

from the seaport role and demanding extensive linear land areas, marked the new fixation line, for ropewalks had been established both to the north of Morfa Swnd, where a lease had been granted in 1778, and to the south of Trefechan (1810). Land ownership, land tenure, a specific land use and sharp breaks of slope all contributed to the emergence of this new fixation line which was to last from the early nineteenth century, when the development of the Inner Fringe Belt first began by encroachment, until the 1870s when, after the coming of the railway in 1864, the second phase of population growth and physical extension pushed settlement beyond it and into the Middle Fringe Belt. This Middle Belt, beyond the second fixation line, was formed during the middle and later part of the nineteenth century when, related to a whole range of social legislation, towns were generating a variety of associated institutions. It had, therefore, to a much greater degree, the characteristic uses of a fringe belt. It was dominated by a series of quarries worked into the valley side and developed as a source of stone for the phase of building after 1813. It also included the Union Workhouse and a militia barracks from the middle of the century and, by the end, an infirmary, gasworks and the town cemetery, as well as schools and playing fields (Fig. 62). After 1880 these were interspersed with the extending frontier of housebuilding, as sites on the northern valley side were used. It is difficult to place Morfa Mawr in this context. Physically it was part of the Inner Fringe Belt, but it remained undeveloped until the later part of the century when it was characterized by Middle Belt uses, including recreation grounds, railway yards, the smithfield, a drill hall and a school. To the south of the river the situation was simpler, for the very steep Rheidol slope meant that the first and second fixation lines were conterminous; there was no distinction between an Inner and a Middle Fringe Belt.

By the end of the nineteenth century, therefore, the town was structured into three distinctive areas — Core, Inner Fringe Belt and Middle Fringe Belt. The physical evidence of the first fixation line, the town walls, and of the second, the ropewalks, had been removed, but the influence of the two lines was clearly apparent. No town, however, can be considered simply in terms of outward extension and as the successive fringe belts were developed so there were related developments in the inward-lying areas. In 1780 the built-up area of the town was skeletal, being little more than the cross streets established in the initial layout of 1277. The phase of extension into the Inner Fringe Belt was preceded and accompanied by a process of infilling in the core. Thus back streets had emerged as housebuilding began on the distal ends of burgage lots. Small cottages were, in this manner, erected on the ends of the burgages which ran back from the main street — Great Darkgate Street — and brought into being Heol y Moch (Pig Street), so called because it overlooked the Pig Market, held on what had been open intra-mural ground. As early as 1762 this had been declared a nuisance by the Court Leet and the market was shifted. The street then changed its name to Barker's Lane and eventually acquired even further dignity as Queen Street. In the next phase of

Table 2. The fringe belts of nineteenth-century Aberystwyth and their development

Growth phase	Core	Inner fringe belt	Middle fringe belt
Medieval genesis	Outline or skeletal form	Common land in agricultural use	Agriculture use
First growth phase 1813–50	Infill	Outline	Agricultural use
Second growth phase 1864–1900	Repletion	Infill	Outline
Early 20th century to 1914	Redevelopment	Repletion	Infill

development, which saw housing extend into the Middle Fringe Belt, the process of infill within the walls was completed. Thus land in the south-east quadrant belonging to the Powell family was developed in a series of short working-class terraces, partly related to the growth of railway employment after 1864. Yet again, with extension into and beyond the Middle Fringe Belt a further process of infill, especially of the Inner Fringe Belt, took place by means of courts and alleys established even in this small resort town behind the main streets. And so the process continued as set out in Table 2 producing a complex structure but one which can be unravelled by using the analytical concepts of growth phase, fringe belt and fixation line.

CONCLUSION

There is little doubt as to what the proper conclusion to this chapter should be. Taking one example, presumably Cardiff in light of its status in the array of towns and cities as examined in the first section, an attempt should be made to weave together the operation of the processes, the role of the elements, and the impact of the structures which were identified in the second section, and thus to provide a complete analysis of the city. That would not be a fundamentally difficult task for most, although not all, of the necessary data are available. It would, however, be a very complex and lengthy piece of work, well beyond the scope of a circumscribed chapter where the prime purpose has been to set out certain analytical procedures which provide insight into the way Welsh towns underwent massive transformation during a critical century and a half. Much of what the period created remains. After 1914 extensive suburbanization, together with municipal housebuilding and the later onset of comprehensive redevelopment, were all to make major modifications but, at root, it was the period 1750–1914 which created the urban character of Wales.

NOTES

[1] H. Carter, *The Growth of the Welsh City System* (Cardiff, 1969).

[2] L. Owen, 'The Population of Wales in the Sixteenth and Seventeenth Centuries', *T.C.S.*, (1959), 99–113.

[3] H. Carter, *An Introduction to Urban Historical Geography* (1983), Chapter 5, 96–113.

[4] C.R. Lewis, and H. Carter, 'Processes and Patterns in Nineteenth-century Cities', Open University, Historical Sources and the Social Scientist, Units 14–15, *Aspects of Historical Geography 1* (Milton Keynes, 1983).

[5] G.E. Evans, *Aberystwyth and its Court Leet* (Aberystwyth, 1902), 163–4.

[6] *The Tourists Guide* (Llandudno, 1849).

[7] Ibid.

[8] P.E. Jones, 'The City of Bangor and its Environs at the Time of the Tithe Survey 1840', *T.C.H.S.*, 31 (1970), 68.

[9] Ibid., 68.

[10] Ibid., 67.

[11] M.J. Daunton, *Coal Metropolis, Cardiff 1870–1914* (Leicester, 1977).

[12] Ibid., 79.

[13] J. Davies, *Cardiff and the Marquesses of Bute* (Cardiff, 1981).

[14] Ibid., 199–200.

[15] H. Carter, and S. Wheatley, *Merthyr Tydfil in 1851. A study of the spatial structure of a Welsh industrial town*, Univ. Wales, Board of Celtic Studies, Social Science Monographs, No. 7, (Cardiff, 1982).

[16] Idem, 'Residential Patterns in mid-Victorian Aberystwyth', in I.G. Jones (ed.), *Aberystwyth 1277–1977* (Llandysul, 1977).

[17] Idem, *Merthyr Tydfil in 1851*, 55 for a full account of this analysis.

[18] H. Carter, 'Transformations in the Spatial Structure of Welsh Towns in the Nineteenth Century', *T.C.S.*, (1980), 175–200.

[19] G. Rees, *St Michael: a history of Marks and Spencer* (1969).

[20] E.L. Chappell, *Cardiff's Civic Centre. A historical guide* (Cardiff, 1946), 13.

[21] Examples are: S.D. Chapman (ed.), *The History of Working-class Housing, 1780–1918* (1971); E. Gauldie, *Cruel Habitations. A History of Working-class Housing 1780–1918* (1974).

[22] J.B. Lowe, *Welsh Industrial Workers Housing 1775–1875* (Cardiff, 1977), 9.

[23] Idem. 'Catslide Roofed Outshot Houses in Merthyr Tydfil and Related Areas', *Iron Industry Housing Papers No. 5*, (n.d.) 31.

[24] H.T. De La Beche, Report on the sanitary condition of Merthyr Tydfil, Glamorganshire. *Second Report of the Commissioners Inquiring into the State of Large Town and Populous Districts*. Parl. Papers (1845), XVIII (610), Vol. 5, Appendix, Part 1, 146.

[25] Anon., *Labour and Poor*, letters to the *Morning Chronicle* (1850), letter IX,. April 29th, 5.

[26] J.B. Lowe, op. cit., 49.

[27] Ibid., 61.

[28] C.R. Lewis, 'Housing Areas in the Industrial town: a case study of Newport, Gwent', *N.L.W. Jnl.*, XXIII (1984).

[29] Ibid.

[30] I am grateful to Mr Paul Vining for information on these developments.

[31] I.G. Jones, *The Religious Census of 1851. A calendar of the returns relating to Wales* 2 vols., (Cardiff, 1976, 1981).

[32] J.B. Hilling, *Cardiff and the Valleys* (London, 1973), 127.

[33] G. Davies, 'Community and Social Structure in Bethesda', *T.C.H.S.*, 41 (1980), 12.

[34] I.G. Jones, 'Denominationalism in Caernarvonshire in the Mid-nineteenth Century as shown in the Religious Census of 1851', *T.C.H.S.*, 31 (1970), 98–9.

[35] Idem, 'Ecclesiastical Economy: aspects of church building in Victorian Wales', in R.R. Davies *et alia* (eds.), *Welsh Society and Nationhood. Historical essays presented to Glanmor Williams* (Cardiff 1984), 216.

[36] Ibid., 218.

[37] G. Davies, *T.C.H.S.*, 41 (1980), 112.

[38] S. Lewis, *Topographical Dictionary of Wales* (Caernarvon, 1833), unpag. entry.

[39] Ibid., unpag. entry, Haverfordwest.

[40] Anon, *Labour and the Poor*, letters to the *Morning Chronicle*, letter VI, April 8th, 5.

[41] M.J. Daunton, *Coal Metropolis*, 54.

[42] P.N. Jones, *Colliery Settlement in the South Wales Coalfield 1850 to 1926*, University of Hull, Occasional Papers in Geography No. 14, (Hull, 1969).

[43] Ibid., 63.

[44] J.W.R. Whitehand (ed.), *The Urban Landscape: historical development and management. Papers by M.R.G. Conzen*, Inst. Brit. Geog., Special Publication, No. 13, (1981).

[45] See p. 273.

Select Bibliography

INTRODUCTION

The selection of items for the bibliography is based upon an assessment of the significance of an individual work in relation to the main themes of the volume. One is aware that the inclusion of a large number of publications on related subjects would be justified in a comprehensive and exhaustive bibliography. Several of the selected items have also been cited in the detailed references which accompany each chapter. Some of the contributors have identified, in a composite reference/bibliographic note, those publications which are considered to be of critical importance with regard to the subject under review.

The bibliography is divided into the following six sections:

1. REFERENCE WORKS
2. PRIMARY SOURCES AND ANTIQUARIAN WORKS
3. GENERAL STUDIES
4. AGRARIAN STUDIES
5. TOWNS AND INDUSTRY
6. COUNTY AND LOCAL COMMUNITY STUDIES

Entries in four sections (1, 3, 4 and 5), are arranged into two groups with 'general' works [A] followed by those which relate specifically to Wales [B]. Some of the works cited could justifiably be placed in more than one group. Antiquarian local studies have been placed in Section 2 rather than in Section 6, which has been reserved for comparatively recent publications. Material relating to domestic/vernacular architecture (apart from the inventories of the Royal Commission on Ancient and Historical Monuments in Wales, and the volumes by R. Haslam and E. Hubbard in the Buildings of Wales series, which appear in Section 6), have been listed in Section 3B and include the volumes by P. Smith and E. Wiliam which might possibly have been located in Section 4B. Section 3 also contains works explicitly concerned with settlement-studies although a case might have been presented for placing them in Section 4.

The grouping of citations into sections, together with the presentation of detailed references accompanying each chapter, are envisaged as bibliographical aids for the reader. However, the editor is aware that he bears the full responsibility for the selection and arrangement of the bibliography.

1. REFERENCE WORKS

A

BARLEY, M.W., *A Guide to British Topographical Collections* (1974).

BRITISH MUSEUM, *Catalogue of Printed Maps, Charts, and Plans to 1964* (1967).

Dictionary of Land Surveyors and Local Cartographers of Great Britain and Ireland, 1550–1850, 3 vols., P. Eden and A. Thomas, (eds.), (Folkestone 1975–9).

EMMISON, F.G., *Archives and Local History* (1966).

— and GRAY, I., *County Records* (1967).

HARLEY, J.B., *The Historian's Guide to Ordnance Survey Maps* (1964).

— *Maps for the Local Historian* (1972).

KAIN, R.J.P., *An Atlas and Index of the Tithe Files of Mid Nineteenth-Century England and Wales* (Cambridge, 1986).

— and PRINCE, H.C., *The Tithe Surveys of England and Wales* (Cambridge, 1985).

KIRBY, J.L., *A Guide to Historical Periodicals in the English Language* (1970).

Maps and Plans in the Public Record Office. 1. British Isles, c. 1410–1860 (1967).

NORTON, J.E., *Guide to National and Provincial Directories of England and Wales, excluding London, published before 1856* (1950).

RIDEN, P., *Local History* (1983).

— *Record Sources for Local History* (Chichester, 1987).

ROGERS, A., and ROWLEY, T. (*eds.*), *Landscapes and Documents* (1974).

SKELTON, R.A. and HARVEY, P.D.A. (eds.), *Local Maps and Plans from Medieval England* (Oxford, 1986).

SMITH, A.H., *English Place-Name Elements* (English Place-name Society, 1956).

STEPHENS, W.B., *Sources for English Local History* (Cambridge, 1975).

TATE, W.E., *The Parish Chest* (Cambridge, 1969).

WEST, J., *Village Records* (1962).

B

BASSETT, D.A., *A Source-Book of Geological, Geomorphological and Soil Maps for Wales and the Welsh Borders* (1800–1966) (Cardiff, 1967).

A Bibliography of the History of Wales (Cardiff, 1962), with supplements for period 1959–1971 in *B.B.C.S.* XX (1963); XXII (1966); XXIII (1969); XXV (1972).

CARTER, H. (ed.), *National Atlas of Wales* (Cardiff, 1980–).

CHARLES, B.G., *Non-Celtic Place Names in Wales* (1938).

DAVIES, E. (ed.), *A Gazetteer of Welsh Place-Names* (Cardiff, 1967).

DAVIES, M., *Wales in Maps* (Cardiff, 1958).

Dictionary of Welsh Biography (Oxford, 1959).

EVANS, O.C., *Maps of Wales and Welsh Cartographers*, The Map Collectors' Circle, 13 (1964).

Geiriadur Prifysgol Cymru (Cardiff, 1950–).

JACK, R.I., *Medieval Wales* (1973).

LLOYD-JONES, J., *Enwau Lleoedd Sir Gaernarfon*, (Cardiff, 1928).

PIERCE, G.O., *The Place-Names of Dinas Powys Hundred* (Cardiff, 1968).

REES, W., *An Historical Atlas of Wales* (Cardiff, 1972).

RICHARDS, G.M., *Welsh Administrative and Territorial Units* (Cardiff, 1969).

STEPHENS, M. (ed.), *The Oxford Companion to the Literature of Wales* (Oxford, 1986).

THOMAS, C., 'Estate Surveys as Sources in Historical Geography', *N.L.W. Jnl.*, XIV (1966), 451–68.

THOMAS, R.J., *Enwau Afonydd a Nentydd Cymru* (Cardiff, 1938).

WILLIAMS, C.J. and WATTS-WILLIAMS, J., (comp.), *Cofrestri Plwyf Cymru/Parish Registers of Wales* (Aberystwyth, 1986).

WILLIAMS, I., *Enwau Lleoedd* (Liverpool, 1945).

2. PRIMARY SOURCES AND ANTIQUARIAN WORKS

BRADNEY, J.A., *A History of Monmouthshire* 4 vols (1904–1933).

FENTON, R., *A Historical Tour through Pembrokeshire* (1811).

GERALD OF WALES, *The Journey through Wales and the Description of Wales*, trans. with introd. by Lewis Thorpe (1978).

JONES, E.D., *Victorian and Edwardian Wales from Old Photographs* (1972).

The Religious Census of 1851. A Calendar of the Returns Relating to Wales. Vol. 1. *South Wales*, I.G. Jones and D. Williams, (eds.), (Cardiff, 1976); Vol. 2. *North Wales*, I.G. Jones, (ed.), (Cardiff, 1981).

JONES, T., *History of the County of Brecknock*, vol. 1, 1805; Vol. II, 1809 (rept. Brecon, 1898).

LELAND, J., *Itinerary in Wales*, L. Toulmin Smith, (ed.), (1906).

LEWIS, S., *A Topographical Dictionary of Wales*, 2 vols. (1840).

LLWYD, A., *History of the Island of Anglesey* (Rhuthun, 1832).

MALKIN, B.H., *The Scenery, Antiquities and Biography of South Wales*, 2 vols. (1807).

The Meirioneth Lay Subsidy Roll, 1292–3. K. Williams Jones, (ed.), (Cardiff, 1976).

MERRICK, R., *Morganiae Archaiographia, A Book of the Antiquities of Glamorganshire*, Brian Ll. James, (ed.) (Barry, 1983).

MEYRICK, S.R., *History and Antiquities of the County of Cardigan* (1808).

OWEN, G., *The Description of Penbrockshire* H. Owen, (ed.) Cymmrodorion Record Series, 4 vols., (1902–36).

PENNANT, T., *Tours in Wales* (ed.), J. Rhŷs, 3 vols. (Caernarfon, 1883).

SPEED, J., *Theatre of the Empire of Great Britain* (1611).

The Times Tercentenary Handlist of English and Welsh Newspapers, Magazines and Reviews, 1620–1919 (1920).

VINOGRADOFF, P. and MORGAN, F. (eds.), *Survey of the Honour of Denbigh, 1334* (1914).

WILLIAMS, D., *History of Monmouthshire* (1796).

WILLIAMS, J., *General History of the County of Radnor* (Tenby, 1859).

3. GENERAL STUDIES

A

ALCOCK, N.W., *Cruck Construction; an introduction and catalogue* (1981).

ASTON, M. and ROWLEY, T., *Landscape Archaeology* (1974).

BAKER, A.R.H. and HARLEY, J.B., *Man Made the Land, Essays in English Historical Geography*, (Newton Abbot, 1973).

BERESFORD, M. and HURST, J.G. (eds.), *Deserted Medieval Villages* (1971).

— and ST. JOSEPH, J.K.S., *Medieval England: an Aerial Survey* (1979).

BRUNSKILL, R.W., *Illustrated Handbook of Vernacular Architecture* (1970).

— *Vernacular Architecture of the Lake Counties* (1974).

— *Timber Building in Britain* (1985).

DARBY, H.C., *A New Historical Geography of England* (1973).

DODGSHON, R.A. and BUTLIN, R.A., (eds.), *An Historical Geography of England and Wales* (1978).

DYMOND, D., *Writing Local History* (1981).

EVANS, J.G., *The Environment of Early Man in the British Isles* (1975).

—, LIMBREY, S. and CLEERE, H. (eds.), *The Effect of Man on the Landscape in the Highland Zone*. C.B.A. Research Rept., 11 (1975).

EVERITT, A., *Ways and Means in Local History* (1971).

FINBERG, H.P.R. (ed.), *Approaches to History* (1965).

— and SKIPP, V.H.T., *Local History. Objective and Pursuit* (Newton Abbot, 1967).

FOX, C., *The Personality of Britain* (Cardiff, 1952).

GELLING, M., *Signposts to the Past: Place-Names and the History of England* (1978).

— *Place-Names in the Landscape* (1984).

— NICOLAISEN, W.F.H. and RICHARDS, M., *The Names of Towns and Cities of Britain* (1970).

GOODWIN, H., *The History of the British Flora* (Cambridge, 1975).

HALL, R. DE Z., *A Bibliography of Vernacular Architecture* (1972).

HILTON, R.H., *A Medieval Society, the West Midlands at the End of the Thirteenth Century* (1967).

HOSKINS, W.G., *The Making of the English Landscape* (1955).

— *Local History in England* (1959).

— *Provincial England* (1963).
— *English Landscapes. How to Read the Man-Made Scenery of England* (1973).
LASLETT, P., *The World we have Lost* (1971).
MACFARLANE, A., *Reconstructing Historical Communities* (Cambridge, 1977).
MEIRION-JONES, G.I., *The Vernacular Architecture of Brittany* (Edinburgh, 1982).
MERCER, E., *English Vernacular Architecture* (1984).
PENNINGTON, W., *The History of British Vegetation* (1974).
PLATT, C., *Medieval Britain from the Air* (1984).
PUGH, R.B., *How to Write a Parish History* (1954).
— (ed.), *Victorian History of the Counties of England. General Introduction* (1970).
RACKHAM, O., *Trees and Woodlands in the British Landscape* (1976).
— *Ancient Woodland* (1980).
— *The History of the Countryside* (1986).
RENFREW, C. (ed.), *British Prehistory* (1974).
REYNOLDS, S. *Kingdoms and Communities in Western Europe* (Oxford, 1984).
ROGERS, A., *Approaches to Local History* (1977).
— (ed.), *Group Projects in Local History* (Folkestone, 1978).
SALWAY, P., *Roman Britain* (Oxford, 1981).
SAWYER, P.H., (ed.), *Medieval Settlement* (1976).
— (ed.), *English Medieval Settlement* (1979).
SKIPP, V., 'Local History: a New Definition' *Local Historian*, 14, 6 and 7, 325–31, 392–9.
SMITH, A.H., *English Place-Name Elements* 2 vols. (1956).
SMITH, C.T., *An Historical Geography of Western Europe before 1800* (1967).
TAYLOR, C., *Roads and Tracks in Britain* (1979).
— *Village and Farmstead* (1983).
WAINWRIGHT, F.T., *Archaeology and Place-Names and History* (1962).
WALKER, D. and WEST, R.G. (eds.), *Studies in the Vegetational History of the British Isles* (Cambridge, 1970).
WRIGLEY, E.A. (ed.), *An Introduction to English Historical Demography from the Sixteenth to the Nineteenth Century* (1966).
— *Nineteenth Century Society* (1972).
— and SCHOFIELD, R.S., *The Population History of England, 1541–1871* (1981).

B
ALCOCK, L., *Economy, Society and Warfare among the Britons and Saxons* (Cardiff, 1987).
BASSETT, T.M., *Bedyddwyr Cymru: The Welsh Baptists* (Swansea, 1966).
BOON, G.C. and LEWIS, J.M. (eds.), *Welsh Antiquity* (Cardiff, 1976).
BOWEN, E.G. (ed.), *Wales: A Physical, Historical and Regional Geography* (1957).
— *The Settlements of the Celtic Saints in Wales* (Cardiff, 1954).
— *Saints, Seaways and Settlements in the Celtic Lands* (Cardiff, 1969).
BROOKE, C.N.L., *The Church on the Welsh Border in the Central Middle Ages* (Woodbridge, 1986).
BROWN, E.H., *The Relief and Drainage of Wales* (Cardiff, 1960).
CARTER, H., and DAVIES, W.K.D. (eds.), *Geography, Culture and Habitat, Selected Essays (1925–1975) of E.G. Bowen* (Llandysul, 1976).
COLYER, R., *Roads and Trackways of Wales* (Ashbourne, 1984).
COWLEY, F.G., *The Monastic Order in South Wales, 1066–1349* (Cardiff, 1977).
DAVIES, E. (ed.), *Celtic Studies in Wales* (Cardiff, 1963).
DAVIES, J., *Cardiff and the Marquesses of Bute* (Cardiff, 1981).
DAVIES, R.R., *Conquest, Coexistence and Change in Wales, 1063–1415* (Oxford, 1987).
— *Lordship and Society in the March of Wales, 1282–1400* (Oxford, 1978).

Davies, R.R. *et alia* (eds.), *Welsh Society and Nationhood. Historical Essays presented to Glanmor Williams* (Cardiff, 1984).

Davies, W., *Wales in the Early Middle Ages* (Leicester, 1982).

Dodd, A.H., 'Welsh History and Historians', in Elwyn Davies (ed.), *Celtic Studies in Wales* (Cardiff, 1963).

— *Life in Wales* (1972).

Ellis, R.G. (ed.), *Flowering Plants of Wales* (Cardiff, 1983).

Emery, F.V., *Wales. The World's Landscapes 2* (1969).

Evans, E., *The Personality of Wales* (Cardiff, 1973).

Evans, E.D., *A History of Wales, 1660–1815* (Cardiff, 1976).

Foster, I.Ll. and Alcock, L. (eds.), *Culture and Environment: Essays in Honour of Sir Cyril Fox* (1963).

— and Raglan, Lord, *Monmouthshire Houses*, 3 vols, (Cardiff, 1951–4).

Grimes, W.F., *The Prehistory of Wales* (Cardiff, 1951).

Herbert, T. and Jones, G.E., (eds.), *Tudor Wales* (Cardiff, 1988).

— *People and Protest: Wales 1815–1880* (Cardiff, 1988)

Hilling, J.B., *Cardiff and the Valleys* (1973).

— *The Historic Architecture of Wales* (Cardiff, 1976).

Howe, G.M., *Wales from the Air* (Cardiff, 1957).

— and Thomas, P., *Welsh Landforms and Scenery* (1963).

Hyde, H.A. and Harrison, S.G., *Welsh Timber Trees* (Cardiff, 1977).

Jarrett, M.G. (ed.), *The Roman Frontier in Wales* (Cardiff, 1969).

Jenkins, G.H., *Literature, Religion and Society in Wales, 1660–1730* (Cardiff, 1978).

— *Hanes Cymru yn y Cyfnod Modern Cynnar, 1530–1760,* (Cardiff, 1983).

— *The Foundations of Modern Wales, 1642–1780* (Oxford, 1987).

Jenkins, P., *The Making of the Ruling Class: the Glamorgan Gentry 1640–1790* (Cambridge, 1983).

Jenkins, R.T., *Hanes Cymru yn y Ddeunawfed Ganrif* (Cardiff, 1928).

— *Hanes Cymru yn y Bedwaredd Ganrif ar Bymtheg* (Cardiff, 1933).

Jones, D.J.V., *Before Rebecca: Popular Protests in Wales, 1793–1835* (1973).

Jones, G.E., *Modern Wales: A Concise History, 1485–1979* (Cambridge, 1984).

Jones, G.R.J., 'The Tribal System in Wales: a Re-Assessment in the Light of Settlement Studies', *W.H.R.*, 1 (1961).

— 'The Distribution of Bond Settlements in North-West Wales', *W.H.R.*, 2 (1964).

Jones, I.G., *Explorations and Explanations* (Llandysul, 1981).

— *Communities: Essays in the Social History of Victorian Wales* (Llandysul, 1987).

Jones, R.B. (ed.), *Anatomy of Wales* (Peterston-Super-Ely, 1972).

Jones, R.M., *The North Wales Quarrymen, 1874–1922* (Cardiff, 1981).

Jones, R.T., *Hanes Annibynwyr Cymru* (Swansea, 1966).

Lewis, G.J., 'The Geography of Religion in the Middle Borderlands of Wales in 1851', *T.C.S.*, (1980), 123–42.

Linnard, W., *Welsh Woods and Forests: History and Utilization* (Cardiff, 1982).

Lloyd, H.A., *The Gentry of South-West Wales, 1540–1640* (Cardiff, 1968).

Lloyd, J.E. *A History of Wales from the Earliest Times to the Edwardian Conquest*, 2 vols. (1911).

Millward, R. and Robinson, A., *Landscapes of North Wales* (Newton Abbot, 1978).

Moore, D. (ed.), *Wales in the Eighteenth Century* (Swansea, 1976).

Morgan, K.O., *Rebirth of a Nation: Wales 1880–1980* (Cardiff, 1981).

Morgan, P. and Thomas, D., *Wales: The Shaping of a Nation* (Newton Abbot, 1984).

Nash-Williams, V.E., *Early Christian Monuments of Wales* (Cardiff, 1950).

Owen, D.H., 'Tenurial and Economic Developments in North Wales in the Twelfth and Thirteenth Centuries', *W.H.R.*, VI (1972).

OWEN, L., 'The Population of Wales in the Sixteenth and Seventeenth Centuries', *T.C.S.*, (1959).

OWEN, T.M., *Welsh Folk Customs* (Cardiff, 1968).

— 'Community Studies in Wales: An Overview' in I. Hume and W.T.R. Pryce (eds.), *The Welsh and their Country* (Llandysul, 1986).

OWEN, T.R. (ed.), *The Upper Palaeozoic and Post Palaeozoic Rocks of Wales* (Cardiff, 1974).

PARRY, T., *A History of Welsh Literature* (Oxford, 1955).

PEATE, I.C., *The Welsh House* (Liverpool, 1946).

— *Tradition and Folk Life: a Welsh View* (1972).

PIERCE, T. JONES, *Medieval Welsh Society*, J.B. Smith (ed.), (Cardiff, 1972).

PUGH, T.B. (ed.), *The Marcher Lordships of South Wales, 1415–1536* (Cardiff, 1963).

REES, J.F., *Studies in Welsh History* (Cardiff, 1965).

REES, W., *South Wales and the March, 1285–1415. A Social and Agrarian Study* (Oxford, 1924).

REEVES, A.C., *The Marcher Lordships* (Swansea, 1983).

RICHARDS, M., 'Ecclesiastical and Secular in Medieval Welsh Settlement', *Studia Celtica*, II (1968).

— 'Places and Persons of the Early Welsh Church', *W.H.R.*, 5 (1971).

ROBERTS, G.M. (ed.), *Hanes Methodistiaeth Calfinaidd Cymru*, 1 (Caernarfon, 1974), II (Caernarfon, 1978).

ROBERTS, G., *Aspects of Welsh History* (Cardiff, 1969).

RODERICK, A.J. (ed.), *Wales through the Ages*, 2 vols. (Llandybïe, 1959, 1961).

ST JOSEPH, J.K.S., 'Aerial Reconnaissance in Wales', *Antiquity*, (1961), 263–75.

SAVORY, H.N., 'Welsh Hillforts: A Reappraisal of Recent Research' in D.W. Harding (ed.), *Hillforts* (1976), 238–93.

SMITH, D.B. (ed.), *A People and a Proletariat* (1980).

— and FRANCIS, H., *The Fed. A History of South Wales Miners in the Twentieth Century* (1980).

SMITH, P., *Houses of the Welsh Countryside* (1975).

— 'The Architectural Personality of Wales', *A.C.*, (1980), 1–36.

TAYLOR, A.J., *The King's Works in Wales 1277–1330* (1974).

TAYLOR, J.A. (ed.), *Culture and Environment in Prehistoric Wales—B.A.R. British Series 76*, (Oxford, 1980).

THOMAS, C., 'Patterns and Processes of Estate Expansion in the Fifteenth and Sixteenth Centuries', *Jnl. Mer. H.R.S.*, VI (1972).

THOMAS, D. (ed.), *Wales: A New Study* (Newton Abbot, 1977).

THOMAS, H., *A History of Wales, 1485–1660* (Cardiff, 1972).

WALKER, D.G. (ed.), *A History of the Church in Wales* (Penarth, 1976).

— *The Norman Conquest* (Swansea, 1977).

WHEELER, R.E.M., *Prehistoric and Roman Wales* (Oxford, 1925).

WILIAM, E., *Farm Buildings of North-East Wales, 1550–1900* (Cardiff, 1982).

— *Historical Farm Buildings of Wales* (Edinburgh, 1986).

WILLIAMS, D., *John Frost* (Cardiff, 1939).

— *The Rebecca Riots: A Study in Agrarian Discontent* (Cardiff, 1955).

— *A History of Modern Wales* (Cardiff, 1977).

WILLIAMS, G., *The Welsh Church from Conquest to Reformation* (Cardiff, 1962).

— *Religion, Language and Nationality in Wales* (Cardiff, 1979).

WILLIAMS, G.A., *When Was Wales?* (Harmondsworth, 1985).

WILLIAMS, M., *The Making of the South Wales Landscape* (London, 1975).

4. AGRARIAN STUDIES

A

Agrarian History of England and Wales, Vol. 1 ii, A.D. 43–1042 H.P.R. Finberg (ed.), (Cambridge, 1972) Vol. IV, 1500–1640, J. Thirsk (ed.), (Cambridge, 1967) Vol. V, 1640–1750, J. Thirsk (ed.), (Cambridge, 1984) Vol. VIII, 1914–39 E.H. Whetham (ed.), (Cambridge, 1978).

BAKER, A.R.H. and BUTLIN, R.A. (eds.), *Studies of Field Systems in the British Isles* (Cambridge, 1973).

BARLEY, M.W., *The English Farmhouse and Cottage* (1961).

BERESFORD, M.W., *The Lost Villages of England* (1954).

— and HURST, J.G. (eds.), *Deserted Medieval Villages* (Woking, 1971).

CHISHOLM, M., *Rural Settlement and Land Use* (1962).

DODGSHON, R.A., *The Origin of British Field Systems* (1980).

DUBY, G., *Rural Economy and Country Life in the Medieval West* (English trans. by C. Postan) (1968).

FOWLER, P.J. (ed.), *Recent Work in Rural Archaeology* (1975).

HOOPER, M.D. *et al.*, *Hedges and Local History* (1971).

JENKINS, J.G., *The Wool Textile Industry in Great Britain* (1972).

MILES, D. (ed.), *The Romano-British Countryside, Studies in Rural Settlements and Economy,* B.A.R. British Series, 103 (ii), (1982).

ROBERTS, B.K., *Rural Settlement in Britain* (Folkestone, 1977).

ROWLEY, T., *Villages in the Landscape* (1978).

— (ed.) *The Origins of Open-Field Agriculture* (1981).

RUSSELL, R.C., *The Logic of the Open-Field Systems* (1974).

TAYLOR, C., *Fields in the English Landscape* (1975).

TODD, E.M. (ed.), *Studies in the Romano-British Villa* (Leicester, 1978).

B

BOWEN, I., *The Great Enclosures of Common Lands in Wales* (1914).

COLYER, R.J., *The Welsh Cattle Drovers* (Cardiff, 1976).

DAVIES, E. and REES, A.D. (eds.), *Welsh Rural Communities* (Cardiff, 1960).

DAVIES, M. 'Field Patterns in the Vale of Glamorgan', *T. Cardiff Nat. Soc.,* (1954–5), 5–14.

DAVIES, W., *A general view of the agriculture and domestic economy of North Wales* (1810).

— *A general view of the agriculture and domestic economy of South Wales,* 2 vols., (1814).

EMERY, F., 'West Glamorgan Farming circa. 1580–1620', *N.L.W. Jnl.,* (1955–6).

HOWELL, D.W., *Land and People in Nineteenth-Century Wales* (1978).

— *Patriarchs and Parasites* (Cardiff, 1986).

HOWELLS, B.E., 'Pembrokeshire Farming, circa. 1580–1620', *N.L.W. Jnl.,* 9, (1955–6).

— 'Open Fields and Farmsteads in Pembrokeshire', *Pembs. Hist.,* 3 (1971).

JENKINS, D., *The Agricultural Community in South-West Wales* (Cardiff, 1971).

JENKINS, J.G. (ed.), *Studies in Folk Life: Essays in Honour of Iorwerth C. Peate* (Cardiff, 1969).

— *Life and Tradition in Rural Wales* (1976).

JONES, G.R.J., 'Rural Settlement in Anglesey' in Eyre, S.R. and Jones, G.R.J. (eds.), *Geography as Human Ecology* (1966).

JONES, I.E., *The Arwystli (Montgomeryshire) Enclosures 1816–1828,* U. of Birmingham, Dept. of Geography, Occasional Pub., 18 (Birmingham, 1985).

OWEN, T., *Welsh Folk Customs* (Cardiff, 1978).

PAYNE, F.G., *Yr Aradr Gymreig* (Cardiff, 1954).

— *Cwysau: Casgliad o Erthyglau ac Ysgrifau* (Llandysul, 1980).

REES, A.D., *Life in a Welsh Countryside* (Cardiff, 1950).

ROBERTS, R.O., *Farming in Caernarvonshire around 1800* (Denbigh, 1973).

SYLVESTER, D., *The Rural Landscape of the Welsh Borderland* (1969).

THOMAS, C., 'Enclosures and the Rural Landscape of Meirioneth in the Sixteenth Century', *T. Inst. Brit. Geog.*, 42, (1967).

— 'Social Organisation and Rural Settlement in Medieval North Wales', *Jnl. Mer. H.R.S.*, 6 (1970), 121–31.

THOMAS, D., *Agriculture in Wales during the Napoleonic Wars* (Cardiff, 1963).

5. TOWNS AND INDUSTRY

A

ASTON, M. and BOND, J., *The Landscape of Towns* (1976).

BARLEY, M.W. (ed.), *The Plans and Topography of Medieval Towns in England and Wales* (1976).

BERESFORD, M.W., *New Towns of the Middle Ages* (1967).

CARTER, H., *An Introduction to Urban Historical Geography* (1983).

CLARK, P., (ed.), *The Early Modern Town: a Reader* (1976).

— and SLACK, P., *English Towns in Transition, 1500–1700* (Oxford, 1976).

DYOS, H.J., *The Study of Urban History* (1968).

LOBEL, M.D., (ed.), *Historic Towns: Maps and Plans of Towns and Cities in the British Isles*, I (1969).

THIRSK, J., 'Industries in the Countryside', in F.J. Fisher (ed.), *Essays in the Economic and Social History of Tudor and Stuart England* (1961).

TRINDER, B.S., *The Making of the Industrial Landscape* (1982).

WACHER, J., *The Towns of Roman Britain* (1974).

B

CARTER, H., *The Towns of Wales: A Study in Urban Geography* (Cardiff, 1965).

— *The Growth of the Welsh City System* (Cardiff, 1969).

— *Urban Essays: Studies in the Geography of Wales* (Harlow, 1970).

— 'Transformations in the Spatial Structure of Welsh Towns in the Nineteenth Century', *T.C.S.*, (1980), 175–200.

DODD, A.H., *The Industrial Revolution in North Wales* (Cardiff, 1971).

GRIFFITHS, R.A. (ed.), *Boroughs of Mediaeval Wales* (Cardiff, 1978).

JACK, R.I., 'The Cloth Industry in Medieval Wales', *W.H.R.*, X (1979–80).

JENKINS, J.G., *The Welsh Woollen Industry* (Cardiff, 1969).

JOHN, A.H., *The Industrial Development of South Wales* (Cardiff, 1950).

JONES, P.N., *Colliery Settlements in the South Wales Coalfield: 1850 to 1926* (Hull, 1969).

LEWIS, E.A., 'The Development of Industry and Commerce in Wales during the Middle Ages', *T.R.H.S.*, XVII (1903).

— *The Medieval Boroughs of Snowdonia* (1912).

LEWIS, W.J., *Lead Mining in Wales* (Cardiff, 1967).

LOWE, J.B., *Welsh Industrial Workers' Housing 1775–1875* (Cardiff, 1977).

MINCHINTON, W.E., *Industrial South Wales, 1750–1914* (1969).

REES, D.M., *The Industrial Archaeology of Wales* (Newton Abbot, 1975).

REES, W., *Industry before the Industrial Revolution*, 2 vols. (Cardiff, 1968).

SOULSBY, I., *The Towns of Medieval Wales* (Chichester, 1983).

6. COUNTY AND LOCAL COMMUNITY STUDIES

BARNES, T. and YATES, N. (eds.), *Carmarthenshire Studies* (Carmarthen, 1974).

Bowen, D.Q., *The Llanelli Landscape* (Llanelli, 1980).

Carr, A.D., *Medieval Anglesey* (Llangefni, 1982).

Carter, H. and Wheatley, S., *Merthyr Tydfil in 1851* (Cardiff, 1982).

Daunton, M.J., *Coal Metropolis, Cardiff 1870–1914* (Leicester, 1977).

Dodd, A.H., *A History of Wrexham* (Wrexham, 1957).

—— *A History of Caernarvonshire, 1285–1900* (Caernarfon, 1968).

Gardner, W. and Savory, H.N., *Dinorben: a Hill-fort occupied in Early Iron Age and Roman Times* (Cardiff, 1964).

GLAMORGAN COUNTY HISTORY: I *Natural History,* W.M. Tattersall (ed.); (1936, 1971); II *Early Glamorgan,* H.N. Savory (ed.) (Cardiff 1984); III *The Middle Ages* T.B. Pugh (ed.) (Cardiff, 1971); IV *Early Modern Glamorgan,* G. Williams (ed.) (Cardiff, 1974); V *Industrial Glamorgan,* A.H. John and G. Williams (ed.) (Cardiff, 1980).

Gresham, C.A., *Eifionydd, A Study in Landownership from the Medieval Period to the Present Day* (Cardiff, 1973).

Griffiths, M., 'The Vale of Glamorgan in the 1543 Lay Subsidy Returns', *B.B.C.S.,* XXIX (1980–2), 709–48.

—— 'The Manor in Medieval Glamorgan: the Estates of the de Ralegh Family in the Fourteenth and Fifteenth Centuries', *B.B.C.S.,* XXXII (1985).

Haslam, R., *Powys: The Buildings of Wales* (Harmondsworth, 1979).

Hubbard, E., *Clwyd; The Buildings of Wales* (Harmondsworth, 1986).

James, T., *Carmarthen: An Archaeological and Topographical Survey* (Carmarthen, 1980).

Jenkins, E. (ed.), *Neath and District: A Symposium* (Neath, 1974).

John, B., *Pembrokeshire* (Newton Abbot, 1976).

Jones, E.D. (ed.). *History of Meirioneth,* Vol. 1 (Dolgellau, 1967).

Jones, F., *Historic Carmarthenshire Homes and their Families* (Carmarthen, 1987).

Jones, I.G. (ed.), *Aberystwyth 1277–1977* (Llandysul, 1977).

Jones, S.R., 'Cileos-Isaf: a Late Medieval Montgomeryshire Long-House', *Mont. Coll.,* (1969–70), 115–31.

—— and Smith, J.T., 'The Houses of Breconshire', *Brycheiniog,* (1963–9).

Lewis, E.D., *The Rhondda Valleys* (1959).

Lewis, W.J., *Born on a Perilous Rock: Aberystwyth Past and Present* (Aberystwyth, 1980).

Lloyd, J.E. (ed.), *A History of Carmarthenshire,* 2 Vols. (Cardiff, 1935, 1939).

Michael, D.P.M., *The Mapping of Monmouthshire* (Bristol, 1985).

Moore, D. (ed.), *Barry: The Centenary Book* (Barry, 1984).

PEMBROKESHIRE COUNTY HISTORY: 3 Early Modern Pembrokeshire 1536–1815, B.E. Howells (ed.), (Haverfordwest, 1987).

Phillips, D.R., *A History of the Vale of Neath* (Swansea, 1925).

Ramage, H., *Portraits of an Island, Eighteenth Century Anglesey* (Llangefni, 1987).

Randall, H.J., *The Vale of Glamorgan — Studies in Landscape and History* (Newport, 1961).

Rees, J.F. (ed.), *The Cardiff Region* (Cardiff, 1960).

Rees, W., *Cardiff: A History of the City* (Cardiff, 1969).

Robinson, D.M., *Cowbridge: the Archaeology and Topography of a small Market Town in the Vale of Glamorgan* (Swansea, 1980).

Royal Commission on Ancient and Historical Monuments in Wales *An Inventory of the Ancient Monuments in Caernarvonshire* I (1956), II (1960) III (1964).

—— *An Inventory of the Ancient Monuments in Glamorgan* I, pts. 1, 2 and 3 (1976), IV, pt. 1 (1981), III, pt. 2 (1982), IV, pt. 2 (1988).

Sylvester, D., *A History of Gwynedd* (Chichester, 1983).

Symons, M.V., *Coal Mining in the Llanelli Area* Vol. I: 16th Century to 1829 (Llanelli, 1979).

Williams, S., *The Glamorgan Historian,* I–XII (Barry, 1963–81).

Williams, W.O., *Tudor Gwynedd* (Caernarfon, 1958).

Index

[Note: Figures in italics refer to illustrations]